Warships of the World
to 1900

WARSHIPS

of the World to 1900

Lincoln P. Paine

A Mariner Original

HOUGHTON MIFFLIN COMPANY

BOSTON · NEW YORK

2000

BOOKS BY LINCOLN P. PAINE

SHIPS OF THE WORLD: AN HISTORICAL ENCYCLOPEDIA

SHIPS OF DISCOVERY AND EXPLORATION

WARSHIPS OF THE WORLD TO 1900

For information about permission to reproduce selections from
this book, write to Permissions, Houghton Mifflin Company,
215 Park Avenue South, New York, New York 10003.

Visit our Web site: www.houghtonmifflinbooks.com.

Library of Congress Cataloging-in-Publication Data
Paine, Lincoln P.
Warships of the World to 1900 / Lincoln P. Paine.
p.   cm.
Includes bibliographical references and index.
ISBN 0-395-98414-9
1. Warships — History. I. Title.
V799 .P28 2000
623.8'225'09 — dc21   00-040793
Printed in the United States of America

Book design by Robert Overholtzer

QUM 10 9 8 7 6 5 4 3 2 1

To Commander Eric J. Berryman, USNR (Retd.)

———————

It is their attachment to their government, from the sense
of the deep stake they have in such a glorious institution, which
gives you both your army and your navy, and infuses into
both that liberal obedience, without which your army would be
a base rabble, and your navy nothing but rotten timber.

— Edmund Burke, *Second Speech on Conciliation
with America* (1776)

Contents

Illustrations

Preface

Warships of the World to 1900 is based in large part on *Ships of the World: An Historical Encyclopedia,* published in 1997. Seventeen new articles help round out some eras and naval traditions overlooked in the earlier book. Several entries have been rewritten or corrected in light of new scholarship and suggestions made by reviewers and other informed readers of *Ships of the World.* I am grateful to them for their courtesy and tact.

A great number of people contributed to this effort in various ways. For help in pulling together information, illustrations, and maps from a variety of disparate sources, and for reading some of the new material, I would like to thank David Blanchard, editor of the *Nautical Research Journal;* Norman Brouwer, curator of ships at the South Street Seaport Museum Library; Lars Bruzelius; Francisco C. Domingues; Andrew Elkerton, Mary Rose Trust; A. Fitzsimmons, Pepys Library; Iain Gunn-Graham; Wim Klooster, for his research into the career of Piet Heyn's *Amsterdam;* Dr. C. S. Knighton; Arthur Layton; Steve McLaughlin; Frances McSherry; David Meagher; Michael Phillips; Nuno J. V. Rubim; and P. C. van Royen, Institute for Maritime History, Royal Netherlands Navy. The administrators of the Maritime History Information Exchange Group (MARHST-L) and Queens University, Toronto, are to be commended for maintaining such a lively international forum for the discussion of maritime history; MARHST's many subscribers have helped answer countless questions and turned light to dark corners. I especially want to thank Rosemary Mosher for her excellent maps.

No research project of this scope can be undertaken without consulting a wide variety of sources, and I am grateful to those librarians upon whom I have relied at the University of Southern Maine, Portland, the New York Public Library, the National Maritime Museum, Greenwich, and South Street Seaport, New York.

On a personal note, I would like to thank Elizabeth Mitchell and Alex Krieckhaus, and Chris Graves and JoAnn Ward, and their children, for their hospitality; John Wright, my agent (*provocateur*) and friend; my collaborators on *Ships of the World,* Jim Terry, Hal Fessenden, and especially Eric Berryman, to whom I dedicate this volume; and above all my wife, Allison, and our daughters, Kai and Madeleine.

Lincoln P. Paine
Portland, Maine

Introduction

This book tells the stories of more than 200 individual fighting ships built before 1900. For the most part, these ships represent a naval tradition that has its roots in the ancient Mediterranean. The reason for this particular focus lies in the historiography of the subject: either the documentary evidence from other early naval traditions is incomplete, or researchers have yet to unearth the sort of information contained in this book.

The focus of this book is on vessels built or used primarily for organized naval warfare as we understand it today, that is, ships operating in concert with other ships or individually, but within a discernible hierarchy of command and control determined by the state. It should be stressed, however, that collectively these ships' stories touch on only a few highlights of world naval history before 1900.

The history of the warship before 1900 can be divided broadly into three periods. Although sailing ships are of great antiquity, until the medieval period, naval warfare was confined chiefly to oar-powered galleys that relied on sails only for auxiliary propulsion. The end of the galley's domination coincides with — but did not result from — the development of the gun in the fourteenth century. At the same time, there was a synthesis of northern and southern European shipbuilding traditions that gave rise to the square-rigged warship from which the ship of the line and frigates of the early 1800s are direct descendants. The final stage in the evolution of naval warfare under discussion was marked by unprecedented changes in materials, ordnance, design, and, above all, propulsion.

Taken together, these affected the size, shape, handling, and function of warships to a greater degree than all other previous developments combined.

The development of the fighting ship alternately parallels that of ships used for civil pursuits, chiefly merchantmen and fishing vessels, and takes off on trajectories of specialized refinement which end, inevitably, with the collapse of the governments and military bureaucracies that standing navies require for their maintenance. The earliest warships were doubtless merchantmen requisitioned for military purposes, usually as troop transports. Sea battles probably began when a defender first attempted to prevent an aggressor from making a successful landing. This could be achieved most easily by boarding an opponent's ship and killing its soldiers and crew. Fought at close quarters on a drifting battlefield, the first sea fights were not unlike infantry battles fought ashore. Among the first weapons peculiar to sea fighting was probably the grapnel, a hook that could be thrown onto an enemy ship so that the two combatants could be joined hull to hull. One of the most vivid accounts of such a battle is found in Snorri Sturluson's thirteenth-century account of the Norwegian king Olav Tryggvason, whose ORMRINN LANGI was the setting for just such a battle in the year 1000.

This form of combat was essentially antipersonnel in nature. Ships might be damaged, but they were rarely sunk in such a melee. The easiest way to sink a ship is to punch a hole in it below the waterline, which is hard to do with hand weapons. Before the advent of long-range weapons, the easiest way to sink a ship was to ram it. The earliest pictorial evidence of the ram dates from about the ninth century BCE. It may have begun as a forward extension of the keel, but sailors soon began to fit a bronze ram to the end. To support the weight of the ram, and to prevent the ramming ship from being shattered by the impact of driving repeatedly into other vessels, the hulls had to be more heavily constructed. A pentecontor (50-oared ship, the largest of the period) with all the rowers on the same level would be 100 feet or longer: such a vessel was heavy, difficult to maneuver or defend, and an unnecessarily large target for enemy ships. It is not surprising that the same period saw the development of the first two-decked ships, which carried the same number of oarsmen in a hull half as long. The earliest depiction of two-decked pentecontors is in an eighth-century BCE relief showing the Phoenician evacuation of Sidon and Tyre to Cyprus. With stronger hulls, ships could also incorporate a raised deck for infantry, archers, and spear-throwers which gave them a further offensive capability.

By the fifth century BCE, the Mediterranean warship *par excellence* was the three-decked trieres, or trireme, a vessel with much greater strength, speed, and hitting power. It is estimated that the trireme was as much as 30 percent faster than the pentecontor, which remained the standard warship for smaller city-states lacking the resources to build or man triremes, which had crews of 200 men. Although larger vessels were built, the trireme seems never to have been improved upon for speed. Exactly how the larger polyreme galleys functioned is open to question. As types, they are referred to in ancient literature by numbers: fives, eights, twelves, and so on, up to a forty. Careful study of the constraints on design and comparisons with better documented Renaissance galleys, such as those of the Venetians, suggest that these polyremes never had more than three banks (horizontal rows) of oars. The numbers probably refer to the number of oarsmen in each column of oars. That is to say, a four might have had two banks of oars, with two men per oar, and an eight might have had three banks of oars, with the top and middle oars pulled by three men each, and the bottom oar by two

men. The maximum number of oarsmen per oar was probably eight, and the highest such rating in a single hull would therefore be a twenty-four.

Warship design in antiquity reached its apogee following the death of Alexander the Great. The most notable innovator was Demetrius the Besieger (336–283 BCE), a Macedonian king who is credited with being the first to put more than one man on each oar. The immediate reason for the need for stronger, bigger ships was to accommodate catapults, the first shipboard artillery. Alexander the Great had used shipborne catapults during the siege of Tyre, but the seagoing catapult did not come into its own until the development of supergalleys by Demetrius and his successors. The most extreme of these Hellenistic-era vessels was the unnamed forty of Ptolemy IV Philopator (Macedonian king of Egypt from 210 to 180 BCE), which maritime historian Lionel Casson interprets as a catamaran warship made up of two twenties with a raised platform deck spanning the two hulls. The dimensions given by Athenaeus (who wrote in the second century CE) seem fantastic but credible: 50 feet wide, 400 feet long, with room for 4,000 oars, 2,850 marines, and 400 deckhands of various sorts. It is also likely that thirties, and possibly some smaller vessels, were also twin-hulled. Nor were such vessels complete rarities. The only catamaran galley known by name is Demetrius's eight, LEONTOPHOROS, of the early third century BCE, but the 336 vessels in the fleet of Ptolemy II Philadelphus (r. 308–246 BCE) included two thirties and a twenty.

At this time, the focus of naval activity was shifting to the west, where Rome vied with Carthage for control of Sicily and the western Mediterranean in the three Punic Wars (264–41, 218–201, and 149–46 BCE). Originally a Phoenician trading colony with roots in the eastern Mediterranean, Carthage dominated the trade routes of the western Mediterranean. After three years of inconsequential fighting on land, the Romans — never enthusiastic seamen — decided to build a fleet of 100 quinqueremes (with 300 crew per ship) and 20 triremes (170). The Carthaginian ships were better built and their crews more experienced, so to take advantage of their infantry, the Romans invented a combination grapnel and boarding plank called a *corvus*. When lowered onto the deck of the opposing ship, it held fast while soldiers rushed across. The *corvus* was used to brilliant effect at Mylae, in August 260, when the Romans captured 44 ships and killed or took prisoner 10,000 Carthaginian sailors. Through imitation and persistence and an almost endless supply of men and materiel, the Romans eventually defeated the Carthaginians, the decisive blow coming at the Battle of the Aegates Islands in March of 241.

For hundreds of years, Rome relied on naval power to keep the Mediterranean free of pirates and open to trade, especially along the vital grain ship route from Alexandria to Rome. Octavian consolidated his position in a brilliant naval campaign that culminated in the Battle of Actium in 31 BCE, and as the emperor Augustus he established Rome's first standing navy, with bases at Misenum on the west coast of Italy and Ravenna on the Adriatic. As the empire expanded, subsidiary naval bases were established in the eastern Mediterranean, in the Black Sea, and on the Danube and Rhine Rivers. Excavations at Mainz, Germany, have yielded the remains of fourth-century patrol craft typical of these imperial riverine outposts.

The economic downturn that accompanied the decline of the Roman Empire forced Constantine (285–337) to adopt smaller thirty- and fifty-man ships, which evolved into the *dromon* ("racer") of the fifth century, and later still the *moneres* and *galea* of the Byzantine navy in the tenth century. Designed for fighting at close quarters, their armament included antiship weapons such as catapults and Greek fire. This seventh-century flamethrower consisted of a flammable liquid pumped from a bronze siphon, and it is credited with having given the Byzantines a crucial edge over Arab fleets in the Aegean Sea and the Sea of Marmara.

Like the Romans, the Arabs did not have an indigenous naval tradition to draw on, but they were masters of recruitment and imitation. In 641, an Arab army captured the Byzantine navy's homeport at Alexandria. Arab fleets captured Cyprus and raided Rhodes and Sicily, and in 655 a Syro-Egyptian fleet of 200 ships routed a Byzantine armada of 500 ships in the Battle of the Masts, or dhu-al-Sawari, off the coast of Lycia in Asia Minor. In an engagement reminiscent of the Battle of Mylae, the lubberly Arabs triumphed by creating a situation in which their superior infantry might prevail. Lashing their ships to those of the enemy, the Arabs carried the day in a series of classic boarding actions that left "the water of the sea saturated with blood."[1] The fleets of the Caliph resumed their assault on the heart of the Byzantine Empire in 669, and Arab fleets threatened Constantinople off and on until the early 700s.

The campaigns against the Byzantine Empire had been conducted by a unified caliphate. After 750, Islamic states on the periphery began to break away, the first to secede being the Ummayad Caliphate of Córdoba in Spain. The development of an Umayyad fleet could not have been more timely, for in 844 a Viking fleet of some eighty ships sailed up the Guadalquivir River and looted Seville. The Muslims reacted swiftly: they sank thirty Norse ships in a battle off Talayata.

Scandinavians had begun to expand out of the Baltic and its tributaries in the eighth and ninth centuries. In the east, they established trading centers at Novgorod, which gave them access to the Dnieper River, which flows to the Black Sea, and the Volga, which flows to the Caspian. Westward expansion began in 793, with the raid on Lindisfarne Abbey in Scotland and soon, as the *Annals of Ulster* record, "no haven, no landing-place, no stronghold, no fort, no castle might be found, but it was submerged by waves of Vikings and pirates."[2] On the Continent, Charlemagne ordered the creation of a defense force to guard the Frisian coast, but after his death the Norse exploited his divided legacy ruthlessly, sailing their ships up the Rhine, the Scheldt, the Seine, the Loire, and the Gironde to conquer such prosperous centers as Hamburg, Utrecht, Paris, Nantes, and Bordeaux. By the time the seafaring Vikings reached the Mediterranean, via Muslim Spain, they had overreached themselves. The Vikings tended to move in relatively small numbers, and a relatively high proportion of them settled among the people they raided. However, they retained the seafaring skills honed over generations. During the Norman invasion of Britain in 1066, William the Conqueror sailed with his MORA and perhaps one thousand other vessels to seize the English throne then occupied by Harold. This was a logistical triumph, but by no means the first such seaborne invasion. Julius Caesar had achieved much the same end in Britain in the first century BCE, and there are numerous other examples of seaborne invasions from antiquity and the medieval period throughout the Mediterranean and in Asia.

The period from the 1100s to the 1400s saw a number of complementary developments that together would make the conduct of naval warfare almost unrecognizable to any previous generation of sailors. The Crusades opened the commerce of the eastern Mediterranean and Black Seas and the spice trades (among others) beyond. The primary beneficiaries of this expansion were the Venetians and Genoese, who built large merchant fleets and navies to protect them. They also began trading with northern Europe, first overland and then, by the 1200s, by sea to the Low Countries.

This brought about the first direct meeting of the distinct Mediterranean and northern European shipbuilding traditions, and a technical revolution in ship design. Two distinct ship types had evolved in the Mediterranean, the galley, or long ship, used for warfare (and in the medieval period as merchant ships), and the round ship, a wide, high-sided vessel with large volume and multitiered "castles" fore and aft. As important, Mediterranean shipwrights built ships by constructing a skeleton frame to which they fastened the outer skin of planks laid edge-to-edge. Mediterranean sailors had also abandoned the square sail common in antiquity in favor of the fore and aft lateen sail, and the largest ships had two or even three masts. Although such a rig enabled ships to point closer to the wind, they were cumbersome when tacking and required large crews.

In northern Europe, the hull was formed first, with overlapping planks fastened to one another with clenched (bent) nails. This technique, which resembles a clapboard house, is known as clinker or lapstrake construction. When the shell was complete, framing pieces were inserted in the hull to provide stiffening. This method can be traced from the Viking-era ships to the more capacious and deeper-hulled merchant cogs favored by the traders of the Hanseatic League. Driven by a single square sail, northern European ships also featured a centerline rudder, a new invention in the west that made ships more maneuverable. Prior to this, European boats and ships were turned by steering oars mounted singly or in pairs on either side of the hull at the stern.

The hybrid that resulted from this combination of techniques was called a carrack, the original full-rigged ship. This can be seen as a framed cog, with a centerline rudder and a rig that incorporated both square and small lateen sails on two or more masts. This blended rig made it possible for carracks to sail somewhat into the wind and tack more easily, and better able to make use of a following wind. Their greater capacity enabled them to carry more provisions — and trade goods — for longer, more profitable voyages. Their high fore- and sterncastles, in which archers and soldiers were stationed in combat, were also an integral part of the hull. By the end of the 1500s, the high-charged carrack had given way to the race-built galleon, which eliminated the towering forecastle. The galleon, in turn, evolved into the ship of the line and frigate, which were the mainstay of the world's navies through the first half of the nineteenth century.

The second major development was the invention of the gun and its adoption for use on ships in the 1300s. At first, guns tended to be relatively lightweight weapons for use against people at close range; sixteenth-century English inventories include guns called "murderers." Like the ram in antiquity, guns were heavy, and the recoil from them created enormous stresses on the fabric and joinery of the ship, a problem that the builders of the heavily built carrack could take in stride. The increased weight of ships' guns also required that they be situated as low in the hull as possible, a problem not satisfactorily overcome until the development of the watertight gunport in the early 1500s. But gunports were something of an Achilles' heel for the capital ships of the day. The MARY ROSE and WASA are only the best known ships to have sunk because of water flooding through their open gunports.

The Portuguese, thanks especially to the Genoese seamen in their employ, had mastered the wind systems of the mid-Atlantic latitudes sailing mainly in the small fore-and-aft rigged *caravela latina*. When they entered the Indian Ocean, it was in the larger carracks, or as the Portuguese called them, *naos*. The merchant sailors of Gujarat and the Persian Gulf, among others whom they encountered, were superb seamen who had pioneered seaborne trade with China in the seventh century. The Portuguese advantage in the Indian Ocean was based not on superior seamanship but on their opponents' lack of an offensive technology comparable to their own. Even when the mariners of the Indian Ocean did adopt guns, their sewn ships could not withstand the recoil, although the coir rope used to fasten their so-called sewn boats was quickly replaced by iron fastenings. With technological parity, they could prove formidable opponents. From the 1620s to the 1660s, the Sultans of Oman challenged the Portuguese along a broad arc from East Africa to India almost continuously.

The Europeans also had the advantage of impeccable timing, especially in East Asia. In the first three decades of the fifteenth century, the Chinese had dispatched seven enormous fleets of treasure junks that sailed as far as the Red Sea and East Africa. From the 1430s, though, China's formidable sea power went into recession, prompted by dramatic changes in domestic priorities. Nor did these elaborate trade missions represent an isolated phenomenon in the history of Asian naval endeavor. In the late thirteenth century, Kublai Khan mounted two major invasions of Japan. Both failed when his Chinese-Korean fleets were destroyed in typhoons, which the Japanese called *kamikaze,* or divine wind. He also launched seaborne invasions of Vietnam and Java. Later still, between 1592 and 1598, Korea's Admiral Yi Sun-shin waged an ultimately successful naval campaign to rid his homeland of a Japanese invasion.

The primary challenge to Europeans operating in Asia, the Americas, and home waters was other Europeans. The early sixteenth century witnessed a trend toward gigantism in northern European ships. One of the first examples of this was James IV of Scotland's monumental carrack MICHAEL. "The greattest sheip and maist of strength that ewer saillit in Ingland or France" is thought to have influenced the building of Henry VIII's better-known HENRY GRACE À DIEU among other ships. As had happened in antiquity, though, these immense ships quickly gave way to smaller, more compact vessels with better sailing qualities and stouter construction.

Henry's greatest contribution to the English navy, and by extension those of other northern European countries, was not merely the construction of large ships and large numbers of them. In his reign can also be seen the nascent bureaucratic infrastructure that, once in place, would maintain the fleet in both war and peace. Whereas Scotland's ambitious naval buildup died with James IV, the English navy remained on a solid footing through the sixteenth century and after. No longer an extension of personal power and prestige, navies were evolving into a reliable instrument of national policy. This does not mean that the Crown no longer exercised its personal prerogative: Elizabeth had no compunction about lending her ships for private commercial ventures, which could prove quite profitable. Private initiatives also enabled the Queen to challenge her enemies covertly, as she did through John Hawkins's voyage to the Spanish Caribbean in the JESUS OF LÜBECK, and through Francis Drake's circumnavigation in the GOLDEN HIND seven years before the Spanish Armada.

Privatized naval warfare probably reached its apogee in the United Provinces, where the United (Dutch) East India Company, or VOC (for Verenigde Oostindische Compagnie), and its less heralded sibling the West India Company had the authority to maintain navies and use them freely. The intent of this policy was to enable these companies to protect their own trade, especially in Asia, without being a burden on the state. In its first decade, the West India Company's notion of opening trade included attacking the Portuguese settlement of Bahía, Brazil, and plundering the Spanish treasure fleets in the Caribbean. Its greatest coup came in 1628 at the hands of Piet Heyn. Sailing in the AMSTERDAM at the head of a fleet of thirty-five ships, Heyn corralled a Spanish treasure fleet in the Bay of Matanzas, Cuba, and looted the ships of about forty-six tons of silver, as well as gold and other commodities bound for Spain.

Naval warfare in Europe passed a watershed in the sixteenth century, which saw the last major sea battle fought between fleets of galleys at Lepanto in 1571, and the first between fleets of square-rigged ships, the weeklong match between the Spanish Armada and the English fleet in 1588. There were material differences between the two fleets that would fade significantly as this sort of naval warfare matured. The English ships tended to be smaller — 150 tons on average, compared with 350 tons on the Spanish side — and so more maneuverable. The longer range of their guns frustrated Spanish attempts to close with them to exchange gunfire and, ultimately, to board their ships.

Even as naval guns and gunnery improved, boarding actions remained a mainstay of sea fighting in the age of sail. The artillery mounted on wooden ships was well suited to reducing an opposing ship's effectiveness as a fighting or sailing unit and to killing people; most casualties resulted from wounds caused by splintered wood. Sinking a wooden ship was still not easily accomplished, and most ship losses in this period were due to accidents — fire, wrecking on shore, or foundering at sea. Battle damage often contributed to the latter. In the Armada, only four Spanish ships (11 percent of the total confirmed losses) were captured or destroyed outright by English gunnery, three of them after they had run aground or been abandoned. Of the 151 ships that originally set out, 91 returned to Spain and 31 were lost in storms; the fate of the other 25 is unknown.[3]

These figures are comparable to statistics for the Royal Navy from the time of the Dutch Wars through the end of the Napoleonic Wars. In the course of ten major wars fought between 1652 and 1815, the Royal Navy lost 1,452 ships. Only 204 (14 percent) were lost in action, a figure that includes ships that blew up, caught fire or burned, were in-

tentionally scuttled or expended as fire ships, or were sunk in battle. More than half of the navy's losses were the result of accidents — mainly shipwreck and foundering — and captures accounted for one-third of the Royal Navy's lost ships.[4] That such figures do not square with modern impressions of naval warfare is perfectly understandable. During World War II, for instance, 1,694 surface warships were lost by all combatants; 81 percent were sunk as the result of enemy action, 9 percent were scuttled, 5 percent were lost in accidents, and 5 percent were captured.[5]

By the seventeenth century, the ships and guns of the major navies had attained a form that would change relatively little over the next 200 years. Improvements in naval architecture — which gradually became more scientific — led to an increase in the size and strength of ships. By the time of the Anglo-Dutch Wars in the 1650s, the line of battle was the preferred tactic for fleet engagements, as it allowed a heavy concentration of broadside fire on a specific part of the enemy's line. The preferred maneuver was "crossing the T," so that one's broadsides raked the enemy ships from stem to stern while the enemy could respond with only a handful of guns mounted in the bows. Fleet administration also became more systematic, with the establishment of rates and classes of ships. In their heyday, the largest ships of the line (first rates) had three full gun decks and mounted 100 or more guns, although the backbone of the battle fleet was the two-decker of 60 to 90 guns. Fleet actions were only one aspect of the navies' mission. The increased size of individual fleets reflected the expansion of imperial commitments and a broader range of assignments. If battle tactics remained relatively unchanged after the seventeenth century, strategy became ever more complex, involving not just the occasional fleet action but convoy protection, extended blockades, commerce warfare, scouting, patrols in remote corners of the empire, and diplomatic missions. Much of this work was taken up by frigates, fast, one-deck ships too small for the line of battle but capable of extended assignment on independent duty.

The operational heyday of the sailing warship

reached its acme during the French Revolutionary and Napoleonic Wars (1793–1815), although ship design continued to improve in the decades of peace that followed. However, the emergence of completely new and distinct technologies in the 1800s rendered the sailing warship obsolete by mid-century. The most obvious was the development of the steam engine and, toward the end of the century, the steam turbine. First harnessed to the paddlewheel and later to the less exposed screw, steam power made ships faster and more maneuverable than they had ever been. One drawback was the need for coal, which had a significant impact on operational endurance and gave a decided advantage to countries with forward bases overseas where coal could be stored. This necessity, coupled with the inefficiency and unreliability of steam engines, led to a generation of auxiliary steam sailing ships that ended with the launch of the first mastless capital ship, HMS DEVASTATION, in 1871. Steam power also made possible the development of the rotating turret, which increased the arc of fire of individual guns. Most ships with two or more turrets could fire across a total combined arc of 360 degrees without reorienting the hull as was necessary in sailing ships with fixed broadside batteries.

The application of iron and, from about the 1880s, steel to ship construction had a twofold effect on ship design. Both metals have greater tensile strength than wood, and it became possible to build much bigger ships. At first, the use of iron was limited to composite construction, wood planking over an iron frame. Later, iron hull plates were mounted to iron frames. Whereas the all-wood HMS VICTORY (1765) was only 226 feet, the French GLOIRE — an iron-clad composite hull — was 256 feet, and the first iron-hulled warship, HMS WARRIOR (1861) was 418 feet long. Iron also provided greater protection against gunfire, and in the American Civil War, it was used extensively in ship construction either by itself or as armor plating for wooden hulls. Its efficacy in this regard can be seen in the casualty figures from the four-hour Battle of Hampton Roads in 1862: USS MONITOR had one wounded, and CSS VIRGINIA

lost two dead and nineteen wounded. By comparison, the fifteen-minute engagement between the frigates USS CHESAPEAKE and HMS SHANNON in 1812 left 78 dead and more than 150 wounded.

Although explosive shells were first developed in the early nineteenth century, they were not terribly effective. The introduction of armor spurred the need for improved antiship ordnance, as distinct from the solid-shot or antipersonnel canister and grape used to repel or clear the way for a boarding action. The shell-gun came into its own thanks not only to more destructive shells but also to the switch from muzzle-loading to breech-loading guns and from smoothbore to rifled gun barrels, and to improvements in the chemistry of propellants. By the end of the nineteenth century, however, the ship's gun was entering what would prove to be the final stages of its 600-year development. The ship's gun would reach its apotheosis in the twentieth century, but by the end of the nineteenth century, entirely new weapons had emerged to threaten its primacy: the submarine boat, the mine, and the torpedo.

The submarine made its first operational debut during the American Civil War. The best known was the Confederate Navy's H. L. HUNLEY, the first submarine to sink a surface ship, the USS HOUSATONIC, although the *Hunley* was herself sunk in the attack. The weapon employed was a spar torpedo, which consisted of an explosive charge carried on the end of a long spar and detonated when placed alongside the opposing ship's hull. (In this period, a torpedo referred to what we now call a mine.) Whether delivered by a submarine or a half-submerged "David" boat (so called because it stood in relation to the larger ships of the U.S. Navy as David did to Goliath) or left on moorings, torpedoes were a cheap and reasonably effective means for an inferior naval power such as the Confederacy to combat a superior one such as the United States. But the Confederacy waged a defensive naval war largely confined to rivers, harbors, and bays. To achieve their potential as offensive weapons, both submarines and torpedoes required mechanical propulsion.

The first "locomotive torpedo," driven by compressed air, was devised in 1866. It was quickly realized that this new weapon was an inexpensive and potent threat to even the largest capital ships. Torpedoes could easily be mounted on purpose-built torpedo boats that were smaller and faster than their prey and difficult to hit with guns designed for use against other capital ships. Ships therefore had to be armed with smaller-caliber guns to counter these smaller boats, and an entirely new class of ship, the torpedo boat destroyer, was developed to protect the larger ships against this new threat. In time, ships of all sizes would be armed with torpedoes, and in the twentieth century, destroyers would be the primary defense against the ultimate torpedo boat, the submarine.

Development of the submarine proceeded steadily in the nineteenth century. Robert Fulton designed and built one in 1801, though the Royal Navy was steadfastly against its further development. Referring to the prime minister's interest in Fulton's machine, First Sea Lord Admiral the Earl St. Vincent declared, "Pitt was the greatest fool that ever existed to encourage a mode of warfare which those that command the sea did not want, and which, if successful, would deprive them of it." One consequence of this entrenched opposition was that development of the practical submarine remained almost exclusively the preserve of private enterprise until the end of the century. Although the first steam-powered submarine was built in England, the world's leading designer was the Irish-American John P. Holland, who built six sub-

marines between 1878 and 1898. The last, the HOLLAND, was commissioned by the U.S. Navy in 1900 and was the prototype for many of the world's first generation submarines. Future events would prove Lord St. Vincent's fears more than justified.

One unanticipated consequence of the industrial age was the rapid diffusion of naval shipbuilding technology. By the end of the nineteenth century, Britain and France were exporting large numbers of ships to Latin America and Asia, especially China and Japan. Likewise, the United States and to a lesser extent Russia, Italy, and Germany embarked on ambitious programs to cultivate their own shipbuilding industries. The resulting competition would ensure that naval warfare would remain savage and brutal, as it had always been, but savage and brutal in entirely new ways.

Notes

1. Philip K. Hitti, *History of the Arabs,* 10th ed. (New York: St. Martin's, 1971), p. 201, citing al-Tabari's *Annals of the Apostles and Kings.*
2. Quoted in Gwyn Jones, *A History of the Vikings* (New York: Oxford University Press, 1968), p. 204n1.
3. M. J. Rodríguez-Salgado et al., *Armada 1588–1988: An International Exhibition to Commemorate the Spanish Armada* (London: Penguin Books, 1988), pp. 154–58.
4. David J. Hepper, *British Warship Losses in the Age of Sail, 1650–1859* (Rotherfield, Sussex: Jean Boudriot, 1994), pp. 211–13.
5. David Brown, *Warship Losses of World War II,* rev. ed. (Annapolis: Naval Institute Press, 1990), pp. 229, 236.

Warships of the World
to 1900

NOTE

Each entry comprises three parts: basic specifications, narrative history, and source note. Complete publication data for all works cited in the source notes can be found in the Bibliography.

The first paragraph includes basic information about the vessel in question, including:

L/B/D: Length, beam, and draft, or depth in hold (dph), given in feet and meters.

Tons: Usually given in gross registered tons (grt) or displacement (disp).

Hull: Hull material, usually wood, iron, or steel.

Comp.: Complement, including crew and/or passengers if known.

Arm.: Armament, including the number of guns and caliber or weight of projectile, in either standard or metric measurement. Numbers in parentheses indicate the number of turrets and guns per turret: $4 \times 10''$ (4×2) means four 10-inch guns, in two turrets mounting two guns each.

> *carr.:* Carronade
> *pdr.:* Pounder
> *TT:* Torpedo tube

Armor: Maximum thickness of belt (or side) and deck armor.

Mach.: Machinery, including type of propulsion, horsepower, number of screws, and speed.

Des.: Designer.

Built: Builder, place, and year of build.

FLEET DESIGNATIONS

CSS: Confederate States Ship
HMS: Her/His Majesty's Ship
USS: United States Ship
USRC: United States Revenue Cutter

A

Adventure Galley

Galley (3m). *L:* ca. 124' (38m). *Tons:* 285 bm. *Hull:* wood. *Comp.:* 152. *Arm.:* 34 × 12pdr. *Built:* Castle Yard, Deptford, Eng.; 1695.

Adventure Galley was a three-masted ship equipped with thirty-six oars as auxiliary propulsion. In 1696, Captain William Kidd was made captain and, armed with a privateer's commission from William III, set out from England to capture enemy commerce, mainly that of France and Spain. Of obscure background, the Scottish-born Kidd had settled in New York after years as a pirate in the Caribbean. In 1695, he had sailed his merchant ship *Antigua* to London with a view to acquiring a letter of marque that would enable him to sail as a privateer. His brief also included the right to attack pirates of any nationality, especially those who preyed on the valuable trade routes of the Indian Ocean.

Adventure Galley sailed on April 6, 1696, and captured a French fisherman in the North Atlantic. On September 6, having recruited a further ninety crew in New York, she sailed for the Indian Ocean via Madeira and the Cape Verde Islands, landing at Tulear, Madagascar, on January 27, 1697. En route, Kidd fell in with a squadron of Royal Navy ships and impressed the officers as a would-be pirate rather than a privateer with the King's commission. Rumors of this spread quickly, and British merchants kept their distance. After repairs in the Comoros, *Adventure Galley* sailed for the Bab al-Mandab Strait at the mouth of the Red Sea to intercept one of the richly laden ships of the Muslim pilgrim fleet, which sailed under the protection of European traders. On August 15, *Adventure Galley* slipped in among a convoy guarded by two Dutch ships and the East India Company's *Sceptre,* whose captain intimidated Kidd into withdrawing. Kidd then headed for the Malabar Coast of India, where he captured a number of prizes, fought off two Portuguese warships from Goa, and had several run-ins with the East India Company. In March 1698, *Adventure Galley* — in company with the prizes *Quedah Merchant* and *Rupparell* — sailed for the island of Saint Marie off the northeast coast of Madagascar. *Adventure Galley* was in wretched condition and eventually sank there. Kidd left the island in *Quedah Merchant,* which ran aground and was burned on Hispaniola after Kidd had sold off what remained of her valuable cargo of textiles.

Upon his return to North America, Kidd was imprisoned and returned to England. A valuable pawn in a political game between William III's Whig supporters, who had backed his venture, and the opposition Tories, who were now in the ascendancy, Kidd was tried for and found guilty of murder and piracy, and then twice hanged (the rope broke the first time). His remains were put on display at Tilbury Point on the Thames as a warning to others.

Ritchie, *Captain Kidd and the War against the Pirates.*

HMS Agamemnon

3rd rate 64 (3m). *L/B:* 160' × 45' (48.8m × 13.7m). *Tons:* 1,348 bm. *Hull:* wood. *Comp.:* 520. *Arm.:* 26 × 24pdr, 26 × 12pdr, 12 × 6pdr. *Built:* Henry Adams, Buckler's Hard, Eng.; 1781.

HMS *Agamemnon* first saw action in the West Indies with Rear Admiral Richard Kempenfelt's squadron when it captured fifteen ships from a French convoy under Admiral Count Luc Urbain de Guichen, who was bound for the Caribbean.

Four months later she was in Admiral Sir George Rodney's squadron at the Battle of the Saintes, April 11, 1782, in which the British defeated the French fleet under Rear Admiral Count François J. P. de Grasse, recouping a little of the glory (but none of the colonies) they had lost at the Battle of the Chesapeake the previous summer. When the revolutionary French government declared war on Great Britain in 1793, *Agamemnon* came under command of Captain Horatio Nelson. Nelson sailed with Lord Howe's Mediterranean Fleet in the blockade of Toulon and in the capture of the Corsican ports of Bastia and Calvi, where Nelson was partially blinded in his right eye. *Agamemnon* remained in the Mediterranean until 1796, a period during which Nelson molded his "band of brothers" and began to establish himself as an innovative, resolute, and daring commander. Nelson was quite fond of his command and described *Agamemnon* as "without exception the finest 64 in the service."

The following year, *Agamemnon* was with the Channel Fleet when her crew were implicated in the mutiny of the Nore. Present at Nelson's great victory in the Battle of Copenhagen in 1801, her next significant assignment was in 1805, when she sailed with Vice Admiral Sir John Orde's fleet off Cadiz. In July, she took part in Admiral Sir Robert Calder's action with the Combined Fleet off El Ferrol. Her squadron later came under the command of Admiral Lord Nelson. During the Battle of Trafalgar against the Franco-Spanish fleet, *Agamemnon* sailed in Nelson's weather column but escaped with relatively few casualties. After further service off Cadiz, she sailed for the West Indies, where she took part in several engagements against French naval units and privateers. Over the next few years, she sailed variously in the West Indies, the Baltic, off Portugal, and off South America. On June 20, 1809, while putting into the River Plate in a storm, she grounded on an unmarked reef and was lost, though without loss of life.

Hepper, *British Warship Losses*. Mackenzie, *Trafalgar Roll*.

HMS Agamemnon

James Watt–class battleship (1f/3m). *L/B/D:* 230.3′ × 55.3′ × 24.1′ (70.2m × 16.9m × 7.3m). *Tons:* 5,080 disp. *Hull:* wood. *Comp.:* 860. *Arm.:* 34 × 8″, 56 × 32pdr, 1 × 68pdr. *Mach.:* Penn trunk engine, 2,268 ihp, single screw; 11.24 kts. *Built:* Woolwich Dockyard, Eng.; 1852.

Laid down in 1849, launched in 1852, and commissioned the following year, the ship-rigged steam battleship *Agamemnon* was the first warship built with screw propulsion, though other sailing vessels had been fitted with engines after commissioning. *Agamemnon*'s success was such that she remained the basic model for the first decade of Britain's steam battlefleet. As flagship of Rear Admiral Sir Edmund Lyons's Black Sea fleet (Captain William Mends commanding) during the Crimean War, she took part in the bombardment of Sevastopol on October 17, 1854. She also took part in the shelling of Fort Kinburn, at the mouth of the Dnieper, one year later.

In 1857, the British government fitted out *Agamemnon* to carry 1,250 tons of telegraphic cable for the Atlantic Telegraph Company's first attempt to lay a transatlantic cable. Although this was unsuccessful, the following year the project was resumed. *Agamemnon* and her American counterpart, USS *Niagara*, spliced their cable ends in mid-Atlantic on July 29 and then sailed for their respective continents. With William Thompson, the future Lord Kelvin, monitoring the progress of the 1,020 miles of cable, *Agamemnon* reached Valentia Bay in County Kerry, Ireland, on August 5, 1858. *Niagara* reached Trinity Bay, Newfoundland, the same day. Eleven days later, Queen Victoria sent a ninety-nine-word message to President James Buchanan, a process that took more than sixteen hours. (Three weeks later, the cable failed and service was interrupted for eight years.) After service on the Caribbean and North American stations, *Agamemnon* was paid off in 1862 and sold in 1870.

Clarke, *Voice across the Sea.* Lambert, *Battleships in Transition.*

Aid

Ship. *Tons:* 300. *Hull:* wood. *Comp.:* 115–120. *Arm.:* 2 × 6pdr, 4 × 4pdr, 4 small. *Built:* Deptford Dockyard, Eng.; 1562.

The Queen's ship *Aid* was one of three built in 1562 as war with France threatened. In the fall of the same year, *Aid* was assigned to help supply the English garrison at Le Havre until the capture of the Huguenot-held port by loyalist forces in August 1563. *Aid*'s next important mission came in 1577, when the Adventurers to the North-West for the Discovery of the North-West Passage, or the Company of Cathay, was formed to follow up Sir Martin Frobisher's discovery of Frobisher Bay on Baffin Island in *Gabriel* the previous year. The inlet promised to be the much sought after Northwest Passage, but more important was his discovery of what was widely believed to be gold. *Aid* sailed as flagship of an expedition that included *Gabriel* and *Michael* and about 150 men. Departing in mid-May, the ships arrived at Baffin Island on July 17. They returned home at the end of the summer with three Eskimos — a man and a woman with her child, all of whom died after a month in England — and 200 tons of ore assayed as yielding a profit of £5 in gold and silver per ton.

On the basis of this hopeful but erroneous assessment, Frobisher sailed at the head of sixteen ships with a view to exploring the Northwest Passage, mining ore, and establishing a manned settlement. After taking possession of Greenland — renamed West England — in the name of the Queen, Frobisher and company continued to the west. In 1578, Frobisher Bay was filled with ice, and after losing one ship to a floe, they sailed west into what they called Mistaken Strait, now Hudson Strait. The fleet doubled back to Frobisher Bay, where *Aid* was hulled below the waterline by an ice floe and repaired with a sheet of lead. After mining 1,350 tons of ore and erecting a house for future use (immediate plans for leaving a party to winter there were abandoned), they sailed home. The five-year effort to extract precious metals from the ore brought home on the second and third voyages was fruitless; the Company of Cathay went under, and the Baffin Island rocks were "throwne away to re-payre the high-wayes."

As tensions between Spain and England worsened, *Aid* was rebuilt and in November 1580 took part in the reduction of Fort Smerwick in Ireland, where a combined Spanish-Papal force had taken refuge. Again under Frobisher's command, *Aid* was one of two Queen's ships contributed to Sir Francis Drake's twenty-five-ship expedition to the Spanish West Indies in 1585. In October, the fleet anchored at Bayona, Spain, where Drake compelled the governor to allow his ships to water and provision before they departed again on October 11. Proceeding to the Cape Verde Islands, Drake burned Santiago, Porto Praya, and Santo Domingo when their inhabitants failed to ransom the towns. The English went on to ransom Santo Domingo and Cartagena and sacked St. Augustine, Florida. They then sailed for Sir Walter Raleigh's colony at Roanoke, North Carolina, and returned to England with the colonists in July 1586.

Two years later, *Aid* was one of six ships in Drake's western squadron based at Plymouth to await the arrival of the Spanish Armada. She remained with the English fleet from the day of the first action on July 31 through the final defeat of the Spanish ships at the Battle of Gravelines on August 8. In 1589, *Aid* again sailed with Drake as part of the poorly executed "Counter-Armada." The triple aim of this venture was to destroy the remaining Armada ships in their home ports in Spain and Portugal, restore the pretender Dom Antonio to the Portuguese throne, and seize the Azores as a base from which to attack the Spanish treasure fleets from the West Indies. The overly ambitious plan failed in all its primary objectives and returned to England. In 1590, *Aid* was broken up after a quarter-century of service to the Elizabethan navy.

Glasgow, "Navy in the French Wars." Stefansson, *Three Voyages of Martin Frobisher.* Sugden, *Sir Francis Drake.*

CSS Alabama

(ex-*Enrica*) Auxiliary bark (1f/3m). *L/B/D:* 220′ × 31.75′ × 14′ (67.1m × 9.7m × 4.3m). *Tons:* 1,050 tons. *Hull:* wood. *Comp.:* 148. *Arm.:* 6 × 32pdr, 1 × 110pdr, 1 × 68pdr. *Mach.:* direct-acting engine, 600 ihp, 1 screw; 13 kts. *Built:* Laird Bros., Ltd., Birkenhead, Eng.; 1862.

In the history of commerce warfare, CSS *Alabama* was the most successful raider in terms of numbers of vessels seized — capturing and burning fifty-five ships and seizing and bonding ten more. James Dunwoody Bulloch, the Confederate naval agent in Europe responsible for creating a viable high-seas fleet from scratch, ordered Hull No. 290; she was christened *Enrica* and put down the Mersey River on July 29, 1862. Charles Francis Adams, the U.S. minister in London, insisted that the sale of the ship violated Britain's 1861 declaration of neutrality. In a manner of speaking, it did not, for it was not until after the ship had been armed from the supply ships *Agrippina* and *Bahama* off the Azores that Captain Raphael Semmes commissioned her as CSS *Alabama* on August 24, 1862.

Cruising from the Azores to Newfoundland, and south to the Caribbean, *Alabama* sank twenty-seven ships between September and December of 1862. On January 11, 1863, she sank the auxiliary schooner USS Hatteras of the Gulf Coast Blockading Squadron about twenty miles south of Galveston, Texas. After putting the captured Union crew ashore in Jamaica, *Alabama* continued on her way. On June 20, while cruising off Brazil, she overhauled the Philadelphia merchant bark *Conrad,* which Semmes armed and commissioned as CSS *Tuscaloosa,* Lieutenant John Low commanding. (*Tuscaloosa* cruised in the South Atlantic for six months before being seized by the British in Simon's Bay, South Africa, on December 26.) Visiting South Africa in the autumn of 1863, *Alabama* sailed into the Indian Ocean and as far east as Singapore. Semmes then returned to Europe for an extensive refit, anchoring at Cherbourg on June 11, 1864.

Semmes fully intended to remain at Cherbourg for several months, but the Union government had recently persuaded the French to impose a twenty-

▲ "The Fight between the **Alabama** and the **Kearsarge**," a woodcut from the *Illustrated London News* showing the end of the Confederacy's most successful commerce raider off Cherbourg, France, June 19, 1864. *Courtesy Library of Congress.*

four-hour limit on the stay of Confederate-flag ships in French ports. In the meantime, the screw sloop USS Kearsarge under Captain John A. Winslow arrived at Cherbourg from Flushing, Belgium, on June 14. After attempting to embark U.S. sailors landed from *Alabama,* Winslow was told he was violating French neutrality and left. Preferring that his ship suffer honorable defeat rather than an ignominious blockade, Semmes is reported to have told his lieutenant, John M. Kell, "Although the Confederate government has ordered me to avoid engagement with the enemy cruisers, I am tired of running from that flaunting rag!" On June 19, *Alabama* sailed out of Cherbourg and, still within sight of the spectators lining the shore, opened fire on *Kearsarge* at 1057. After so long at sea, *Alabama* was no match for *Kearsarge* and was reduced to a sinking condition in an hour. Semmes repeatedly struck his flag, but before *Kearsarge* could act, he and some forty others were rescued by the British yacht *Deerhound* — a crime for which Semmes was arrested in December 1865 on orders from U.S. Navy Secretary Gideon Welles. While the sinking of *Alabama* did not affect the outcome of the Civil War, her loss was a blow to Confederate morale.

The devastation caused by *Alabama* and her sister raiders, especially FLORIDA and SHENANDOAH, has frequently been cited as one cause of the decline of U.S. international shipping in the latter half of the nineteenth century. An immediate consequence of their efforts was the 900 percent rise in insurance rates for U.S.-flag ships, and the resulting transfer of some 900 ships to foreign registry. Following the war, the United States insisted that Britain be held liable for the destruction wrought by British-built commerce raiders. These proceedings came to be known as the *Alabama* claims, as *Alabama* alone accounted for as much as $5 million in losses. After several false starts, the claims were finally resolved under the Treaty of Washington (1871), by which the United States and Great Britain submitted to arbitration by an international tribunal composed of representatives from Britain, the United States, Italy, Switzerland, and Brazil. The tribunal found that Britain had not exercised "due diligence" and awarded the United States $15.5 million in damages.

Alabama's story did not end there. On November 7, 1984, French divers from the minesweeper *Circé* discovered the remains of the ship lying in about 195 feet of water six miles off Cherbourg. The site is under the protection of a joint French and American authority.

Dalzell, *Flight from the Flag*. Guérout, "Engagement between the C.S.S. *Alabama* and the U.S.S. *Kearsarge*." Leary, "*Alabama* vs. *Kearsarge*." Robinson, *Shark of the Confederacy*. Semmes, *Memoirs of Service Afloat*. Silverstone, *Warships of the Civil War Navies*.

HMS Alecto

Steam sloop (1f/3m). *L/B/D:* 164′ × 32.7′ × 12.6′ (50m × 10m × 3.8m). *Tons:* 796 bm. *Hull:* wood. *Mach.:* direct-acting engine, 280 ihp, sidewheels; 8.5 kts. *Built:* Chatham Dockyard, Eng.; 1839.

Named for one of the furies of Greek mythology, *Alecto* was a brigantine-rigged sidewheel steamer. She served for six years with the Mediterranean Fleet. Built at a time when the Admiralty were beginning to believe that screw propulsion was more efficient than paddlewheels, *Alecto* is best remembered for her role in a series of trials against HMS RATTLER, a near sister ship fitted with a single screw instead of paddles. In the spring of 1845, the Admiralty sponsored a series of twelve trials between the two ships. These included races under steam, under sail alone, one under steam towing the other not under power, and the most famous, a tug-of-war held on April 3. In this, the two ships were joined by a line running from stern to stern. *Alecto* got steam up first, towing *Rattler* at about 2 knots before the latter's engines were engaged. Within five minutes, *Rattler* had brought *Alecto* to a standstill and soon managed to pull the sidewheeler stern first at about 2.8 knots. Although the results seem to have been a foregone conclusion — the Admiralty had already ordered several screw ships — the demonstrations were good publicity for its adoption of the screw as the preferred means of auxiliary, and later primary, propulsion. At the end of 1845, *Alecto* resumed more regular assignments, including five years on the American station and several years on the coast of Africa. She was broken up in 1865.

Brown, *Before the Ironclad*.

Alfred

(ex-*Black Prince*) Ship (3m). *Tons:* 440. *Comp.:* 220. *Arm.:* 20 × 9pdr, 10 × 6pdr. *Built:* John Wharton(?), Philadelphia; 1774.

The merchantman *Black Prince* made two voyages to England before being requisitioned for a warship by the Continental Congress on November 4, 1775. Renamed for Alfred the Great, the ninth-century British king credited with building England's first fleet, *Alfred* was put under command of Captain Dudley Saltonstall. She was made flagship of Commodore Esek Hopkins's eight-ship squadron (including *Columbus, Cabot,* ANDREW DORIA, PROVIDENCE, *Fly,* HORNET, and WASP), which occupied Fort Nassau, the Bahamas, for two weeks in March 1776. On October 26, Captain John Paul Jones (a lieutenant on her first voyage) left New London for a cruise off Nova Scotia during which

Alfred captured nine ships before returning to Boston on December 26. The following August, under Captain Elisha Hinman, *Alfred* and *Raleigh* sailed for France for military supplies. Returning via the West Indies, the two ships were engaged by the British ships HMS *Ariadne* (20 guns) and *Ceres* (14) on March 29, 1778. *Alfred* was captured and acquired by the Royal Navy at Barbados. She was sold out of service in 1782.

McCusker, *"Alfred," the First Continental Flagship;* "American Invasion of Nassau in the Bahamas."

Alliance

(ex-*Hancock*) Frigate (3m). *L/B/D:* 151′ × 36′ × 12.5′ (46m × 11m × 3.8m). *Tons:* 900. *Hull:* wood. *Comp.:* 300. *Arm.:* 28 × 12pdr, 8 × 9pdr. *Built:* William & James K. Hackett, Essex, Mass.; 1777.

Launched as *Hancock,* but renamed in recognition of the French entry into the American Revolution against Britain, *Alliance* was one of the most celebrated American ships of the war. Her first mission, under Captain Pierre Landais, was to carry the Marquis de Lafayette to France to plead for more support for the colonists. She left Boston on January 4, 1779. A mutiny by pro-British crew was discovered and suppressed, and the ship went on to capture two prizes before landing at Brest after twenty-three days at sea. Benjamin Franklin then assigned the ship to Captain John Paul Jones's squadron. Landais resented the assignment, and he is believed to have deliberately rammed the flagship, BONHOMME RICHARD, during the convoy's passage from Brest to Bourdeaux in June. While taking part in Jones's raiding cruise around the British Isles in August and September, Landais was repeatedly insubordinate, though *Alliance* captured three ships before rounding the north of Scotland. During *Bonhomme Richard*'s epic fight with HMS *Serapis* on September 23, Landais at first stood off from the battle and then fired broadsides into the grappled ships that caused as much damage and death to the Americans as to the British. After the battle, *Alliance* sailed with Jones's squadron to the Netherlands, where Landais was relieved of command.

On December 27, flying Jones's flag, *Alliance* slipped the British blockade off the Texel and sailed down the English Channel and then south to La Coruña, Spain, before returning to Brest. Although Franklin urged Jones to load a cargo of arms and supplies and return to the United States at once, Jones delayed and traveled to Paris. While he was away, Landais appeared at Brest and usurped command of his old vessel. Although the French offered to stop *Alliance,* by force if necessary, Jones let the ship sail under Landais, whose shipmates later locked him up because they thought he was insane.

Captain John Barry assumed command of *Alliance* at Boston in September 1780, but the ship was not ready for sea until February 1781. When she sailed for France, her passengers included George Washington's former aide-de-camp Colonel John Laurens and Thomas Paine. After only three weeks at Brest, she sailed for home in company with the former French East Indiaman *Marquis de Lafayette* and loaded with arms and supplies for the Continental Army. On April 2, *Alliance* captured the privateer brigs *Mars* and *Minerva*. Prize crews were put aboard both, but again the French proved fickle allies. *Minerva* sailed for France, and *Marquis de Lafayette* later abandoned Barry, only to be captured by the British.

On May 27, still struggling for home, *Alliance* was engaged by the British sloops HMS *Trepassy* and *Atalanta* (both 14 guns). Unmaneuverable in the light airs, *Alliance* could not position herself against the British ships, which pounded her repeatedly from positions astern. Barry was seriously wounded but refused to surrender, and when the wind sprang up he worked his ship between his opponents and forced them both to surrender. *Alliance* finally returned to Boston on June 6.

The American Revolution ended with the surrender of General Cornwallis's army at Yorktown, and on December 24, the Marquis de Lafayette embarked in *Alliance* for his return to France, arriving at Brest on January 17, 1782. Two months later, she sailed for home with dispatches from Benjamin Franklin, but contrary weather made for a long crossing to New London, where she arrived on May 13. *Alliance* put to sea again in August and, as peace still was not formally declared, took eight prizes.

Two were returned to the United States, and the others accompanied *Alliance* to France, where they arrived in October. Two months later, Barry was ordered to the West Indies for a consignment of gold, only to find that it had already been loaded aboard the American warship *Duc de Lauzan*. Sailing as an escort, *Alliance* fought off an attack by the frigates HMS *Alarm* (32 guns) and *Sybil* (28) and the sloop of war *Tobago* (14) on March 11, 1783. None of the combatants knew that peace had been achieved through the Treaty of Paris in January. These were the last shots of the American Revolution.

Alliance returned to Newport and in June was ordered by Congress to carry a cargo of tobacco from Philadelphia to France. The ship grounded leaving Newport, but no damage was detected until after she had left the Delaware River, when a leak forced her back to Philadelphia. Funds were unavailable for her repair, and the last ship of the Continental Navy was sold out of service, in August 1785, to John Coburn, who in turn sold her to Robert Morris, formerly Agent of Marine of the Continental Congress. Morris converted her for merchant service to China, and under Captain Thomas Read, *Alliance* sailed for Canton in June 1787, becoming the eighth U.S.-flag vessel to enter that port, on December 22. She returned to Philadelphia on September 17, 1788. Her subsequent career is unknown, except that she was finally abandoned on Petty Island on the Delaware.

U.S. Navy, *DANFS*.

HMS Amphion

Amphion-class 5th rate 32 (3m). *L/B/D:* 144.0′ × 37.5′ × 12.5′ (43.9m × 11.4m × 3.8m). *Tons:* 910 bm. *Hull:* wood. *Comp.:* 254. *Arm.:* 26 × 18pdr, 6 × 6pdr, 6 × 24pdr. *Des.:* Edward Rule. *Built:* Betts, Mistlythorn, Eng.; 1798.

Named for a son of Zeus credited in some Greek myths with the founding of Thebes, HMS *Amphion* was commissioned in 1800, when she was attached to the fleet of Admiral Sir Hyde Parker in the Atlantic. In 1801, Lord Nelson sailed in *Amphion* to take up his post as commander-in-chief of the Mediterranean Fleet. He shifted his flag to HMS VICTORY off Toulon, bringing with him *Amphion*'s captain, Thomas Masterman Hardy, who was succeeded by Captain Sutton.

On October 5, 1804, *Amphion* was in a squadron of four ships dispatched to intercept a Spanish squadron en route from Montevideo bearing silver and other valuables worth £2 million. *Medea* (40 guns), *Fama*, *Clara*, and *Mercedes* (all 34s) were intercepted about 100 miles west of Cadiz. As Spain and Britain were not at war, Captain Graham Moore (HMS *Indefatigable*) was under orders to detain the fleet and not to fire unless fired upon. Rear Admiral Don Joseph Bustamente refused to heed the British signals, and *Mercedes* opened the battle with a broadside against *Amphion*. Ten minutes later, *Mercedes* blew up; all but forty of the nearly three hundred crew and passengers were killed, including the wife of Captain Alvear and eight of their children. Within the hour, the three other Spanish ships were captured after putting up stout resistance. Alvear and one son had transferred to *Medea* just before the battle started; in addition to his wife and children, Alvear lost a personal fortune of £30,000 he had amassed during thirty years abroad. By way of compensation, the British government repaid him in full for his financial loss. Worse for the British, this action off Cape Santa Maria did much to push Spain to declare war on Britain on December 12.

In October 1805, *Amphion*'s ailing Captain Sutton was succeeded by one of Nelson's favorite midshipmen, Captain William Hoste. Ordered to Algiers, *Amphion*'s crew did not learn of Nelson's death at Trafalgar until after their return to Gibraltar on November 9. Hoste was much affected by the news and wrote to his father:

> Not to have been in the battle is enough to make one mad; but to have lost such a friend besides is really sufficient to almost overwhelm me. . . . I like my ship very much; as the last gift of that excellent man I shall ever consider her, and stay in her during the war.

Although Trafalgar had removed the threat of large-scale fleet actions by the French and Spanish navies, the Royal Navy remained busy in the Mediterranean. In March 1806, *Amphion*'s crew were ordered to protect Sicily from a French invasion, and on July 4, her crew supported soldiers under Major General Sir John Stuart in the British army's first victory over a Napoleonic army, at the Battle of Maida, an event commemorated in the naming of Maida Vale in London.

Amphion underwent a refit in England in the last half of 1807, and in May 1808 she destroyed the French transport *Balleine* in the Bay of Rosas, Spain. Hoste was then dispatched to the Adriatic, a major artery of supply for Napoleon's forces in Illyria, his main base being on the island of Lissa (now Vis), south-southwest of Split in Bosnia-Herzegovina.

On March 13, 1811, a combined Franco-Venetian squadron of four 40-gun and two 32-gun frigates and five smaller vessels under Commodore Bernard Dubourdieu approached the island intent on its recapture. Against this force, Hoste had *Amphion*, *Active* (38 guns), *Cerberus* (32), and *Volage* (22). Outnumbered 300 guns to 150, and 2,500 men to 900 men, British prospects were dim. Nonetheless, flying the signal "Remember Nelson," Hoste put his ships in line-ahead formation as the French bore down in two divisions. Dubourdieu, in *Favorite* (40), hoped to cross ahead of Hoste's squadron to bring the English ships under fire from two sides. *Amphion* proved too fast, and an attempted boarding action was abandoned when Hoste fired a 5.5-inch mortar loaded with 750 musket balls onto *Favorite*'s forecastle, killing most of the boarding party, including Dubourdieu, the captain, and several other officers. The French ship continued to drive ahead into shallow water when Hoste's squadron suddenly wore. *Favorite* ran aground and was later blown up by her crew. *Amphion* was taken under fire by *Flore* (40) and *Bellona* (32), but through deft ship handling, Hoste forced both to strike their colors. (*Flore* later escaped, a move Hoste protested in a letter to the French captain.) By the end of the battle, the British had captured two Venetian ships — *Corona* (40; renamed HMS *Daedalus*) and *Bellona* (32; later the troopship *Dover*).

Hoste's lopsided victory over a vastly superior force became the stuff of legend; British casualties numbered 45 dead and 145 wounded against French losses of about 700 men and three ships. Lissa was also a strategically decisive battle that marked the turning point in the struggle for control of the Adriatic. Following repairs in England, *Amphion* saw duty in the North Sea. From 1815 to 1818, she was based variously at Bermuda, Portsmouth, and Brazil. In 1820, she was sunk as a breakwater at Woolwich.

Henderson, *Frigates*. Hoste, *Memoirs and Letters of Captain Sir William Hoste*. Lyon, *Sailing Navy List*.

Amsterdam

Ship (3m). *Tons:* 500 lasten. *Hull:* wood. *Comp.:* 166 crew, 84 soldiers. *Arm.:* 22 bronze guns, 28 iron guns. *Built:* Amsterdam; 1628.

The Dutch West India Company (WIC) was established to foster Dutch trade and settlement in the Americas, but the charter of 1621 allowed the company to maintain an army and a fleet — as did the East India Company (VOC) — and its earliest undertakings were directed more toward plunder than plantations. In 1624, an expedition of 3,300 men led by Jacob Willekens captured the Portuguese colony at Bahía, Brazil, where Dutch traders had been active since the 1580s. In retaliation, Spain dispatched a force numbering more than 12,000 soldiers, and the Dutch were forced to surrender the town in 1625. The Dutch were also active in the Caribbean, where the great prize was the Spanish silver fleet.

Established in the 1560s, the Spanish fleet system consisted in the yearly dispatch of two supply convoys to the Americas, one intended to serve the markets of New Spain (Mexico) and the other those of Peru. The first fleet, the *flota*, sailed in April bound for Puerto Rico and Veracruz, Mexico. The "fleet of the Tierra Firme" — known in the 1600s as the *galeones*, for the six to eight warships that sailed as escorts — put to sea in August, heading for Cartagena de Indias (Colombia) and Portobelo on the isthmus of Panama. In March of the

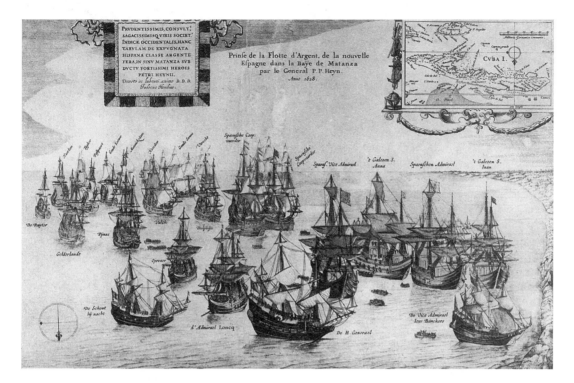

▲ Piet Heyn's flagship, **Amsterdam,** is depicted in the foreground of this view of the Dutch fleet at the Battle of Matanzas Bay, where Heyn corralled the Spanish treasure fleet in 1628. *Courtesy Instituut voor Maritieme Historie, Marinestaf, 's-Gravenhage, Netherlands.*

following year, both fleets rendezvoused off Havana, Cuba, for the return to Spain. An annual venture proved unworkable, and in the two centuries of its operation, the *flota* was dispatched every two years and the *galeones* every three years.

The WIC's first attempt to capture the *flota* was led by Boudewijn Hendricksz in 1625–26. The fleet reached Bahía just after it had been retaken, and overawed by the strength of the Spanish presence, the Dutch sailed north to the Caribbean. In September, Hendricksz captured San Juan, Puerto Rico, but failing to take Morro Castle, the Dutch left after five weeks. With little to show for his efforts, Hendricksz remained in the Caribbean hoping to capture the treasure fleet, but he died in June and his now mutinous crew sailed for home. In the

meantime, the WIC had dispatched Piet Heyn with fourteen ships to link up with Hendricksz's fleet. To Heyn's dismay, he had to watch as the silver fleet passed before him in the Strait of Florida. Heyn then turned for Bahía, where his ships captured or sank twenty-six ships, "by which happy result [the WIC] — by so many preceding disasters and damages so much weakened — began to recover her breath and bounded back on her feet." The profits from these and other initiatives in the Caribbean and on the "Wild Coast" of South America not only enabled the WIC to send out three fleets in 1628 but put the Spanish on their guard.

The first fleet of 1628 captured about a dozen significant prizes in Brazil. At the same time, Pieter Adriaenszoon Ita sailed with thirty-six ships to the Caribbean, where on August 1 he detained two Honduran galleys, burning one and capturing the other off Havana. This was a doubly rich prize, for after the action Ita headed home, leading the Spanish to believe that the Dutch were gone for the year. In fact, on August 8, Heyn had reached the Strait of

Florida in *Amsterdam* (under Captain Witte de With). Heyn's fleet of thirty-one ships lay in wait for the Spanish off the Dry Tortugas, Florida. On August 22, authorities in Havana learned of Heyn's presence and dispatched advice boats to warn the ships of the *flota* from San Juan de Ulúa, Mexico.

The warnings were never received, and on the evening of September 8, the Dutch first saw the Spanish fleet of Don Juan de Benavides — about twenty-two ships, including four galleons, two of them unarmed. Fickle winds made it impossible for Benavides to bring his ships into Havana, and the next morning he decided to run for the Bay of Matanzas, fifty miles to the east. Heyn divided his fleet, sending ahead Vice Admiral Joost van Trappen (called Bankert) with nine ships so that Benavides was now trapped between two wings of the Dutch fleet. Benavides had little choice but to enter the bay, although in such disorder that several ships grounded. The first Dutch ships on the scene anchored in the mouth of the bay and fired on the Spanish as they attempted to off-load their cargoes. When Bankert arrived, the Dutch entered the bay, and Benavides allowed the passengers and crew to leave the ships.

Heyn arrived in *Amsterdam* after dark and with his customary discipline and organization lit seamarks at the entrance to the bay. When he judged it safe, he ordered his men to board the Spanish ships and to give quarter to any Spaniard who surrendered. As Cornelis Goslinga has written, although Heyn was praised for his charitable treatment of prisoners, there was no reason for him to do otherwise: "The admiral understood perfectly well that his masters at home were interested in profit, not in glory and blood." After systematically looting the Spanish ships, which took eight days, the Dutch burned all but four galleons and one smaller ship before sailing from Matanzas on September 17. Two small ships were sent ahead with the good news, and the States General sent a fleet to convoy Heyn's fleet past the Dunkirk pirates.

The Dutch landed at Falmouth, England, on December 28, 1628, and the reassembled fleet returned in triumph to Hellevoetsluis in January 1629. The value of the gold, 46 tons of silver, and merchandise was valued at between 11.5 and 14 million guilders; the WIC made a net profit of some 7 million guilders and paid a dividend of 50 percent. The consequences of Benavides' disorganization and defeat were fatal: he was tried and executed in 1634. His great nemesis predeceased him. Having been made admiral of the war-navy of the United Provinces, Heyn was killed in action against the Dunkirk pirates in 1629.

Flush with money after the capture of the silver fleet, the WIC decided to launch an attack on Pernambuco, a sugar-producing captaincy in northern Brazil. Since Heyn was no longer in the service of the WIC, Hendrick Cornelisz. Loncq, Heyn's former second-in-command, was appointed as the general of the Dutch fleet. A fleet of twenty ships and six yachts put to sea between May 17 and June 27, when *Amsterdam* sailed from Goere (Zeeland) as flagship under command of Captain Pieter Willemsz.

In the early morning of August 23, between Gran Canaria and Tenerife, *Amsterdam* and seven other Dutch ships and yachts suddenly found themselves surrounded by the royal Spanish fleet of forty sail under Don Federico de Toledo. Despite heavy fire, the Dutch lost only a few men, and their fleet escaped practically unharmed. Why Toledo failed to destroy the Dutch has never been explained. In early September, Loncq anchored off St. Vincent in the Cape Verde Islands to refresh his scorbutic crew. While there, they were joined by reinforcements from the Netherlands, and on December 26, a fleet of fifty-two ships and thirteen sloops left for Brazil. The landing in February 1630 was followed by a successful conquest, and on May 8, Loncq returned to the Dutch Republic with eight ships, including *Amsterdam,* and one yacht.

On September 4, 1631, *Amsterdam* was back in Recife. The officers tried to meet up with the fleet commanded by General Adriaen Jansz. Pater, but Pater had left. *Amsterdam* then sailed north, and shortly thereafter, west of Cabo S. Agustin, an exchange of fire took place with a Spanish fleet of twenty-four sail. *Amsterdam* escaped to Recife and in December of that year took part in a failed expedition to conquer Paraíba. In April 1632, *Amster-*

dam sailed with twenty-one other ships from Pernambuco to the West Indies to "harm the enemy." It is not clear when she returned to the Netherlands, but on July 3, 1634, she sailed from Amsterdam for Pernambuco, arriving on October 7. The next month, she was part of a successful expedition against Paraíba. There is no mention of *Amsterdam* after October 11, 1635, when she sailed again from Amsterdam to Pernambuco.

Goslinga, *Dutch in the Caribbean.* Klooster, *Dutch in the Americas.*

Andrew Doria

(ex-*Defiance*) Brigantine (2m). *L/B/D:* ca. 75' × 25' × 10' (22.9m × 7.6m × 3m). *Tons:* ca. 190. *Hull:* wood. *Comp.:* 112. *Arm.:* 14 × 4pdr. *Built:* <1775.

The Continental Congress authorized the purchase of the merchant brig *Defiance* in October 1775. Armed and renamed *Andrew Doria* in honor of the fifteenth-century Venetian admiral, she was placed under command of Captain Nicholas Biddle. In January 1776, she took part in Commodore Esek Hopkins's capture of Fort Nassau in the Bahamas and returned with the fleet to New London in April. Over the next six months, *Andrew Doria* captured ten ships, including four supply vessels belonging to Virginia's Loyalist governor, John Murray, Earl of Dunmore. In October, Biddle took command of the frigate RANDOLPH and was succeeded by Captain Isaiah Robinson who was dispatched to St. Eustatius, Dutch West Indies, for military stores. Her arrival at the port on November 16, 1776, was met with the first salute to the American flag rendered by a foreign power in a foreign port. On the same voyage, *Andrew Doria* captured the British sloop *Racehorse* (12 guns) — which entered the Continental Navy as *Surprize* — and a merchant ship. *Andrew Doria* never left the Delaware after her return to Philadelphia. Following the loss of Fort Mercer, New Jersey, Captain Robinson ordered his ship burned to prevent her falling into British hands.

Fowler, *Rebels under Sail.* U.S. Navy, DANFS.

USS Argus

Brig (2m). *L/B/D:* 95.5' × 27' × 12.7' (29.1m × 8.2m × 3.9m). *Tons:* 31 bm. *Hull:* wood. *Comp.:* 142. *Arm.:* 18 × 24pdr, 2 × 12pdr. *Built:* Edmund Hartt, Boston; 1803.

One of two ships, with USS HORNET, authorized by Congress in 1803, USS *Argus* was launched and commissioned the same year and sailed for the Mediterranean station under Lieutenant Stephen Decatur, who relinquished command to Lieutenant Isaac Hull at Gibraltar. *Argus* remained in the Mediterranean for three years and was present at many of the defining moments in the Barbary Wars: the bombardment of Tripoli in August 1804; the ill-fated attempt to destroy the Tripolitan fleet with the bomb ship INTREPID, which she escorted into the port; and the capture of Derna. In 1804, Colonel William Eaton conceived a plan to restore the deposed Pasha Hamet Karamanli to the throne of Tripoli. Raising a mixed force of Greeks, Italians, Arabs, and ten Americans, Eaton marched 600 miles across North Africa from Egypt to Derna, where, supported by gunfire from *Argus* and *Hornet,* they captured the fort on April 27, 1805. (This action inspired "The Marine Hymn" verse about "the shores of Tripoli.")

The following year, *Argus* returned to the United States, and after a brief layup, she was assigned to home waters along the East Coast. She remained in this work through the opening of the War of 1812. In the fall of that year, she captured six British prizes. On June 19, 1813, Minister to France William H. Crawford embarked in *Argus* for the voyage to L'Orient, France, where she arrived on July 11. Nine days later, Lieutenant William H. Allen embarked on a commerce-destroying mission in the English Channel and then into the Irish Sea. *Argus*'s crew captured twenty ships — eleven of them after August 10 — of which thirteen were sunk and the remainder used as cartel ships, manned, and kept. At dawn on the fourteenth, *Argus* was brought to battle by HM Brig *Pelican* (18 guns), under Commander John Fordyce Maples. The contest was brief, *Pelican* gaining the weather gauge and rendering the American ship unmaneuverable within fifteen minutes. *Argus* lost ten men (including Allen), and thirteen were wounded. She was brought back to Plymouth and sold to an unknown buyer.

Dye, *Fatal Cruise of the "Argus."* U.S. Navy, *DANFS.*

CSS Arkansas

Arkansas-class ironclad. *L/B/D:* 165′ × 35′ × 11.5′ (50.3m × 10.7m × 3.5m). *Hull:* wood and iron. *Comp.:* 200. *Arm.:* 2 × 9″, 2 × 9″, 2 × 6″, 2 × 32pdr, 2 × 64pdr. *Armor:* 18″ iron and wood. *Mach.:* low-pressure engines, 900 ihp, 2 screws; 8 mph. *Built:* J. T. Shirley, Memphis, Tenn.; 1862.

CSS *Arkansas* was a powerful casemate ironclad ram distinguished particularly for what she accomplished, despite being so imperfectly and incompletely finished that a junior officer, George W. Gift, described her as a "hermaphrodite iron-clad." Plated over with railroad iron and iron plate, she had a nine-ton ramming beak and was considered fast for her size. Laid down at Memphis, Tennessee, and completed at Yazoo City, Mississippi, she was commissioned in May 1862, Lieutenant Isaac Newton Brown commanding. On July 15, she engaged the ironclads *Tyler, Belle of the West,* and CARONDELET, the last being run aground near the mouth of the Yazoo River with thirty-five casualties. She then entered the Mississippi and ran through Flag Officer David Farragut's fleet above Vicksburg to take refuge beneath the batteries of that city. Admiral David G. Farragut was determined to destroy the Confederate ram and invoked the memory of Nelson at Trafalgar when he declared that "no one will do wrong who lays his vessel alongside the enemy or tackles the ram. The ram must be destroyed." Despite repeated attacks, Union forces were unable to inflict serious damage before withdrawing downriver a week later. *Arkansas* left for Baton Rouge on August 3, but her engines failed three days later, and she was abandoned and set afire to avoid capture by USS *Essex.*

Milligan, *Gunboats down the Mississippi.* Still, *Iron Afloat.*

Ark Royal

(ex-*Ark Raleigh*) Galleon (4m). *Tons:* 694 burthen. *Hull:* wood. *Comp.:* 4 × 60pdr, 4 × 30pdr, 12 × 18pdr, 12 × 9pdr, 6 × 6pdr, 17 small. *Built:* Deptford Dockyard, Eng.; 1587.

Built for Sir Walter Raleigh at Deptford, *Ark Raleigh* was taken over by Queen Elizabeth before completion and renamed. During the Spanish Armada the following year, *Ark Royal* sailed as flagship of Charles Howard, Lord Howard of Effingham. With high sterncastles but a cut-down forecastle that made her more weatherly than the high-charged vessels of the previous century, she had four masts; the fore and main were square rigged and set topsails, while the mizzen and bonaventure set single lateen sails.

When the Spanish Armada arrived in the English Channel on July 30, 1588, Howard led his fleet of more than fifty-six ships out of Plymouth. The following day, his ships came astern of the larger, less maneuverable Spanish fleet, and *Ark Royal* was the first English ship to engage the Spanish, attacking the 820-ton *Rata Santa Maria Encoronada* until other Spanish ships could come to her aid. On August 2, the Spanish fleet was caught off Portland Bill between the English fleet and the land. Martín de Bertendona's *Regazona* attempted to board *Ark Royal*, which slipped away. When the wind changed in Howard's favor, he attacked Medina Sidonia's flagship, SAN MARTÍN, though to little effect.

The following three days brought only light winds, and the two fleets made their way slowly toward Calais, where they anchored on August 6. The next night, Howard ordered a fleet of fire ships sent down on the Spanish fleet, which escaped in disorder but otherwise relatively unscathed. The next morning, Howard led an English force in boarding the galleass *San Lorenzo,* which had grounded on a sandbar in the escape, and *Ark Royal* missed the main action of the Battle of Gravelines. By the next day, the Spanish fleet had been blown past the rendezvous with the land forces of the Duke of Parma and into the North Sea. Although the English could not destroy the Spanish fleet, the elements did.

Ark Royal's next major engagement came in 1596, when she was part of a fleet that attacked the Spanish at Cadiz. She was readied to repel another Spanish threat in 1599, although the anticipated invasion never happened. In 1608, *Ark Royal* was rebuilt as *Anne Royal,* and as such she remained on the navy list until she sank at Tilbury Hope in 1636.

Mattingly, *Armada.* Sugden, *Sir Francis Drake.*

HMS Asia

2nd rate 84 (3m). *L/B/D:* 196.1′ × 51.1′ × 22.5′ (64.3m × 17.1m × 7.4m). *Tons:* 2,898 bm. *Hull:* wood. *Comp.:* 700. *Arm.:* 32 × 32pdr, 38 × 24pdr. *Des.:* Sir Robert Seppings. *Built:* Bombay Dockyard, Bombay, India; 1824.

By the close of the Napoleonic Wars, the Royal Navy had come to rely heavily on the potential of India as a source for shipbuilding facilities and material, especially teak, a wood that is resistant to marine borers and seasons quickly. Exploitation of these resources was frustrated by an uncooperative East India Company (whose yards were used), inadequate skilled labor, and high costs. However, several ships were built in Bombay, among them HMS *Asia.* Like many others of the postwar period, this two-decker was based on the design of the French ship *Canopus,* which had been captured at the Battle of the Nile in 1798. It also incorporated a number of Sir Robert Seppings's shipbuilding innovations, including diagonal bracing, which gave ships greater longitudinal strength and used less wood, and rounded sterns, which were stronger and increased the arc of fire of guns mounted aft.

In 1826, HMS *Asia* became the flagship of Vice Admiral Sir Edward Codrington, commander-in-chief of the Mediterranean Fleet. At that time, Greek nationalists had been fighting for independence from the Ottoman Empire for five years. Britain, France, and Russia sought to bring the belligerents to the negotiating table, and by the Treaty of London, the three countries had agreed to work for an armistice and the pacification of Greece, and the elimination of piracy. By the end of September 1827, the Greeks and the Turks had agreed to an armistice.

No sooner was this done than Ibrāhīm Pasha, commander of a Turkish-Egyptian force based at Navarino (Pylos, in the western Peloponnesus), requested permission to move supplies toward Patras, which was under threat from Greek forces led by Lord Cochrane, a Royal Navy veteran who had distinguished himself in the struggles for Chilean and Brazilian independence. Codrington denied the request, and the Turkish-Egyptian ships returned to Navarino Bay. The allies requested that the troops be ordered ashore, whereupon they began marauding the countryside. At this juncture, Codrington, French Rear Admiral Henri de Rigny, and Russian Rear Admiral Count Heiden decided to enter Navarino Bay and anchor there to enforce Turkish adherence to the armistice. Codringon's orders of October 18 stated that

> no shot is to be fired from the combined fleet without a signal being made for that purpose, unless shot be fired from any of the Turkish ships; in which case the ships so firing are to be destroyed immediately.

The Turkish-Egyptian fleet numbered between sixty-five and eighty-nine ships, including at least two 84-gun ships, one 76, four 64s, thirteen 48-gun frigates, and various smaller units. The allied fleet consisted of twenty-seven ships (twelve British, seven French, eight Russian) including three 84s, eight ships of between 60 and 80 guns, and the remainder of 50 guns or less.

As *Asia* sailed into the bay on October 20, a message was brought from Ibrāhīm Pasha requesting the allied departure. To this, Codrington replied: "I am come not to receive orders but to give them; and if any shot be fired at the allied fleet, the Turkish fleet shall be destroyed." Neither side sought an engagement, and the Turks allowed more than half the allied fleet to anchor — *Asia* lying between the Turkish and Egyptian flagships — before hostilities began. Turkish marines fired on a ship's boat that had been sent to request that some Turkish ships move, and the action quickly became general. The battle lasted two and a half hours, during which *Asia* sank both flagships. Once engaged, the Turks fought with tenacity, and only one ship reportedly struck its colors; the remainder were either sunk or scuttled to avoid capture. Estimates of Turkish losses range from thirty-six to seventy-three ships. The last major fleet engagement of the age of sail was not without controversy, and Codrington was soon recalled from the Mediterranean.

After a refit in Portsmouth, *Asia* returned to the Mediterranean and took part in the combined British-Austrian bombardment of Beirut during the Syrian Crisis. During Portugal's Miguelite Wars, *Asia* was briefly stationed in Lisbon to protect British trade. In 1842, she became the flagship of Rear Admiral Hornby in the Pacific, where she remained until 1852. Returning to Portsmouth, *Asia* was made a guardship in 1859. She was broken up at Dunkirk in 1906.

Clowes, *Royal Navy*. Lambert, *Last Sailing Battlefleet*. Lyon, *Sailing Navy List*. Phillips, *Royal Navy*.

HMS Association

2nd rate 90 (3m). *L/B/D:* 165' × 45.3' × 18.2' dph (50.3m × 13.8m × 5.6m). *Tons:* 1,459 bm. *Hull:* wood. *Comp.:* 680. *Arm.:* 26 × 32pdr, 26 × 18pdr, 26 × 9pdr, 18 × 6pdr. *Des.:* Bagwell. *Built:* Portsmouth Dockyard, Eng.; 1699.

The flagship of Admiral Sir Cloudisley Shovell when he was sent out to the Mediterranean in the War of the Spanish Succession, *Association* took part in the capture of Gibraltar on August 4, 1704, and the subsequent battle of Malaga, against a French fleet, on August 24. The ship is best remembered for the tragedy that befell Shovell's squadron upon its return from the Mediterranean in the autumn of 1707 under Captain Edmund Loades. After lying-to near the mouth of the English Channel while waiting for a fresh breeze, the twelve ships proceeded on the evening of October 22. However, the ships were off course, and they soon ran aground on the Bishop and Clerks Rocks off the Scilly Isles. *Association* was quickly smashed on the rocks, with the loss of her entire complement of 800 men. Three other ships were also lost that night: the 3rd-rate *Eagle,* under Captain Robert Hancock, with more than 500 men; the 4th-rate *Romney,* under Captain William Coney, with about 250 crew; and the fire ship *Firebrand,* under Commander Francis Piercey, from which there were 24 survivors.

Hepper, *British Warship Losses.* Powell, "Wreck of Sir Cloudesley Shovell."

Athlit ram

Built: 2nd cent. BCE.

In 1980, while conducting a routine underwater survey near Athlit on the Israeli coast, marine archaeologist Yehoshua Ramon discovered a bronze ram from an ancient warship. The partially covered ram lay about two hundred meters offshore at a depth of three meters. The ram was lifted and is now on permanent display at the National Maritime Museum, Haifa. A team from the University of Haifa later investigated the seafloor in the area, but no ship or related artifacts have yet been found.

The ram measures 2.26 meters long, 0.76 meters wide, and 0.96 meters wide, and weighs about

▼ The **Athlit ram,** found on the seabed off the coast of Israel, was a massive, blunt instrument to punch holes through the hulls of enemy ships below the waterline. *Courtesy National Maritime Museum, Haifa.*

465 kilograms. The surviving wooden armature to which the bronze was fitted was built up of sixteen pieces of cedar, elm, and pine. The central, wedge-shaped ramming timber was connected by mortise-and-tenon joinery to the ship's stem; a second heavy timber, raked aft, formed an angle of seventy-one degrees with the top of the ramming timber. This armature was enclosed in a bronze jacket averaging two centimeters in thickness and fastened with copper nails. The asymmetries of the construction suggest that the bronze piece was custom-cast to fit the preexisting bow timbers.

The Athlit ram is of a type familiar from pictorial representations of the classical and Hellenistic periods. Three bladelike protrusions run horizontally along each side. At the head, the three horizontal blades are crossed down the center by a solid vertical section, forming a gridlike striking surface. Driven by oar power, this ancient "warhead" was designed to smash the enemy ship's planking at the waterline. The ram is decorated with a variety of symbols in relief that have been identified with the Hellenistic king of Egypt Ptolemy V Epiphanes and his successor, Ptolemy VI Philometor, who reigned 204–164 BCE. A date for the ram in the first half of the second century BCE is supported by tree-ring analysis of the wood.

Basch, "Athlit Ram." Casson & Steffy, *Athlit Ram*.

CSS Atlanta

(ex-*Fingal;* later *Triumph*) Casemate ironclad (1f). *L/B/D:* 204′ × 41′ × 15.8′ (62.2m × 12.5m × 4.8m). *Tons:* 1,006 grt. *Hull:* iron. *Comp.:* 145. *Arm.:* 2 × 7″, 2 × 6.4″, spar torpedo. *Armor:* 4″ casemate. *Mach.:* vertical direct-acting engines, 3 screws; 8 kts. *Built:* J. & G. Thomson, Govan, Scot.; 1861.

The casemate ironclad CSS *Atlanta* began life as the schooner-rigged Scottish coastal steamer *Fingal.* Chartered by Confederate agent James D. Bulloch, she sailed from Scotland, picked up Bulloch in Holyhead (where she inadvertently rammed and sank the brig *Siccardi*), and sailed for Savannah. Her cargo included 14,000 Enfield rifles, one million cartridges, sabers, uniforms, and other materiel. By the time *Fingal* was ready to return to England with a cargo of cotton, Union forces had blockaded Savannah, and in the spring of 1862 she was purchased by the Confederate government. Cut down to the waterline and converted to a casemate ironclad by Nelson and Asa Tift, she was armed with two 7-inch and two 6.4-inch guns, a ram, and spar torpedo.

Commissioned CSS *Atlanta* in 1862, on June 17, 1863, *Atlanta* (Lieutenant William A. Webb, commanding) attempted to attack the Union fleet in Wassau Sound. As she moved down on the Union monitors *Nahant* and *Weehawken,* she ran aground and came under devastating fire that compelled Webb's surrender. After repairs at Philadelphia, *Atlanta* was commissioned in the U.S. Navy and assigned to the North Atlantic Blockading Squadron in 1864, with which she saw extensive service on the James River below Richmond. Decommissioned after the Civil War, she is believed to have been sold to Haitian interests in June 1869 and, renamed *Triumph,* lost at sea off Cape Hatteras in December.

Silverstone, *Warships of the Civil War Navies.* Still, *Iron Afloat.* U.S. Navy, *DANFS.*

B

USS Baltimore (C-3)

Protected cruiser (2f/2m). *L/B/D:* 335' × 48.7' × 20.5' (102.1m × 14.8m × 6.2m). *Tons:* 4,413 disp. *Hull:* steel. *Comp.:* 386. *Arm.:* 4 × 8", 6 × 6", 4 × 6pdr, 2 × 3pdr, 2 × 1pdr. *Armor:* 4" belt, 4" deck. *Mach.:* triple expansion, 2 screws; 10,750 ihp; 20 kts. *Built:* William Cramp & Sons Ship & Engine Building Co., Philadelphia; 1890.

USS *Baltimore* first gained renown in the so-called *Baltimore* affair, during the Chilean civil war of 1891. Shortly after the start of hostilities in January, *Baltimore* was one of several ships dispatched to Chilean waters to protect American interests. In the spring of that year, the U.S. government had detained the steamer *Itata* and a cargo of weapons and ammunition smuggled out of the country by Chilean insurgents led by Admiral Jorge Montt. Somewhat later, the *Baltimore* stood guard while repairs were made to a privately owned submarine cable — an operation the insurgents viewed as favorable to President José Manuel Balmaceda. These and similar actions convinced Chilean rebels that the United States favored the Balmaceda regime,

---

▼ A busy day in port aboard **USS Baltimore,** with laundry drying on lines strung to the yard on the foremast, and crews setting up or already working on gangplanks the length of the hull, notably just below the forward 8-inch gun, and just forward of the aftermost 6-inch gun. *Courtesy U.S. Naval Historical Center, Washington, D.C.*

which fell in September. Later that fall, *Baltimore* was ordered to Valparaiso to provide protection for the U.S. legation at Santiago. There, on October 16, a mob attacked 117 sailors on shore leave, and two sailors were killed. After a two-month trial, in which three Chileans and one American sailor were sentenced to jail, *Baltimore* was ordered to San Francisco. Diplomatic wrangling between Chile and the United States dragged on until January 1892.

In 1898, amid escalating tension between the United States and Spain, *Baltimore* was dispatched with ammunition to Commodore George Dewey's Asiatic Squadron at Hong Kong, arriving there on April 22. Five days later, the squadron sailed for the Philippines, and at the Battle of Manila Bay on May 1, *Baltimore* sank the Spanish *Don Antonio de Ulloa*. Over the next twenty-five years, *Baltimore* was in and out of commission several times. During World War I, she operated as part of the Northern Barrage, the Allied effort to close the 350-mile gap between the Orkney Islands and Norway to German submarines. She was sold out of the Navy in 1942.

Goldberg, *"Baltimore" Affair.* Hopkins, "Six *Baltimore*s."

Banshee

(later *J. L. Smallwood, Irene*) Sidewheel steamship (2f/2m). *L/B/D:* 214′ × 20.3′ × 10′ (65.2m × 6.2m × 3m). *Tons:* 325 grt. *Hull:* iron and steel. *Comp.:* 60–89. *Arm.:* 1 × 30pdr, 1 × 12pdr. *Mach.:* oscillating engines, sidewheels; 12 kts. *Built:* Jones Quiggin & Co., Liverpool; 1862.

Built as a blockade-runner for the Anglo-Confederate Trading Company, *Banshee* was the first steel-hulled ship to cross the Atlantic. Her design set the pattern for about a hundred further paddlewheel blockade-runners, including over thirty built of steel, that followed from British and Scottish shipyards. Captured on her fifteenth trip by USS *Grand Gulf* and the U.S. armed transport *Fulton* bound from Nassau, Bahamas, to Wilmington on November 21, 1863, she was condemned by a prize court and bought by the U.S. Navy on March 12, 1864.

Commissioned as USS *Banshee* in June, she was assigned to the North Atlantic Blockading Squadron and took part in the unsuccessful attack on Fort Fisher, North Carolina, on December 24–25. Reassigned to the Potomac River Flotilla in January 1865, she was sold on September 30, 1865, and carried fruit and other cargo under the name *J. L. Smallwood*. Sold again to British interests and renamed *Irene*, in 1867, she is believed to have survived until 1885, although she may have sunk in a collision as early as 1868, and her registration was not closed until 1915.

Silverstone, *Warships of the Civil War Navies.* Spratt, *Transatlantic Paddle Steamers.* Taylor, *Running the Blockade.*

HMS Barfleur

2nd rate 90 (3m). *L/B/D:* 177.5′ × 50.2′ × 21′ (54.1m × 15.3m × 6.4m). *Tons:* 1,947 bm. *Hull:* wood. *Comp.:* 750. *Arm.:* 28 × 32pdr, 30 × 18pdr, 30 × 12pdr, 2 × 6pdr. *Des.:* Sir Thomas Slade. *Built:* Chatham Dockyard, Eng.; 1768.

HMS *Barfleur* was named for the Anglo-Dutch victory over the French at Cape Barfleur in 1692. In September 1780, she was made flagship of Vice Admiral Samuel Hood, second-in-command to Admiral George Brydges Rodney on the West Indies station. In August 1781, *Barfleur* and thirteen ships sailed to New York, Hood now serving as second-in-command to Rear Admiral Thomas Graves in HMS LONDON (90 guns). Charged with preventing the French Admiral François Joseph Paul de Grasse, flying his flag in the 120-gun VILLE DE PARIS, from cutting off Major General Charles Cornwallis, then dug in on the Yorktown peninsula, the nineteen British ships turned south on August 30 and arrived off the mouth of Chesapeake Bay on September 5. Although *Barfleur* was supposed to sail fourth in line, as the French fleet stood out of the bay Graves ordered his ships to wear, so that Hood's squadron was now in the rear. As a result of a cautious adherence to one of two conflicting signals from Graves, few of his ships actually engaged the French fleet, whose continued control of the bay forced the surrender of Cornwallis six weeks later.

Though American independence was all but assured, war between Britain and France continued in the West Indies. On January 25, 1782, Hood seized the anchorage at Basse Terre from de Grasse, although the English garrison on St. Kitts was forced to surrender on February 12. Two nights later, Hood slipped away from the superior French fleet (twenty-nine ships to his twenty-two), and on February 25, he rendezvoused with twelve ships under Rodney. Their objective was to prevent de Grasse from joining a Franco-Spanish force at Haiti, which would have given the latter a fleet of fifty-five ships of the line and twenty thousand troops with which to attack Jamaica. On April 9, the fleets met off Dominica, each about thirty ships strong, but light winds allowed them only a minor skirmish, and the French withdrew to protect their convoy.

Three days later, the thirty-six ships under Rodney in *Formidable* (90 guns), with Hood again second-in-command, met de Grasse's thirty-one ships off The Saintes, a group of three islands south of Guadeloupe. At 0700 the French were sailing south in line ahead while the British were sailing north. Battle began at 0740, the two fleets passing each other on opposite tacks. At 0905, the wind hauled to the south-southeast, and gaps opened in the French line. Seizing the initiative, Rodney luffed and with six ships passed through the French line four ships astern of *Ville de France.* At the same time, HMS *Bedford* led the thirteen ships of Hood's rear squadron through the French line between *Dauphin* and *Royal César,* second and third ships ahead of *Ville de Paris.* Unable to regroup, the French were at the mercy of the concentrated fire of the British ships. At 1800, *Ville de Paris* was surrounded by nine British ships and struck her flag to *Barfleur;* four other French ships followed suit. Though the battle forestalled a French invasion of Jamaica, the overcautious Rodney restrained Hood from capturing more ships and thereby destroying French seapower in the Caribbean.

Peace was achieved in 1783, but ten years later Britain joined the First Coalition against Revolutionary France. *Barfleur* was part of Admiral Richard Howe's fleet at the Glorious First of June 1794 against Rear Admiral Villaret-de-Joyeuse, and on June 23, 1795, she was in Admiral Alexander Hood's action against Villaret-de-Joyeuse off Ile de Groix. *Barfleur* flew the flag of Vice Admiral W. Waldegrave at the Battle of Cape St. Vincent, fought on February 14, 1797. Her last significant action came in 1805, when she took part in the blockade of Rochefort and, on July 22, 1805, in Vice Admiral Sir Robert Calder's desultory action against Vice Admiral Pierre Villeneuve off Cape Finisterre, Spain. *Barfleur* continued in service for more than a decade and was broken up in 1819.

Clowes, *Royal Navy.* Larrabee, *Decision at the Chesapeake.* Mahan, *Influence of Sea Power upon History.*

La Belle Poule

Frigate (3m). *L/B:* 140′ × 38′ (42.7m × 11.6m). *Tons:* 902 bm. *Hull:* wood. *Comp.:* 260. *Arm.:* 26 × 12pdr, 4 × 6pdr. *Built:* Bourdeaux; 1768.

Launched during the relatively long peace between the end of the Seven Years' War and the American Revolution, *La Belle Poule* was a fast frigate and one of the first French warships with a copper bottom. By 1778, relations between France and Britain had become strained owing to the former's support for the American colonists' fight for independence. On June 16, a squadron composed of the frigate *La Belle Poule* and *La Licorne* and the lugger *Le Coureur* were cruising in the western approaches to the English Channel when it came in sight of Rear Admiral Augustus Keppel's Channel Fleet, which had been ordered to blockade Brest. Rather than close with the superior force, Captain Isaac Jean Timothée Chadeau de la Clocherie signaled for his consorts to scatter. The fast British frigate *Arethusa* (28 guns) caught up with *Belle Poule* and *Coureur* and demanded their surrender. When Chadeau de la Clocherie refused, *Arethusa* opened fire at 1800. The battle lasted five hours as the ships drifted toward the coast of Brittany. *Arethusa* finally withdrew to the safety of the British fleet. The next morning, *Belle Poule* eluded two

other British ships and returned to Brest with forty dead and sixty-one wounded; *Licorne* and *Coureur* were both captured.

Chadeau de la Clocheterie's success in the unprovoked attack won him instant celebrity at court, and *Belle Poule* was assigned to a new captain. On July 15, 1780, she was captured by HMS *Nonsuch* off the Loire and brought into the Royal Navy rated as a 36-gun 5th-rate frigate. Sometime after 1781, she became a receiving ship. She was sold out of the service in 1801.

Culver, *Forty Famous Ships*.

HMS Bellerophon

Arrogant-class 3rd rate 74 (3m). *L/B/D:* 168′ × 46.8′ × 19.8′ (51.2m × 14.3m × 6m). *Tons:* 1,643 bm. *Hull:* wood. *Comp.:* 550. *Arm.:* 28 × 32pdr, 28 × 18pdr, 18 × 9pdr. *Des.:* Sir Thomas Slade. *Built:* Greaves & Co., Frindsbury, Eng.; 1786.

Named for the mythical Greek hero who was the companion of the winged horse Pegasus, HMS *Bellerophon* was the second ship of the name. Her first fleet action was with Lord Howe at the Glorious First of June 1794 against the French fleet of Admi-

▲ The third-rate 74-gun **HMS Bellerophon** was the veteran of many naval actions during the Napoleonic Wars. John James Chalon painted her at Plymouth, where she housed the imprisoned Napoleon from July 25 to August 14, 1815, prior to his permanent exile on the remote island of St. Helena. *Courtesy National Maritime Museum, Greenwich.*

ral Villaret-de-Joyeuse, during which she forced the 74-gun *Eole* to strike. She subsequently distinguished herself in several actions during the blockade off France. In 1797, under Captain Henry d'Esterre Darby, she was assigned to Rear Admiral Horatio Nelson's squadron sent to find the French fleet bound for Egypt. At the Battle of the Nile on the evening of August 1, 1798, *Bellerophon* engaged the 120-gun L'ORIENT. Within the hour, she was dismasted and had to disengage, coming under fire from TONNANT (80 guns) as she did so. Her casualties included 193 killed or injured.

Over the next four years, she served variously in the Mediterranean, with the Channel Fleet, and in the West Indies. At the Battle of Trafalgar on October 21, 1805, "Billy Ruffian," as she was known among the lower deck, sailed in the lee division. Inspired by Nelson's signal that "England expects that every man will do his duty," her gun crews chalked on the gun barrels "*Bellerophon:* Death or Glory." Despite casualties numbering 132, including Captain John Cooke, she took the French *Aigle* (74 guns).

From 1806 to 1809, she sailed with the Channel Fleet and in the Baltic. Following his loss at Waterloo in 1815, Napoleon was compelled to surrender to *Bellerophon's* Captain Frederick Lewis Maitland at Rochefort, and she carried the defeated emperor to England prior to his exile to St. Helena. The following year, she became a prison hulk, which she remained until broken up in 1836. Among others who served in *Bellerophon* as young men were Matthew Flinders, a midshipman at the Glorious First of June, who surveyed Australia in HMS *Investigator* (1801–3), and John Franklin, who commanded the ill-fated Arctic expedition in HMS *Erebus* and *Terror* (1845–47).

Culver, *Forty Famous Ships.* Mackenzie, *Trafalgar Roll.* Schom, *Trafalgar.*

HMS Birkenhead

Paddle frigate (1f/2m). *L/B/D:* 210′ × 36.7′ (60.5′ew) × 15.8′ (64m × 11.2m [18.4m] × 4.8m). *Tons:* 1,918 disp. *Hull:* iron. *Comp.:* 250 crew. *Arm.:* 4 × 10″, 4 × 68pdr. *Mach.:* side-lever steam engines, 536 nhp, 2 paddles; 13 kts. *Des.:* J. Laird. *Built:* Laird Bros., Birkenhead, Eng.; 1845.

Named for the British port, HMS *Birkenhead* was the Royal Navy's first iron-hulled frigate, originally rigged as a brig but converted to a barkentine. On August 27, 1847, she was used to free Brunel's *Great Britain,* which had stranded in Belfast Lough the year before. Gunnery trials led the Admiralty to the conclusion that iron was unsuitable for warship construction because it could be pierced or shattered by shot, and *Birkenhead* was converted to use as a troopship in 1848. In January 1852, under Master Robert Salmond, she sailed for South Africa with 487 officers and men of the 74th Highlanders and other regiments commanded by Colonel Alexander Seton, together with 25 women and 31 children. After touching at Cape Town, the ship sailed on to Algoa Bay. At 0200 on the morning of

February 26, *Birkenhead* hit a rock in False Bay. Three boats were launched from the ship, and as *Birkenhead* began to break up and sink the soldiers held their ranks in a legendary display of valor and chivalry. In all, 438 men lost their lives; the 193 survivors included all the women and children. The remains of the ship, which had broken into three pieces, were discovered by divers in the 1980s.

Bevan, *Drums of the "Birkenhead."* Brown, *Before the Ironclad.* Hepper, *British Warship Losses.*

Le Bon

3rd rate ship (3m). *L/B:* 135.5′ × 36′ (41.3m × 11m). *Tons:* 850 bm. *Hull:* wood. *Comp.:* 500. *Arm.:* 50 guns. *Built:* Hubac, Brest, Fr.; 1672.

Built during the expansion of the French navy under Louis XIV's Minister of Marine Jean-Baptiste Colbert, *Le Bon* ("The Good") first saw action during the Franco-Dutch War of 1672–80. At the two battles of Schooneveldt (June 7 and 14, 1673) and the Texel (August 21), she fought with the combined Anglo-French fleet against the Dutch. She remained in the Brest fleet and was flagship of Vice Admiral François-Louis Rousselet de Châteaurenault in skirmishes with the Dutch off Ushant in 1677 and 1678. Following the Peace of Nijmegen in February 1679, she was stationed with the fleet of Vice Admiral Jean d'Estrées in the French West Indies.

Returning to Europe, in 1683 *Le Bon* sailed under command of Count Ferdinand de Relingue in the Baltic before joining the French Mediterranean squadron. At the time, France was at war with Spain, particularly with respect to Spanish territories in Italy. In 1684, the French captured Genoa, and in response, Spain allied with Naples, Sicily, and Sardinia to combat the French threat. On July 10, *Le Bon* and a convoy were becalmed off northern Corsica when a combined fleet of thirty-three galleys under the Marquis de Centurione surrounded the French warship, twelve lying astern and twenty-one blocking her advance. In the course of a brilliantly fought five-hour battle, de Relingue outshot and outmaneuvered the galleys, two of which he sank, one by ramming and another by gunfire, and three of which were completely disabled. Badly damaged herself, with ninety of her crew dead, *Le Bon* limped into Livorno pursued by the galleys, who only called off their attack when a Dutch warship threatened to defend *Le Bon*.

The ship's next major engagement was during the French campaign to restore the Catholic James II to the English throne in place of the Dutch Protestant William II of Orange. On July 10, 1690, she was part of Comte de Tourville's fleet in the French victory over the English at the Battle of Béveziers (Beachy Head). She later joined d'Estrées's Mediterranean squadron, but while en route to rejoin Tourville at Brest before the battles of Barfleur and La Hogue, she wrecked off Ceuta, Spain, in May 1692.

Culver, *Forty Famous Ships.*

Bonhomme Richard

(ex-*Duc de Duras*) Frigate (3m). *L/B/D:* 145′ × 36.8′ × 17.5′ (47m × 11.9m × 5.7m). *Tons:* 700 burthen. *Hull:* wood. *Comp.:* 322. *Arm.:* 6 × 18pdr, 28 × 12pdr, 6 × 8pdr, 10 swivels. *Des.:* N. Groignard. *Built:* M. Segondat-Duvernet, L'Orient, Fr.; 1765.

Built for La Compagnie des Indes and originally named for one of the French East India Company's shareholders, *Duc de Duras* made two round-trips to China before the company was dissolved in 1769. Taken over by the French government, she made one voyage to Ile de France as a troop transport before being sold to Sieur Bernier and Sieur Bérard — the latter eventually taking full ownership. During the American Revolution, the Continental Navy officer John Paul Jones — a veteran of the fledgling republic's ALFRED, PROVIDENCE, and RANGER — had been promised a ship by the French government, and in 1778, the merchant Leray de Chaumont intervened with the government to secure *Duc de Duras* for him.

After ordering his ships refit with twenty-eight 12-pdr. and six 8-pdr. guns and ten 3-pdr. swivels, Jones named his ship *Bonhomme Richard* after

Benjamin Franklin's translation of *Poor Richard's Almanac.* On August 14, 1779, *Bonhomme Richard* sailed at the head of a seven-ship squadron, including ALLIANCE (36 guns), *Pallas* (32), and *Vengeance* (12). Jones's squadron spent three weeks raiding merchant shipping in and around the Irish Sea, and then sailed around Ireland and northern Scotland into the North Sea. After sailing into the Firth of Forth to threaten Edinburgh, on September 23, they were off Flamborough Head when they encountered a convoy of forty-one merchant ships homeward bound from the Baltic and escorted by HMS *Serapis*, a 44-gun, two-deck, fifth-rate frigate under Captain Richard Pearson, and by the armed merchant ship *Duchess of Scarborough* (20). Alerted to the presence of enemy ships, the convoy was ordered to scatter. Jones maneuvered *Bonhomme Richard* toward *Serapis* but refused to answer the latter's signals until the two ships were less than fifty meters apart.

The battle erupted with simultaneous broadsides at about 1915. On the second round, two of *Bonhomme Richard*'s 18-pdr. guns exploded, and Jones ordered the gundeck cleared. Within half an hour, *Serapis*'s repeated 18-pdr. broadsides on the starboard hull and stern had devastated *Bonhomme Richard,* leaving sixty dead and as many wounded, and seven holes along the waterline. At about 2000, the two ships were lying starboard-to-starboard, and realizing that their only advantage lay in keeping *Serapis* close, Jones ordered his men to grapple the British ship. Nonetheless, *Serapis* guns continued to fire, so destroying *Bonhomme Richard*'s hull that much of the shot passed through the hull without hitting anything before falling into the water. One observer later remarked, "One might have driven in with a coach and six [horses], at one side of this breach, and out the other."

Serapis continued firing with such intensity that both ships were soon ablaze. Meanwhile, the French marines in the tops had effectively cleared the British tops and prevented the British crew from securing the quarterdeck, across which the Americans were now attempting board. At about 2110, *Alliance*, which had been standing off from the action, closed the two ships and fired broadsides of canister and grape shot that inflicted serious injuries on both combatants. Although *Bonhomme Richard* was now effectively reduced to two 18-pdr. guns, when asked by *Serapis*'s Captain Richard Pearson if he wanted to surrender, Jones replied, "No. I'll sink, but I'm damned if I'll strike."

At 2200, *Bonhomme Richard*'s quartermaster released the 100 or so British prisoners in the hold. At the same time, a grenade thrown into the main hatch of *Serapis* exploded in the gundeck, knocking out the entire battery. Reckoning that he had secured the safety of his convoy, and that further fighting would only result in the needless slaughter of his men — half of whom were already dead — Captain Pearson struck his flag. Jones accepted Pearson's surrender with grace, inviting him to share a glass of wine in what was left of his quarters after three or four broadsides.

Of the 322 crew with whom Jones had started the battle, 140 died during or shortly after the battle. *Bonhomme Richard* was so badly holed that Jones transferred his flag to *Serapis* the following morning. On January 25, *Bonhomme Richard* sank in about 200 meters a few miles off Flamborough Head, from which the entire night engagement had been watched. *Serapis* landed at Texel, the Netherlands, on October 4, and from 1779 to 1781 she was on the lists of the French navy. The victory of *Bonhomme Richard* over *Serapis* was achieved by neither superior tactics nor superior training, nor certainly by better ships. As Captain Edward Beach has written, it was "due to sheer power of will." But of such intangibles are legends made, and above any other achievement, it is for the Battle of Flamborough Head, neither strategically nor tactically significant in itself, that John Paul Jones is remembered as the father of the United States Navy.

There have been several attempts to find the wreck of Jones's command, both funded by the American author Clive Cussler. The first was mounted in 1978 by English historian Sydney Wignall. The next year, an expedition headed by Lieutenant Commander Eric Berryman, USN, "covered ten times as much territory with a cost factor less than half the first effort," according to Cussler. But "even with a top-rated team, we failed to find the elusive *Bonhomme Richard*."

Boudriot, *John Paul Jones and the "Bonhomme Richard" 1779*. Cussler, *Sea Hunters*. Morison, *John Paul Jones*. U.S. Navy, *DANFS*.

Bordein

River steamer. *Hull:* iron. *Mach.:* steam, sidewheel. *Built:* Bulaq Dockyard, Egypt; 1869.

Built for Sir Samuel Baker's expedition to the Upper Nile in 1869, *Bordein* was subsequently employed as a river ferry on the Nile between Dongala and Khartoum. She was also one of a fleet of steamers used to clear the Bahr el-Jebel for navigation. In 1884, she was pressed into service by Britain's General Charles George "Chinese" Gordon for his ascent up the Nile to Khartoum during the Sudanese War. One of several steamers sent up the Blue Nile on foraging expeditions for food, she became Gordon's only lifeline to the outside world when the Mahdi's forces besieged Khartoum. On November 25, she was sent north for the last time, bearing urgent dispatches about the plight of the garrisons at Omdurman and Khartoum, as well as six volumes of Gordon's journal. On January 25, 1885, Bordein was southbound again with the steamer *Talatwein* and twenty desperately needed Redcoats and two hundred native soldiers when the vessel hit a rock at the Sixth Cataract of the Nile about fifty-five miles north of Khartoum. *Bordein* remained fast for twenty-four hours and finally reached the vicinity of Khartoum on January 28, two days after the sack of Khartoum by the forces of the Mahdi. She was scuttled by the British but repaired for service under the Mahdi, until recaptured by the Anglo-Egyptian Army after the Battle of Omdurman in 1898. The steamer continued in service for several years in the Sudan, and her hull and paddleboxes were eventually preserved ashore at Khartoum, under the auspices of the River Transport Corporation.

Brouwer, *International Register of Historic Ships*. James et al., *Juan Maria Schuver's Travels*. Nutting, *Gordon of Khartoum*.

HMS Bounty

(ex-*Bethia*) Ship (3m). *L/B/D:* 91′ × 24.3′ × 11.3′ dph (27.7m × 7.5m × 3.5m). *Tons:* 220 burthen. *Hull:* wood. *Comp.:* 46. *Arm.:* 4 × 4pdr, 10 swivels. *Built:* Hull, Eng.; 1784.

In 1775, the Society for West India Merchants proposed that breadfruit trees, native to the South Pacific, be transplanted to the West Indies to be grown as a food staple for slaves. Twelve years later, the Royal Navy purchased the merchant ship *Bethia* especially for the purpose of sailing to the Society Islands, "where, according to the accounts which are given by the late Captain Cook, and Persons who accompanied him during his Voyages, the Bread Fruit Tree is to be found in the most luxuriant state." After the vessel was approved for the purpose by the botanist Joseph Banks, a veteran of Captain James Cook's first voyage, *Bethia* was purchased from Messrs. Wellbank, Sharp, and Brown in May 1787. At Deptford Dockyard, the ship was refitted to carry 300 breadfruit trees, its upper deck being rebuilt "to have as many Gratings . . . as conveniently can be to give air; likewise to have Scuttles through the side for the same reason." Half the trees were destined for Jamaica, and half for the Royal Botanical Garden at St. Vincent; at his discretion, Lieutenant William Bligh could take some trees for Kew Gardens on his return to Britain. The Admiralty also ordered the ship sheathed in copper. Three boats were also ordered from naval contractor John Burr, a sixteen-foot jolly boat, a twenty-foot cutter, and the twenty-three-foot BOUNTY LAUNCH.

On August 17, Bligh was appointed to command HM Armed Vessel *Bounty,* as the ship was officially designated. A veteran of Cook's third voyage to the Pacific, during which he served as master of HMS *Resolution,* Bligh was an accomplished hydrographer. Sailing from Portsmouth on December 23, 1787, *Bounty* went to Tahiti, arriving there on October 26, 1788. After five months in the island paradise, which the crew seem thoroughly to have enjoyed except for Bligh's increasingly harsh discipline, *Bounty* weighed anchor on April 6, 1789, with more than a thousand breadfruit trees. Twenty-two days later, five members of the forty-three-man crew seized the ship in a bloodless mu-

tiny. The ringleader was Fletcher Christian, whom Bligh had appointed the ship's second-in-command and who now put Bligh and nineteen of his supporters into the ship's launch, which Bligh sailed to the Dutch entrepôt at Timor.

Christian attempted a landing on Tubuai, about 400 miles south of Tahiti, where *Bounty* arrived on May 28. The crew met with a poor reception and soon returned to Tahiti, where they stayed ten days while they loaded 460 hogs and 50 goats and embarked 28 Tahitians — nine men, eight boys, ten women, and one girl. A second visit to Tubuai was no better, and after a pitched battle with about 700 Tubuaians, 66 of whom were killed, the mutineers and their Tahitian shipmates departed on September 17. Accompanied by the Tubuaian chief Taroa, three men, and twelve women, who had befriended them, they arrived back at Tahiti on September 20. Sixteen of the mutineers (some of whom seem to have been unwilling accessories from the start) remained on the island, and the next day Christian sailed with the Tubuaians, a few Tahitians, and eight of the crew. Navigating with a defective chronometer and in search of an uninhabited island whose published position was 200 miles east of its actual position, the mutineers reached Pitcairn Island in January or February of 1790. The next day, they burned their ship and attempted to settle the island. As the English promptly divided the island among themselves and relegated the Tahitians to second-class status, relations between the men turned violent and several were killed. The survivors gradually acclimated themselves to their new situation. Eighteen years later, on February 6, 1808, Pitcairn was visited by the Nantucket sealer *Topaz* under Captain Matthew Folger. The sole male survivor of the original band of settlers was Alexander Smith, whom Folger gave the new name John Adams, to lessen his chance of arrest should the island be visited by a British warship. Following the publication of Captain Frederick William Beechey's report of his visit aboard HMS *Blossom* thirteen years after that, Pitcairn came under the protection of the British Crown in 1825.

Fourteen mutineers were eventually arrested in Tahiti by the men of HMS PANDORA, which had been dispatched for the purpose. On August 28,

1791, *Pandora* struck the Great Barrier Reef and sank; four of the mutineers were drowned. *Pandora's* survivors sailed to Timor, and the ten surviving mutineers were ultimately brought to trial in England. Thomas Ellison, John Milward, and Thomas Burkitt were hanged. Bligh was also given a second chance to complete his mission, which he did in HMS PROVIDENCE in 1792. (*Providence* was later wrecked, on May 17, 1797, when, under command of Commander William Broughton, she ran aground in the Sakashima Islands east of Taiwan during a surveying voyage of the North Pacific.)

The story of the mutiny on the *Bounty* has inspired countless retellings and fictional accounts. The first of several movies of the mutiny, *The Mutiny on the Bounty,* appeared in 1935, starring Charles Laughton and Clark Gable, and featured the *Lilly* as the *Bounty*. Replicas of *Bounty* were built for the 1962 remake starring Marlon Brando and Trevor Howard and for *Bounty* (1985) with Mel Gibson and Anthony Hopkins.

Barrow, *Mutiny and Piratical Seizure of HMS "Bounty."* Bligh, *Narrative of the Mutiny on the "Bounty."* Knight, "H.M. Armed Vessel *Bounty*." Smith, "Some Remarks about the Mutiny of the *Bounty*."

Bounty launch

Launch (1m). *L/B/D:* 23′ × 6.8′ × 2.8′ dph (7m × 2.1m × 0.8m). *Hull:* wood. *Comp.:* 20. *Built:* John Samuel White, Cowes, Isle of Wight, Eng.; 1787.

When Fletcher Christian rallied his supporters to mutiny aboard HMS BOUNTY on April 28, 1789, there was no thought of killing Lieutenant William Bligh. Instead, they put him and nineteen supporters into the ship's launch together with twenty-eight gallons of water, five bottles of wine, four quarts of rum, 150 pounds of biscuit, and twenty pounds of pork. Bligh was also given a sextant and four cutlasses. Fully loaded, the twenty-three-foot-long launch had a freeboard of only seven inches. The day after the mutiny, the launch landed at the nearby island of Tofoa, in the Fiji Islands, but one

of the crew was killed by the inhabitants as they prepared to leave the next day. With rations limited to one ounce of bread and four ounces of water daily (later reduced to half an ounce of bread and one ounce of water), Bligh decided to sail direct for the Dutch settlement at Timor, 3,600 miles to the west. The launch passed through the New Hebrides (May 14–15), along the Great Barrier Reef (May 16–June 4), through the Torres Strait between Australia and New Guinea, and on to Timor, arriving on June 12. Miraculously, in sailing forty-three days through uncharted waters in an open boat overcrowded with desperately ill-provisioned men, Bligh had not lost a single one of his crew. Recognized then and now as an outstanding feat of navigation, the voyage of the *Bounty* launch remains almost without peer in the history of navigation.

Bligh, *Narrative of the Mutiny on the "Bounty."* Fryer, *Voyage of the "Bounty" Launch.*

Brederode

Ship (3m). *L/B/D:* 132′ × 32′ × 13.5′ (40.2m × 9.8m × 4.1m). *Tons:* 800. *Hull:* wood. *Arm.:* 56 guns. *Built:* Rotterdam; 1644.

Named for Johan Wolfert van Brederode, brother-in-law of stadtholder Frederick Hendrick and president of the Admiralty of Rotterdam, *Brederode* sailed as flagship for a succession of admirals in the first Anglo-Dutch War of the mid-seventeenth century. After three years under the flag of Vice Admiral Witte de With, in 1647 she was put under command of Admiral Maarten Harpertszoon Tromp. Four years later, as antagonism between British and Dutch merchants grew, the British instituted the Navigation Acts, on October 9, 1651. Among other things, these restricted British goods to British ships and called for foreign ships in the English Channel to dip their flags to British warships as a mark of respect. A few minor incidents occurred over the winter, but on May 18, 1652, Tromp's fleet was in the channel protecting convoys of Dutch traders when it was forced to seek shelter in the Downs. Ordered to leave, Tromp sailed for France, but the next day saw the English fleet under Admiral Robert Blake bearing down on him. Tromp, his fleet in some disarray, turned to meet the English. He almost had the better of the English until Admiral Nehemiah Bourne arrived with nine ships from the Downs. The Battle of Dover cost the Dutch two ships, but Tromp had carried out his orders, namely, to protect Dutch trade and to do nothing to discredit his own flag.

Shortly after the official declaration of war on July 8, Tromp was relieved of his command for his failure against English squadrons under Blake and Admiral Sir George Ayscue. His successor was Michiel Adrienszoon de Ruyter, whom the English naval historian William Laird Clowes described as "the greatest naval leader of his century." Political considerations led to de Ruyter's serving under Witte de With in September, but this move was so unpopular that when the Dutch fleet attacked the British in the Thames estuary on October 8, Brederode's crew refused to allow Witte de With to shift his flag to the ship. The Dutch fought listlessly at the Battle of the Kentish Knock — twenty ships refused to fight altogether — and Admiral Blake's fleet sank three Dutch ships and damaged many others. On December 10, with Tromp again at the head of the fleet in Brederode, the Dutch attacked a much smaller force under Blake in the Battle of Dungeness. Although his flagship was nearly captured, Tromp took five English ships (out of forty-two) and then shepherded one outbound and one inbound convoy through the English Channel. According to legend, he returned to port with a broom lashed to the mast to signify that he had swept the channel clean.

Such confidence was short-lived, and on February 18, 1653, the English attacked Tromp as he escorted an outbound convoy past Portland. The so-called Three Days' Fight cost the Dutch four warships captured, five sunk, and three burned, and thirty to fifty merchantmen captured, although Blake was severely wounded in the action. The next and most decisive engagement of the war came at the Battle of the North Foreland on June 2. The Dutch had been off the English coast with about ninety-eight ships and six fire ships, and the English off the Dutch coast with more than 100

ships. (The English advantage was greater than the numbers imply, because many of the Dutch ships were converted or hired merchantmen, and Dutch warships tended to be smaller owing to the shallow draft necessitated by the shallow Dutch waters.) The fleets met off North Foreland, England, the English under Admiral Sir William Penn (in the James). The battle seems to have taken place between two more or less parallel battle lines, and Tromp is often credited with having developed this tactic, which the English adopted and refined over the next 250 years. The flagships closed with one another, but neither Tromp nor Penn could gain the upper hand. At the end of the day, the Dutch retired to the south, their ammunition almost exhausted, but the next day the English bore down on them in light airs, and by the end of June 3 they had sunk six Dutch ships, burned two, and captured eleven together with 1,350 prisoners. De Ruyter was so disgusted with the outcome that he left the navy until improvements were made.

In the meantime, Admiral Tromp refit his fleet in the Maas and on July 24 sailed out to lift the blockade. Two days later, Witte de With left the Texel, whereupon the English moved to prevent a junction of the fleets. Although they failed in this and were outnumbered by about seventeen ships, the English fought well and Tromp was killed. Both fleets suffered heavily, but the Dutch could ill afford their losses, and the Battle of Scheveningen proved the last major fight of the war. The English losses forced them to lift their blockade, although many Dutch merchant ships subsequently fell prey to English privateers, and there were a number of single ship actions before peace was finally concluded in April 1654.

The Dutch had been supported by Denmark, and three years later they sent ships to support Denmark in its war against Sweden's Karl X Gustaf. In the fall of 1658, the Swedes besieged Copenhagen, and the Dutch dispatched thirty-five ships under Jacob Wassenaer van Obdam in Eendracht. On November 8, the Dutch and Swedish fleets met in the Battle of the Sound off Helsingør. Although the Dutch lost five ships — Brederode among them — to the Swedes' three, Copenhagen was relieved, and the Dutch maintained control of the sound until peace was negotiated in 1660.

Clowes, *Royal Navy.* Hainsworth & Churches, *Anglo-Dutch Naval Wars.*

USS Brooklyn (AC-3)

Brooklyn-class armored cruiser (3f/2m). *L/B/D:* 400.5' × 64.7' × 26.2' (122.1m × 19.7m × 8m). *Tons:* 9,215 disp. *Hull:* steel. *Comp.:* 516. *Arm.:* 8 × 6", 12 × 5", 12 × 6pdr, 4 × 1pdr, 4 × mg, 2 × 3"; 4 × 18"TT. *Armor:* 3" belt, 6" deck. *Mach.:* 4 triple expansion, 18,770 ihp, 2 screws; 22 kts. *Built:* William Cramp & Sons, Philadelphia; 1896.

An improved version of the *New York*–class armored cruiser, USS *Brooklyn* was the first American ship whose contract specified that all major components be made in the United States rather than being imported from abroad — the rule before the country's industrial maturity. Though her hull was distinguished by a pronounced tumblehome and ram bow, *Brooklyn*'s design was innovative in several respects. More heavily armed than other cruisers, she carried eight rather than four 6-inch guns, mounted in turrets forward, aft, and two wing turrets amidships. This configuration enabled her to train six guns forward, aft, or on either broadside. In addition, *Brooklyn* was the first ship to employ electricity to turn the turrets, which were previously trained by either hydraulic or steam power. The experiment was a great success, and electric-powered turrets were adopted for subsequent warships.

Commissioned in 1896, *Brooklyn* represented the U.S. Navy at ceremonies marking Queen Victoria's Diamond Jubilee. Returning to the United States, she patrolled on the Atlantic coast and in the West Indies until 1898, when she became flagship of Commodore W. S. Schley's Flying Squadron during the Spanish-American War. At the end of May, Schley instituted blockades first of Cienfuegos and then of Santiago, where the bulk of Admiral Pascual Cervera's fleet of antiquated cruisers lay. On July 3, Cervera attempted a breakout from the port and, after nearly ramming USS TEXAS, *Brooklyn* led the chase that resulted in the destruc-

tion of four armored cruisers and 350 Spanish dead on the Cuban coast. The *Brooklyn* suffered one fatality — the only U.S. crewman killed in the battle.

From 1899 to 1902, *Brooklyn* was flagship of the Asiatic Squadron based at Manila, from where she visited China, the Dutch East Indies, and Australia. In 1902, she returned to Havana for ceremonies marking the transfer of government from the United States to a native Cuban government and thereafter divided her time between the North Atlantic Fleet and the European Squadron. In 1905, she was dispatched to France to receive the remains of Revolutionary War Captain John Paul Jones for entombment at the U.S. Naval Academy in Annapolis. *Brooklyn* was in and out of commission from 1906 to 1914, when she joined the Neutrality Patrol off Boston before a second assignment as flagship of the Asiatic Fleet. She remained in the Pacific until 1921, when she was sold out of the navy.

Emerson, "Armoured Cruiser USS *Brooklyn.*" U.S. Navy, *DANFS.*

Bucintoro

State barge. *L/B/D:* 143.7' × 23.9' × 27.6' (43.8m × 7.3m × 8.4m). *Hull:* wood. *Comp.:* 168 oarsmen. *Built:* Arsenale, Venice; 1728.

In 1000, the Venetian Doge Pietro Orseolo II began the consolidation of Venetian power with the defeat of Dalmatian pirates who had long infested the Adriatic trade routes. As the power of the Most Serene Republic grew, her annual rite of the blessing of the sea evolved into a more complex and elaborate ceremony by which Venice was spiritually wed to the Adriatic. The *sposalizia* — literally, the wedding — annually took place on Ascension Day, the anniversary of the departure of Orseolo's fleet. The Doge, his retainers, members of the clergy, and the various ambassadors to Venice would put out in the *Bucintoro*, rowed by 168 oarsmen pulling on 42 oars. After the blessing of the ring by the Patriarch of San Elena, the *Bucintoro* would continue past the Lido, and the Doge would drop the marriage ring into the Adriatic with the words: "Disponsamus te, Mare, in signum veri perpetuique dominii" (We wed thee, Adriatic, as a sign of our true and perpetual dominion). The presence of ambassadors ensured that this was no idle covenant, and indeed the Holy Roman Emperor Frederick III, among others, sought permission for his ships to pass through the Adriatic.

Just when the *sposalizia* formally began is unknown. There was a ritual blessing of the Adriatic in Orseolo's time, and this would have taken on added importance following his victory over the pirates. Two centuries later, in 1177, the stature of Venice was further enlarged with Pope Alexander III's official recognition of her role in mediating a long-standing dispute between the papacy and the Holy Roman Empire. "Bucintoro" is also of uncertain origin. One theory is that it refers to a figurehead combining elements of a cow and a centaur. It may also be a corruption for either *ducentorum,* meaning a boat carrying 200 men, or *cinto d'oro,* meaning girdled with gold, as the later vessels certainly were. The last of the state barges to bear the name *Bucintoro* was built in 1728. In addition to the *sposalizia,* she was also used for important ceremonies of state. Her end came in 1797 when the French seized the Republic of Venice. In a rite of ritualistic humiliation, General Napoleon Bonaparte ordered his troops to melt down the gold decoration and destroy the barge's adornments. The hull was spared and fitted out as a floating battery in the Austrian navy. The renamed *Hydra* may have remained in service until 1824.

Senior, "*Bucentaur.*"

Buffel

Turret-ram (1f/2m). *L/B/D:* 205.8′ × 40.4′ × 15.9′ (62.7m × 12.3m × 4.8m). *Tons:* 2,198 disp. *Hull:* iron. *Comp.:* 159. *Arm.:* 2 × 9.2″, 4 × 30pdr. *Armor:* 6.1″ belt. *Mach.:* compound engine, 2,000 ihp, 2 screws; 12.4 kts. *Built:* Robert Napier & Sons, Glasgow; 1868.

Designed for coastal defense service in the North Sea, the turret-ram *Buffel* was one of several such ships built for the Royal Netherlands Navy between 1866 and 1890, and the only one to have survived until the end of the twentieth century. As the name implies, the turret-ram carried two distinct weapons. The submerged bow ram was an instrument the origins of which can be traced to antiquity. Its function was to disable an enemy warship either by making holes in it below the waterline or by sheering off its rudder. The rotating turret-mounted gun was a new development that increased the arc of fire while providing a protective shelter for the gun and gunners. *Buffel* (the name is Dutch for buffalo) carried no sails, but she was intended for work in home waters within easy reach of coal supplies.

After seventeen years in active service, *Buffel* became an accommodation ship berthed first at Gellevoetsluis and later at Den Helder. She survived World War II laid up at Amsterdam, and today she is preserved at the Maritiem Museum Prins Hendrick in Rotterdam.

Heine, *Historic Ships of the World.* Silverstone, *Directory of the World's Capital Ships.*

C

USS Cairo

Cairo-class ironclad gunboat. *L/B/D:* 175′ × 51.2′ × 6′ (53.3m × 15.6m × 1.8m). *Tons:* 512 disp. *Hull:* wood. *Comp.:* 251. *Arm.:* 3 × 8″, 6 × 42pdr, 6 × 32pdr, 1 × 12pdr. *Armor:* 2.5″ casemate. *Mach.:* horizontal engines, center wheel; 9 kts. *Des.:* John Lenthall, Samuel M. Pook & James B. Eads. *Built:* James Eads & Co., Mound City, Ill.; 1862.

Cairo was one of seven river gunboats known as "Pook Turtles" after the designer Samuel M. Pook and completed by James B. Eads for service with the U.S. Army's Western Gunboat Flotilla. Named for the Ohio River port in Illinois, *Cairo* was originally commissioned as a U.S. Army ship but was transferred to the U.S. Navy's Mississippi Squadron on October 1, 1862. The ironclad saw extensive action on the Cumberland and Mississippi Rivers from February on, and on June 6, 1862, *Cairo* was one of seven Union gunboats that sank five and severely damaged one of eight Confederate gunboats during the capture of Memphis. In October 1862, she was transferred to the U.S. Navy's Mississippi Squadron, and her armament was changed so that she mounted three 42-pdr. guns instead of six and carried an additional 30-pdr. *Cairo* saw little further action until the end of the year when, as part of an expedition on the Yazoo River under Commander Thomas O. Selfridge, she hit two stationary torpedoes and sank below Haines Bluff, Mississippi, on December 12, 1862. In 1956, the remains of the *Cairo* were found and identified by Edwin C. Bearss of the Vicksburg National Military Park, where the vessel is now on public display.

Bearss, *Hardluck Ironclad.*

USRC Caleb Cushing

Revenue cutter (2m). *L/B/D:* 100.3′ × 23′ x 9.6′ (30.6m × 7m × 2.4m). *Tons:* 153 disp. *Hull:* wood. *Arm.:* 1 × 32pdr, 1 × 12pdr. *Built:* J. M. Hood, Somerset, Mass.; 1853.

The U.S. revenue cutter *Caleb Cushing* was the last in a long line of captured Union ships that began with the Confederate raider CSS FLORIDA's seizure of the Baltimore-bound brig *Clarence* (ex-*Coquette*) on May 6, 1863. Armed as a commerce raider under Lieutenant Charles W. Read, *Clarence* went on to capture six more ships until Read decided to transfer his crew to the bark *Tacony* (known briefly as *Florida 2*) on June 12. Cruising New England waters, *Tacony* captured fifteen vessels, mostly fishing schooners, over the next twelve days. On June 24, Read transferred his crew to the fishing schooner *Archer* and burned *Tacony*. Learning that the revenue cutter *Caleb Cushing* and a passenger steamer were lying off Portland, Maine, in Casco Bay, Read decided to capture the revenue cutter first, and then to seize the passenger boat. He succeeded in the former effort on July 29, but the next day the presence of a superior Union fleet forced him to burn his prize and take to his boats, although he and his crew were quickly captured. In a curious twist, the revenue cutter's namesake, a distinguished congressman and diplomat who negotiated the Treaty of Whangia opening Chinese ports to U.S. shipping, later played a leading role in negotiating the settlement of the ALABAMA's claims with Great Britain.

Canney, *U.S. Coast Guard and Revenue Cutters.* Smith, *Confederates Downeast.*

HMS Calliope

(later *Helicon*) *Calliope*-class corvette (1f/3m). *L/B/D:* 235′ × 44.5′ × 19.1′ (71.6m × 13.6m × 5.8m). *Tons:* 2,770 disp. *Hull:* steel. *Comp.:* 317. *Arm.:* 4 × 6″ (4 × 1), 12 × 5″, 6 mg; 2 × 14″TT. *Mach.:* compound engine, 4,023 ihp, 1 screw; 14.7 kts. *Des.:* Nathaniel Barnaby. *Built:* Portsmouth Dockyard, Eng.; 1884.

One of the last two corvettes powered by steam and sail (she carried a bark rig) in the Royal Navy, HMS *Calliope* was similar to the *Comus*-class corvettes commissioned for long-range commerce protection between 1879 and 1881. Dispatched to the Australian station from 1886 to 1890, she achieved lasting fame in 1889 as the only one of seven warships to escape serious damage when a hurricane hit Apia. *Calliope* had been sent to protect British interests in Samoa in the face of mounting tension between the United States and Germany. On March 14, the weather began to deteriorate, but advised by local pilots that the storm season was over, the fleets prepared to ride out the storm at anchor. The storm continued unabated through the sixteenth, wrecking twelve of the thirteen ships in the harbor, including three German and three American warships. Only *Calliope* was able to get under way and, narrowly missing both the reefs and USS *Trenton,* struggle into open waters. Four days later, she returned to a scene of utter devastation; Robert Louis Stevenson described the aftermath: "no sail afloat and the beach piled high with the wrecks of ships and debris of mountain forests."

The "Hurricane Jumper," as she came to be known, returned to Britain in 1890 and was laid up for seven years. After eight years as a tender, she became a reserve training ship in the Tyne in 1906. Renamed *Helicon* from 1915 to 1936, she remained there until broken up in 1951.

Brown, "Seamanship, Steam and Steel." Osbon, "Passing of the Steam and Sail Corvette."

HMS Camperdown

Admiral-class battleship. (2f/1m). *L/B/D:* 330′ bp × 68.5′ × 28.4′ (100.6m × 20.9m × 8.7m). *Tons:* 10,600 disp. *Hull:* steel. *Comp.:* 525–36. *Arm.:* 4 × 13.5″ (2 × 2), 6 × 6″, 12 × 6pdr, 10 × 3pdr; 5 × 14″TT. *Armor:* 18″ belt, 3″ deck. *Mach.:* compound engine, 7,500 ihp, 2 screws; 15.7 kts. *Built:* Portsmouth Dockyard, Eng.; 1889.

HMS *Camperdown* — the name celebrates a British victory over a Dutch fleet on October 11, 1797 — was one of four *Admiral*-class barbette ships (later classified as battleships) laid down in 1882–83. *Camperdown* spent six months as flagship of the Mediterranean Fleet and was next flagship of the Channel Fleet until 1892, when she returned to the Mediterranean. On June 22, 1893, *Camperdown* was flying the flag of Rear Admiral A. H. Markham during maneuvers off Tripoli, Lebanon. The ships were steaming in two columns about six cables apart when Vice Admiral Sir George Tryon, Commander-in-Chief, Mediterranean, ordered the two divisions to turn inward, a maneuver that most officers on the bridge could see would result in a collision. *Camperdown* rammed VICTORIA, which sank with the loss of 358 of her officers and crew, Tryon among them. *Camperdown* nearly sank, too, but staggered into port. Following repairs, she was put into reserve. After a turn as a Coast Guard ship and submarine berthing ship at Harwich, she was broken up in 1911.

Parkes, *British Battleships.*

HMS Canopus

Canopus-class battleship (2f/2m). *L/B/D:* 418′ × 74′ × 26.5′ (127.4m × 22.6m × 8.1m). *Tons:* 14,320 disp. *Hull:* steel. *Comp.:* 750. *Arm.:* 4 × 12″, 12 × 6″, 12 × 12pdr, 6 × 3pdr; 4 × 18″TT. *Armor:* 6″ belt; 2.5″ deck. *Mach.:* triple expansion, 13,500 ihp, 2 screws; 18.3 kts. *Built:* Portsmouth Dockyard, Eng.; 1899.

Named for the ancient Egyptian city near Alexandria where Nelson defeated the French at the Battle of the Nile, *Canopus* was the first of six lightly built pre-Dreadnought battleships ordered in 1896. *Canopus* spent two tours in the Mediterranean (1903 and 1908), and the outbreak of World War I found her laid up and scheduled for scrapping in 1915. The British Admiralty sent *Canopus,* Captain Heathcote Grant commanding, to reinforce Rear Admiral Christopher Cradock's South American Squadron against Vice Admiral Graf von Spee's

East Asia Cruiser Squadron. But Cradock detached her to escort colliers, and she missed the disastrous Battle of Coronel. First Sea Lord Fisher then ordered the ship beached at Stanley as a defense for the Falkland Islands port. On December 8, *Canopus* fired the opening shots of the battle of the Falklands against the scouting *Gneisenau* and *Nurnberg*. After service in the Dardanelles in 1915, she was taken out of active service and broken up in February 1920.

Marder, *From the "Dreadnought" to Scapa Flow.*

HMS Captain

Canada-class 3rd rate 74 (3m). *L/B/D:* 170′ × 46.7′ × 20.5′ (52.4m × 14.5m × 6.2m). *Tons:* 1,632 bm. *Hull:* wood. *Comp.:* 550. *Arm.:* 28 × 32pdr, 28 × 18pdr, 18 × 9pdr. *Des.:* William Bately. *Built:* Batson, Limehouse, Eng.; 1787.

The third of six ships to bear the name, HMS *Captain* was launched midway between the American and the French Revolutions. At the start of the latter, she was part of Vice Admiral Samuel Hood's Mediterranean Fleet when French Royalists threw open the port of Toulon to the British between August and December 1793. On March 14, 1795, she was heavily damaged off Genoa when thirteen ships in Vice Admiral Hotham's squadron bested a French force of fifteen ships under Vice Admiral Comte Martin. On June 11, 1796, Commodore Horatio Nelson was transferred from HMS AGAMEMNON into *Captain* on orders of Admiral John Jervis. Nelson's squadron was first deployed off Livorno during Napoleon Bonaparte's march through northern Italy at the head of the Armée d'Italie, and in September Nelson oversaw Britain's strategic withdrawal from Corsica.

By February 1797, Nelson had rejoined Jervis's fleet twenty-five miles west of Cape St. Vincent at the southwest tip of Portugal, just before it intercepted a Spanish fleet under Admiral Don José de Cordoba on February 14. The Spanish were en route from Cartagena to the English Channel to support a Franco-Spanish amphibious invasion of England; they had planned to stop at Cadiz but overshot the port and were now doubling back. Jervis's fleet consisted of fifteen ships of the line while Cordoba commanded twenty-seven ships. The Spanish crews were inexperienced and poorly trained, which Jervis did not know; the fleet's disorganization was apparent, however, and he lost no time in exploiting his advantage.

The battle opened with the British sailing south-southwest to pass between two groups of Spanish ships. The bulk of the fleet was heading north-northwest while eight ships sailed north-northeast with a view to circling behind the British to rejoin the main group. At about 1300, the British line began turning to chase the larger Spanish squadron. Realizing that they were in danger of losing the Spanish fleet to leeward, and to prevent a possible junction with the eight ships to the east, Nelson on his own initiative wore ship — *Captain* was third from the last in line — to intercept the Spanish van. Jervis immediately approved the move by ordering *Excellent,* in the rear of the British line, to join *Captain* against Cordoba's immense flagship, *Santísima Trinidad,* which mounted 136 guns on four decks. The battle quickly became general, and *Captain* came under fire from seven Spanish ships, suffered many killed and wounded, and had much of her rigging shot away. At 1530, she was closely engaged with *San Nicolás* (80 guns) when the Spaniard was disabled by a broadside from *Excellent* and ran into *San José* (112). With *Captain* no longer maneuverable, Nelson ran his ship alongside *San Nicolás,* which his crew seized in a boarding action in which he participated. He was preparing to order his men into *San José* when the captain of that ship signaled his intent to surrender. "I desired him," wrote Nelson,

> to call on his officers, and on the quarter-deck of a Spanish first-rate, extravagant as the story may seem, did I receive the swords of vanquished Spaniards, which, as I received, I gave to one of my bargemen, who put them with the greatest sangfroid under his arm.

Later in the evening, Nelson was invited aboard VICTORY, where Jervis, soon to be Earl St. Vincent, embraced him and said "he could not sufficiently thank me, and used every kind expression, which could not fail to make me happy."

Having been responsible for half the Spanish ships captured off Cape St. Vincent, *Captain* was the most severely damaged of the British ships and the only one dismasted. She returned to service following repairs, but her only other battle honors were for her part in the capture of Martinique in 1809. The same year she was put into harbor service, and four years later she burned at Plymouth while undergoing conversion to a sheer hulk.

Bennett, *Nelson the Commander.*

HMS Captain

Captain-class turret ship (1f/3m). *L/B/D:* 334′ × 53.3′ × 25.5′ (101.8m × 16.2m × 7.8m). *Tons:* 7,767 disp. *Hull:* iron. *Comp.:* 500. *Arm.:* 4 × 12″ (2 × 2), 2 × 7″. *Armor:* 7″ belt. *Mach.:* trunk engines, 5,400 ihp, 2 screws; 14.25 kts. *Des.:* Cowper Coles. *Built:* Laird Bros., Ltd., Birkenhead, Eng.; 1870.

HMS *Captain* was the inspiration of the Royal Navy's Captain Cowper Coles, an early advocate of centerline turrets for warships. Unlike the traditional broadside battery, turrets enabled a ship's guns to be brought to bear without changing the ship's heading. Coles's ideas were not readily accepted by the naval establishment, which had modified his ideas in their development of HMS *Monarch.* But public support from the British press and members of Parliament finally pressured the Admiralty into accepting his design for HMS *Captain,* which was laid down by Laird Bros. in 1867.

Although designed with a freeboard of only 8.5 feet — the intent was to minimize the area of hull exposed to enemy fire — *Captain* was so heavily built that her upper deck rested only 6.5 feet above the waterline at full draft, which made her a wet ship in all but the calmest weather. The primary armament was contained in two revolving centerline turrets on the upper deck, but a forecastle and poop on the same deck effectively reduced the arc of fire of the four 12-inch guns to broadside positions. Although Coles was in favor of eliminating sail propulsion altogether — among his other innovations was the adoption of twin screws — the Admiralty insisted that *Captain*'s limited coal capacity be augmented by an auxiliary sail rig for ocean voyaging. For his masterpiece, Coles insisted on a rig that spread 50,000 square feet of sail. Tripod masts eliminated a mass of standing rigging, but they virtually guaranteed that the ship would capsize before the masts would break.

With her excessive draft and her lofty and rigid masting, the ship had a maximum stability angle of only twenty-one degrees — as against more than sixty degrees for virtually all other Royal Navy capital ships. These problems notwithstanding, the ship was accepted and joined the Channel Squadron in the summer of 1870 under Captain Hugh Burgoyne; Coles himself sailed in her as an observer. The squadron sailed to Gibraltar to join Admiral Sir Alexander Milne's Mediterranean Fleet for maneuvers in the Atlantic. On September 6, Milne boarded *Captain* in the Bay of Biscay to observe gunnery practice. Toward evening the wind freshened, and he returned to his flagship, *Lord Warden.* The fleet was about twenty miles west of Cape Finisterre, Spain, when shortly after midnight a blast of wind whipped through the fleet, blowing out sails aboard all eleven ships in the fleet except *Captain.* She was knocked down and sank with the loss of all but 18 of her 499 crew in about 43°N, 9°06′E.

In the court-martial that followed, blame for the tragedy flowed freely between the Admiralty, Coles and his supporters, and the builders. The court avoided castigating any of the principals involved with the controversial ship. Its muted finding asserted: "The *Captain* was built in deference to public opinion expressed in Parliament and through other channels." Although HMS *Captain* can hardly be said to have vindicated all of Coles's innovations — the Royal Navy has never again used the name for one of its ships — centerline turreted guns quickly became the norm for capital ships.

Ballard, *Black Battlefleet.* Hawkey, *Black Night Off Finisterre.* Sandler, "'In Deference to Public Opinion.'"

USS Carondelet

Cairo-class ironclad gunboat (2f/2m). *L/B/D:* 175′ × 51.2′ × 6′ (53.3m × 15.6m × 1.8m). *Tons:* 512. *Hull:* wood. *Comp.:* 251. *Arm.:* 6 × 32pdr, 3 × 8″, 6 × 42pdr, 1 × 12pdr. *Armor:* 2.5″ casemate. *Mach.:* horizontal beam engines, centerwheel; 4 kts. *Built:* James Eads & Co., St. Louis, Mo.; 1862.

Named for a village in St. Louis County, Missouri, USS *Carondelet* first saw action with the U.S. Army's Western Gunboat Flotilla at the capture of Fort Henry, on the Tennessee River, on February 6, 1862. A week later, she was at the fall of Fort Donelson, on the Cumberland. Moving to the Mississippi, under Commander Henry Walke, *Carondelet* contributed to the capture of Island No. 10 — a Confederate stronghold on the Mississippi — Fort Pillow, and Memphis, Tennessee. In July, she ran aground and was heavily damaged on the Yazoo River in an engagement with CSS Arkansas when that ironclad escaped down the Yazoo and past the Union fleet above Vicksburg, Mississippi. In October 1862, the Western Gunboat Flotilla was transferred to the navy and became the Mississippi Squadron. *Carondelet* subsequently took part in several engagements on the Yazoo, Mississippi, and Red Rivers aimed at weakening Vicksburg's defenses. By the beginning of 1864, her armament consisted of two 100-pdr., one 50-pdr., one 30-pdr., three 9-inch, and four 8-inch guns. (The 8-inch guns were later removed.) The surrender of Vicksburg on July 4, 1864, and of Port Hudson, Louisiana, two days later, gave the Union complete control of the Mississippi, and *Carondelet* returned to the Cumberland. Her last major engagement was at Bell's Mill, below Nashville, on December 3, 1864. Sold in November 1865, her hull was later incorporated into a wharf at Gallipolis, Ohio.

Anderson, *By Sea and by River.* Silverstone, *Warships of the Civil War Navies.* U.S. Navy, *DANFS.*

HMS Centurion

4th rate 60 (3m). *L/B:* 144′ × 40′ (43.9m × 12.2m). *Tons:* 1,005 bm. *Hull:* wood. *Arm.:* 24 × 24pdr, 26 × 9pdr, 10 × 6pdr. *Built:* Portsmouth Dockyard, Eng.; 1732.

At the start of the War of the Austrian Succession in 1739, Commodore George Anson took command of a squadron that was given the task of harassing Spanish shipping on the coast of South America and capturing the Manila galleon, the annual shipment of gold and silver from Mexico to the Philippines. His six ships were HMS *Centurion, Severn* (50 guns), *Pearl* (40), *Wager* (28), *Tryal* (8), and the supply ship *Anna Pink.* Despite the support of First Lord of the Admiralty Sir Charles Wager, Anson was unable properly to man his ship. Short 300 sailors, Anson was given only 170: 32 from Chatham hospital, and 98 marines, many of them novices. In lieu of a land force of 500 men, he was given "invalids to be collected from the out-pensioners of Chelsea college . . . who from their age, wounds, or other infirmities, are incapable of service in marching regiments." Of these, all but 259 deserted before they were embarked in the ships.

These and other delays postponed the sailing date to September 1740, by which time the Spanish had dispatched to the Pacific a squadron of six ships under Don Joseph Pizarro. After stops at Madeira, Brazil, and Argentina, the British ships were separated in a withering autumn rounding of Cape Horn. Worse, the crews began to suffer from scurvy, and the disease was so virulent that *Centurion*'s lieutenant "could muster no more than two Quarter-masters, and six Fore-mast men capable of working; so that without assistance of the officers, servants and the boys, it might have proved impossible for us to have reached [Juan Fernández] Island, after we had got sight of it," on June 9, 1741. They were joined there by *Tryal, Gloucester* (which had "already thrown over-board two thirds of their complement"), and *Anna Pink.* (*Wager* was lost on the coast of Chile on May 15, though many of her crew survived. *Severn* and *Pearl* turned back from the horn.) By the time the surviving ships left Juan Fernández, they had lost a staggering 626 of the 961 crew they had sailed with; the remaining 335 men and boys were "a number, greatly insufficient for the manning of *Centurion* alone."

On September 9, *Centurion* left the island and three days later captured the merchantman *Nuestra Señora del Monte Carmelo,* from which Anson learned that Pizarro was still in the Atlantic. Over the next two months, the English took three Spanish merchantmen, one of which, *Nuestra Señora del Arranzazú,* was renamed *Tryal Prize* and used as a replacement for the abandoned *Tryal.* On November 13, they seized Paita, burning the town, sinking five ships, and taking one. From there they sailed north to keep watch off Acapulco in the vain hope of capturing the Manila galleon. After destroying their prizes and making what repairs they could manage on the hostile Mexican coast, on May 6, 1742, *Centurion* and *Gloucester* sailed for China. By August 15, the latter was in such a state of decay that she had to be scuttled; eleven days later, *Centurion* landed at Tinian, which was in regular contact with the Spanish garrison at Guam. Half of the crew were ashore, Anson included, when a typhoon struck on September 21. The ship's cables parted, and *Centurion* disappeared. Believing they might never see her again, Anson and his 113 crew set about to lengthen a small Spanish "bark" in which they planned to sail to China. Three weeks later, *Centurion* returned, and on October 21 the reunited crew sailed for Macao, where they arrived on November 12.

As the Chinese looked on all ships not engaged in trade as pirates, fitting out at Macao proved extremely difficult, and *Centurion* was not ready for sea until April 6. Rather than sail directly for England, Anson intended to intercept the Manila galleon off the Philippines. Keeping station off Cape Espiritu Santo for a month, on June 20 they overhauled *Nuestra Señora de la Covadonga* (36 guns) six leagues from the cape (in about 12°35′N, 125°10′E). The Spanish ship was no match for the determined *Centurion,* and Captain Jerónimo de Montero lost sixty-seven crew killed and eighty-four wounded compared with only two English killed and seventeen wounded. The two ships arrived at Canton on July 11, and Anson's efforts to provision his ship were again frustrated. *Covadonga* was sold for $6,000 to local merchants, and *Centurion* sailed for home on December 15, 1743.

Centurion's nearly four-year circumnavigation ended at Spithead on June 15, 1744. Despite the loss of three ships and more than 1,300 crew (only four to enemy action), Anson's capture of the Manila galleon with 1,313,843 pieces of eight and 35,682 ounces of virgin silver outshone any other achievement of England's ten-year war with Spain and was ranked the equal of Drake's circumnavigation in GOLDEN HIND 160 years before. Anson achieved flag rank the following year, and *Centurion* was in a squadron commanded by him at the Battle of Cape Finisterre in which the English defeated Admiral de la Jonquière on May 3, 1747, and captured seven merchantmen, four ships of the line, and two frigates. During the Seven Years' War, *Centurion* was at the capture of Louisbourg in 1758, and of Quebec the next year. In 1762, she participated in the capture of Havana. She was broken up seven years later. In addition to eyewitness accounts of Anson's circumnavigation, Patrick O'Brian's *The Golden Ocean* is a readable and accurate, though fictional, account of the voyage.

Anson, *Voyage round the World.*

HMVS Cerberus

(later HMAS *Platypus I*) Coastal defense monitor (1f/2m). *L/B/D:* 225′ × 45′ × 15.3′ (68.6m × 13.7m × 4.6m). *Tons:* 3,340 disp. *Hull:* iron. *Comp.:* 155. *Arm.:* 4 × 10″ (2 × 2). *Armor:* 8″ belt, 1.5″ deck. *Mach.:* horizontal steam, 1,369 ihp, 2 screws; 9.75 kts. *Built:* Palmer Shipyard, Jarrow, Eng.; 1870.

Named for the three-headed dog of Greek myth who guards the underworld, HMVS *Cerberus* was one of seven near sister ships designed for coastal defense around the empire. The first British warship designed without masts, she was further distinguished by a low freeboard, breastwork armor, and a central superstructure with turrets fore and aft. *Cerberus*'s main armament consisted of four 10-inch guns mounted in two turrets, forward and aft, which could be trained over an arc of 270 degrees. She also had ballast tanks that could be filled to sink the hull and lower her freeboard to further reduce her profile in battle. Describing the class of ungainly ships, Admiral G. A. Ballard wrote that "no contemporary opponent of their own tonnage . . . would have stood much chance against them. They might be said to resemble full-armed knights riding on donkeys, easy to avoid but bad to close with."

First assigned to Her Majesty's Victoria (State) Navy and in 1901 to the fledgling Australian Navy, *Cerberus* was intended for the defense of Melbourne's Port Philip Bay. During World War I, she was used as a port guard and munitions ship. In 1921, renamed HMAS *Platypus I,* she was employed as a submarine depot ship. In 1926, her hull was purchased by the city of Sandringham and sunk as a breakwater for the Black Rock Yacht Club. She remains there in a deteriorated state.

Ballard, *Black Battlefleet.* Herd, *HMVS "Cerberus."*

Chasseur

(later *Cazador, Almirante*) Schooner (2m). *L/B/D:* 85.7' keel × 26' × 12.6' (26.1m × 7.9m × 3.8m). *Tons:* 356 burthen. *Hull:* wood. *Comp.:* 115. *Arm.:* 16 × 12pdr. *Built:* Thomas Kemp, Fells Point, Baltimore; 1812.

Built as a privateer during the War of 1812, *Chasseur* was the most famous of the so-called Baltimore clippers, sharp, heavily — even dangerously — canvassed, but lightly sparred vessels built around Chesapeake Bay in the late eighteenth and early nineteenth centuries. *Chasseur*'s exploits on both sides of the Atlantic earned her the nickname "Pride of Baltimore." While privateering in English waters, Captain Thomas Boyle impetuously declared a blockade of the British Isles, and on her last cruise of the war, she took eighteen prizes. The last was the 16-gun schooner HMS *St. Lawrence* (Lieutenant James Gordon) off Mantazas, Cuba, on February 26, 1815, two months after the Treaty of Ghent had ended the war.

Upon her return to Baltimore, *Chasseur* was

sold to the merchants George Patterson and George Stevenson to sail in the China trade. Rerigged as a brig and under command of Captain Hugh Davey, she cleared Baltimore on May 19, 1815. After a stop at Boston to take on more cargo, she sailed for Canton on June 12. Her progress was good, and she passed the equator twenty-five days out (as against the thirty-five or forty days it normally took) and rounded the Cape of Good Hope on August 1. From there she was another thirty-five days to Java Head (where she stopped briefly for provisions) and was at Whampoa on September 25. After three months in port, she cleared on December 30 and, returning the way she had come, sailed home in a record ninety-five days from Canton to Boston, and eighty-four days from Java Head; these records were not bettered until 1832.

Although the voyage was a profitable one, *Chasseur* was sold to Thomas Sheppard for trade to the West Indies. After one voyage to Havana, one of the few Spanish-American ports open to foreign ships during this revolutionary period, *Chasseur* was sold to the Spanish navy. Armed with 21 guns and manned by a crew of 180, she was renamed *Cazador* (Spanish for *chasseur,* or hunter). Because there was already a *Cazador* in the Spanish navy, she was carried on the lists as *Almirante.* On August 27, 1816, *Cazador* was part of a squadron that fired on USS *Firebrand,* a New Orleans–based schooner suspected of escorting smugglers in the pay of Mexican revolutionaries. The next year, on June 29, 1817, *Cazador* and *Consulado* attempted to capture *Hotspur* off Morro Castle, but the Colombian privateer managed to escape. The next year, she succeeded in capturing a privateer that had itself just captured a slaver. The whole crew were hanged and the slaves returned to Havana.

Cazador remained on the Spanish lists until 1824; her subsequent fate is unknown. The same year, a Spanish vessel of that name was reported at Charleston in distress, but it is not known if this was the same ship. In 1835, a suspected slaver of the same name was seized at Gibraltar and two years later auctioned by the Royal Navy at Lloyds.

However, the connection between the *Cazador/Chasseur* and this vessel has eluded confirmation.

Hopkins, "*Chasseur:* The Pride of Baltimore." Roosevelt, *Naval War of 1812.*

USS Chesapeake

Frigate (3m). *L/B/D:* 152.5′ bp × 40.9′ × 13.8′ dph (46.5m × 12.5m × 4.2m). *Tons:* 1,244 bm. *Hull:* wood. *Comp.:* 340. *Arm.:* 28 × 18pdr, 20 × 32pdr. *Des.:* Josiah Fox. *Built:* Gosport Navy Yard, Norfolk, Va.; 1800.

The last and least fortunate of the original six frigates ordered by Congress to deal with the Barbary corsairs in the Mediterranean, USS *Chesapeake's* construction proceeded fitfully. Laid down in 1795, she was only completed after the start of the Quasi-War with France. The frigates included the heavily built UNITED STATES, CONSTITUTION, and PRESIDENT, rated as 44-gun frigates, and *Chesapeake,* CONSTELLATION, and *Congress,* rated as 38s and designed to carry twenty-eight 24-pdrs. and eighteen to twenty 12-pdrs.

Chesapeake sailed from Norfolk on June 6, 1800, under Captain Samuel Barron to patrol the West Indies during the Quasi-War with France. She took one French privateer before the cessation of hostilities in 1801. In April 1802, she was flagship of the Mediterranean Squadron under Commodore Richard V. Morris until his replacement by Commodore Edward Preble, in *Constitution.* Among the other complaints leveled against the ineffectual Morris was that he paid more attention to his pregnant wife, who sailed with him, than to prosecuting the war against the corsairs.

Chesapeake was laid up at Washington from mid-1803 to 1807, when she was readied for a two-year assignment as flagship of Commodore James Barron (younger brother of Samuel) in the Mediterranean. In addition to the supplies needed for the lengthy spell on foreign station, the ship carried a number of important passengers and their belongings, which customarily took priority over the battle readiness of American warships not sailing through hostile waters. As the country was at peace, there was little to fear. However, the Royal Navy was hard-pressed in its war against Napoleonic France, and in its effort to keep its ships manned had resorted to impressment, first at home and among its merchant fleets, and then among U.S.-flag ships. Shortly before *Chesapeake* sailed, two French ships had sought shelter from a storm in the Chesapeake and a British squadron had anchored in Lynhaven Roads to prevent their escape. In the meantime, five British deserters had joined *Chesapeake* and, despite an apparent diplomatic settlement of the issue (and the fact that four had subsequently deserted *Chesapeake*), HMS LEOPARD had been dispatched from Halifax with orders to take the men from *Chesapeake* when she sailed.

On June 22, *Chesapeake* cleared the bay whose name she carried, and *Leopard* followed her past the three-mile limit. When Barron refused to accede to the British demand to have his ship searched for Royal Navy deserters, *Leopard* fired seven unanswered broadsides into the unready *Chesapeake* — only a single gun was fired in reply — killing four men, wounding eighteen, including Barron, and damaging the ship severely. Her boarding party then carried off five men. One was hanged, two died, and the two survivors were returned at Boston in 1812 — shortly after the commencement of hostilities for which their capture was but a distant prelude. After repairs at Norfolk, *Chesapeake* was assigned to patrol New England waters to enforce the embargo laws, under command of Captain Stephen Decatur.

With the outbreak of the War of 1812, *Chesapeake,* Samuel Evans commanding, made an extended cruise against British shipping; between December 1812 and April 1813, she ranged from the West Indies to Africa, taking five British prizes and, through skillful seamanship, evading the pursuit of a British 74. Back at Boston, Captain James Lawrence took command and, on June 1, put to sea to meet HMS *Shannon,* a crack 38-gun frigate under command of Captain Philip Bowes Vere Broke. Accepting an implicit challenge from Broke (who had actually issued a written one, which Lawrence never received), Lawrence sailed for a rendezvous outside of Boston Harbor and shortly after 1600 came alongside *Shannon*. Meticulously prepared for this battle, *Shannon's* crew killed or fatally wounded most of *Chesapeake's* officers, including Lawrence (whose dying words were "Don't give up the ship"), shot away her head sails, boarded her, and hauled down the American flag to replace it with their own. The bloodiest naval battle of the war, and one of the shortest — it lasted only fifteen minutes — had cost the lives of forty-eight U.S. crew and thirty British, with ninety-eight wounded in *Chesapeake* and fifty-six in *Shannon*.

Chesapeake was taken to Halifax, where she was repaired and brought into the Royal Navy. By a strange twist of fate, she was the site of the court-martial of Captain Edward Crofton, HMS *Leopard* (converted to a troopship in 1812), who had run his ship aground on Anticosti Island in the Gulf of St. Lawrence in June 1814. Later that year, *Chesapeake* sailed for England and ran aground off Plymouth. By mid-1815, she was at Cape Town, where she learned that Britain and the United States were no longer at war. She was sold at Portsmouth and broken up in 1820. The same year, the ghost of the ill-starred *Chesapeake* stirred one last time when her most disgraced captain, James Barron, killed her most admired, Stephen Decatur, in a duel.

Chapelle, *History of the American Sailing Navy*. Dennis, "Action between the *Shannon* and the *Chesapeake*." Pullen, *"Shannon" and the "Chesapeake*." Strum, "*Leopard-Chesapeake* Incident of 1807." Tucker & Renter, *Injured Honor*.

HMS Colossus

Leviathan-class 3rd rate 74 (3m). *L/B/D:* 172.3′ × 48′ × 20.3′ dph. (52.5m × 14.6m × 6.3m). *Tons:* 1,716 burthen. *Hull:* wood. *Comp.:* 640. *Arm.:* 28 × 32pdr, 28 × 18pdr, 18 × 9pdr, 2 carr. *Built:* Cleverly, Gravesend, Eng.; 1787.

The third-rate ship of the line HMS *Colossus* saw extensive action in the wars with Revolutionary France, including the capture of Toulon in 1793 and the Battle of Groix in 1795. The following year, she joined Admiral Sir John Jervis's fleet under Captain George Murray, a friend of Commodore Horatio Nelson. On February 14, 1797, while on blockade of the Spanish coast between the Tagus and Cadiz, *Colossus* was severely damaged at the Battle of Cape St. Vincent, where Admiral Sir John Jervis, with fifteen ships of the line, overwhelmed a Spanish fleet of thirteen ships of the line and fourteen frigates.

Her battle damage repaired, *Colossus* joined Nelson's squadron at Naples as an armed storeship. Following the Battle of the Nile on August 1, 1798, *Colossus* was used to transport the wounded, both British and French, as well as the treasure taken from the defeated French fleet. Though victorious, the British ships were badly damaged at the Nile, and *Colossus* herself was so cannibalized that Murray even surrendered his spare anchor to Nelson's Vanguard.

Ordered home with a convoy of merchant ships, before leaving Naples *Colossus* loaded a cargo of antiquities that had been collected by Sir Edward Hamilton. This was made possible by both Hamilton's position as the British minister to Naples and his and his wife Emma's friendship with Nelson. After stopping at the Tagus for five days, on December 7, Captain Murray led his convoy into the anchorage at St. Mary's Island in the Scilly Islands. Three days later, a gale struck, the anchor cable parted, and the sheet and bower anchors would not hold — and there was no spare. *Colossus* went ashore on Southward Well Rock, and the next morning all but one man were rescued. Much of the ship was salvaged soon after, but Hamilton's vases were not. In 1968, Roland Morris began diving on the site (in 49°55′N, 06°21′W) and six years later recovered fragments from Hamilton's collection. Over the years, these were reassembled by the British Museum; the most famous reconstructed artifact is the so-called Colossus Vase dating from fifth-century BCE Athens.

Morris, *HMS "Colossus*."

HMS Confiance

5th rate 36 (3m). *L/B/D:* 147.4' × 37.2' × 7' dph (44.9m × 11.3m × 2.1m). *Tons:* 1,200 disp. *Hull:* wood. *Comp.:* 270–300. *Arm.:* 27 × 24pdr, 2 × 18pdr, 4 × 32pdr carr., 6 × 24pdr carr. *Built:* Isle aux Noix, Ont.; 1814.

The largest warship ever constructed on Lake Champlain, HMS *Confiance* was built in answer to the American Commander Thomas Macdonough's ambitious shipbuilding program, itself designed to thwart British advances into Vermont and New York during the War of 1812. Captain George Downie's flagship at the Battle of Plattsburg, on September 11, 1814, *Confiance* was forced to strike after a two-hour battle with Macdonough's SARATOGA, during which she sustained at least 105 hits by round shot. Forty of her crew were killed, including Downie, and another eighty-three wounded. Taken into the U.S. Navy at Whitehall, New York, in 1815, she was never fitted, and she was eventually sold out of the navy in about 1825.

Heinrichs, "Battle of Plattsburg."

Congress

Galley (2m). *L/B/D:* 72.3' × 19.6' × 6.2' dph (22m × 6m × 1.9m). *Tons:* 123 tons. *Hull:* wood. *Arm.:* 1 × 18pdr, 1 × 12pdr, 2 × 9pdr, 6 × 6pdr, swivels. *Built:* Skenesborough, N.Y.; 1776.

The Continental Navy's *Congress* was one of four lateen-rigged galleys — the others were *Washington, Trumbull,* and *Gates* — built for General Benedict Arnold's Lake Champlain flotilla, with which he intended to halt the British advance from Canada to the Hudson River Valley. Launched just five days before the Battle of Valcour Island, on October 11, 1776, *Congress* was severely damaged on the first day of the battle; the same action saw the loss of the schooner *Royal Savage* and the gundalow PHILADELPHIA. The following day, she led the retreat south through the British line and around Crown Point. Pursued by the British on October 13, Arnold was forced to run four more gundalows and his flagship aground and burn them. Twenty of *Congress*'s crew had died in the three-day run-

ning battle. Despite Arnold's losses, though, he had delayed the British advance for the season, and when they advanced the next October, the Americans scored a resounding victory at Saratoga.

Chapelle, *History of the American Sailing Navy.* Fowler, *Rebels under Sail.*

USS Congress

Frigate (3m). *L/B/D:* 164' × 41' × 13.3' (50m × 12.5m × 4.1m). *Tons:* 1,867 disp. *Hull:* wood. *Comp.:* 480. *Arm.:* 4 × 8pdr, 49 × 32pdr. *Built:* Portsmouth Navy Yard, Kittery, Me.; 1841.

The fourth vessel of the name, USS *Congress* saw duty in the Mediterranean and then, in the fall of 1844, protected American interests at the beginning of the eight-year siege of Montevideo by Argentine dictator Juan Manuel de Rosas. The next year she embarked Commodore Robert Stockton en route to Monterey, where she became flagship of the Pacific Squadron. During the Mexican War (1846–48), she patrolled the coast of California and Mexico and her crew played an active role in defeating Mexico and adding California to the territory of the United States. From 1850 to 1853, she served again on the Brazil station, where she oversaw U.S. interests in South America and enforced bans on the African slave trade. From 1855 to 1857, she was flagship of the Mediterranean Squadron, and 1859 found her again in Brazilian waters until the outbreak of the Civil War.

After her recall to the United States, she was assigned to the North Atlantic Blockading Squadron in 1861. On March 8, 1862, she was on blockade in Hampton Roads when the ironclad CSS VIRGINIA sailed out of Norfolk. After sinking USS CUMBERLAND, *Virginia* turned on *Congress,* whose commanding officer, Lieutenant Joseph Smith, intentionally grounded his ship under the protective fire of batteries near Signal Point. Unfortunately, she could bring only two of her guns to bear against *Virginia*'s devastating fire, which claimed the lives of more than 120 of her crew. Unable to take the stranded vessel in tow owing to the shallow water,

Virginia riddled the stricken *Congress* with incendiary shot, and shortly after midnight the resulting fires ignited the magazines and the ship blew up.

Still, *Iron Afloat*. U.S. Navy, *DANFS*.

USS Constellation

Frigate (3m). *L/B/D:* 164′ bp × 40.5′ × 13.5′ dph (50m × 12.3m × 4.1m). *Tons:* 1,265 disp. *Hull:* wood. *Comp.:* 340. *Arm.:* 38 guns. *Des.:* Josiah Fox, Joshua Humphreys. *Built:* David Stodder, Sterrett Shipyard, Baltimore; 1797.

Known as the "Yankee Race Horse," USS *Constellation* was the second frigate completed under the congressional authorization of 1794. She first saw action during the Quasi-War with France as part of the West Indics Squadron under Captain Thomas Truxton. On February 9, 1799, she captured the frigate *L'Insurgente* (40 guns) in an hour-long engagement off Nevis. Her next major contest, on February 1, 1800, was against *Vengeance* (52) in a five-hour night action off Guadeloupe during which the French frigate struck her colors twice but eventually escaped the partially dismasted *Constellation* under cover of darkness. During the Barbary Wars, in 1802, *Constellation* was assigned to the Mediterranean Squadron and took part in the evacuation of Derna and in actions against Tunis in 1805. Blockaded in the Chesapeake during the War of 1812, she returned to the Mediterranean as part of Stephen Decatur's squadron and took part in the capture of the Algerian frigate *Mashuda* in June 1815. From 1819 to 1845, *Constellation* served on a variety of stations, including Brazil, the Pacific, the Mediterranean, the West Indies, and last, as flagship of the East India Squadron during the Opium War. *Constellation* was in ordinary from 1845 to 1853.

There is a great deal of confusion as to *Constellation*'s subsequent fate. It is quite clear that the navy establishment felt *Constellation* ought to be maintained in some form, and it is possible that some timbers from the ship of 1797 were incorporated in the construction of the sloop of war CONSTELLATION in 1854. But as early as 1872, the his-torian Admiral George H. Preble wrote that the original *Constellation* was "now represented by a new ship bearing the same name." Until recently, the navy unofficially regarded the *Constellation* of 1854 as a rebuilt version of the frigate of 1797.

Dunne, "Frigate *Constellation* Clearly Was No More: Or Was She?" Randolph, "Fouled Anchors? Foul Blow"; "USS *Constellation*." Wegner, "An Apple and an Orange." Wegner et al., *Fouled Anchors*.

USS Constellation

Sloop of war (3m). *L/B/D:* 176′ × 42′ × 19.3′ (53.6m × 12.8m × 5.9m). *Tons:* 1,278 disp. *Hull:* wood. *Comp.:* 227. *Arm.:* 16 × 8″, 4 × 32pdr, 1 × 30pdr, 1 × 20pdr, 2 × 12pdr. *Built:* Gosport Navy Yard, Portsmouth, Va.; 1854.

The U.S. Navy's last ship built to be driven solely by the wind, the 24-gun sloop of war *Constellation* slid down the ways at the Norfolk Navy Yard in 1854. After a three-year tour of duty in the Mediterranean, she had become flagship of the Africa Squadron, patrolling against slavers, by the outbreak of the Civil War. During the war, she was reassigned to the Mediterranean. In 1865, she returned to Newport and was decommissioned. *Constellation* spent the next seventy-five years as a training and receiving ship. During this period, she undertook a number of special assignments. She sailed to Europe for the Paris Exposition of 1878 and the Columbian Exposition of 1892, to Ireland with food aid in 1880, and to Baltimore for the centenary of "The Star-Spangled Banner" in 1914. *Constellation* was renamed *New Constellation* from 1917 to 1925, to free the name for a cruiser that was eventually scrapped under the Washington Naval Agreement of 1922. Recommissioned in 1940, *Constellation* served as relief flagship for the Atlantic Fleet and Battleship Division Five from 1941 to 1943. Decommissioned and stricken from the navy lists in 1955, *Constellation* is currently a museum ship in Baltimore.

Dunne, "Frigate *Constellation* Clearly Was No More: Or Was She?" Randolph, "Fouled Anchors? Foul Blow"; "USS *Constellation*." Wegner, "An Apple and an Orange." Wegner et al., *Fouled Anchors*.

USS Constitution

Frigate (3m). *L/B/D:* 175′ × 43.5′ × 22.5′ (53.3m × 13.3m × 6.9m). *Tons:* 2,200 tons. *Hull:* wood. *Comp.:* 450. *Arm.:* 32 × 24pdr, 20 × 32pdr, 2 × 24 pdr. *Des.:* Joshua Humphreys, Josiah Fox, William Doughty. *Built:* Edmund Hartt, Boston; 1797.

One of the U.S. Navy's six original frigates, authorized by Congress specifically as a counter to the Barbary corsairs in the Mediterranean, USS *Constitution* was launched in 1797. Though all six were fast, heavily built frigates with a flush spar deck above the gundeck, UNITED STATES, *Constitution,* and PRESIDENT were nominally rated as 44s but mounted thirty 24-pdr. and twenty to twenty-two 12-pdr. long guns (later replaced by short-range 42-pdr. carronades). The slightly smaller CONSTELLATION, CHESAPEAKE, and *Congress,* rated as 38s, carried 28 long guns and 18 to 20 carronades. In the words of James Henderson, an authority on British frigates: "Class for class, they had no superior."

A temporary peace with the Barbary States was achieved before she was finished, but *Constitution* was commissioned in time for the Quasi-War with France, during which she captured a number of smaller ships and privateers in the West Indies. Returning to the Charlestown Navy Yard in 1801, she was placed in ordinary. The United States' next foreign entanglement was with the deys of Algiers, Morocco, Tunis, and Tripoli. In 1803, *Constitution* sailed as flagship of the Mediterranean Squadron maintaining a tight blockade on Tripoli, which was bombarded in August and September 1804, that finally forced the deys of Algiers and Tunis to sign treaties exempting American ships from tribute payments. While the Barbary Wars produced few opportunities for decisive ship-to-ship engagements, the Americans were much admired, and Lord Nelson is said to have observed that "there is in the handling of those transatlantic ships a nucleus of trouble for the navy of Great Britain."

Following repairs at New York, in 1809 *Constitution* joined Commodore John Rodgers's North Atlantic Squadron, and the following year Isaac Hull, her most illustrious captain, assumed command. The start of the War of 1812 found her at

Annapolis, Maryland, and she put to sea on July 5. By July 17, *Constitution* was off the New Jersey coast when she spotted ships that all assumed to be Rodgers's squadron. It soon transpired that they were in fact HMS *Africa* (64 guns), the frigates *Shannon,* GUERRIÈRE (38s), *Belvedira* (36), and *Aeolus* (32), and the recently captured U.S. brig NAUTILUS (12), under command of Captain Sir Philip Broke. In a remarkable sixty-six-hour chase that began in light airs, *Constitution* kept out of range of the British ships by kedging ahead with her anchors, by towing with the ship's boats, and, when the wind finally came up, by what Broke described as "very superior sailing."

On August 19, *Constitution* was cruising the Grand Banks south of Newfoundland when she encountered *Guerrière* in position 41°42′N, 55°48′W. Captain James Dacres was a willing combatant and had only recently invited Rodgers to meet "U. States frigate *President . . .* or any other American frigate of equal force for the purpose of having a few minutes tête-à-tête." At 1700, *Guerrière* opened fire at long range; Hull closed the range until 1805, when at a distance of half a pistol shot he gave the order to fire. The first broadside smashed into *Guerrière,* and Hull exclaimed, "By heaven, that ship is ours!" Twenty-five minutes later, the dismasted *Guerrière* was wallowing in the heavy seas. *Constitution*'s casualties were seven dead and seven wounded; *Guerrière* had seventy-eight dead and wounded and was so shattered that Hull ordered her blown up the next day. It was during this battle that *Constitution* earned the nickname "Old Ironsides," after shot was seen bouncing off her hull. *Constitution* returned to a Boston — and a nation — thrilled with the stunning victory. As the *London Times* observed,

> It is not merely that an English frigate has been taken, . . . but that it has been taken by a new enemy, an enemy unaccustomed to such triumphs, and likely to be rendered insolent and confident by them.

Family affairs compelled Hull to hand over command to the much maligned William Bainbridge, who had lost USS PHILADELPHIA at Tri-

◄ The **USS Constitution** during a visit to New York City in the summer of 1931. She is seen in the Hudson River alongside Pier 113 at the foot of West 79th Street. *Photo by Burnell Poole, courtesy of the family of Burnell Poole.*

poli in 1803. En route to join USS ESSEX and HORNET in the South Pacific, on December 29, 1812, *Constitution* was off the coast of Brazil, in 13°6'S, 31°W, when she encountered HMS *Java* (38 guns) under Captain Henry Lambert. Battle was joined at about 1400, and *Constitution* opened fire at about half a mile. *Java* had the better of it at first, but by 1725, *Constitution's* overwhelming firepower and superior gunnery had reduced *Java* to a mastless hulk, with 124 of her crew killed or wounded, including Captain Lambert. *Constitution's* casualties were 34 (or 52, according to British estimates) dead and wounded. *Java* was so riddled with shot she had to be blown up. Dramatic though the victory was, damage to *Constitution* prevented Bainbridge from continuing his cruise against British shipping.

Constitution put back to Boston, where the wounded Bainbridge was replaced by Captain Charles Stewart. After a brief cruise to the Caribbean in early 1814, she put back to Boston, where she remained until December 1814, when she again slipped the British blockade. On February 20, 1815 — a week after the war formally ended — she sailed into action against HMS CYANE (22) and *Levant* (20) off Madeira. She forced both ships to strike, and both ships were taken as prizes, though *Levant* was recaptured by a British squadron on March 11. *Constitution* arrived at New York on May 15, the most celebrated ship in the U.S. Navy.

Out of commission for the next six years, she returned to the Mediterranean between 1821 and 1828. Two years later, she was saved from the scrapyard after a public outcry sparked by the publication of a poetic encomium by Oliver Wendell Holmes. *Constitution* emerged from her rebuilding in 1835 and thereafter sailed on a number of diverse assignments, including the Mediterranean and Home Squadrons, and on the South Pacific station, and, in 1844–46, a twenty-nine-month circumnavigation of the world. During the Civil War, she saw duty as a navy training ship. Rebuilt in the

1870s, she sailed again as a training ship until 1881, after which she was used as a receiving ship in New Hampshire. In 1897, she was brought to Boston for preservation. She made an extended goodwill voyage in 1931–34, when she was towed to seventy-six ports along the Atlantic, Gulf, and Pacific coasts. Maintained as a museum ship at Boston, USS *Constitution* is the oldest commissioned ship in the U.S. Navy, and the oldest commissioned warship afloat in the world. To ensure equal weathering on both sides of her hull, she leaves her dock for a turnaround cruise in Boston Harbor every July 4.

Gillmer, *Old Ironsides*. Martin, *A Most Fortunate Ship*. Roosevelt, *Naval War of 1812*.

HMS Conway

HM Schoolship *Conway* is the name given to a series of vessels used as stationary schoolships for Britain's Mercantile Marine Service Association. The *Conway* program was designed to prepare students for careers in Britain's merchant navy and the Royal Navy. The curriculum combined the study of liberal arts and nautical science with an Outward Bound segment for the mastery of practical seamanship skills.

The school's first ship was the sixth-rate frigate HMS *Conway*, which was in commission from 1832 to 1857. After a two-year refit, she opened as a schoolship on the Mersey with accommodations for 150 cadets. The institution proved such a success that the Admiralty replaced the *Conway* with the fourth-rate HMS *Winchester*, a *Java*-class frigate of 1822. To preserve a sense of institutional continuity, she was renamed *Conway*. (The original *Conway* was renamed *Winchester* and employed as a naval reserve drillship at Aberdeen.) The program continued to prosper, and in 1875 it acquired the second-rate 92-gun ship HMS *Nile*. This veteran of the Baltic campaign in the Crimean War had a long gestation. Laid down in 1827, she was not launched until 1839, and not commissioned until 1852. Almost immediately, she was fitted with an engine and single screw. The new *Conway* opened in 1875 with accommodations for 265 trainees. (The second *Conway* was renamed *Mount Edgecomb* and remained in service with the Devonport and Cornwall Industrial Training Ship Association until 1920.)

The new *Conway* remained on the Mersey until World War II. After several incendiary bombs landed on the ship, she was towed to Plas Newydd, the manor house of the Marquis of Anglesey. She remained there on the Menai Strait after the war. In 1949, the ship was given an extensive refit, and the establishment was expanded to include a shoreside facility. Four years later, she was being towed to Liverpool for dry-docking when she stranded in the Menai Strait. The wreck of the last *Conway* burned in 1956.

Fay, "Career of the *Conway.*" Masefield, "*Conway.*"

La Cordelière

(ex-*La Marie Cordelière, La Mareschalle*) Nef (4m). *Tons:* 1,000 tons. *Hull:* wood. *Comp.:* 900. *Arm.:* 16 great guns, 60 lesser guns. *Built:* Morlaix, France; 1448.

La Mareschalle was a nef built at the end of the Hundred Years' War shortly before Charles VII succeeded in forcing the English to relinquish all their French holdings except Calais. More than six decades later, French incursions into Italy under Louis XII brought into being the Holy League, consisting of the Papal States, Venice, Spain, and, in 1512, England's Henry VIII. Among the ships lent to Louis for the defense of the realm was the Breton nef now called *La Cordelière,* commanded by the veteran corsair Hervé de Portznoguer, known also as Primaguet. In August 1512, a fleet of twenty-one ships was gathered at Brest under Admiral René de Clermont. On August 9, Portznoguer was entertaining about 300 people on board *La Cordelière* when an English fleet of some fifty ships under Sir Edward Howard was reported approaching the roadstead. Clermont ordered his fleet to weigh anchor to avoid being bottled up in port, and *La Cordelière* sailed with her guests still aboard and anchored between Capes St. Mathieu and Toulinquet.

The next morning, Clermont ("a worse than

bad sailor," according to one French historian) ordered *La Cordelière* and another ship to cover the withdrawal of the French ships as the English attacked. Howard's MARY ROSE was disabled and run aground before three other ships fell on *La Cordelière: Mary James, Sovereign,* and *Regent,* the last commanded by Howard's brother-in-law Sir Thomas Knyvet. Portznoguer ran his ship aboard the *Regent,* and Knyvet was killed early in the fighting. The English ships kept up a withering fire until *La Cordelière*'s magazine blew up and the ship sank with the loss of all but 20 of her 1,200 soldiers, seamen, and guests. The old ship did not die entirely in vain, for she was soon followed to the bottom by *Regent,* which also exploded with the loss of all but a few of her men.

Clowes, *Royal Navy.* Culver, *Forty Famous Ships.*

Corsair

(later USS *Gloucester*) Screw schooner (2f/1m). *L/B/D:* 241.5′ × 27′ × 13′ (73.6m × 8.2m × 4m). *Tons:* 560 grt. *Hull:* steel. *Mach.:* triple expansion, 2,000 ihp, 1 screw; 17 kts. *Des.:* J. Beavor-Webb. *Built:* Neafie & Levy, Philadelphia; 1890.

The second of four yachts of the same name owned by J. Pierpont Morgan (who owned the first three) and J. Morgan, Jr. (who built the fourth, in 1930), *Corsair* had a celebrated career both as the personal yacht of the financier and philanthropist and as a commissioned ship in the U.S. Navy. During Morgan's tenure as commodore of the New York Yacht Club in 1897–98, *Corsair* served as flagship of that distinguished fleet. It is interesting to note that despite her great size, she was by no means the largest yacht in the club. That same year, there were four vessels longer than 300 feet: W. K. Vanderbilt's *Valiant* (332 feet), Ogden Goulet's *Mayflower* (320 feet) and *Nahma* (306 feet), and Eugene Higgins's *Varuna* (304 feet).

At the start of the Spanish-American War, in April 1898, Morgan presented *Corsair* to the U.S. Navy. She was commissioned as USS *Gloucester* under command of Lieutenant Commander Richard Wainwright. Fitted with four 6-pdr. guns, she joined the North Atlantic Blockading Squadron. At the Battle of Santiago Bay on July 3, she helped sink the Spanish torpedo boats *Pluton* and *Furor*. She was later credited with the single-handed capture of Guanica, Puerto Rico, and aided in the capture of Arroyo. Following the war, *Gloucester* served as a Naval Academy training ship and between 1902 and 1905 sailed in the West Indies and South America as tender to the commander-in-chief of the South Atlantic Squadron. After service with the New York and Massachusetts state militias, *Gloucester* was recommissioned in 1917. Sold out of the service in 1919, she was wrecked in a hurricane off Pensacola, Florida.

Parkinson, *History of the New York Yacht Club*. U.S. Navy, *DANFS*.

La Couronne

Ship (3m). *L/B/D:* 165' lod × 46' × 19' dph (50.3m × 14m × 5.8m dph). *Tons:* 2,100 bm. *Hull:* wood. *Arm.:* 68 guns. *Built:* Charles Morieux, La Roche-Bernard, France; 1635.

Laid down in 1629 on the banks of the Seudre River in Brittany, *La Couronne* was the largest French warship built to that time, twenty-five feet longer and seven feet broader in the beam than the next largest of the King's ships. As significant, she represented a major shift in French policy, being French-built rather than an import from Holland, as was usual at the time. The inadequacy of contemporary French shipbuilding can be gauged by the fact that *La Couronne* was not launched until 1635. Sometime later she was dismasted, but in the spring of 1639, she was Isaac de Launay Razilly's flagship when the French fleet sailed from Brest for La Coruña, Spain. The French fleet sailed again in June, and after storms arrived at Laredo in July, where they captured an admiral's ship. Subsequently laid up at Brest, *La Couronne* was broken up in 1641, either because too many of her timbers were rotten to make repairs possible, or possibly because a jealous naval officer denied command of the ship arranged for her scrapping.

She was reputedly a good sailer, and much admired in England, Holland, and the other countries she visited in her brief career. Despite her great size, her arming was anachronistic when compared with Dutch and English practice. Although the inadequacy of galleys against larger ships had been confirmed during the siege of the Huguenot stronghold of La Rochelle in 1627–28, *La Couronne* was armed with 12 guns in the stern and 8 in the bows, as protection against the more maneuverable galleys. Moreover, she was lightly armed; England's Sovereign of the Seas (1637) carried 102 guns on a hull about 20 feet shorter than *La Couronne*'s.

It is interesting to note that the timbers used for construction of *La Couronne* were taken from the forests of the defeated Huguenot leader Duc de Rohan. Asked her opinion of the new ship, the Duchess de Rohan remarked, with a partisan lack of enthusiasm, "I truly believe that the two forests of Monsieur de Rohan which have been used to build this ship were more beautiful than what I see."

Culver, *Forty Famous Ships*. Hancock, *"La Couronne."*

USS Cumberland

Frigate (3m). *L/B/D:* 175' bp × 45' × 22.3' (53.3m × 13.7m × 6.8m). *Tons:* 1,726 tons. *Hull:* wood. *Comp.:* 400. *Arm.:* 40 × 32pdr, 10 × 64pdr. *Built:* Boston Navy Yard; 1846.

Laid down in 1826, USS *Cumberland* was not commissioned until 1842, as a frigate mounting 50 guns. Her varied service included tours with the Mediterranean Squadron (twice as flagship) and as flagship of the Home Squadron during the Mexican War. In 1856, she was razeed (her spar deck was removed) and reclassified as a sloop of war mounting 24 guns. She sailed as a squadron flagship twice more with the African Squadron (1857–59), and again with the Home Fleet in 1860.

Shortly after the start of the Civil War, on April 20, 1861, *Cumberland* narrowly escaped destruction at the Norfolk Navy Yard when Union soldiers burned as many ships as they could, including USS *Merrimack*, to prevent their capture by Confederate forces. Assigned to the North Atlantic Blockading Squadron, she captured eight prizes and took part in Silas Stringham's capture of Forts

Clark and Hatteras at Hatteras Inlet on August 18–19. On March 8, 1862, she was anchored at the mouth of the James River off Newport News when CSS VIRGINIA — as the salvaged, engined, and iron-clad *Merrimack* was now known — sortied from Norfolk on her destructive maiden voyage. *Virginia* opened fire on USS CONGRESS at 1400 before closing with the more heavily armed *Cumberland,* mounting twenty-two 9-inch and one 10-inch smoothbore guns and one 70-pdr. rifled gun, and under temporary command of Lieutenant George Morris. Ninety minutes later, *Cumberland* sank, her flag still flying. In the interim, *Virginia*'s broadsides had raked the wooden ship's hull with devastating effect, while *Cumberland*'s defiant return fire ricocheted off her opponent. *Virginia* then rammed *Cumberland* on her starboard side. The loss of *Cumberland* and *Congress* that day signaled the beginning of the end of the "wooden walls" from behind which men had fought at sea for all of recorded history.

Selfridge, *Memoirs of Thomas O. Selfridge, Jr.* Silverstone, *Warships of the Civil War Navies.* U.S. Navy, *DANFS.*

HMS Cyane

6th rate 22 (3m). *L/B/D:* 110′ × 31.5′ × 17.3′ dph (33.5m × 9.6m × 5.3m). *Tons:* 539 tons. *Hull:* wood. *Comp.:* 180. *Arm.:* 22 × 32pdr, 10 × 18pdr, 2 × 12pdr. *Built:* Bass, Topsham, Eng.; 1806.

Originally named *Columbine,* HMS *Cyane* was one of two frigates taken by the USS CONSTITUTION in a single action while covering a convoy en route from Gibraltar to England in company with HMS *Levant.* Although nominally rated as a 22-gun ship, she mounted a total of 34 guns, while *Levant* mounted 21. On the afternoon of February 20, 1815, while off Madeira, *Cyane* sighted a ship on the horizon and sailed toward her until failure of the unknown ship to answer recognition signals persuaded Captain Gordon Falcon to rejoin *Levant.* The mystery ship, the USS *Constitution* — nominally a 44, but mounting 50 guns — caught up with the pair at about 1800 and opened fire with her 32-pdrs. well out of range of the British ships' carronades. *Constitution* forced first *Cyane*

(six dead, twenty-nine wounded) and then *Levant* (six dead, sixteen wounded) to strike. Although *Levant* was recaptured by HMS *Acasta* on March 11, *Cyane* returned to the United States and was purchased by the U.S. Navy. From 1819 to 1821, she cruised between the West Indies and the newly founded West African colony of Liberia. She also saw duty in the Mediterranean (1824–25) and on the Brazil station (1825–27). Laid up at the Philadelphia Navy Yard, she was broken up in 1836.

Hepper, *British Warship Losses.* U.S. Navy, *DANFS.*

USS Cyane

Sloop of war (3m). *L/B/D:* 132.3′ bp × 36.3′ × 16.5′ (40.3m × 11m × 5m). *Tons:* 792 om. *Hull:* wood. *Comp.:* 200. *Arm.:* 18 × 32pdr, 4 × 24pdr. *Built:* Boston Navy Yard; 1838.

First assigned to the Mediterranean Squadron, the second USS *Cyane* was dispatched to the Pacific Squadron in 1841, a period of strained relations between the United States, Mexico, and Great Britain. Acting on erroneous information, on October 19, 1842, *Cyane*'s Captain William Mervine seized Monterey and raised the U.S. flag, only to take it down when he learned there was no war. After a voyage to the East Coast, *Cyane* returned in time to take part in the Mexican War in 1846. On July 6, 1847, *Cyane* again seized Monterey — permanently — and then embarked Lieutenant Colonel John C. Frémont's California Battalion for San Diego. In company with USS *Warren,* *Cyane* attempted to enforce a blockade along 2,500 miles of Mexican coastline, seizing thirty Mexican vessels and taking part in the capture of Mazatlán on November 11 with USS CONGRESS and INDEPENDENCE. From 1852 to 1857, *Cyane* was assigned to the Home Squadron and cruised between Nova Scotia and Panama. She returned to the Pacific in 1858 and served on the West Coast between Panama and Alaska until laid up at Mare Island in 1871. She was sold in 1887.

Johnson, *Thence round Cape Horn.* U.S. Navy, *DANFS.*

D

HMS Danae

(ex-*La Vaillante*) 6th rate 20 (3m). *L/B/D:* 119.2′ × 30.9′ × 8.9′ (36.3m × 9.4m × 2.7m). *Tons:* 507 bm. *Hull:* wood. *Comp.:* 155. *Arm.:* 20 × 32pdr, 6 × 12pdr, 6 × 12pdr. *Built:* Bayonne, France; 1796.

The first mission of the French frigate *La Vaillante* was to carry reactionaries arrested in the coup d'état of September 4, 1797, to Cayenne, French Guinea. Sailing on September 24, 1797, she made the passage out in about six weeks, and by January 1798 was back in France. Sent out again on August 6, 1798, with fifty-two *déportés,* including four women and a child, she was captured two days later by Captain Sir Edward Pellew's HMS *Indefatigable.* Taken into the Royal Navy and renamed *Danae* (for a woman in Greek myth), she was rearmed with twenty 32-pdr. carronades, ten 12-pdr. carronades, and two 6-pdr. "longs," the weight of which made her top-heavy.

Although *Danae*'s complement was technically 155, British ships of the era were chronically undermanned, and by March 1799, *Danae* had only seventy-one crew. Assigned to operate against French merchantmen and privateers between Le Havre and Brest, she returned periodically to Plymouth, and in November of that year she joined the Channel Fleet to cruise off Ushant. All along, Captain Lord Proby had augmented her crew by signing on men captured from French ships or impressed from English merchantmen and privateers. By the end of February 1800, *Danae*'s crew had grown to 130 crew and marines, including five French prisoners and seven crew claiming U.S. citizenship. On the night of March 14, 1800, about forty of the crew mutinied and seized the ship off Le Conquet, near Brest, and the next morning *Danae* sailed into Le Conquet accompanied by the frigate *La Colombe.* Proby and his loyal crew were exchanged. There were forty-six mutineers, many of American or Irish origin, most of whom returned to sea. Only three were captured by the British and tried; found guilty, two were hanged, and one pardoned.

The French considered *Danae* no longer suitable for naval duty, and she was sold to a Morlaix merchant named Cooper, who chartered her to the French government as a transport. *Danae* made one voyage to Haiti during the uprising led by Toussaint L'Ouverture in 1801. The ship's fate after 1802 is unknown.

Lyon, *Sailing Navy List.* Pope, *Devil Himself.*

CSS David

Spar torpedo boat. *L/B/D:* 50′ × 6′ × 5′ (15.2m × 1.8m × 1.5m). *Comp.:* 4. *Des.:* F. D. Lee. *Built:* T. Stoney, Charleston, S.C.; 1863.

Presumably named for the Israelite David in recognition of his battle with Goliath, CSS *David* was built by T. Stoney of Charleston, South Carolina. Shaped like a cigar and designed to operate very low in the water, *David* and the ten other Confederate torpedo boats built at Charleston were intended to sink Federal blockade ships by detonating an explosive charge against the ships' hulls, the explosive being carried on the end of a spar projecting from the bow.

On the night of October 5, 1863, Lieutenant W. T. Glassell commanding, *David* attacked the casemate ironclad steamer USS NEW IRONSIDES. The torpedo detonated under *New Ironsides*'s starboard quarter, causing serious damage but throwing up a column of water that extinguished *David*'s boiler fires. All but the pilot, W. Cannon, abandoned ship, though Assistant Engineer J. H. Tomb returned to the vessel. The engines were eventually restarted, and *David* made it to safety. (Glassell and J. Sullivan were captured.) *David* is known to have staged two more attacks, neither successful. The first was on March 6, 1864, against USS *Memphis*, and the second was on April 18, when she tried to sink USS *Wabash*. Her ultimate fate is unknown.

Perry, *Infernal Machines*. Silverstone, *Warships of the Civil War Navies*.

De Braak

Brig-sloop (2m). *L/B/D:* 84′ × 28.9′ × 11.2′ (25.6m × 8.8m × 3.4m). *Tons:* 255 bm. *Hull:* wood. *Comp.:* 86. *Arm.:* 16 × 24pdr, 2 × 6pdr. *Built:* Britain(?); <1784.

One of the most inept maritime archaeological excavations ever undertaken, the bungled salvage of HMS *Braak* incidentally helped ensure the passage of legislation to develop a rational approach to the preservation of historic underwater sites. The origins of the cutter *De Braak* (Dutch for "The Beagle") are obscure. Although it was long believed that she was Dutch-built, analysis of the hull remains suggests that she was probably built in Britain. During the 1780s, she sailed against England under the Dutch flag, operating with a Mediterranean squadron out of Toulon, France. In 1793, she took part in the defense of Willemstad, Curaçao, against a French Revolutionary army, and at the end of 1794, *De Braak* was ordered to escort a convoy of East Indiamen to Batavia. Not realizing that their country was again at war with England, the Dutch put into Falmouth, where the twenty-four merchantmen and six warships were seized.

Brought into the Royal Navy as HM Sloop of War *Braak,* the cutter was rerigged as a brig and rearmed with sixteen 24-pdr. carronades. She entered service under Captain James Drew on June 13, 1797, and remained on duty until dismasted in a storm at the end of the year. Upon her return to service in February 1798, *Braak* joined a convoy bound for the Virginia Capes, but on April 2, off the Azores, she was separated from the other ships. At the end of the month, she captured a Spanish ship worth £160,000 in prize money, and on May 25, Captain Drew put into Delaware Bay. Shortly after a pilot boarded off Cape Henlopen, "a sudden flaw of wind" threw the brig on her beam ends, and *Braak* sank, with the loss of thirty-five of her crew, including Drew, and twelve Spanish prisoners.

In time, *De Braak*'s seven-week solo cruise and the certain fact that she had captured one valuable prize became encrusted with myth. Over the years, more than a dozen individuals and groups attempted to find the ship, and by the 1980s, estimates of the value of the treasure aboard the humble convoy escort exceeded $500 million. Would-be salvors ran the gamut from salvage experts to charlatans, "sportsmen and socialites," and a convicted felon who initiated his research from the Michigan State Penitentiary. Success of a sort finally came in 1984 when Harvey Harrington's Sub-Sal, Inc., raised a cannon, an anchor, and a ship's bell bearing the name "La Patrocle." Sub-Sal became legal custodian of the wreck on behalf of the U.S. District Court and with a one-year lease began working round-the-clock to retrieve as much as possible from the site. With almost total disregard for archaeological practice, divers tagged a portion of what they recovered and disposed of anything they considered worthless, including human remains, a rare stove, and objects too small to warrant their consideration.

In 1985, Sub-Sal was taken over by a New Hampshire investment group led by L. John Davidson. The state of Delaware began to take a more active interest in the project and assigned Claudia Melson to tag retrieved artifacts, which ultimately included 26,000 items ranging from ship fittings, weapons, and ammunition to toothbrushes, combs, dominoes, a syringe, compasses and dividers, a mahogany telescope, an octant, a sink, 150 shoes, a sailor's "Monmouth" hat, three anchors, storage vessels, and hundreds of specimens of organic foodstuffs including peas, corn, and beans. Determined at all costs to find the ship's treasure, Davidson secured permission to move the 200-year-old hull ashore and excavate the surrounding bottom with a clamshell bucket. During this "historic humiliation," as one archaeologist described it, the hull was raised at a rate of thirty feet per minute (rather than one and a half feet per minute, regarded as the maximum safe speed). The lifting cables cut into the hull "like a hot knife through butter" and tons of artifact-rich mud and individual artifacts slipped back into the sea. To crown this folly, the surrounding mud was sifted through a road construction rock sorter. All told, the "unmitigated archaeological disaster" of De Braak's salvage cost $2.5 million and yielded a "treasure" of 650 gold, silver, and other coins. The majority of the artifacts were housed in the Zwaanendal Museum in Lewes, Delaware, and the hull was eventually moved to a special facility in Cape Henlopen State Park.

While the underfunded conservation of artifacts continued, the excavation brought to the fore the inadequate state of legal protection for underwater archaeological sites. The law then held that historic shipwrecks and their contents enjoyed no more protection than any other property abandoned at sea; historical value was not considered as it would be in the case of, for example, a Navajo pueblo on dry land. To correct this, archaeologists and preservationists helped draft legislation to protect historic underwater sites. Testifying before Congress in support of the Abandoned Shipwreck Act of 1987, President of the National Trust for Historic Preservation J. Jackson Walter alluded to the De Braak site when he argued that

> we would not tolerate a commercial enterprise that bulldozed Gettysburg and then dumped the remains through a sifting machine to recover valuable objects. Yet this is exactly what current law allows treasure hunters to do to our nation's maritime legacy.

Signed into law in April 1988, the act gives the Federal government title to historic shipwrecks in state waters.

Shomette, *Hunt for HMS "De Braak."*

HMS Defence

Arrogant-class 3rd rate 74 (3m). *L/B/D:* 168′ × 46.8′ × 19.8′ (51.2m × 14.3m × 6m). *Tons:* 1,630 bm. *Hull:* wood. *Comp.:* 530. *Arm.:* 28 × 32pdr, 28 × 18pdr, 18 × 9pdr. *Hull:* wood. *Des.:* Sir Thomas Slade. *Built:* Devonport Dockyard, Eng.; 1763.

Launched in the last year of the Seven Years' War between France and Britain, HMS *Defence* was the first — and most decorated — Royal Navy ship to bear the name. She did not see action for the first two decades of service, but thereafter her honors include most of the major engagements of the Franco-British contest for supremacy. In 1782, *Defence* was part of Admiral Sir Edward Hughes's fleet at the battle of Cuddalore, India (a subsidiary theater of the American Revolution), against Admiral Pierre de Suffren de St. Tropez. Her first major engagement in European waters was on the Glorious First of June in 1795, when as part of Admiral Lord Howe's Channel Fleet she managed to break the French line under Admiral Louis Thomas Villaret de Joyeuse. On February 14, 1797, *Defence* was with Admiral Sir John Jervis's Mediterranean Fleet when it engaged the Spanish fleet under Admiral Don José de Cordoba at the Battle of Cape St. Vincent. The following year, she was in Rear Admiral Horatio Nelson's fleet at the Battle of the Nile (August 1, 1798), and three years after that at the Battle of Copenhagen (April 2, 1801) as part of Admiral Sir Hyde Parker's squadron. Under Captain George Hope, *Defence* sailed in Admiral Collingwood's lee column at the Battle of Trafalgar on October 21, 1805, where she engaged the French *Berwick* and forced the surrender of the Spanish *San Ildefonso,* which sustained 165 dead and wounded to her own 36. Later detailed to the Baltic Fleet, on Christmas Eve 1811, while en route from the Baltic to Britain in company with Rear Admiral Robert Reynolds's flagship, St. George, *Defence* ran aground and was lost near Ringkøbing, Denmark; only five of her company survived.

Hepper, *British Warship Losses.* Schom, *Trafalgar.*

Defence

Brigantine. L/B: 72' × 20' (21.9m × 6.1m). *Tons:* 170 burthen. *Hull:* wood. *Arm.:* 16 × 6pdr. *Built:* John Cabot and Israel Thorndike, Beverly, Mass.; 1779.

Defence was one of an estimated 1,600 vessels issued with letters of marque and reprisal to sail as privateers against British merchant ships during the American Revolution. Her career was very short-lived, for on her maiden voyage she joined the Penobscot expedition. This disastrous undertaking, led by Captain Dudley Saltonstall in WARREN, was intended to push the British out of their new stronghold on the Bagaduce Peninsula in Penobscot Bay (the site of present-day Castine, Maine), 175 miles northeast of Boston. Saltonstall's force consisted of forty ships, including *Defence,* whose owners intended to continue from Maine to the rich privateering grounds of the Gulf of St. Lawrence. Despite early successes, on August 13, 1779, Saltonstall's forces collapsed in the face of a powerful British force and burned or scuttled their whole fleet to avoid capture. *Defence* sank into the soft preserving mud of Stockton Harbor and remained there undisturbed until 1972. That summer, students from the Maine Marine Academy located the remains of the ship with a homemade sonar device. Archaeologists from the Institute of Nautical Archaeology excavated the site for seven seasons during which they recovered extensive amounts of ship fittings and personal possessions. The latter included bottles of French origin, ceramic products of domestic manufacture, five complete mess kits, notions such as buttons and buckles, and shoes and other items that offer a rare glimpse into shipboard life in the late colonial period.

Smith, "Life at Sea." Switzer, "Privateers, Not Pirates."

HMS Defiance

Elizabeth-class 3rd rate 74 (3m). *L/B/D:* 168.5' × 46.8' × 19.8' (51.4m × 14.3m × 6m). *Tons:* 1,613 bm. *Hull:* wood. *Comp.:* 550–600. *Arm.:* 28 × 32pdr, 28 × 18pdr, 18 × 9pdr. *Des.:* Sir Thomas Slade. *Built:* Messrs. Randall & Co., Rotherhithe, Eng.; 1783.

Launched in 1783, the Royal Navy's tenth HMS *Defiance* was first commissioned, into the Channel Fleet, in 1794. Living up to her name, the ship was involved in three separate mutinies: in 1794, when five of her crew were hanged; 1797, the year of the Spithead mutinies; and 1798, when twenty members of the United Irishmen in her crew were hanged. From 1799 to 1801, *Defiance* sailed with Lord St. Vincent's Mediterranean Fleet. In the latter year, she sailed with Admiral Sir Hyde Parker to the Baltic to break up Napoleon's Northern Coalition. On April 2, *Defiance* was part of the British fleet commanded by Rear Admiral Nelson at the Battle of Copenhagen. During the engagement against the Danish fleet and shore batteries, *Defiance's* casualties included seventy-five dead and wounded.

In 1804, *Defiance* joined Admiral Sir Robert Calder's blockading force between El Ferrol and Cadiz. Under Captain Charles Durham, she took part in the inconclusive action of July 22, 1805, against Vice Admiral Pierre Villeneuve's Combined Fleet off El Ferrol. Nelson replaced Calder in September, and on October 21, he led his fleet against the Combined Fleet at Trafalgar, *Defiance* in the lee column. After first engaging *Principe de Asturias* (112 guns), she closed with the French *L'Aigle* (74), which struck after a furious engagement that left more than 400 of *L'Aigle's* crew dead or wounded. *Defiance* later captured *San Juan Nepomuceno* (74). Trafalgar cost *Defiance* seventy dead and wounded, and she was all but dismasted in the action.

An interesting postscript to the ship's Trafalgar experience occurred in 1841, when Queen Victoria ordered that surviving members of the lower deck be acknowledged for their service to the Royal Navy between 1793 and 1840. As Robert H. Mackenzie relates,

> Amongst the claimants for the medal and clasp was Jane Townsend, a woman who was present in the ship [at Trafalgar]. As the regulations for the award of the medal contained no reservations as to sex, and as her services were reported as highly satisfactory and useful, her claim was at first admitted; but on reconsideration refused, as it appeared to the Board that complication would arise

on account of there being so many other women in the ships of the fleet whose services were reported as equally useful.

Defiance returned to duty in 1806. She sailed in the Bay of Biscay and landed Lieutenant General Arthur Wellesley (later the Duke of Wellington) at La Coruña, Spain, at the start of the Peninsular Campaign in 1808. On February 22, 1809, she took part in an action with three French frigates off Sable d'Olonne and suffered thirty dead and wounded. After repairs, her squadron sailed into El Ferrol and captured five Spanish ships, which the British rigged and sailed as prizes to Cadiz. *Defiance* was used as a prison ship at Chatham from 1813 to 1816, when she was broken up.

Kennedy, "Bligh and the *Defiance* Mutiny." Longridge, *Anatomy of Nelson's Ships.* Mackenzie, *Trafalgar Roll.*

the first true capital ship under any flag without a single sail, and . . . the first complete application to a sea-going battleship of the principle of mounting the main armament on top of the hull instead of inside it.

Her four 12-inch guns — the largest muzzle-loaders ever — were mounted in two turrets each with an arc of fire of 280 degrees. In 1891, these were replaced by 10-inch breech-loaders with twice the range and three times the rate of fire. In the same year, she also received triple-expansion engines, the increased efficiency of which enabled her to cross the Atlantic both ways without refueling.

Devastation's first two commissions were divided between home waters and the Mediterranean. After a two-year refit, she spent four years in reserve before being assigned to the First Reserve Fleet in Scotland. She was later made a port guardship at Portsmouth and then at Gibraltar. Re-

HMS Devastation

Breastwork turret ship (2f/1m). *L/B/D:* 307′ × 62.3′ x 26.5′ (93.6m × 19m × 8.1m). *Tons:* 9,188 disp. *Hull:* steel. *Comp.:* 400. *Arm.:* 4 × 12″ (2 × 2). *Armor:* 12″ belt, 3″ deck. *Mach.:* Penn trunk engines, 800 nhp, 2 screws; 13 kts. *Built:* Portsmouth Dockyard, Eng.; 1871.

By the 1870s, steam power was well established among the world's leading naval powers, and a number of smaller coast defense vessels that relied solely on mechanical propulsion had been built. There had also been an increasing tendency toward turreted guns in place of the broadside arrangement typical of sailing ships of the line. However, so long as seagoing ships relied on masts for even auxiliary power, a turret's arc of fire was necessarily limited. All this changed with the commissioning of HMS *Devastation,*

▶ Warship design passed through many phases during the transition from sail to steam. The first oceangoing capital ship built without auxiliary sails was the **HMS Devastation**, commissioned in 1873 and seen here off Southend during Queen Victoria's Diamond Jubilee, June 28, 1897. *Courtesy National Maritime Museum, Greenwich.*

tired again in 1902, the first mastless capital ship was broken up in 1908.

Ballard, *Black Battlefleet.* Gardiner & Lambert, eds., *Steam, Steel and Shellfire.*

D. Fernando II e Glória

Frigate (3m). *L/B/D:* 160′ × 42′ × 20′ (48.8m × 12.8m × 6.1m). *Tons:* 1,849 disp. *Hull:* wood. *Comp.:* 145–379; 270 pass. *Arm.:* 20 × 32pdr, 22 × 18pdr, 2 × 12pdr. *Built:* Damão Shipyard, Portuguese India; 1843.

D. Fernando II e Glória was the last sailing frigate to serve in the Portuguese navy and the last to serve on the run between Portugal and India. Built at the Portuguese shipyard at Damão, a seaport on the Gulf of Cambay about 100 miles north of Mumbai (Bombay), her hull was constructed of teak from the forests of Nagar-Aveli, just east of Damão, which was one of the three constituent parts of Portuguese-administered territory in India, together with Goa and Diu. (The Portuguese had long built ships in India and Brazil, where the wood was better than that available in Portugal itself.) Following her launch, *D. Fernando* was towed to Goa, about 350 miles to the south, for fitting out as a full-rigged ship.

The name *D. Fernando II e Glória* was a tribute both to Dom Fernando Saxe-Coburg-Gotha, the consort of Queen Maria II of Portugal, and to Our Lady of Glory, a figure of special devotion among the inhabitants of Goa. She sailed for twenty years on the old Carreira da India — the India run dating from 1500 — carrying military personnel, colonial administrators, and their families between Portugal and her colonial outposts in India, Angola, and Mozambique. She was noted especially for her relatively spacious accommodations, a critical factor on voyages that could take six months or more without an intermediate port of call.

In 1865, the *D. Fernando* became an artillery schoolship, replacing the old *Vasco da Gama* in that role. On her last training voyage, in 1878, she rescued the crew of the American bark *Lawrence Boston,* which had caught fire off the Azores. Fol-

lowing this voyage, the frigate was permanently moored at Lisbon as the Naval Artillery School and underwent significant modifications in 1889. In 1938, she housed the Fragata D. Fernando Welfare Institution, which provided general education and sail training opportunities for underprivileged youth.

In 1963, *D. Fernando II e Glória* was partially destroyed by fire and all but abandoned. She lay in the mud of the Mar da Palha in the River Tagus until 1990, when the Portuguese navy and the National Commission for the Commemoration of the Portuguese Discoveries began a collaborative effort to restore the ship to her appearance as she was in the 1850s. The restoration was carried out at Ria Marine in Aveiro and received widespread public and private support. Refloated in 1992, her restoration was completed six years later, when she was opened as a floating museum under the auspices of the Museu da Marinha in Lisbon.

Brouwer, *International Register of Historic Ships.* Hollins, "Fragata from the Fire." Rubino, *"Dom Fernando II."*

USS Dolphin

Dispatch vessel (1f/3m). *L/B/D:* 256.5′ × 32′ × 14.2′ (78.2m × 9.8m × 4.3m). *Tons:* 1,486 disp. *Hull:* steel. *Comp.:* 152. *Arm.:* 1 × 6″, 2 × 6 pdr, 4 × 47mm. *Mach.:* compound engine, 2,255 ihp, 1 screw; 16 kts. *Built:* John Roach & Sons, Chester, Pa.; 1885.

In 1883, the U.S. Navy convinced Congress that it was time for the nation to develop expertise in the construction of steel warships. To this end, it secured authorization for the construction of three armored cruisers, USS *Atlanta, Boston,* and *Chicago,* and the gunboat *Dolphin,* collectively known as the ABCD ships. Although designed in part to demonstrate U.S. technological capabilities, *Dolphin* was built with a very dominant bark rig. Over the years, this was changed to a three-masted, and ultimately a two-masted schooner. The first "New Navy" ship commissioned, *Dolphin* was sent out to the Pacific Station for two years before returning via ports in Asia, the Indian Ocean, and Europe in 1888. She then joined the ABC ships in the "Squadron of Evolution" to develop tactics and maneuvers. In 1895, *Dolphin* was assigned to the Special Service Squadron. After carrying President William McKinley's entourage to the dedication of Grant's Tomb in 1897, she was laid up at New York. Recommissioned in 1898, she sailed on blockade duty during the Spanish-American War, and from 1899 until 1917, *Dolphin* worked as a special dispatch ship for the navy. *Dolphin* was en route to take possession of the Danish Virgin Islands, which Denmark had sold to the United States, when America entered World War I. *Dolphin* remained in the Caribbean as part of the Special Service Squadron until 1922, when she was sold.

Millett, "State Department's Navy." U.S. Navy, *DANFS*.

Duke

Frigate (3m). *L/B:* ca. 80′ keel × 26′ (24m × 8m). *Tons:* 320 tons. *Hull:* wood. *Comp.:* 183. *Arm.:* 30 guns. *Built:* England(?); <1708.

Duke was one of two Bristol-owned privateers — the other was *Duchess* — fitted out for an expedition against Spanish shipping in the Pacific Ocean, which at the time was widely regarded as "a Spanish lake." The ships sailed on August 2, 1708; the officers included William Dampier, veteran of two circumnavigations, including one in *Roebuck* (1699–1700), and Woodes Rogers. After stopping at Cork and the Canary and Cape Verde Islands, the ships came to the island of Grande, off Brazil. About January 15, 1709, they rounded Cape Horn, in the process sailing to 61°53′S, "which for aught we know is the furthest that any one has yet got to the southward." The ships made next for the island of Juan Fernández, where on February 1 the castaway Alexander Selkirk greeted them. Four years before, he had sailed as master of the privateer *Cinque Ports* in an expedition commanded by Dampier, who sailed in the *St. George*. Preferring the uncertainty of exile to work with the *Cinque*

Ports' Captain Thomas Stradling, Selkirk was put ashore and left to fend for himself. On Dampier's recommendation, Rogers appointed Selkirk mate in the *Duke*, which sailed next to the coast of Peru. Here Dampier and company captured several ships, including *Havre de Grace*, which they armed and renamed *Marquis.*

On April 22, the English seized the city of Guayaquil, Ecuador, and eight ships, which they ransomed for the payment of 30,000 pieces of eight. They cruised between the coast of Peru and the Galápagos Islands until mid-September, when they sailed for the Tres Marias Islands, 100 miles south of Mazatlán, Mexico. There they awaited the Manila galleon — Spain's annual shipment of gold and silver from the Americas to the Philippines — until December 21, when they captured one of a pair, *Nuestra Señora de la Encarnación Disenganio*, which they renamed *Batchelor.* Six days later, they engaged the 450-ton *Bigonia* but could not capture her. From here, the ships turned west across the Pacific. Their run from Port Segura to Guam lasted from January 11 to March 11, 1710; their best day's run was 161 miles, their worst only 41. They were well received by the Spanish governor, and after provisioning, they continued on their long voyage home, with stops at the Portuguese-held Butung Island (May 26), the Dutch entrepôts at Batavia (June 20), and the Cape of Good Hope (December 29). Sailing with a Dutch convoy, Rogers's four ships returned to Erith on October 14, 1711.

The voyage of the *Duke* and *Duchess* was a financial success — it grossed about £800,000 for a £14,000 investment — and spurred further incursions into the Pacific. Rogers's *Cruising Voyage round the World* also publicized the remarkable story of Selkirk's stay on Juan Fernández and became the inspiration for Daniel Defoe's novel *Robinson Crusoe* and William Cowper's "Lines on Solitude," which begins, "I am monarch of all I survey."

Rogers, *A Cruising Voyage round the World.*

E

HMS Elephant

Arrogant-class 3rd rate 74 (3m). *L/B/D:* 168′ × 46.8′ × 19.8′ (51.2m × 14.3m × 6m). *Tons:* 1,604 bm. *Hull:* wood. *Comp.:* 550. *Arm.:* 28 × 32pdr, 28 × 18pdr, 18 × 9pdr. *Des.:* Sir Thomas Slade. *Built:* Parsons, Bursledon, Eng.; 1786.

The second Royal Navy ship of the name, HMS *Elephant* saw little service until 1800, when she was assigned to the Channel Fleet for operations off Brest. In December of that year, Russia, Denmark, Sweden, and Prussia embargoed British shipping in their ports and denied the Royal Navy the right to search neutral vessels suspected of trading in contraband with France, with whom Britain had been at war since 1793. Diplomatic overtures to Denmark were unsuccessful, and in March 1801, Admiral Sir Hyde Parker and Vice Admiral Horatio Nelson were dispatched to the Baltic with a fleet of thirty-nine ships. To prepare for operations in the shallow waters around Copenhagen, Nelson shifted his flag from the first-rate HMS ST. GEORGE to *Elephant.* The fleet came under fire from the Danish fort at Helsingör as it passed through the Øresund, but the Swedish guns at Helsingborg, on the opposite side of the narrows, were quiet.

Having assessed the strength of the shore batteries and naval units around the Danish capital, Nelson persuaded Parker to let him attack Copenhagen with a force of twelve 3rd- and 4th-rate ships, seven frigates, seven bombs, and two fire ships. On April 1, this force sailed south of the city through the Hollaenderdyb, and then turned north into the narrow confines of the Kongedyb between Copenhagen and the shoals of the Middel Grund. Copenhagen was defended by twenty-five vessels of between 6 and 74 guns and a dozen 4-gun

xebecs, anchored in a line between the channel and the city. There were also seven powerful shore batteries.

Nelson split his force into three divisions: Captain Riou, in HMS *Amazon,* with four other frigates and two fire ships was to take on the Trekroner forts at the north end of the Kongedyb; six gun brigs were to take on the batteries to the south; and seven bomb vessels were to anchor on the fringe of the Middel Grund and fire over the third-rate 74s lying in mid-channel: DEFIANCE, *Monarch, Ganges, Elephant, Glatton* (54 guns), *Ardent* (64), and *Edgar.*

Nelson's ships began moving into position at 0930, although the 74s *Bellona, Russell,* and AGAMEMNON ran aground in the narrow channel before they could get in position. The battle began at 1005, and all ships were engaged by 1130. An hour and a half later, Admiral Parker, who was anchored with eight ships four miles to the northeast, signaled Nelson to break off the engagement. Told of the signal, Nelson reportedly erupted:

> "Leave off action? Now damn me if I do! You know, Foley," turning to the Captain, "I have only one eye: I have a right to be blind sometimes"; and then, putting the glass to his blind eye, in that mood of mind which sports with bitterness, he exclaimed, "I really do not see the signal." Presently he exclaimed, "Damn the signal! Keep mine for closer battle flying! That's the way I answer such signals. Nail mine to the mast."

In point of fact, Parker probably intended the signal to be read as discretionary, and under withering fire from the forts, Riou ordered his frigates to withdraw just before he was killed by a cannon shot. Firing subsided by 1400, and after an exchange of messages between Nelson and the Danish Crown Prince, a truce was concluded that afternoon. An estimated 350 British officers and seamen were killed at Copenhagen, including two captains, and about 1,700 Danes, including 270 from the *Dannebrog*, a dismasted 62-gun ship that blew up opposite the *Elephant* at about 1530.

Following the battle, Nelson returned to the *St. George*, but *Elephant* remained in his squadron when five weeks later he sailed for Reval to show the flag in Russian waters. On May 17, the Russians and Swedes joined the Danes in lifting their embargo on British ships, and Nelson returned to England in June.

From 1803 to 1806, *Elephant* operated variously off Jamaica and in home waters, and in 1807, she was decommissioned at Portsmouth. She returned to service in 1811, and on December 28, 1812, she captured the American privateer schooner *Swordfish* after a 100-mile chase. In 1818, *Elephant* was cut down as a frigate with an armament of twenty-eight 18-pdrs., twenty-eight 42-pdrs., and two 12-pdrs.; her crew was cut by 100 men. She was broken up in 1830.

Clowes, *Royal Navy*. Phillips, *Royal Navy*.

Enchantress

(ex-*Putnam*) Brig. *Hull:* wood. *Comp.:* 14. *Built:* Baltimore; <1861.

On June 28, 1861, the Confederate privateer brig *Jefferson Davis* (ex-*Putnam*) sailed from Charleston, South Carolina, to cruise against Northern merchantmen. One of her prizes was the brig *Enchantress*, bound from Boston to Santiago de Cuba with general cargo. The ship was seized in 38°52′N, 69°15′W (about 300 miles east of Delaware), and a prize crew was put aboard for the return to Charleston. The only member of the original crew to remain was the black cook, Jacob Garrick. On July 22, the ship was being followed by USS *Albatross* off Hatteras Inlet when Garrick leaped into the sea and began shouting that the vessel was a Confederate prize. The ship's master, William Smith, had no choice but to surrender, and he and

the crew of thirteen were brought to Philadelphia.

The Lincoln administration refused to recognize either the Confederate government or, by extension, letters of marque signed by President Jefferson Davis for Confederate privateers, and Smith and his men were tried for piracy, a capital offense. In anticipation of such a move, the Confederate Congress granted Davis sweeping powers to retaliate, and when Smith and four of his crew were sentenced to die, he ordered a high-ranking Union officer transferred from a prisoner-of-war camp to a common prison, "to be treated in all respects as if [a convicted felon], and to be held for execution in the same manner as may be adopted by the enemy for the execution of the prisoner of war Smith." In February 1862, Lincoln reluctantly remanded Smith and his confederates to a prisoner-of-war camp. Later exchanged for Union POWs, they returned to great acclaim in Charleston.

Robinson, *Confederate Privateers*.

USS Enterprise

Schooner (2m). *L/B/D:* 84.6′ lod × 22.5′ × 10′ dph (25.8m × 6.9m × 3m). *Tons:* 135 bm. *Hull:* wood. *Comp.:* 70. *Arm.:* 12 × 6pdr. *Built:* Henry Spencer, Eastern Shore, Md.; 1799.

The third ship of the name, USS *Enterprise* was built during the Quasi-War with France. On her first cruise, she sailed to the Caribbean under Lieutenant John Shaw, and by the end of the war, she had captured eight French privateers and freed eleven U.S. merchantmen. In the summer of 1801, *Enterprise* joined the "Squadron of Observation" sent to the Mediterranean to protect American shipping from the Barbary corsairs of North Africa. Although she alternated between assignments as a dispatch vessel, convoy escort, and blockade ship, she fought a number of Tripolitan vessels in single ship engagements and participated in the bombardment of Tripolitan forts. Most notable, on December 23, 1803, *Enterprise* and CONSTITUTION captured the Tripolitan ketch *Mastico*, which was taken into the squadron as USS INTREPID. Rearmed with 12-pdr. guns at Venice in 1804, *Enterprise* remained in the Mediterranean until the winter of 1807.

Laid up from 1809 to 1811, after service on the East Coast, *Enterprise* was refitted as a brig and armed with fourteen 18-pdr. carronades and two 9-pdr. longs, putting to sea just before the start of the War of 1812. On September 5, 1813, off Portland, Maine, she fought HM Brig *Boxer* (12 guns), which she took in a forty-five-minute action that resulted in the death of both commanders, Lieutenant William Burrows and *Boxer*'s Captain Samuel Blyth. *Enterprise* next sailed to the Caribbean in company with USS *Rattlesnake*, but the two were forced to separate in the face of a more heavily armed opponent, and *Enterprise* returned to Wilmington, North Carolina, having jettisoned most of her guns to avoid capture.

Enterprise spent the remainder of the war as a guardship at Charleston. After four months with the newly formed Mediterranean Squadron in 1815, she sailed on the West Indies Station operating against smugglers and slavers until July 9, 1823, when she stranded and broke up on Little Curaçao Island.

Culver, *Forty Famous Ships.* U.S. Navy, *DANFS.*

Erzherzog Ferdinand Max

Erzherzog Ferdinand Max–class broadside ironclad (1f/3m). *L/B/D:* 274.8' × 52.3' × 23.4' (83.7m × 16m × 7.1m). *Tons:* 5,130 disp. *Hull:* steel. *Comp.:* 511. *Arm.:* 16 × 48pdr, 4 × 8pdr, 2 × 3pdr. *Armor:* 123mm belt. *Mach.:* horizontal compound engine, 1 screw, 2,925 ihp; 12.5 kts. *Des.:* Joseph von Romako. *Built:* Stabilimento Tecnico Triestino, Trieste; 1865.

Named for Archduke Ferdinand Max, the first commander-in-chief of the Austro-Hungarian navy (and later Emperor Maximilian of Mexico), *Erzherzog Ferdinand Max* was one of two ironclad ships modeled on France's GLOIRE built for the Austro-Hungarian navy; the other was *Habsburg*. Launched too late for the last fleet engagement between wooden ships, the Battle of Helgoland between Austrian and Danish forces in 1865, she was Vice Admiral Baron Wilhelm von Tegetthoff's flagship the following year at the Battle of Lissa, the first fleet engagement between ironclads.

In 1866, Otto von Bismarck sought to reconfigure the North German League as a German confederation under Prussian leadership and minus Austria-Hungary. The Seven Weeks' War that ensued pitted the Dual Monarchy against Prussia and a newly unified Italy. An Italian victory at sea appeared to be a foregone conclusion, but Tegetthoff was not to be put off. Although he possessed only seven ironclads to twelve Italian, he drilled his crews hard, and when the hesitant Admiral Count Carlo Bellion di Persano kept his fleet in port, Tegetthoff stood off Ancona all but taunting him to come out. The Austrians returned to Pola, and on July 8, Persano finally put to sea. A week later, he was ordered to invade the island of Lissa, off the Dalmatian coast. Landings began on the eighteenth, but Persano failed to capitalize on his initial success, and the undermanned Austrian garrison at San Giorgio held fast.

Tegetthoff sailed from Pola on July 19, and by 0800 the next morning, the Austro-Hungarian fleet was approaching Lissa in a triple chevron formation, *Erzherzog Ferdinand Max* in the van. Persano's squadron was moored in line abreast parallel to the shore, while Albini's transports were moored in two lines abreast, stern to the island. The Italians opened fire at 1045, killing the captain of the ironclad *Drache* in the opening minutes of the battle.

Ferdinand Max and *Habsburg* had been designed to mount two 8-inch Krupp guns, but their delivery was delayed owing to the political situation, so Tegetthoff had mounted old 48-pdr. smooth-bore guns to oppose RE D'ITALIA's 8-inch guns. To compensate for this inferiority, Tegetthoff told his officers, "When we get into the battle, ram anything in gray." (His own ships were painted black.) As the second echelon of Austrian ships approached the Italian line, the 90-gun ship of the line *Kaiser* was brought under fire by the *Affondatore,* but Persano ordered his ship to turn away. (Persano had transferred from *Re d'Italia* to the turret ship *Affondatore,* but virtually no one in either fleet knew.) *Kaiser* next came under fire from *Re di Portogallo,* which she rammed, losing her own foremast and funnel in the process. Captain Anton von Petz turned for the security of San Giorgio Harbor, and *Affondatore* allowed the *Kaiser* to escape.

At about 1120, *Re d'Italia* was crossing ahead of *Ferdinand Max.* The Italian flagship's steering gear was damaged, and in order to avoid ramming an Austrian ship, Captain Faà di Bruno put his engines in reverse. The ship came to a complete standstill, and *Ferdinand Max* drove into her port side. Captain Max von Sterneck pulled away from his adversary, and two minutes later, *Re d'Italia* sank with the loss of 383 lives. This action effectively brought the battle to a close, although the burning armored gunboat *Palestro* exploded and sank at 1430. In addition to the two ships, the Italians lost a total of 636 officers and men. Austrian losses amounted to 38 men, and all Tegetthoff's ships returned to Pola.

Ferdinand Max's bow was repaired at the British dockyard in Malta, and she finally received her 8-inch guns in 1869. She remained in service until 1886, after thirty years as a tender to a gunnery training ship. She was scrapped in 1916. Though it had proved effective, ramming was nothing more than a last resort from a resourceful and determined leader. Nonetheless, naval strategists drew the wrong conclusions from the Battle of Lissa, and even as gun ranges and ship speeds increased, ramming — a standard method of warfare in antiquity — enjoyed a brief revival in the late nineteenth century.

Chesneau & Kolesink, *Conway's All the World's Fighting Ships 1860–1905.* Sokol, *Imperial and Royal Austro-Hungarian Navy.* Sondhaus, *Habsburg Empire and the Sea.*

USS Essex

Frigate (3m). *L/B/D:* 140′ bp × 31′ × 12.3′ dph (42.7m × 9.4m × 3.7m). *Tons:* 850 bm. *Hull:* wood. *Comp.:* 319. *Arm.:* 40 × 32pdr, 6 × 18pdr. *Des.:* William Hackett. *Built:* Enos Briggs, Salem, Mass.; 1799.

Built by the citizens of Essex County, Massachusetts, who presented her to the U.S. government, USS *Essex* was commissioned under command of Captain Edward Preble. On her first voyage in 1800, during the Quasi-War with France, *Essex* helped convoy a fleet of Dutch East Indiamen through the Indian Ocean. In 1801, she was one of several ships sent to the Mediterranean to contain the Barbary corsairs harassing American shipping. She sailed first under Captain William Bainbridge and then under Captain James Barron. Following the war, she was laid up from 1806 to 1809.

At the beginning of the War of 1812, under command of Captain David Porter, *Essex* captured ten prizes, including HMS *Alert* (18 guns), between July and September. On October 28, 1812, *Essex* left the Delaware River to rendezvous with USS CONSTITUTION and HORNET for a cruise into the South Pacific. After waiting in vain on the coast of Brazil, in January 1813, Porter took the initiative and continued on his own. By way of encouragement, he told his crew that

> the unprotected British commerce, on the coast of Chili[*sic*], Peru, and Mexico, will give you an abundant supply of wealth; and the girls of the Sandwich Islands, shall reward you for your sufferings during the passage round Cape Horn.

The passage was bleak, but the rewards matched Porter's promise. During the course of 1813, *Essex* virtually destroyed Britain's South Pacific whale fishery and took fifteen prizes, including the whaleship *Atlantic,* which the Americans armed with ten 6-pdr. long guns and ten 18-pdr. carronades and renamed *Essex Junior.* In October, the two ships sailed to Nuka Hiva in the Marquesas Islands. On February 3, 1814, they returned to Valparaiso, where the ships were blockaded by Captain James Hillyard's HMS *Phoebe* (36) and *Cherub* (18), which had been dispatched to the Pacific for the purpose. On March 28, Porter attempted to break out of Valparaiso, but *Essex* lost her main topmast in a gale. Disregarding Chilean neutrality, Hillyard attacked and, taking advantage of his guns' superior range, slowly but surely re-

▲ The frigate **USS Essex** (left) devastated British merchant interests in the Pacific during the War of 1812. But she stood no chance against the long-range guns of **HMS Phoebe** and **Cherub** when brought to battle off Valparaiso in March 1814, as seen in this painting by Captain William Bainbridge Hoff. *Courtesy U.S. Naval Historical Center, Washington, D.C.*

duced *Essex,* whose primary armament consisted only of short-range carronades. Three hours later, Porter was forced to strike; one of the last flags flying was one proclaiming "Free trade and sailors' rights" — the slogan that had impelled the United States to war. *Essex* lost fifty-eight killed, thirty-one drowned, and seventy wounded; British losses were five dead and ten wounded. *Essex* was taken into the Royal Navy as a 42-gun frigate. In 1823, she was made a convict ship, and she was sold in 1837. *Essex Junior* sailed to New York as a cartel ship, where she was sold.

Porter, *Journal of a Cruise.* U.S. Navy, *DANFS.*

USS Experiment

Schooner (2m). *L/B/D:* 88.5′ × 23.5′ × 6.1′ dph (27m × 7.2m × 1.9m). *Tons:* 176 burthen. *Hull:* wood. *Arm.:* 2 × 12pdr. *Des.:* William Annesley. *Built:* Washington Navy Yard, Washington, D.C.; 1832.

As traditional framing was expensive, heavy, and took up space, naval architect William Annesley devised a way of planking a ship that would do away with frames and published his research in *A New System of Naval Architecture* in 1822. Nine years later, he secured a contract to build a schooner — his fourth vessel — for the U.S. Navy. The hull consisted of five layers of planks, the first, third, and fifth running longitudinally, and the second and fourth running laterally; the deck was laid in a similar fashion. Another departure from normal practice was the elliptical hull shape, which Annesley based on his observation of ducks. Although she sailed well downwind, *Experiment* worked badly to windward. As Linda Maloney observes, "In his admiration for the duck [Annesley] failed to note that speed and seaworthiness are not its foremost attributes." Poorly fastened, she leaked, which heightened her crew's reluctance to sail in a ship without frames. Although her commander, Lieutenant William Mervine, thought her fit for any service, his conservative superiors felt otherwise, and she was confined to coastal survey work. Nevertheless, *Experiment*'s greatest failing was the sheer novelty of her frameless construction. In later years, lamination would be used widely in iron, steel, and wood and fiberglass hulls.

Experiment spent two years in the Caribbean, and three years stationed at New York, where she was employed as a surveying ship. She served as a receiving ship at Philadelphia from 1839 to 1848, when she was sold.

Maloney, "A Naval Experiment." U.S. Navy, *DANFS*.

Fenian Ram

Submarine. *L/B/D:* 31′ × 6′ × 7.3′ (9.4m × 1.8m × 2.2m). *Tons:* 9 disp. *Hull:* iron. *Comp.:* 3. *Arm.:* pneumatic bow gun. *Mach.:* gasoline engine, 17 hp, 1 screw; 9 kts. *Des.:* John P. Holland. *Built:* Delamater-Robinson, Delamater Iron Works, New York; 1881.

The Irish-born schoolteacher and inventor John P. Holland was a longtime believer in the possibilities of submarine technology and wanted only money to put his ideas into practice. His first opportunity came in 1876, when he met John J. Breslin upon the latter's return to New York from rescuing six Irish convicts from Australia in the bark *Catalpa*. The Clan na Gael (United Irish Brotherhood) agreed to fund Holland's idea, and on May 22, 1878, Holland launched a 14.5 feet long by 3 feet wide prototype on the Passaic River in Paterson, New Jersey. After remaining submerged for up to an hour and otherwise demonstrating the soundness of her builder's concept, she was scuttled in the Passaic. (*Holland No. 1* was later raised and exhibited at Paterson.)

Work on his next project began shortly thereafter, and *Fenian Ram*, as it was dubbed by the *New York Sun*, was launched in 1881. The name indicated not only its financial backers, but the use to which it was expected to be put; Holland's first project had been similarly referred to as a "wrecking boat." Holland modeled the hull for this and his subsequent designs, including USS HOLLAND, on the form of a porpoise, which gave the vessel a submerged speed almost equal to that of its surface speed. (Interestingly, this shape was abandoned until the advent of nuclear submarines in the 1950s. One of the great deficiencies of the submarines of World Wars I and II was their poor speed underwater.) *Fenian Ram* was taken to a depth of sixty feet in and around New York Harbor and could remain submerged for as long as two and a half hours. Her armament, a single pneumatic gun tube set at an angle, successfully fired an early form of torpedo. Although these were supplied through the offices of the U.S. Navy's forward-looking John Ericsson, who had designed USS MONITOR, Holland had reason to be pessimistic about others in the profession. Reflecting on the skepticism that his *Fenian Ram* elicited from the builders at Delamater Iron Works, he later observed:

> Many objections were raised against her, especially by men who should have known better, but the trouble with them was almost the same as I encountered later among the staff officers of the navy, viz: they were, almost without exception, of English, Welsh, or Scotch descent, experienced in all kinds of shipbuilding.

Destined never to see service against British warships, as had been intended, *Fenian Ram*'s active career was short-lived. Fearing that she might be seized in the course of a court proceeding over money, Breslin arranged for the submersible to be taken to New Haven. There the vessel was laid up until 1916, when she was returned to New York for use as an exhibit to raise funds for victims of the failed Easter Rebellion in Ireland. Later moved to the New York State Maritime Academy, in 1927 she was purchased by Edward A. Browne, who put her on exhibit in Paterson.

Morris, *John P. Holland.*

CSS Florida

(ex-*Oreto*) Screw steamer (3m schooner). *L/B/D:* 191′ × 27.4′ × 13′ (58.2m × 8.4m × 4m). *Tons:* 700 burthen. *Hull:* iron. *Comp.:* 52. *Arm.:* 2 × 7″, 6 × 6″, 1 × 12pdr howitzer. *Mach.:* horizontal direct-acting steam engines; 9.5 kts. *Built:* William C. Miller & Sons, Liverpool; 1862.

Known as the "Prince of Privateers," CSS *Florida* was the second most successful Confederate raider after ALABAMA. Laid down in June 1861, the Confederacy's first foreign-built commerce raider departed Liverpool on March 22, 1862, and was commissioned at Green Cay, Bahamas, Lieutenant John Newland Maffitt commanding. From there, she sailed to Cuba and through the Federal blockade into Mobile, where she arrived on September 4. She remained in port until January 16, 1863, when she broke through the blockade to begin a lucrative seven-month cruise during which she captured twenty-two vessels, including the clippers *Red Gauntlet* and *Southern Cross,* and facilitated the capture of another twenty-three, among them the revenue cutter CALEB CUSHING. After a five-month refit in Brest, during which command was transferred to Lieutenant Charles M. Morris, she captured eleven ships before putting into Bahia, Brazil, on October 4, 1864, a few days after USS WACHUSETT. Morris pledged to observe Brazilian neutrality and was granted four days in which to make necessary repairs. The Brazilians, anxious to prevent a confrontation between *Wachusett* and *Florida,* moored some of their own ships of the line between the two antagonists. But on October 7, *Wachusett* rammed the Confederate raider with the intention of sinking her. Wilson had granted about half his crew leave, and after assessing the situation, Lieutenant T. K. Porter surrendered the ship and the remaining crew, who were put in irons. The ship was towed out of Bahia and back to Newport News, where she sank in a collision with the transport *Alliance.*

Owsley, CSS *"Florida."*

Fulton Steam Frigate

Steam frigate. *L/B/D:* 156′ × 56′ × 11′ (47.5m × 17.1m × 3.4m). *Tons:* 2,475 disp. *Comp.:* 200. *Arm.:* 24 × 32pdr. *Mach.:* single-cylinder inclined engine, 120 hp, center wheel; 6 kts. *Built:* Adam & Noah Brown, New York; 1815.

Known also as *Demologos* and *Fulton the First,* the *Fulton Steam Frigate* was the first steam-powered warship built for the U.S. Navy, and the last vessel designed by Robert Fulton. On Christmas Eve 1813, Fulton met with a small but eminent gathering of military men and merchants to present his idea for a floating battery to break the British blockade of New York during the War of 1812. Among the naval officers who endorsed the project were Oliver Hazard Perry and Stephen Decatur. Funds for the frigate were approved by Congress on March 9, 1814, and on October 28, a crowd of 20,000 New Yorkers watched as the ship was launched into the East River and towed across the Hudson to Fulton's New Jersey workshops.

The ship was of innovative design, consisting of two pontoon hulls that came together at the gun deck; a sixteen-foot paddlewheel was mounted between them. The pontoons were double-ended, the engine was reversible, and there were two sets of rudders so that the ship could be sailed either end first; even the auxiliary rig was double-ended, consisting of a lateen sail and jib at either end.

In February 1815, shortly after news that the Treaty of Ghent was signed, Fulton died of pneumonia. Work on the steam frigate continued, and trials in the summer demonstrated that the principle of a steam-powered warship was entirely sound. Despite suggestions that she be used as a training ship, the *Fulton Steam Frigate* was laid up, except for a brief tour of New York Harbor by President James Madison in 1818. With her engines and armament removed in 1821, she was used as a receiving ship at the Brooklyn Navy Yard until June 6, 1829, when the ship accidentally blew up, with the loss of twenty-nine crew killed and twenty-three wounded. It was not until 1836 that the U.S. Navy ordered a second steam warship, named *Fulton II.*

Chapelle, *Fulton's "Steam Battery."* Philip, *Robert Fulton.* Tyler, "Fulton's Steam Frigate."

G

Gaspée

Schooner (2m). *L/B:* 68′ × 20′ × 9′ (20.7m × 6.1m × 2.7m). *Tons:* 102 bm. *Hull:* wood. *Comp.:* 30. *Built:* Canada(?); 1763.

With the conclusion of the French and Indian War (or Seven Years' War), Britain annexed French Canada in 1763. To help patrol against smugglers working in the Gulf of St. Lawrence, the British government purchased six schooners and sloops in 1764, including *Gaspée.* The patrol soon expanded to cover the ports of New England. On June 9, 1772, *Gaspée* ran aground on Namquit Spit seven miles from Providence, Rhode Island, while pursuing the ship *Hannah,* which was suspected of avoiding payment of customs duties. News of the stranded vessel quickly reached Providence, and that night eight boatloads of colonists, led by the merchant brothers John and Nicholas Brown, moved to seize the vessel. As the colonists approached, they were ordered to identify themselves, but the only reply was, "God damn your blood, we have you now!" *Gaspée* was boarded, and the nineteen crew, including Lieutenant William Dudingston, who was wounded in the attack, were landed before the schooner was put to the torch. A commission of inquiry was convened in January 1773, but even the posting of a £500 reward failed to produce any reliable witnesses. Hence one of the American colonists' first acts of defiance to the British Crown went unpunished.

May, "*Gaspée* Affair." Miller, *Sea of Glory.* Staples, *Documentary History of the Destruction of the "Gaspée."*

General Armstrong

Topsail schooner (2m). *Tons:* 246 bm. *Hull:* wood. *Comp.:* 90. *Arm.:* 1 × 24pdr, 8 × 9pdr. *Built:* New York; <1814.

Named for Brigadier General John Armstrong, a distinguished soldier and statesman of the American Revolution, the topsail schooner *General Armstrong* sailed as a privateer under command of Captain Samuel C. Reid during the War of 1812. On September 26, 1814, she was lying in the roads at the neutral port of Fayal, Azores, when a British squadron comprising HMS *Plantagenet* (74 guns), *Rota* (36), and *Carnation* (10) came into the anchorage. That afternoon, British boats approached *General Armstrong* and, suspicious of their intentions, Reid warned the British off, opening fire only as a last resort. Reid repositioned *General Armstrong* in shallower waters and prepared for an attack. At midnight, 180 men in seven boats supported by *Carnation* began their assault on *General Armstrong.* The American defense was withering; two boats were sunk, two captured, and the British claimed thirty-four dead and eighty-six wounded for only two American dead and seven wounded. Reid cleared his ship for action the next morning, but after repulsing *Carnation,* he realized that his position was hopeless. Rather than sacrifice his men, he scuttled his ship. *General Armstrong's* splendid fight is especially notable given that her crew were merchant rather than naval seamen.

Roosevelt, *Naval War of 1812.*

CSS Georgia

(ex-*Japan*) Commerce raider (1f/2m). *L/B/D:* 212′ × 27′ × 13.8′ (64.6m × 8.2m × 4.2m). *Tons:* 648 grt. *Hull:* iron. *Comp.:* 75. *Arm.:* 2 × 100pdr, 2 × 24pdr, 1 × 32pdr. *Mach.:* steeple condensing engines, 900 ihp, 1 screw; 13 kts. *Built:* William Denny & Bros., Ltd., Dumbarton, Scotland; 1862.

Laid down as a merchant vessel, the unfinished *Japan* was purchased for the Confederate Navy in 1863. Sailing on April 1, 1863, under Commander W. L. Maury (cousin of the celebrated oceanographer Matthew Fontaine Maury, who arranged the ship's purchase), CSS *Georgia* was commissioned at sea eight days later. After a brief cruise that took her to Bahia and the Cape Colony, with nine prizes to her credit, she put into Cherbourg on October 28 and was decommissioned. She sailed for Liverpool and was sold there. Seized by USS *Niagara* off Portugal on August 15, she was condemned as a prize at Boston. Resuming service as a merchant ship in 1865, she was sold to Canadian interests in 1870, then lost off Tenants Harbor, Maine, on January 14, 1875.

Silverstone, *Warships of the Civil War Navies.* Stephens, "C.S.S. *Georgia.*"

La Girona

Galleass (3m). *Hull:* wood. *Comp.:* 349. *Built:* Naples(?); <1588.

The first Armada shipwreck in Ireland identified and excavated in modern times was that of *La Girona,* one of four galleasses that had sailed in Don Hugo de Moncada's Neapolitan Squadron. Galleasses were oared sailing ships — a cross between a galleon and an oared galley — ill suited to work in the North Atlantic, and *Girona* sustained heavy damage en route from Lisbon to La Coruña. She contributed little to the fighting in the English Channel, but in the retreat home from the North Sea she was forced into the port of Killibegs, in Donegal, Ireland, for repairs to her rudder. While there, she took aboard about 800 survivors from two other Spanish shipwrecks. The Genoese carrack *La Rata Santa Maria Encoronada* had gone ashore in Blacksod Bay, County Mayo, and her crew had embarked in the hulk *Duquesa Santa Ana,* which then went aground at Loughros Mor Bay, Donegal. When *Girona* was repaired, Don Alonso de Leiva ordered her to Catholic Scotland. The next day, October 26, 1588, her jury rudder broke, and she was driven violently ashore off Lacada Point, County Antrim, in 55°14′N, 06°30′W; fewer than ten of the estimated thirteen hundred people aboard survived the last of the twenty-four Armada shipwrecks in Ireland.

In 1967, Belgian archaeologist Robert Sténuit began excavation on the site, and in the following two seasons divers removed two brass cannon, shot for guns up to fifty pounds, lead ingots carried for the production of small-arms ammunition, navigational instruments, and an abundance of personal jewelry of gold and precious stones. One of the most famous and intriguing pieces is believed to represent a flying lizard from the Philippines, *draco volans,* the scientific discovery of which was not made until 200 years later. In addition, the site contained crosses, reliquaries, cameo portraits, gold and silver coins from Europe, Mexico, and Peru, as well as more everyday items such as pottery and ships' fittings.

Flanagan, *Shipwrecks of the Irish Coast.* Sténuit, *Treasures of the Armada.*

La Gloire

Broadside ironclad ship (3m). *L/B/D:* 255.6′ × 55.9′ x 27.10′ (77.9m × 17m × 8.5m). *Tons:* 5,630 disp. *Hull:* ironclad wood. *Comp.:* 550. *Arm.:* 36 × 6.4″. *Armor:* 4.7″ belt. *Mach.:* 2-cycle trunk, 2,500 ihp, 1 screw; 12.5 kts. *Des.:* Stanislas Dupuy de Lôme. *Built:* Arsenal de Toulon, Fr.; 1860.

One of the first tests of the effectiveness of ironclad ships in battle conditions occurred during the Crimean War. Impressed especially by their performance against Russian defenses at Fort Kinburn at the mouth of the Dnieper River, the French navy embarked on a program of building ironclad warships. In this, it was strongly supported by Napoleon III. Appointed naval constructor in 1857,

Stanislas Dupuy de Lôme completed plans for six ironclads in 1858. *La Gloire,* the first of these, was essentially a modification of his design for the world's first steam screw warship, *Napoleon* of 1850. Because of their relatively weak industrial base, the French were unable to build an iron-hulled ship. The compromise reached in *Gloire* was for a wooden hull clad with 4.7-inch iron plate and heavily reinforced with iron fastenings. With a single iron deck, *Gloire* was a single-screw, three-masted ship mounting thirty-six 6.4-inch muzzle-loading rifled guns. Designed to operate as a battle-ship in a traditional battle line, *Gloire* had two sister ships, *Invincible* and *Normandie.* These were joined by the iron-hulled *Couronne* and the ten ships of the *Flandre* class (one of which, *Heroïne,* had an iron hull), as well as the two-decker iron-clads *Magenta* and *Solferino,* mounting 50 guns on two decks.

Laid down in May 1858 and commissioned in July 1860, *Gloire* served in the French fleet for nine years before undergoing a thorough overhaul and refit, emerging with six 9.6-inch and two 7.8-inch muzzle-loading rifled guns. She was struck from the navy list in 1879 and broken up four years later. Far from helping the French achieve naval superiority over the British, *Gloire* prompted the conservative British to undertake the development of their own iron-hulled ships. No sooner was *Gloire* laid down than the Admiralty promptly ordered two ironclad and four iron ships of their own. The immediate result was HMS WARRIOR, an all-iron-hull warship that entirely dwarfed *Gloire* and ushered in a new generation of fighting ship.

Baxter, *Introduction of the Ironclad Warship.* Gardiner & Lambert, eds., *Steam, Steel and Shellfire.* Silverstone, *Directory of the World's Capital Ships.*

Gokstad ship

Karvi (1m). *L/B/D:* 76.4' × 17' × 7.2' (23.3m × 5.2m × 2.2m dph). *Tons:* 20.2 disp. *Hull:* oak. *Comp.:* 64–70. *Built:* Norway; ca. 890–95.

Dating from the late ninth century, shortly after the beginning of the Vikings' long-distance raid-

ing, the Gokstad ship is a large clinker-built boat thought to be of a type known as a karvi, similar in construction to the earlier OSEBERG SHIP. Intended for open ocean sailing, the karvi was smaller than the longboat that represented the apogee of Viking ship construction. The Gokstad ship had sixteen strakes (four more than in the Oseberg ship) built up from either side of the single-piece oak keel, and the thirty-two oar holes were fitted with shutters that could be closed to keep out water when the single square sail was set. The shield rack could mount two shields between each oar hole. Unlike the more lavishly carved Oseberg ship, which dates from about three-quarters of a century before, the only ornamentation is a carved animal head on the tiller. After the excavation of the burial mound in which the ship was discovered in 1880, the remains of the vessel were transferred to Oslo. The reconstructed ship has been housed in the Viking Ship Hall at Bygdøy, Oslo, alongside the remains of the Oseberg and Tune ships. In addition to the ship itself, the burial mound near Sandefjord also yielded three smaller boats, the smallest of which was 6.6 meters long. In addition, the site yielded the remains of more than two dozen animals, including twelve horses and six dogs, a bed, and cooking implements. Once thought to have been the grave of Olav Gjerstad, stepson of Queen Åsa, this attribution now seems to be erroneous.

In 1893, a nearly exact replica of the Gokstad ship, named *Viking,* was built at Sandefjord and sailed from Bergen to New York in six weeks with a crew of twelve under Magnus Andersen. *Viking* continued on to the Chicago World's Fair via the Erie Canal and Great Lakes; it has been preserved and is currently in storage in Chicago awaiting new exhibition facilities.

Bonde & Christensen, "Dendrochronological Dating of the Viking Age Ship Burials." Nikolaysen, *Viking Ship Discovered at Gokstad in Norway.* Sjøvold, *Oseberg Find.*

Golden Hind

(ex-*Pelican*) Galleon (3m). *L/B/D:* ca. 70′ bp x 19′ × 9′ (21.3m × 5.8m × 2.7m). *Tons:* ca. 150 burthen. *Hull:* wood. *Comp.:* 80–85. *Arm.:* 18 guns. *Built:* Plymouth, Eng.; 1576.

Destined to become one of the greatest seamen of all time, Francis Drake made two voyages to the Spanish Main between 1566 and 1568 in company with his kinsman John Hawkins. Although lured by the profitable slave trade and South American silver, the Protestant Drake was further motivated by a fervent anti-Catholicism. His hatred increased after the loss of JESUS OF LÜBECK to Spanish duplicity at San Juan de Ulúa. In 1576, Queen Elizabeth approved, albeit secretly, Drake's captaincy of a mission with a threefold aim: to pass through the Strait of Magellan, reconnoiter the Pacific coast of South America, and, if possible, return via the Northwest Passage; to establish relations with people not yet subject to European princes; and to plunder Spanish shipping.

Drake's command consisted of about 180 men in five ships. The flagship, *Pelican,* carried courses, topsails, and topgallants on her main and foremasts, and a lateen mizzen. The other ships were *Elizabeth* (80 tons, 16 guns) under John Winter; *Marigold* (30 tons, 16 guns) under John Thomas; *Swan* (50 tons, 5 guns) under John Chester; and *Christopher* (15 tons, 1 gun) under Tom Moone. After a false start in November, the expedition cleared Plymouth on December 13, 1577. After stopping at Mogador, Morocco, the crew sailed for the Cape Verde Islands, capturing half a dozen Spanish ships and, more important, the Portuguese pilot Nuño da Silva. His *Santa Maria* was renamed *Mary* and put under command first of Thomas Doughty, one of several "gentlemen adventurers" on the voyage, and then of Drake himself, who exchanged *Pelican*'s command with Doughty. The latter proved a troublemaker, and Drake soon relieved him of command altogether.

The ships reached the coast of southern Brazil on April 5, proceeded from there to the River Plate, and then on to Puerto San Julian, where they landed on June 20. The fleet remained at anchor for a month, during which the crisis with the muti-

▲ A replica of the **Golden Hind**, the galleon in which Sir Francis Drake encompassed the world on the first circumnavigation by an English ship. *Photo by Beken of Cowes.*

nous Doughty came to a head. Tried on the spot, Doughty was found guilty and executed in the same place that Ferdinand Magellan had executed the treasonous Gaspar de Quesada in 1520. It was here, too, that Drake delivered his celebrated sermon enjoining the "gentlemen to haul and draw with the mariner, and the mariner with the gentlemen," in order to ensure their mutual success.

After abandoning the other three ships, *Pelican, Marigold,* and *Elizabeth* put to sea on August 17. Three days later, they rounded the Cape of Virgins at the entrance to the Strait of Magellan, where Drake rechristened his ship *Golden Hind.* The choice of name was political, for the golden hind was found on the coat of arms of Sir Christopher Hatton, one of the voyage's principal backers and a friend of the late Thomas Doughty. After only fourteen days in the strait, the English flag first flew in the Pacific on September 6, 1578. The ships' luck failed when a furious storm drove them southward, costing the expedition two ships. *Marigold* was lost with her twenty-nine crew, and John Winter turned back to England. Drake, however, established that the Strait of Magellan did not separate South America from Terra Incognita Australis, as was then believed, but that its southern shore was made up of islands to the south of which lay open ocean, now known as Drake Passage.

When the storm abated, the English struck north along the unsuspecting west coast of Spanish America. Looting the small port of Valparaiso on December 5, they pressed on to Arica, where silver from the mines of Potosí was shipped to Panama. When *Golden Hind* arrived at Callao on February 15, 1579, word of the English presence had preceded them, although there was little the Spanish could do to detain them. Learning that a treasure ship had sailed only three days before, Drake took off in pursuit and on March 1 captured *Nuestra Señora de la Concepción* — nicknamed the *Cacafuego* — off Cape Francisco, Colombia. Sailing out of the main coastal shipping lane, the English transshipped eighty pounds of gold and twenty-six tons of silver bars equal in value to about £126,000 — or about half the English Crown's revenues for a year. Although chiefly interested in returning home with their treasure intact, the English captured a few more ships whose crews were almost unanimous in their respect for Drake's gentility and fairness. Their greatest concern was over his drawings of the coastline, which seemed to suggest that more English would follow, "for everything is depicted so naturally that anyone who uses these paintings as a guide cannot possibly go astray."

In searching for the Strait of Anian, or Northwest Passage, Drake sailed as far as 48°N — just south of the Strait of Juan de Fuca — before turning south. On June 17, 1579, *Golden Hind* anchored in 38°30′N at a "convenient and fit harbor" generally thought to be Drake's Bay, on Point Reyes, California, just north of San Francisco Bay. Drake's dealings with the natives were characteristically evenhanded, and the English found "a goodly countrye, and fruitfull soyle, stored with many blessings fit for the use of man" — fit even to be called New Albion and claimed for her majesty.

On July 25, *Golden Hind* sailed west across the Pacific, making no landfall until September 30, when she landed in either the Palau or Ladrones Islands. By October 16, she was off Mindanao in the Philippines, from where she turned south for the Moluccas. The king of Ternate had recently thrown out the Portuguese, but he allowed Drake to load spices and refit his ship. After a month preparing for the last leg of their journey home, the expedition sailed on December 12 but spent a month caught in the maze of islands and shoals in the Indonesian archipelago. On January 9, 1580, *Golden Hind* struck a coral reef and was held fast for a day before the wind shifted and she slid into deep water. After watering his ship at Tjilatjap on the south coast of Java (previously thought to be connected to Terra Australis), Drake weighed anchor on March 26. A nonstop journey of over 9,700 miles — remarkable for its lack of incident — brought *Golden Hind* to Sierra Leone on July 22. The first English circumnavigation of the globe ended on September 26, 1580, when *Golden Hind* sailed into Plymouth after a voyage of two years, ten months, and eighteen days with fifty-nine of her crew aboard, a great achievement given the record of many later voyages.

Cautioned to lie low while the diplomatic consequences of his voyage were considered at London, Drake was finally received by Queen Elizabeth. On April 4, 1581, Drake was knighted on the decks of *Golden Hind* at Deptford. Elizabeth also ordered the ship displayed in dry dock, and the intrepid ship remained on public view until the 1660s.

Hampden, *Francis Drake, Privateer.* Sugden, *Sir Francis Drake.*

Grace Dieu

Great ship. *L/B/D:* 218′ oa × 50′ × 21.4′ (66.4m × 15.2m × 6.5m). *Tons:* 1400–1500 burthen; 2,750 disp. *Hull:* wood. *Comp.:* 250+. *Built:* William Soper, Southampton, Eng.; 1418.

So far as is known, at her launch *Grace Dieu* was the largest ship ever built in northern Europe, and no English ship exceeded her in size until SOVEREIGN OF THE SEAS more than two centuries later. More than 200 feet long overall, she measured 184 feet (60.3 meters) on deck and 135 feet (41.1 meters) on the keel. For many years, it was thought that *Grace Dieu* never put to sea — that the ship was a failure — and that this was due to the fact that clinker hulls could not be built so big. (Her clinker-laid strakes were fastened by clenched nails and caulked with moss and tar.) Laid down in 1416, she was launched and christened by the Bishop of Bangor in 1418 and put to sea under William Payne in 1420. Her crew seem to have refused to muster, although this was probably due to foul weather, poor provisions, and a policy forbidding shore leave. There is nothing in the record to suggest that the ship handled badly.

Later in 1420, *Grace Dieu* transferred to a berth at Bursledon in the Hamble River with the other royal ships (including her contemporaries *Jesus, Trinity Royal,* and *Holigost*), probably because the ships were extremely expensive to man, and Henry V's navy had swept from the Narrow Seas the very French menace the *Grace Dieu* was designed to meet. This included a number of high-charged Genoese carracks, though none were as lofty as *Grace Dieu,* whose forecastle loomed fifty-two feet above the waterline, and from which her archers and infantrymen could have carried the day against any opponent.

Although *Grace Dieu* appears never to have returned to active service, in 1430 the royal ships were visited by Luca di Maso degli Albizzi, a Florentine captain of the galleys who dined aboard *Grace Dieu* with William Soper. Luca, who later wrote, "I never saw so large and so beautiful a construction," took the only contemporary measurements of *Grace Dieu* to have survived. Among these is the almost incredible figure of 204 feet for the mast, which is nonetheless consistent with pictorial evidence. (The number of masts carried by *Grace Dieu* is not known; it may have been only one or as many as three.) In 1433, she was moved farther upstream and enclosed in a dock. The great ship was struck by lightning on the night of January 6–7, 1439, and burned beyond repair, after which an estimated seven tons of iron and other fittings were salvaged. *Grace Dieu* has lain where she burned ever since (in 50°51′N, 1°17′W), damaged by enthusiastic, if primitive, nineteenth-century archaeologists, but otherwise protected by the mud and accessible only at spring tides.

Loades, *Tudor Navy.* Prynne, "Annual Lecture"; "Notes." Rose, "Henry V's *Grace Dieu* and Mutiny at Sea." Turner, "Building of the *Grace Dieu, Valentine* and *Falconer.*"

El Gran Grifón

Hulk (4m). *Tons:* 650. *Hull:* wood. *Comp.:* 45 crew, 234 soldiers. *Arm.:* 38 guns. *Built:* Rostock (Germany); <1588.

When the Spanish Armada sailed from Lisbon on May 30, 1588, there were twenty-three hulks (or urcas), storeships leased from Hanseatic merchants, in the Baltic. The flagship of the hulks under Juan Gómez de Medina was *El Gran Grifón* — the griffin is the emblem of her home port, Rostock. On August 2, the Armada was off Portland Bill when *Gran Grifón* fell to weather of the main fleet. In an action that cost her seventy dead and wounded, she was nearly captured by Sir Francis Drake's REVENGE before ships of Juan Martinez de Recalde's Biscayan Squadron joined the fray and *Gran Grifón* was towed off by a galleass. On August 6–7, she also took part in the rearguard action off Gravelines before the Spanish turned north, hoping to round Scotland and sail home.

The hulks *Gran Grifón, Barca de Amburg, Castillo Negro,* and the Venetian TRINIDAD VALENCERA were separated from the main fleet north of Scotland on about August 20. *Barca de Amburg* foundered on September 1, and her crew were taken aboard *Trinidad Valencera* and *Gran Grifón*. Three days later, the surviving ships separated; *Castillo Negro* disappeared, and *Trinidad Valencera* was wrecked in Ireland. On September 27, the leaking *Gran Grifón* made Fair Isle, midway between the Orkney and Shetland Islands. As her crew tried to beach the ship, she wrecked in a rocky bay called Stroms Hellier. Most of her company landed, although fifty died of exposure and starvation before they could sail for Scotland, where they secured safe passage home.

The wreck was visited in 1758 by John Row and William Evans, who retrieved two brass cannon. In 1970, divers Colin Martin and Sydney Wignall found the remains of the ship. They recovered all or parts of twelve cannon cast in bronze, cast iron, and wrought iron, which shed new light on the arming of these noncombatant supply ships.

Martin, *Full Fathom Five.*

Great Galley (*see* Princess Mary)

Guadeloupe

Paddle frigate (1f/2m). *L/B/D:* 187′ od × 30.1′ × 9′ (57m × 9.2m × 2.7m). *Tons:* 878 disp.; 788 bm. *Hull:* iron. *Arm.:* 2 × 68pdr, 2 × 24pdr. *Mach.:* 2 cyl, 180 nhp, sidewheels; 9 kts. *Built:* Cammell, Laird & Co., Ltd., Birkenhead Iron Works, Birkenhead, Eng.; 1842.

The world's largest iron ship when built, *Guadeloupe* was built on speculation by John Laird, who intended to sell her to the Royal Navy. The Admiralty was not yet interested in iron warships of such size, and he eventually sold the ship to the Mexican navy, which was contending with secessionist movements in the Yucatán and Texas. When *Guadeloupe* was laid down in 1836, the British were not interested in exploiting the use of iron in shipbuilding because they had not as yet devised a satisfactory way of correcting compass error in iron hulls. (Astronomer George Airey published an explanation of how to do this in 1839.)

Guadeloupe entered service under command of Captain Edward Phillip Charlwood, a Royal Navy captain then on half pay in Britain's peacetime navy. At the time, Mexico was engaged in putting down an insurrection in the Yucatán, which had seceded, and *Guadeloupe* sailed against the insurgents in company with another Laird-built ship, *Montezuma*. In 1843, *Guadeloupe* was actively involved in the campaign against the Texas navy and on May 16 forced the corvette *Austin* to withdraw under fire from her 68-pdr. guns. Following two years of service, Charlwood provided British authorities with detailed observations on the advantages of iron over wood in warships. These included greater buoyancy, more room below decks because the hull was thinner and there were fewer frames, and watertight bulkheads. With respect to fighting the ship, *Guadeloupe* provided a steadier gun platform for the two 68-pdr. pivot guns (mounted fore and aft), and when the hull was penetrated, the hole was clean and did not splinter as it did in wooden ships. Splinters and the resulting infection were a primary cause of death from combat in wooden ships.

Brown, "Paddle Frigate *Guadeloupe.*"

HMS Guerrière

5th rate 38 (3m). *L/B/D:* 155.8′ × 39.8′ × 12.8′ (47.5m × 12.1m × 3.9m). *Tons:* 1,092 bm. *Hull:* wood. *Comp.:* 284. *Arm.:* 16 × 32pdr, 28 × 18pdr, 2 × 9pdr. *Des.:* Lafosse. *Built:* Cherbourg; 1799.

The French navy frigate *Guerrière* ("Warrior") was built during the consulate of Napoleon Bonaparte. In 1801, *Guerrière* escorted a troop convoy dispatched to quell the Haitian uprising led by Toussaint L'Ouverture, and she narrowly escaped capture by a British blockade on her return in 1803. Later engaged in commerce raiding against British shipping, in 1806 she was one of three frigates operating against the Greenland whale fisheries. Three British frigates were dispatched to the Shetland Islands to intercept the French, although HMS *Phoebe* and *Thames* returned prematurely. Captain Thomas Lavie's HMS *Blanche* (36 guns) sailed from the Downs and at 1030 on July 18 came in sight of *Guerrière* near the Faeroe Islands. Captain Hubert closed with *Blanche* until he realized, too late, that she was not one of his ship's own consorts. *Blanche* sailed in pursuit, caught up with *Guerrière* at about midnight, and loosed two broadsides before the Frenchman could reply. After an hour's fight, *Guerrière* had lost her mizzen topmast and struck to the British, who had suffered only four wounded as against twenty dead and thirty wounded as well as heavy damage to the French ship.

Repaired and brought into the Royal Navy as a fifth-rate frigate, during the War of 1812 she was assigned to the North American Station at Halifax. On July 17, 1812, she was in a squadron commanded by Captain Sir Philip Broke in HMS *Africa* (64) when it came upon the frigate USS CONSTITUTION off New Jersey. After a remarkable sixty-six-hour chase in light winds, *Constitution* escaped. On August 19, a solitary *Guerrière* was cruising the Grand Banks south of Newfoundland in position 41°42′N, 55°48′W, when she encountered *Constitution* a second time. Her arrogant captain, James Dacres, had issued a challenge to "U. States frigate *President* . . . or any other American frigate of equal force for the purpose of having a few minutes tete-a-tete," and he was quite pleased by the prospect of an engagement. Opening fire at long range, two of her shot bounced off the hull of *Constitution*, which thereafter was known as "Old Ironsides." Commodore Isaac Hull held his fire until he had closed to a range of less than half a pistol shot before he loosed his first broadside. Twenty-five minutes later, the dismasted *Guerrière* was wallowing in the heavy seas with seventy-eight dead and wounded compared with only seven dead and seven wounded aboard *Constitution*. *Guerrière*'s hull was so shattered that Hull ordered her blown up the next day. The unlucky *Guerrière* was thus the first major British unit lost to the U.S. Navy in the War of 1812. The *London Times* observed, correctly, "It is not merely that an English frigate has been taken, . . . but that it has been taken by a new enemy, an enemy unaccustomed to such triumphs, and likely to be rendered insolent and confident by them."

Allen, *Battles of the Royal Navy.* Roosevelt, *Naval War of 1812.*

H

Hamilton

(ex-*Diana*) Schooner (2m). *L/B:* 73′ × 20′ (22.3m × 6.1m). *Tons:* 112 grt. *Hull:* wood. *Comp.:* 50. *Arm.:* 1 × 32pdr, 1 × 24pdr, 8 × 6pdr. *Built:* Henry Eagle, Oswego, N.Y., 1809.

Built for Matthew McNair of Oswego, *Diana* was one of several schooners acquired for Captain Isaac Chauncey's Lake Ontario squadron during the War of 1812. Armed and renamed *Hamilton,* in honor of Navy Secretary Paul Hamilton, she joined Chauncey's squadron at Sackett's Harbor, New York, in late October. Under Sailing Master Joseph Osgood, she took part in the attacks on Kingston on November 9, 1812, York (now Toronto) on April 27, 1813, and Ft. George, on the Niagara River, on May 27. On the night of August 8, she was overwhelmed in a squall, with the loss of all but four of her crew; the schooner SCOURGE was also lost. In 1973, the *Hamilton* and *Scourge* Foundation of Hamilton, Ontario, located the two schooners at a depth of 300 feet. Photographs showed both vessels to be in a remarkable state of preservation.

Cain, *Ghost Ships.* Nelson, "*Hamilton* and *Scourge.*" Roosevelt, *Naval War of 1812.*

Hancock

Frigate (3m). *L/B/D:* 136.6′ × 35.5′ × 11.5 dph (41.6m × 10.8m × 3.5m). *Tons:* 750. *Hull:* wood. *Comp.:* 290. *Arm.:* 24 × 12pdr, 10 × 6pdr. *Built:* Jonathan Greenley & John & Ralph Cross, Newburyport, Mass.; 1776.

One of the thirteen original frigates ordered by the Continental Congress in 1775, *Hancock* was named for John Hancock, president of the Continental Congress from 1775 to 1777. Under command of Captain John Manley, she sailed with the frigate *Boston* (24 guns) on May 21, 1777. After capturing a small merchant ship on the twenty-ninth, the following day *Hancock* was chased by HMS *Somerset* (64), which gave up only when *Boston* attacked the convoy of transports she was guarding. On June 21, the two ships took on HMS *Fox* (28), which struck after losing her mainmast. After several days repairing their prize, Manley's squadron resumed cruising off the New England coast. On July 6, they were chased by HMS *Rainbow* (44) and *Victor* (10). By the following morning, HMS *Flora* (32) had joined the chase, at which point the Americans split up. *Fox* was retaken by *Flora,* and *Hancock* by *Rainbow; Boston* escaped.

Taken into the Royal Navy as HMS *Iris,* the Massachusetts-built ship was well admired by her captors, who described her as "the finest and fastest frigate in the world." Four years later, she captured the American TRUMBULL (24) before being captured by the French at the Battle of the Virginia Capes, on September 11, 1781. After active service in the French navy, *Iris* was hulked at Toulon, where she was blown up by the British on December 18, 1793.

Chapelle, *History of the American Sailing Navy.* U.S. Navy, *DANFS.*

Hannah

Schooner (2m). *L/B/D:* ca. 61′ × 17′ × 8′ (18.6m × 5.2m × 2.4m). *Tons:* 78 bm. *Hull:* wood. *Arm.:* 4 × 4pdr. *Built:* Marblehead, Mass.; <1775.

John Glover's fishing schooner *Hannah* is commonly accorded the honor of being the first vessel armed and paid for by the Continental Congress during the American Revolution, and thus with the genesis of the American navy. The truth is somewhat less certain. *Hannah* was the first hired on the authority of the Continental Army's General George Washington. Put under command of Army Captain Nicholson Broughton, and crewed by men from John Glover's Marblehead regiment, she sailed on September 5, 1775. The next day she seized the small sloop *Unity*, with a cargo of naval stores and other provisions. She sailed again at the end of the month, but she was run aground while fleeing from HMS *Nautilus*, a 16-gun sloop, near Beverly, Massachusetts, on October 10. Saved from destruction by spirited resistance from local patriots, she was soon decommissioned by Washington, who had meanwhile hired vessels more appropriate to the army's needs.

Fowler, *Rebels under Sail*. Miller, *Sea of Glory*.

USS Harriet Lane

(later *Lavinia*, *Elliott Richie*) Aux. brigantine (1f/2m). *L/B/D:* 180′ × 30′ × 12.5′ dph (54.9m × 9.1m × 3.8m). *Tons:* 639 grt. *Hull:* wood. *Comp.:* 130. *Arm.:* 4 × 9″, 4 × 32pdr, 9″ pivot gun, 20pdr pivot gun. *Mach.:* inclined, direct-acting engine. *Built:* William H. Webb, New York; 1857.

Designed as a revenue cutter, *Harriet Lane* was named for President James Buchanan's niece, who served as the bachelor president's unofficial First Lady. Originally based out of New York, the ship fired the first shot of the Civil War as she tried to stop a ship inward bound to Charleston on the night before the bombardment of Fort Sumter, on April 12, 1861. Transferred to the U.S. Navy on September 17, she saw duty along the East Coast before being transferred to the West Gulf Blockading Squadron, which took Galveston on October 4, 1862. On New Year's Day 1863, Major General John B. Magruder recaptured Galveston and, in the process, *Harriet Lane*, which was rammed by the Confederate "cottonclad" steamers *Bayou City* (Captain Henry S. Lubbock) and *Neptune* (Captain W. H. Sangster). Five crew were killed, including

▲ A lithograph captioned "Surprise and Capture of the United States Steamer **Harriet Lane**, by the Confederates under General Magruder, and the Destruction of the Flagship **Westward**" at Galveston, Texas, on New Year's Day 1863. *Courtesy U.S. Naval Historical Center, Washington, D.C.*

Commander Jonathan M. Wainwright, and twelve wounded. *Harriet Lane* was sold, converted to a blockade-runner, and renamed *Lavinia* in 1864. Sunk at Havana on January 18, 1865, she was raised and rerigged as the ship *Elliott Richie*, remaining in service until wrecked off the Pernambuco River in 1884.

Frazier, "Cottonclads in a Storm of Iron." Yanaway, "United States Revenue Cutter *Harriet Lane*."

USS Hartford

Screw sloop (1f/3m). *L/B/D:* 225′ × 44′ × 17.2′ (68.6m × 13.4m × 5.2m). *Tons:* 2,900 disp. *Hull:* wood. *Comp.:* 310. *Arm.:* 20 × 9″, 20 × 20pdr, 2 × 12pdr. *Mach.:* horizontal double-piston rod engines, 1,204 ihp, 1 screw; 13.5 kts. *Built:* Harrison Loring, Boston; 1859.

USS *Hartford*'s first assignment was as flagship of the East India Squadron under newly appointed

Two views of the screw sloop **USS Hartford**, flagship of Admiral David G. Farragut's West Gulf Blockading Squadron. The photo shows her riding at anchor in Mobile Bay in 1864. The lithograph shows the **Hartford**'s crew serving a 20-pound gun during her close engagement with the ironclad **CSS Tennessee**. *Courtesy U.S. Naval Historical Center, Washington, D.C.*

Flag Officer Cornelius K. Stribling, charged with safeguarding U.S. interests in the Philippines, China, and elsewhere in Asia. Ordered home following the start of the Civil War, *Hartford* fitted out at Philadelphia and sailed at the end of 1861 as flagship of Flag Officer David G. Farragut's West Gulf Blockading Squadron. Although the operations of the Union high command embraced the coast from Pensacola, Florida, to Texas, their primary objective was the capture of New Orleans, the first city of the South. Farragut marshaled his forces at Ship Island, off Biloxi, Mississippi, and his

deep-water ships crossed the Mississippi River bar in April 1862. Forts St. Philip and Jackson were engaged by Commodore David Porter's mortar schooners and steam gunboats for a week before *Hartford* led the advance past the Confederate batteries on April 24. Nearly rammed by the ironclad CSS MANASSAS, she then ran aground trying to avoid a fire ship that landed alongside her near Fort St. Philip. The fires were extinguished, and *Hartford* fought her way upriver. Subsequent resistance was negligible, and New Orleans all but surrendered on April 25.

Farragut's next objective was to secure the Mississippi River. Baton Rouge and Natchez fell easily before the Union fleets. But with its 200-foot-high bluffs crowned by Confederate batteries, Vicksburg, Mississippi, was all but impregnable. Leaving a gunboat force below the city, *Hartford* and the other Union ships returned to New Orleans at the end of May. With orders direct from President Abraham Lincoln, Farragut's force returned to

Vicksburg on June 26, and then ran the gauntlet to join the Western Flotilla above Vicksburg on June 28. A month later, *Hartford* sailed for Pensacola, via New Orleans, for repairs.

Returning in November, Farragut blockaded the Red River, south of Vicksburg, while General Ulysses S. Grant moved overland to take Vicksburg from the rear. On March 14–15, 1863, *Hartford* and *Albatross* ran past Confederate batteries at Fort Hudson, Louisiana, and patrolled between there and Vicksburg, which finally fell on July 4, followed by Fort Hudson, which capitulated on the ninth. In Lincoln's felicitous words, "The father of waters again goes unvexed to the sea" — the Confederacy had been cut in two. Despite the fact that Mobile, Alabama, was, after New Orleans, the Confederacy's largest port, other operations received priority, and Farragut's squadron was relegated to blockade duty for the remainder of 1863. *Hartford* returned to New York for an overhaul in August and was not fit for sea again until January 1864.

In June, *Hartford* was off the Alabama coast with a flotilla reinforced with monitors and ironclads to counter the Confederate ironclad TENNESSEE. The Battle of Mobile Bay finally opened at dawn on August 5. The monitors advanced past Fort Morgan, followed by USS *Brooklyn* at the head of the Union fleet, until she fell out of line and *Hartford* took the lead. Although Farragut's oft-quoted "Damn the torpedoes; full speed ahead" is apocryphal, he was lashed to the rigging, and by leading his column across the Confederate minefield, he quickly got his ships well into Mobile Bay and out of range of Fort Morgan. The only remaining obstacle was *Tennessee*, which at 0845 commenced an attack on Farragut's ships. In the brawl that followed, the Union ships poured fire on the impervious ironclad and attempted to ram her, doing more damage to themselves. Finally, at 1000, with her tiller chains shot away, *Tennessee* was compelled to surrender. The forts surrendered by August 23, 1864. Although the war was over before Mobile fell, as a blockade-runner's haven the port was finished.

Hartford returned to New York for repairs in December 1865 and that July was sent out as flagship of the Asiatic Squadron, with which she served two tours of duty, 1865–68 and 1872–75. In 1887, she became a training ship based at Mare Island, California. Laid up from 1890 to 1899, she resumed work as a training ship in the Atlantic until 1912, when she was moored at Charleston, South Carolina, as a station ship. In 1938, she was moved to Washington, D.C., and after World War II transferred to Norfolk Navy Yard as a "relic." In 1956, she foundered at her berth and was broken up.

Jameson & Sternlicht, *Black Devil of the Bayous.*

USS Hatteras

(ex-*St. Mary's*) Sidewheel steamer (1f/3m). *L/B/D:* 210′ bp × 34′ × 18′ (64m × 10.4m × 5.5m). *Tons:* 1,126 bm. *Hull:* iron. *Comp.:* 126. *Arm.:* 4 × 32pdr, 1 × 20pdr. *Mach.:* beam engine, 500 hp, sidewheels; 8 kts. *Built:* Harland & Hollingsworth Co., Wilmington, Del.; 1861.

Laid down as a merchant steamship, *St. Mary's* was purchased from her builders by the U.S. Navy in September 1861. Assigned to the South Atlantic Blockading Squadron at Key West, Florida, on January 7, 1862, she raided Cedar Keys Harbor, where she sank seven Confederate blockade-runners and burned the railroad wharf. Transferred to Farragut's West Gulf Blockading Squadron on January 26, she engaged CSS *Mobile* the next day, and over the course of the year, she captured seven runners, including the sloop *Poody,* which Commander George F. Emmons brought into the squadron as *Hatteras Jr.*

On January 6, 1863, *Hatteras,* now under Commander Homer C. Blake, was assigned to blockade duty off Galveston. On January 11, she gave chase to a square-rigger about twenty miles south of the port. When challenged, the ship replied that she was the British *Spitfire.* But as a boarding party approached the ship, her captain, Raphael Semmes, broke the Confederate flag and opened fire. *Hatteras* and CSS ALABAMA fought at close quarters for forty minutes before *Hatteras* began to sink.

She had lost two dead and five wounded; the remainder of the crew were taken aboard *Alabama* and paroled at Port Royal, Jamaica. *Hatteras* sank in about nine fathoms.

Silverstone, *Warships of the Civil War Navies.* U.S. Navy, *DANFS.*

HMS Havock

"A"-class destroyer (1f/2m). *L/B/D:* 180′ × 18.5′ × 6.7′ (54.9m × 5.6m × 2m). *Tons:* 240 disp. *Hull:* steel. *Comp.:* 42. *Arm.:* 1 × 12pdr, 3 × 6pdr; 3 × 18″TT. *Mach.:* triple expansion, 3,554 ihp, 2 screws; 26 kts. *Built:* Yarrow & Co., Ltd., Poplar, Eng.; 1893.

One of the least-heralded developments in nineteenth-century naval warfare was that of the free-running torpedo. Although the compressed air–driven torpedo, developed in 1866 by Robert Whitehead and Austrian navy Captain Giovanni Luppis, carried only an eighteen-pound charge at a speed of six knots, it was quickly understood that the torpedo was a potent and inexpensive weapon that could easily sink even the strongest ironclad battleships. To increase the offensive power of these short-range weapons, navies developed lithe, fast torpedo boats capable of launching their torpedoes and getting away quickly.

To counter this threat to their battlefleets, European naval powers began developing vessels variously described as torpedo-boat "catchers," "hunters," and "destroyers." Initial designs proved unsuitable for fleet operations on the high seas. In 1892, newly appointed Third Sea Lord Rear Admiral John A. "Jackie" Fisher directed the development of a new class of seagoing torpedo-boat destroyer, six of which were ordered: *Havock* and *Hornet* from Yarrow, *Daring* and *Decoy* from Thornycroft, and *Ferret* and *Lynx* from Lairds. The trials of *Havock* and the other vessels were a great success. Although *Havock* was sold for breaking up in 1912, several first-generation destroyers were among the 221 in the Royal Navy at the start of World War I.

March, *British Destroyers.*

Henry Grace à Dieu

("Great Harry"; later *Edward*) Carrack (4m). *L/B:* ca. 175–200′ main deck (125–35′ keel) × 50′ (53–61m/38–41m × 15m). *Tons:* 1,500 burthen. *Hull:* wood. *Comp.:* 700 (1,536). *Arm.:* 43 heavy guns, 141 light guns. *Built:* Woolwich Dockyard, Eng.; 1514.

One of Henry VIII's more enduring achievements was his promotion of England's navy. His ambitious shipbuilding program saw the construction of, among others, MARY ROSE (1505), *Henry Grace à Dieu* (often known simply as "Great Harry"), and GREAT GALLEY (1513). One distinguishing characteristic of these ships was that they were built for war rather than as merchant ships that could be converted for martial purposes. The tonnage of Great Harry is given variously as 1,500 tons and 1,000 tons; her linear dimensions have been inferred from these figures, the larger one yielding the approximate dimensions given above.

▼ A rendering of the **Henry Grace à Dieu,** taken from "A Declaracion of the Kynges Maiesties Owne Nave of sundere kyndes of shyppes," compiled by Anthony Anthony, an officer of the ordnance, and presented to Henry VIII in 1546. Some of the detail in the drawing is questionable, but the information for each ship included tonnage; numbers of soldiers and mariners; brass and iron guns; gunpowder; iron, stone, and lead shot; bows, bowstrings, and arrows; and various other materiel. *Courtesy Pepys Library, Magdalene College, Cambridge.*

Her armament consisted mainly of smaller-caliber brass and iron guns, but the large guns were mounted in the waist of the ship; this position not only increased the ship's stability but made the guns more effective against other ships, which could be more easily hulled at or below the water-line. The smaller-caliber guns were designed mainly for use against masts, rigging, and people and were most effective mounted in the forecastle, which rose four decks high, and the sterncastle, which had two decks.

Although *Henry Grace à Dieu* was born of the continual wars between England and France, the period following her building was one of compara-tive peace, and she saw no action until 1545. Dur-ing the French attack on Portsmouth in July of that year (during which the MARY ROSE sank), she was engaged by Admiral Claude d'Annebault's more maneuverable galleys. Upon the accession of Ed-ward VI in 1547, she was renamed for that mon-arch. She remained in peacetime service until Au-gust 25, 1553 (the year of Edward's death), when she was destroyed by fire at Woolwich.

Laughton, "Report: The *Henry Grace à Dieu*." Loades, *Tu-dor Navy*. Robinson, "Great Harry."

HMS Hermione

(later *Santa Cecilia*, HMS *Retribution*) *Hermione*-class 5th rate 32 (3m). *L/B/D:* 129′ x 35.4′ × 15.3′ (39.3m × 10.8m × 4.6m). *Tons:* 717 bm. *Hull:* wood. *Comp.:* 170. *Arm.:* 26 × 12pdr, 6 × 6pdr, 12 swivels. *Des.:* Edward Hunt. *Built:* Teast, Tombs & Co., Bristol, Eng.; 1782.

The scene of "the most daring and sanguinary mu-tiny that the annals of the British Navy can recall," HMS *Hermione* was a Royal Navy frigate built dur-ing the tumultuous era of the French Revolution-ary Wars. In this period, not only was the Royal Navy on guard against the navies of France and her allies, but there was growing disaffection within its own ranks, as indicated by the mutinies at Spithead and the Nore in 1797. Some of the sailors' discon-tent had spread to the more remote West Indies Station, where the pestilential climate was an en-emy more feared than the French or Spanish.

On February 6, 1797, *Hermione* came under command of Hugh Pigot, under whom the ship patrolled the Mona Passage between Santo Domingo and Puerto Rico in company with HM Brig *Diligence*. Pigot was a malevolent officer given to frequent, ruthless, and arbitrary punishment of his crew, who quickly grew to resent and fear his violent rages. At about 1800 on September 21, *Hermione* was struck by a squall, and Pigot ordered the topsails reefed. As the men were not taking in sail fast enough to suit him, Pigot bellowed into the rigging that he would flog the last man down, and in their haste to avoid punishment, three of the youngest mizzentopmen slipped and fell to their deaths. Pigot ordered, "Throw the lubbers over-board," and when this provoked murmurs of dis-belief from the twelve to fourteen men on the maintopyard, he ordered the bosun's mates aloft to flog them.

Shortly before midnight of the same day, the crew mutinied, and within a few minutes four men were dead: Pigot, two lieutenants, and a mid-shipman. At this point, surgeon's mate Lawrence Cronan assumed control of the mutiny and turned it from a more or less spontaneous act of ven-geance into a vehicle for the aspirations of Irish re-publicans. Cronan's first recommendation was to kill all of the officers, and although a number of them were eventually spared, the final death toll was ten. The mutineers appear to have numbered no more than sixty-two of the ship's company, and of these, eighteen were considered ringleaders, chief among them bosun's mate Thomas Jay and seaman Thomas Leech, who had twice deserted His Majesty's ships only to return of his own voli-tion.

The next day, the mutineers decided to sail for La Guaira, Venezuela, where they arrived on Sep-tember 27. According to the governor's report, they claimed to have overthrown the tyrannical Pigot and set him adrift in the ship's launch, but the real story gradually leaked out. Its outline was well known to the captain of the Spanish schooner *San Antonio*, which sailed several weeks later only to be captured by *Diligence*. Word reached Sir Hyde Parker, commander of the West Indies Squadron, who immediately ordered a hunt for the mutineers. By 1799, fifteen had been arrested and hanged, their rotting corpses displayed as a warning to others. Seven years later, the last of the twenty-four *Hermione* mutineers was executed.

In the meantime, the Spanish had renamed their prize *Santa Cecilia*, which they armed with 40 guns and manned with a crew of about 400 men. Her fate was in the hands of indecisive colonial bureaucrats for two years before it was decided to sail her to Havana. Shortly before her projected departure, on October 25, 1799, Captain Edward Hamilton led 100 men from his 28-gun frigate HMS *Surprise* and cut her out from under the 200 guns of Puerto Caballo. The British losses were a dozen men, as against about 100 Spanish dead. Admiral Parker ordered her renamed *Retaliation*, but he was overruled by the Admiralty and she became HMS *Retribution*. She returned to Portsmouth in 1802 but was paid off shortly thereafter; three years later, she was broken up.

Pope, *Black Ship*.

Héros

3rd rate 74 (3m). *L/B/D:* 178.8′ × 46.2′ × 2.3′ (54.5m × 14.1m × 6.8m). *Tons:* 1,800 burthen. *Hull:* wood. *Arm.:* 28 × 36pdr, 30 × 18pdr, 16 × 8pdr. *Des.:* J. M. B. Coulomb. *Built:* Toulon, France; 1778.

Although France began aiding the nominally independent United States in 1776, it was not until February 6, 1778, that a definitive alliance was forged. Britain quickly declared war against France, and she was soon at war with Spain and the Netherlands, too. A conflict that had been confined to North America quickly expanded to include European possessions in the Caribbean, the Mediterranean, and the Indian Ocean. In 1781, the British dispatched a squadron under Commodore George Johnstone to capture the Dutch colony of South Africa. On the way, they were shadowed by a French squadron under Vice Admiral Pierre André, Bailli de Suffren, who had left France at the same time as Comte de Grasse, whose fleet would

force the surrender of General Charles Cornwallis in September. In mid-April, the sixteen British ships were taking on water and supplies at Porto Praya, Cape Verde Islands, when Suffren appeared off the port. His squadron included his flagship *Héros,* another 74-gun ship, and three 64s. Both sides were surprised by the chance encounter, and Suffren's attack was poorly executed by his captains. Nonetheless, he was able to reach the Cape before Johnstone, and he prevented the English from seizing the strategic Dutch colony.

Continuing to the French outpost at Ile de France, upon the death of Commodore Comte d'Orves in February, Suffren assumed command of the French naval forces in the Indian Ocean. His fleet of three 74s, seven 64s, and two 40s reached the coast of Madras, in the Bay of Bengal, a week later. There they sighted the fleet of Vice Admiral Sir Edward Hughes, whose flagship was HMS *Superb* and who commanded in all two 74s, one 68, five 64s, and one 50. The English position was complicated by a war with Hyder Ali, Sultan of Mysore, and by the fact that they hoped to defend the Ceylonese port of Trincomalee, which they had just taken from the Dutch.

On February 17, 1782, the French and English met in an indecisive action off Madras. In April, the British were joined by HMS *Sultan* (74) and *Magnanime* (64), which made the two fleets nearly equal, although the British retained the advantage of having access to better ports and supplies. On April 12, Suffren bore down on Hughes as the latter sailed for Trincomalee. The Battle of Providien (off Ceylon) was hotly contested, and the opposing fleets suffered roughly equal casualties — 137 dead on both sides, though the English had slightly more and the French slightly less than 400 wounded. (The Battle of Providien was fought the same day that, half a world away, the British fleet under Admiral Sir George Rodney defeated de Grasse at the Battle of the Saintes.) The two fleets were too exhausted to continue fighting, and Hughes sailed for Trincomalee while Suffren made for Batacalo, to the south of the English-held port.

In June, the two fleets sailed north, the French to Cuddalore, which had fallen to Hyder Ali, and the English to Negapatam. On July 5, they met off the latter port; Suffren had only eleven ships, as one had been partially dismasted the day before. Casualties were again heavy — 77 English dead, to 178 French — and the capture of two French ships was only narrowly averted. In mid-August, Suffren was reinforced by two new ships at Batacalo, and moving with prodigious speed he laid siege to Trincomalee, which fell on August 31. Two days later, Hughes appeared off the port, now with fourteen ships under his command. As ever, *Héros* was in the thick of the fighting, and she and the *Illustre* lost their main and mizzen masts, but Hughes failed to press home his advantage. Owing to the onset of the winter monsoon, this was the last battle of the year. Hughes took his fleet to Bombay, on the west coast of India, and Suffren, deprived of adequate supplies at Trincomalee, sailed east for the Dutch port at Acheen, on the island of Sumatra. In the interval, he had lost the *Orient* (74) and *Bizarre* (64) in accidents.

Although the Peace of Versailles had been signed by the following spring, this was not known; moreover, the strategic picture in the East had changed dramatically. Hughes now had eighteen ships of the line, including *Gibraltar* (80), to Suffren's fifteen. Moreover, the French ally Hyder Ali had died, and the British decided to retake Cuddalore. Suffren appeared off the port on June 13, 1783. A week of fickle winds prevented either side from engaging, but on June 20, Suffren attacked. The fighting was general, and though no ships were seriously damaged, casualties were high, both sides losing about 100 men dead and 400 wounded. Nonetheless, Suffren had at last won a tactical and strategic victory, his chief object having been to prevent the loss of Cuddalore. Four days later, the frigate HMS *Medea* arrived with news that peace negotiations were under way, and the French and British agreed to end hostilities.

Suffren quit India in *Héros* in October, returning to a hero's welcome in France via Ile de France and the Cape of Good Hope. At the Cape Colony, he was met by the captains of six of Hughes's ships, who readily acknowledged his brilliant conduct of a two-year campaign in which he never wavered in

pressing home his attack, despite the disadvantages of undermanned ships and inadequate supplies. "The good Dutchmen have received me as their savior," Suffren wrote, "but among the tributes which have most flattered me, none has given me more pleasure than the esteem and consideration testified by the English who are here."

At the start of the French Revolution, *Héros* was at Toulon when Royalist officers opened the port to the British Mediterranean Fleet under Vice Admiral Sir Samuel Hood. When the British quit the port in December 1793, *Héros* was burned, along with many other ships.

Cavaliero, *Admiral Satan*. Clowes, *Royal Navy*. Mahan, *Influence of Sea Power upon History*.

CSS H. L. Hunley

(ex-*Fish Boat*) Submarine. *L/B/D:* 30–40′ × 4′ × 4–5′ dph (9–12m × 1.2m × 1.5m). *Hull:* iron. *Comp.:* 9. *Arm.:* spar torpedo. *Mach.:* Hand-cranked propeller. *Built:* Thomas B. Park & Thomas W. Lyons, Mobile, Ala.; 1863.

CSS *H. L. Hunley* was the first submarine to sink an enemy warship in combat. *Hunley* was actually the third vessel, after CSS PIONEER and *American Diver*, built by a group of investors and inventors lured by the Confederate government's promise of prize money equal to 20 percent of the value of any Union warship sunk. Among the hopefuls was the vessel's namesake, Confederate Army Captain Horace Lawson Hunley. Basically a modified iron cylinder steam boiler, *Hunley* was steered by one member of the crew and propelled by eight others turning a propeller shaft. The simple armament consisted of a spar torpedo, a mine carried at the end of a long pole that detonated on contact with an enemy ship. Following successful trials at Mobile in August 1863, *Hunley* was shipped by rail to Charleston, South Carolina.

The original captain was James R. McClintock, a partner in the venture, but his lack of success in attacking Union shipping led to the Confederates' requisitioning the vessel, which was commissioned and crewed by volunteers under Lieutenant John

▶ Drawing of a midships section of the Confederate submersible **H. L. Hunley.** *11,* struts holding the propeller shaft in place; *22,* rod from one diving plane to the other; *23,* diving plane; *25,* crewman; *31,* detachable keel. *Courtesy U.S. Naval Historical Center, Washington, D.C.*

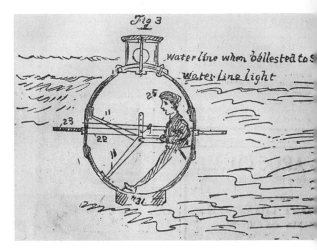

A. Payne. Five of this navy crew were killed when the submarine accidentally sank; another nine people died, Hunley among them, when she sank again on October 15. Despite the ship's predisposition to kill its crews, a third crew was found. On the night of February 17, 1864, CSS *H. L. Hunley* sailed into Charleston Harbor and attacked the screw sloop USS HOUSATONIC, which was sunk with the loss of five men.

Neither *Hunley* nor its crew returned from this mission, and the remains of the world's first successful submarine were presumed lost forever. That same night, however, the Confederate officer Lieutenant Colonel O. M. Dantzler recorded that "the signals agreed upon to be given in case the boat wished a light to be exposed at this post [Battery Marshall] as a guide for its return were observed and answered." Others also reported seeing an exchange of signals forty-five minutes after the sinking of the *Housatonic,* but these facts seem to have escaped the notice of the Office of Submarine Defenses. Captain M. M. Gray, CSA, later wrote, "I am of the opinion that . . . she went into the hole made in the *Housatonic* by the explosion of torpedoes and did not have sufficient power to back out." In 1994, researchers managed to locate the elusive submarine in the waters of Charleston Harbor. There were plans to raise the remains of the submarine in July 2000.

Although *Hunley* was only a qualified success, having killed less than one of the enemy for every four of her own crew, her destruction of USS *Housatonic* ushered in a form of warfare that would find its full, grim expression half a century later in World War I.

Kloepel, *Danger beneath the Waves.* Murphy, *"H. L. Hunley."* Perry, *Infernal Machines.*

USS Holland (SS-1)

Holland-class submarine. *L/B/D:* 53.3′ × 10.3′ × 8.5′/11.4′ (16.2m × 3.1m × 2.6m/3.5m). *Tons:* 63/74 disp. *Hull:* steel; 75′ dd. *Comp.:* 6. *Arm.:* 1 × 18″TT; 1 × 8.4″ pneumatic gun. *Mach.:* gasoline engine/electric motor, 45 bhp/150 shp, 1 screw; 8/5 kts. *Des.:* John P. Holland. *Built:* Crescent Shipyard, Elizabeth, N.J.; 1900.

John Philip Holland's sixth submarine boat design — her predecessors included FENIAN RAM — was the first operationally practical submarine commissioned into the U.S. Navy. *Holland* was "the forerunner of all modern submarines," in the words of British submariner and historian Richard Compton-Hall: "The design and the construction were entirely along the lines of submarines today with frames, plating and general arrangements [that] would not be out of place in any submarine drawing office today." A gasoline engine drove the vessel on the surface while an electric motor powered her when submerged. She had diving rudders fitted on either side of her single four-bladed propeller. The primary armament consisted of three 18-inch torpedoes that were fired from a single torpedo tube in the bow. After surface trials and a thirty-minute static submergence, *Holland*'s first dive underway was made, on March 17, 1898 — St. Patrick's Day, fittingly enough, given Holland's Irish Republican background — in the waters off Staten Island, New York.

▲ The prototype of the world's first successful class of submarines, **USS Holland** was named for her inventor, the engineer John Holland. *Courtesy U.S. Naval Historical Center, Washington, D.C.*

Witnessing her official trials ten days later, Assistant Secretary of the Navy Theodore Roosevelt urged that the navy purchase the vessel, but it was not until April 11, 1900, that she was formally commissioned as USS *Holland* at Newport. The navy also ordered an additional six submarines on the same model. Intended strictly for port defense, the *Hollands* had no crews' quarters or sleeping accommodations. Towed to Annapolis, *Holland* was used to train officers and crew of the U.S. Navy's nascent submarine service until sold for scrap in 1913.

Compton-Hall, *Submarine Boats*. Morris, *John P. Holland*. U.S. Navy, *DANFS*.

Hornet

Sloop. *L/B/D:* ca. 64′ × 18′ × 10′ (19.5m × 5.5m × 3m). *Tons:* 75 bm. *Hull:* wood. *Arm.:* 10 × 4pdr. *Built:* Baltimore(?); 1774.

A merchant sloop owned by Baltimore merchant Captain William Stone, *Hornet* was one of the first vessels (with WASP) chartered by Congress for the Continental Navy. On February 18, 1776, she sailed in a squadron under Commodore Esek Hopkins, flying his flag in ALFRED, to capture British gunpowder at New Providence, the Bahamas. Running afoul of *Fly*, she was forced back to the Delaware. On January 30, 1777, *Hornet* (now under James Nicholson) and *Fly* were ordered to escort a merchant convoy bound for Martinique to secure French military stores bound for the Continental Army.

Following General Sir William Howe's capture of Philadelphia on September 26, *Hornet*, ANDREW DORIA, *Wasp*, and *Fly* were part of the fleet that lay on the Delaware River between the British fleet at Chester and Philadelphia, which had fallen to the British. *Hornet*'s ultimate fate is uncertain. Some believe that she was burned, together with *Andrew Doria* and *Wasp*, following the fall of the Delaware River Forts Mifflin and Mercer on November 20, 1777, to prevent their falling into British hands. It is also possible that she escaped the Delaware, only to be captured off Charleston by the British schooner *Porcupine* after loading a cargo of indigo for Martinique.

Fowler, *Rebels under Sail*. Miller, *Sea of Glory*.

USS Hornet

Brig. *L/B/D:* 106.8' × 31.4' × 14' dph (32.5m × 9.6m × 4.3m). *Tons:* 440 bm. *Hull:* wood. *Comp.:* 50. *Arm.:* 16 × 32pdr, 2 × 12pdr. *Des.:* Josiah Fox. *Built:* William Price, Baltimore; 1805.

USS *Hornet* and WASP were two blue-water fighting vessels ordered by Congress in the midst of President Thomas Jefferson's "gunboat navy" building program at the beginning of the nineteenth century. Under command of Commandant Isaac Chauncey, *Hornet* was assigned to the Mediterranean Squadron in 1806–7, after which she was decommissioned at Charleston, South Carolina. Returning to service in 1808, she patrolled the East Coast enforcing the Embargo Act, which forbade export shipping from U.S. ports. Following the repeal of this act, in 1810 she was rerigged as a ship at the Washington Navy Yard, and her beam was increased by ten inches.

The beginning of the War of 1812 found her with Commodore John Rodgers's squadron at New York. Sailing under Master Commandant James Lawrence, on July 9 *Hornet* seized the British privateer *Dolphin*, which was unfortunately recaptured with her prize crew. On October 30, *Hornet* sailed for the Pacific in company with USS CONSTITUTION. En route, they were to rendezvous with USS ESSEX at Salvador, Brazil. It was at this time that *Constitution* fought her celebrated duel with HMS *Java* and returned to Boston. *Hornet* blockaded British shipping at Salvador until the arrival of HMS *Montagu* (74 guns). On February 24, 1813, off Demerara, British Guiana, she intercepted HM Brig *Peacock* (18). Lawrence "ran him close on board on the starboard quarter, and kept up such a heavy and well directed fire, that in less than 15 minutes she surrendered (being literally cut to pieces)." In recognition of this decisive action, Lawrence was given command of the frigate USS CHESAPEAKE. Blockaded at New York until 1815, under Lieutenant James Biddle *Hornet* sailed with orders to harass British commerce in the Indian Ocean. Unaware that a peace had been signed, *Hornet* fought HMS *Penguin* (18) in a sharp contest on March 23, 1815, about five miles northeast of Tristan da Cunha. The Americans' superior gunnery destroyed *Penguin*, which was later scuttled, and killed between ten and twenty-five of her crew, including Commander James Dickinson.

Hornet arrived at New York on August 23, to great acclaim, despite the fact that the war had been over for eight months. She saw further service in the Atlantic and Mediterranean before assignment to the Caribbean, based at Key West and Pensacola. She remained with the West Indies Squadron until her loss with all hands in September or October 1829 in a gale off Tampico, Mexico.

Aimone, "Cruise of the U.S. Sloop *Hornet* in 1815." Hardin, "Notes." U.S. Navy, *DANFS*.

USS Housatonic

Ossipee-class screw sloop (1f/2m). *L/B/D:* 205' bp × 38' × 16.6' (62.5m × 11.6m × 5.1m). *Tons:* 1,934 disp. *Hull:* wood. *Comp.:* 160. *Arm.:* 1 × 100pdr, 2 × 30pdr, 1 × 11", 2 × 32pdr, 2 × 24pdr hwz, 1 × 12pdr hwz. *Mach.:* horizontal direct-acting engines, 715 ihp, 1 screw; 12 kts. *Des.:* John Lenthall. *Built:* Globe Iron Works, Boston; 1862.

One of four *Ossipee*-class unarmored screw sloops laid down after the start of the Civil War, the bark-rigged *Housatonic* joined the South Atlantic Blockading Squadron in September 1861, stationed off Charleston Harbor. The largest ship on station at the time, the *Housatonic* made her first engagement on January 31, 1863, when she helped fight off an attack by the ironclad rams *Chicora* and *Palmetto State*, which had inflicted serious damage on USS *Mercedita* and *Keystone State*. Their attack was provoked by the recent capture of the blockade-runner *Princess Royal*, inward bound with "the war's most important single cargo of contraband," including two marine engines, ordnance, and ammunition.

That summer, the Union ships adopted a more aggressive posture and began shelling Fort Morgan and other shore installations. On the night of February 17, 1864, while *Housatonic* was moored just off Charleston Harbor, the officer of the watch saw what he later described as "a plank moving in the water." He ordered the anchor slipped and the engine reversed, but two minutes later, the spar

torpedo of the Confederate submarine H. L.
HUNLEY detonated on the starboard hull just forward of the mizzen mast. *Housatonic* filled rapidly
and sank with the loss of five of her crew. Although
H. L. Hunley was the first submarine to sink another ship in combat, she and her crew were lost
following the attack. The remains of the *Hunley*
were not discovered until 1995.

Silverstone, *Warships of the Civil War Navies*. U.S. Navy,
DANFS.

Huascar

Ironclad turret ship (2m). *L/B/D:* 200′ lbp × 35.5′ x 16′ (37.8m ×
10.2m × 3.4m). *Tons:* 1,870 disp. *Hull:* iron. *Comp.:* 193. *Arm.:* 2 ×
300pdr, 1 × 10″, 2 × 40pdr, 1 × 12pdr. *Armor:* 4.5″ belt. *Mach.:*
Maudslay return connecting rod engine, 300 hp, 1 screw; 12 kts. *Des.:*
Cowper Coles. *Built:* Laird Bros., Ltd., Birkenhead, Eng.; 1865.

Ordered by the Peruvian navy during the war with
Spain, *Huascar* was named for the son of the Incan
emperor Huayna Capac. The first turret ship designed as such by the Royal Navy's Captain Cowper
Coles, *Huascar*'s primary armament was housed in
a 22-foot-diameter turret mounted abaft the fore-

mast. She had a 138-degree arc of fire on either
beam. *Huascar* joined the Peruvian-Chilean squadron under Chile's Rear Admiral Manuel Blanco
Encalada and proceeded to Callao to take part in
Peru's final revolution against Spain, but arrived
after hostilities with Spain were over.

In 1877, *Huascar* was seized by supporters of
Nicolas de Piérola, and under command of Manuel
M. Carrasco, she raided as far as Pisagua, Bolivia,
before being engaged by HMS *Shah* and *Amethyst*
off Ilo, Peru, on May 29. Piérola surrendered the
ship to Peruvian authorities the following day. In
April 1879, Peru entered the War of the Pacific as
Bolivia's ally against Chile. Under Commander
Miguel Grau, on May 21 *Huascar* and the ironclad
frigate *Independencia* attempted to raise the Chilean blockade of Iquique by the gunboat *Covadonga*
and the twenty-year-old screw corvette *Esmeralda*,

▼ The ironclad turret ship **Huascar** is one of only a few
warships surviving from the mid-19th century. In addition
to an increased preference for steam over sail, this critical
period saw the first experiments with the turreted, centerline guns that would become a mainstay of 20th-century
capital ship design. *Courtesy Norman Brouwer.*

which *Huascar* sank by ramming. On October 8, *Huascar* encountered the Chilean ships *Cochrane* and *Blanco Encalada* off Agamos Point near Antofagasta. In the hour-and-a-half battle, which pitted Coles's turret ironclad against Edward J. Reed's broadside battery ships, *Huascar* was hit with an estimated 70 rounds that knocked out her steering, penetrated her turret, and killed 64 of her 193 crew, including Grau. Captured and commissioned in the Chilean navy, *Huascar* was put on blockade duty for the remainder of the war. In 1901, *Huascar* was stricken from the active list, but she served as a submarine tender from 1917 to 1930. She was opened to the public as a museum ship at Talcahuano in 1952. (Several years after her engagement with *Huascar*, *Blanco Encalada* was the first ship sunk by a self-propelled torpedo, during the Chilean revolution.)

Seeger, "The Ten Cent War." Wood, "Ironclad Turret Ship *Huascar.*"

HMS Hussar

Mermaid-class frigate (3m). *L/B/D:* 124′ × 33.5′ × 11′ dph (37.8m × 10.2m × 3.4m). *Tons:* 613 bm. *Hull:* wood. *Comp.:* 200. *Arm.:* 24 × 9pdr, 4 × 3pdr, 12 swivels. *Des.:* Sir Thomas Slade. *Built:* Inwood, Rotherhithe, Eng.; 1763.

During the American Revolution, HMS *Hussar* sailed as a dispatch boat on the North American station. By mid-1779, the British position in New York was precarious, as a French army had joined forces with General George Washington's troops north of the city. When Admiral Sir George Brydges Rodney took his twenty ships of the line south in November, it was decided that the army's payroll should be moved to the anchorage at Gardiner's Bay on eastern Long Island. Over his pilot's better judgment, on November 24 *Hussar*'s Captain Charles Pole decided to sail from the East River through the treacherous waters of Hell Gate between Manhattan Island and Long Island.

Just before reaching Long Island Sound, *Hussar* was swept onto Pot Rock and began sinking. Pole was unable to run her aground, and she sank in sixteen fathoms of water. The British immediately denied there was any gold aboard the ship, but despite the difficulty of diving in the waters of Hell Gate, reports of $2 million to $4 million in gold prompted many salvage efforts over the next 150 years. This continued even after the U.S. Army Corps of Engineers "blew the worst features of Hell Gate straight back to hell" with 56,000 pounds of dynamite in 1876. *Hussar*'s remains, if any survive, are now believed to lie beneath landfill in the Bronx.

Hepper, *British Warship Losses.* Rattray, *Perils of the Port of New York.*

I

HMS Implacable

(ex-*Duguay-Trouin*, later HMS *Lion*) 3rd rate (3m). *L/B/D:* 181.5′ × 48.9′ × 22′ (55.3m × 14.9m × 6.7m). *Tons:* 1,896 bm. *Hull:* wood. *Comp.:* 670. *Arm.:* 30 × 32pdr, 12 × 32pdr carr, 30 × 18pdr, 2 × 12pdr. *Built:* Rochefort, France; 1801.

Named for one of the greatest French admirals, René Duguay-Trouin (1673–1736) — who as a privateer in 1711 captured and ransomed the city of Rio de Janeiro — the 74-gun ship *Duguay-Trouin* was launched just after the establishment of Napoleon Bonaparte's consulate in France. In 1801, she helped convoy General C. V. E. Leclerc's army to Santo Domingo for the suppression of the slave rebellion led by Toussaint L'Ouverture. While in the Caribbean, she became flagship of Vice Admiral Louis-René Levassor de Latouche-Tréville. On April 15, 1803, *Duguay-Trouin* grounded off the port of Jérémie, and she could be refloated only after Captain Pierre l'Hermité jettisoned twenty of her heaviest guns, each weighing more than three tons.

Illness in the fleet forced the return of three ships to France, and on July 24, 1803, *Duguay-Trouin*, *Guerrière* (Captain Louis-Alexis Beaudouin), and *Duquesne* (Commodore Querangal) attempted to run the British blockade, though *Duquesne* was captured. On August 29, *Duguay-Trouin* was engaged by the Royal Navy frigate *Boadicea* off El Ferrol, Spain. In an effort to determine how well manned she was, Captain Maitland engaged the larger ship until he was satisfied that the French could fight their lower deck guns. *Duguay-Trouin* was then engaged by Sir Edward Pellew's squadron, which chased her so closely that Pellew's HMS *Culloden* came under fire from shore batteries at La Coruña.

Duguay-Trouin eventually passed under command of Claude Touffet, but remained at La Coruña until August 11, 1805, when she sailed with the Comte de Villeneuve's fleet for Cadiz. Although ordered to Naples by Napoleon, Villeneuve feared an engagement with the British fleet, first under Vice Admiral Sir Cuthbert Collingwood and then under Vice Admiral Lord Nelson in VICTORY. When he learned that Napoleon was relieving him of his command, he took his eighteen French and fifteen Spanish ships of the line out of Cadiz and, on October 21, turned to fight Nelson. As the ships sailed into battle, *Duguay-Trouin* was one of the ten ships in the van under Rear Admiral Pierre Dumanoir Le Pelley in *Formidable*. Except for a few ships whose captains fought as they should in defiance of his orders, Dumanoir kept his squadron out of battle until 1500 — three hours after battle was joined. *Formidable*, *Duguay-Trouin*, *Mont Blanc*, *Scipion*, and the Spanish *Neptuno* sailed to the assistance of Villeneuve's *Bucentaure*. But too late to aid the beleaguered flagship, Dumanoir quit the battle with four of his ships, *Neptuno* having been captured by HMS *Minotaur* and *Spartiate*.

Two weeks later, Dumanoir was cruising in the Bay of Biscay when the French sighted the British frigate *Phoenix*. The chase brought them right into the fleet of Sir Richard Strachan on November 4, and the four French ships were overwhelmed by Strachan's superior force. Aboard *Duguay-Trouin*, Touffet and all his lieutenants were killed or injured, and the ship was surrendered by Ensign de Vaisseau Rigodet.

Taken into the Royal Navy, the 74-gun ship was renamed HMS *Implacable*. In 1808, she sailed under Captain Thomas Byam Martin as part of Sir

James Saumarez's Baltic expedition. Detached to the Swedish fleet, on August 26 *Implacable* and Rear Admiral Samuel Hood's *Centaur* engaged, captured, and blew up the Russian *Vsevolod* (74) practically within range of the whole Russian fleet. Laid up following the Napoleonic Wars, *Implacable*'s next action was with the Mediterranean Fleet. In 1840, she sailed as part of a combined British, Austrian, and Turkish force in an action off the coast of Syria to prevent an Egyptian advance into Turkey.

From July 1855, she served as a Royal Navy training ship at Devonport, and in 1871, she was renamed *Lion*. In 1912, the navy loaned her to Mr. J. Wheatley Cobb for use as a training ship, and her name reverted to *Implacable*. A major overhaul was undertaken in 1925, and she remained a private training ship until World War II. Dry-docked at Portsmouth in 1943, she was commissioned as a training ship and renamed *Foudroyant*; she was paid off for the last time in 1947. A survey of the ship showed that deterioration of the hull during the war was so extensive as to make her restoration prohibitively expensive — more than £200,000 in 1948. As a result, on December 2, 1949, she was towed into the English Channel and scuttled. The loss of the ship galvanized a small fraternity of preservationists, chief among them Frank Carr, director of the National Maritime Museum in Greenwich, who established the World Ship Trust. Today *Implacable* lives on in the mission of the trust: "to advance the education of the public by the preservation and display of historic ships and associated artifacts." Her stern is on display at the National Maritime Museum in Greenwich.

Mackenzie, *Trafalgar Roll*. Schom, *Trafalgar*. Wyllie, "H.M.S. *Implacable*."

USS Independence

Ship of the line (3m). *L/B/D:* 190.8' bp × 54.6' × 24.3' (58.2m × 16.6m × 7.4m). *Tons:* 2,257 bm. *Hull:* wood. *Comp.:* 790. *Arm.:* 90 × 32pdr. *Built:* Edmund Hartt and J. Barker, Boston; 1814.

By 1814, the course of naval operations in the War of 1812 made it apparent that a fleet comprising of

▲ Sailmaker's plan for the American 74-gun ship of the line **USS Independence** prior to the removal of her spar deck in 1836, when she was reconfigured as a 54-gun frigate. *Courtesy U.S. Naval Historical Center, Washington, D.C.*

nothing larger than 44-gun frigates, no matter how well fought, was no match for the largest units of the all-too-effective British blockade. To rectify this, the U.S. Navy ordered three 74-gun ships of the line: USS *Independence, Franklin,* and *Washington.* Launched in June 1814, *Independence* was quickly armed and stationed off Boston Harbor. The war was soon over, and in June 1815, she sailed as flagship of a squadron under Commodore William Bainbridge to the Mediterranean, where she arrived after a new peace had been concluded with the Barbary corsairs. *Independence* returned stateside the same year and remained in service until 1822.

Poorly designed as a three-decker, *Independence* had only three and a half feet of freeboard at her lower gun deck, which made it all but impossible to use those guns in battle. She remained in ordinary at Boston until 1835–36, when she was razeed — that is, her spar deck was removed — and she was recommissioned as a 54-gun frigate. "Thus," in the words of Howard Chapelle, "a ship considered a failure and useless for almost twenty-two years became one of the best ships in the Navy."

Her first assignment after recommissioning in 1837 was to convey to Kronstadt the U.S. minister to Russia, George Dallas, en route to his new post at St. Petersburg. *Independence* then sailed from the Baltic to Rio de Janeiro, where she served as flagship of the navy's Brazil Squadron, responsible for safeguarding U.S. interests along the east coast of South America. Two years later, she became flagship of Commodore Charles Stewart's Home Squadron. Following the outbreak of the Mexican War in 1846, she sailed for Monterey, California, and Commodore William B. Shubrick broke his flag aboard *Independence* in January 1847. The Pacific Squadron, which also comprised the frigate CONGRESS (44) and three sloops, seized the ports of Guaymas (October 20) and Mazatlán (November 11). En route home in 1848, *Independence* called at Honolulu. A mild outbreak of measles among her crew quickly spread to the Hawaiian people with devastating effect: the ensuing epidemic is believed to have killed 10 percent of the native population.

Independence spent three years as flagship of the Mediterranean Squadron, then returned in 1852 to New York, where she was placed in ordinary. Two years later, she sailed for Valparaiso to take up assignment as flagship of the Pacific Squadron for a second time, her duties taking her north to San Francisco and east to Hawaii. On October 2, 1857, she entered the Mare Island Navy Yard at San Francisco and became a receiving ship. Sold in 1914, her hardwood was salvaged and the remainder burned to recover her metal fittings.

Chapelle, *History of the American Sailing Navy.* Johnson, *Thence round Cape Horn.* U.S. Navy, *DANFS.*

USS Indiana (BB-1)

Indiana-class pre-dreadnought battleship (2f/1m). *L/B/D:* 350.1′ × 69.3′ × 27′ (106.7m × 21.1m × 8.2m). *Tons:* 11,688 disp. *Hull:* steel. *Comp.:* 650. *Arm.:* 4 × 13″ (2 × 2), 8 × 8″; 4 × 6″, 20 × 6pdr, 6 × 1pdr. *Armor:* 18″ belt, 3″ deck. *Mach.:* VTE engines, 9,000 ihp, 2 screws; 15.5 kts. *Built:* William Cramp & Sons Ship and Engine Building Co., Philadelphia; 1895.

Authorized in 1890, USS *Indiana* was the name ship of the U.S. Navy's first class of battleships; the others were USS *Massachusetts* and OREGON. Classified as coastal defense battleships, they had

more powerful guns and thicker armor than their contemporaries, and in the words of a British naval architect, they were "distinctly superior to any European vessels of the same displacement, and . . . quite a match for any ships afloat." In 1898, *Indiana* was one of ten ships in Admiral William T. Sampson's squadron sent to intercept a Spanish fleet of four antiquated cruisers and lighter units en route to Cuba. After shelling San Juan, Puerto Rico, on May 12, she withdrew to Key West before proceeding to Santiago, Cuba. When Admiral Pascual Cervera y Topete attempted his desperate breakout on July 3, *Indiana*, *Gloucester* (ex-CORSAIR), and *Iowa* shattered the destroyers *Pluton* and *Furor*.

From 1905 to 1914, *Indiana* worked as a training ship. Decommissioned from 1914 to 1917, she resumed training duty following the U.S. entry into World War I. In 1920, she was sunk as a target ship during tests of aerial bombs.

U.S. Navy, *DANFS.*

HMS Inflexible

Brig-rigged turret ship (2f/2m). *L/B/D:* 320′ × 75′ × 26.5 (97.5m × 22.9m × 8.1m). *Tons:* 11,880 disp. *Hull:* steel. *Comp.:* 440. *Arm.:* 4 × 16″ (2x2), 6 × 20pdr. *Armor:* citadel 16–24″, bulkheads 14–22″. *Mach.:* inverted compound engine, 8,400 ihp, 2 screws; 14.75 kts. *Des.:* Sir Nathaniel Barnaby. *Built:* Portsmouth Dockyard, Eng.; 1881.

The most progressive British battleship to follow HMS WARRIOR, HMS *Inflexible* incorporated a number of innovative design elements, many of which became standard features of later warship architecture. She was the first ship to use an underwater armor deck in place of vertical armor along the waterline, and the 24-inch armor used in the 110-foot-long central box citadel was the thickest ever used in a British warship. *Inflexible*'s 16-inch guns — carried in two turrets mounted en echelon — were also the largest fitted to that time. These muzzle-loading rifles could be loaded only from outside the turrets, a relatively awkward maneuver achieved by depressing the muzzles into a built-up portion of the armored deck directly above the magazines. *Inflexible* was the first ship fitted with electric light. However, because of the labyrinthine

▲ The most advanced ship in the world when commissioned in 1881, **HMS Inflexible** originally sported a brig rig, although this was later removed when it became obvious that it was of no use as a means of propulsion. She is seen here at Malta.

division of the hull spaces that ensured the stability and survivability of the ship, her first captain, John Arbuthnot Fisher, devoted several months to color-coding the passageways and using other devices to enable the crew to maneuver efficiently below decks, in darkness if need be. Nonetheless, it was not until the crew had perfected its sail handling — despite the fact that the auxiliary rig was never intended for use in battle — that *Inflexible* was rated "the best ship in the Fleet." The sails were replaced by fighting tops in 1885.

Seven and a half years under construction, upon her commissioning, *Inflexible* was the most powerful warship in the world. Joining the Mediterranean Fleet in 1881, she was part of the British force sent to Alexandria during the abortive uprising by the Egyptian General Ahmed Arabi (Arabi Pasha) against the pro-European Khedive of Egypt. During the bombardment of July 12, *Inflexible* lost five men killed and forty-four wounded from enemy fire. (Under Fisher, her shore parties later improvised the first armored train for patrolling the outskirts of the city.) She remained in the Mediterranean until 1885 and emerged from a refit to be placed in reserve. She was again in commission in the Mediterranean from 1890 to 1893, and thereafter served as a guard ship at Portsmouth. She was broken up in 1903.

Brown, "Design of HMS *Inflexible*." Massie, *"Dreadnought."* Parkes, *British Battleships.*

Intelligent Whale

Submarine. *L/B/D:* 28.7′ × 7′ × 9′ dph (8.7m x 2.1m × 2.7m). *Tons:* 4,000 lb. *Hull:* iron. *Comp.:* 6–13. *Mach.:* hand crank, single screw; 4

kts. *Des.*: Scovel S. Meriam. *Built:* August Price, Cornelius S. Bushnell, American Submarine Co.; 1863.

The immediate impetus for the development and construction of the experimental submarine *Intelligent Whale* was triggered by Union fears excited by the success of similar vessels in the Confederacy during the Civil War. CSS H. L. HUNLEY and PIONEER were two outstanding examples. Meriam's design called for a manually operated vessel. To dive, water was admitted to the ballast chambers; to surface, the water was expelled again by means of pumps and compressed air. A hand crank geared to a single propeller was the sole means of forward propulsion. Only six people were required to operate the vessel, though it could carry as many as thirteen. *Intelligent Whale* carried no armament per se, but she was intended as a vehicle for sneak attack. In her only known operational test, she was submerged to a depth of sixteen feet, whereupon a General Sweeney exited the hull in a diver's suit, attached an underwater mine to the hull of an anchored barge, and returned to the submarine. The mine was detonated by pulling a lanyard leading to a friction primer on the mine. This trial was only completed in 1872, eight years after the navy purchased *Intelligent Whale* from the American Submarine Company. Although the scow was sunk, the navy was not impressed with the undertaking and declined either to test *Intelligent Whale* further or to pay the fee due on acceptance of the craft. Placed on exhibit at the Brooklyn Navy Yard, the submarine was transferred to the Washington Navy Yard's Navy Memorial Museum in 1966.

Delgado & Clifford, *Great American Ships.* U.S. Navy, *DANFS.*

USS Intrepid

(ex-*Mastico, L'Intrépide*) Ketch (2m). *L/B:* 60′ × 12′ (18.3m × 3.7m). *Tons:* 64. *Hull:* wood. *Comp.:* 64. *Arm.:* 4 guns. *Built:* France; 1798.

Built for Napoleon's Egyptian campaign in 1798, following the defeat of the French fleet at the Battle of the Nile, the bomb-ketch *L'Intrépide* was sold to Tripoli. On October 31, 1803, the renamed *Mastico* took part in the capture of USS PHILADELPHIA when the frigate ran aground off Tripoli Harbor. Two months later, while en route to Constantinople, she was captured by USS ENTERPRISE, under Lieutenant Stephen Decatur, and taken into the American fleet as *Intrepid.* To deny Tripoli any chance of refloating *Philadelphia* itself, Commodore Edward Preble decided to burn the ship. Renamed *Intrepid* and commanded by Decatur, *Intrepid* slipped into the harbor on the night of February 16, 1804. Sixty of her crew overwhelmed *Philadelphia*'s token crew and set the ship ablaze, with no casualties to themselves. Hearing of the brilliant feat, England's Lord Nelson is said to have proclaimed it "the most bold and daring act of the age." *Intrepid* lay idle at Syracuse until August, when it was decided to use her as a "floating volcano" to destroy the Tripolitan fleet at anchor. Packed with gunpowder and manned by twelve volunteers under Lieutenant Richard Somers, *Intrepid* entered the harbor on September 4. The ketch exploded prematurely, and there were no survivors.

U.S. Navy, *DANFS.*

J

HMS Jersey

4th rate 60 (3m). *L/B/D:* 144′ × 41.5′ × 16.9′ (43.9m × 12.6m × 5.2m). *Tons:* 1,068 bm. *Hull:* wood. *Comp.:* 400. *Arm.:* 24 × 24pdr, 26 × 9pdr, 10 × 6pdr. *Built:* Devonport Dockyard, Plymouth, Eng.; 1736.

Built during a period of relative peace in England, HMS *Jersey* was soon in battle. Her first encounter came in Admiral Edward Vernon's failed attack on the Spanish port of Cartagena, Colombia, at the start of the War of Jenkins's Ear in October 1739. (The war was so called because the *casus belli* was the detention of the merchant brig *Rebecca* and the loss of the master's ear to a Spanish officer's knife.) *Jersey*'s next major action came during the Seven Years' War (or French and Indian War). On August 18–19, 1759, Admiral Edward Boscawen's British fleet of fifteen ships of the line at Gibraltar gave chase to twelve ships under Admiral M. de la Clue Sabran sailing from the Mediterranean to the Atlantic. Five French ships escaped to Cadiz, but the others were brought to battle east of Cape St. Vincent, Portugal. One French ship sank, two escaped, and four were run ashore in Lagos Bay, where Boscawen, disregarding Portuguese neutrality, attacked them the next day. De la Clue's flagship *Ocean* and *Redoutable* were burned, and *Téméraire* and *Modeste* were captured.

In March 1771, *Jersey*'s masts and spars were removed, and she was officially classed as a hospital ship moored in Wallabout Bay, later the site of the Brooklyn Navy Yard. During the American Revolution, she was used as a prison ship for captured Continental Army soldiers, and her name is synonymous with the squalor and deprivation to which American prisoners were subject. Thousands of prisoners were crammed below decks, where there was virtually no natural light or fresh air and few provisions for the sick. Political conditions only made things worse, as the British had no interest in legitimizing the cause of independence by exchanging prisoners, and General George Washington had no interest in surrendering professional British soldiers for his ragtag volunteers. The ghastly statistics speak for themselves. While between 4,400 and 6,800 soldiers and sailors are believed to have died in combat during the American Revolution, another 18,500 died in captivity, of disease, or from other causes. The estimated number of fatalities aboard the New York prison ships stands at between 4,000 and 11,000. It was recorded that as many as seven or eight corpses a day were buried from *Jersey* alone before the British surrendered at Yorktown in September 1783. When the British evacuated New York two months later, *Jersey* was abandoned.

Jackson, "Forgotten Saga of New York's Prison Ships." Kemp, ed., *Oxford Companion to Ships and the Sea.*

Jesus of Lübeck

Round ship (4m). *Tons:* 600 tons. *Hull:* wood. *Comp.:* 300. *Arm.:* 26 guns. *Built:* Germany(?); <1544.

Built for trading under the auspices of the Hanseatic League, administratively headquartered in the Baltic Sea port of Lübeck, *Jesus of Lübeck* was a round ship designed chiefly for work in the waters of northern Europe and not for oceanic voyaging. A large and imposing vessel, she had high stern- and forecastles from which her crew could repel boarders. But these same features caught the wind, making her unresponsive to the helm and straining the hull. Henry VIII purchased her in 1544 during his naval buildup, but she was poorly maintained in the decades that followed. In 1564, Queen Elizabeth lent *Jesus of Lübeck* to John Hawkins for an expedition during which he sold African slaves illegally in the Spanish Caribbean. (Slavery was legal, but trading without the proper papers was not.)

Two years later, Hawkins sailed again with six vessels, the royal ships *Jesus of Lübeck* and *Minion* (300 tons), *William and John* (150 tons), *Swallow* (100 tons), *Judith* (50 tons), and *Angel* (33 tons). Clearing Plymouth on October 2, 1567, they arrived on the coast of Guinea in mid-November. After two months spent gathering slaves, either by theft from Portuguese slavers or by trade and conquest, the English sailed for the Caribbean, arriving off Dominica on March 27, 1568. Restrictions on trade made it difficult for Hawkins to offload his cargo, but after selling most of the slaves near Cartagena, he was ready to return to England. Hit by a hurricane in the Gulf of Mexico, *Jesus of Lübeck* was so strained that Hawkins ordered part of the upperworks cut away, a fortuitous move that may have been the genesis of the race-built, weatherly galleons Hawkins promoted for the English navy in the years before the Spanish Armada. Putting into San Juan de Ulúa, Mexico, near Veracruz, on September 15, Hawkins hoped to repair his ships before the arrival of the Spanish *flota*, which appeared two days later bearing the new Viceroy of Mexico, Don Martin Enríquez. Negotiating an armistice, the English continued their repairs, but on September 23, the Spanish launched a surprise attack, sinking *Jesus of Lübeck, Angel, Swallow,* and two Portuguese prizes — though not before the flagship had sunk two Spanish ships. Only *Judith*, by now under command of Francis Drake, and *Minion* survived the voyage, returning to Plymouth in late January 1569 with barely 70 of the 400 men with whom the expedition began.

Hampden, *Francis Drake, Privateer*. Loades, *Tudor Navy*. Sugden, *Sir Francis Drake*.

Jylland

Steam frigate (3m). *L/B/D:* 210.3′ × 43′ × 19.7′ (64.1m × 13.1m × 6m). *Tons:* 2,450 disp. *Hull:* wood. *Comp.:* 437. *Arm.:* 44 × 30pdr, 1 × 18pdr, 1 × 12pdr, 3 × 4pdr. *Mach.:* horizontal steam engine, 400 nhp, 1 screw; 12 kts. *Built:* Nyholm Naval Shipyard, Copenhagen; 1860.

The development of the steam engine and auxiliary power in the nineteenth century helped to revolutionize navigation and naval warfare. However, paddle machinery was vulnerable to enemy fire and took up so much space formerly given over to guns that it was more of a liability than an asset. The widespread adoption of screw propulsion in the 1840s made steam warships a more realistic alternative to windships. *Jylland* (Jutland) was built for the Danish navy in 1860. Initially sailed as a cadet-training ship, on May 9, 1863, she was severely damaged in the Battle of Helgoland between a Danish fleet under Admiral Edouard Suenson and an Austro-Prussian force under Admiral Wilhelm von Tegetthoff. Hostilities had begun after King

▼ The Danish steam frigate **Jylland,** minus her masts, in 1979. From a distance the white stripe might mask the hogged hull (the fact that she is lower at the bow and stern than amidships), but the gently arching row of gunports reveals the curvature of the deck. *Courtesy Norman Brouwer.*

Christian IX attempted to formally annex the duchies of Schleswig and Holstein — historically Danish but with a large German population — into Denmark. On the pretext of enforcing the Treaty of London of 1852, which forbade any such annexation, Prussia's Chancellor Otto von Bismarck — with an Austrian alliance — forced the Danes to back down in 1864.

Denmark, which surrendered the two duchies only to see them annexed by Prussia after the Austro-Prussian War of 1866, remained at peace through the end of the nineteenth century. *Jylland*'s role was largely one of showing the flag, mostly in European waters but also in the Danish West Indies (now the U.S. Virgin Islands). From 1892 to 1908, *Jylland* was used as a stationary barracks and training ship. In 1908, the government decided to save the ship as a museum, although she was used as a barracks during and just after both world wars. The last survivor from the era of wooden-hulled, screw-driven warships has been undergoing restoration in a permanent dry dock at Ebeltoft since 1984.

Brouwer, *International Register of Historic Ships*. Kjølsen, "Old Danish Frigate." Schäuffelen, *Great Sailing Ships*.

K

USS Katahdin

Harbor defense ram (1f/1m). *L/B/D:* 251′ × 43.4′ × 16′ (76.5m × 13.2m × 4.9m). *Tons:* 2,383 disp. *Hull:* steel. *Comp.:* 108. *Arm.:* 4 × 6pdr. *Armor:* 6″. *Mach.:* triple expansion, 4,800 ihp, 2 screws; 16 kts. *Des.:* RAdm. Daniel Ammen. *Built:* Bath Iron Works, Bath, Me.; 1896.

The second U.S. Navy ship named for the highest mountain in Maine, USS *Katahdin* was something of a technological throwback during an era of dramatic change in naval shipbuilding. Rams fitted to the bow of a ship had been one of the principal weapons of galley warfare in antiquity, but in the age of sail, ramming had been rendered obsolete by both a change from shell-first to the more easily repaired plank-on-frame construction and the reliance on wind rather than mechanical propulsion. Steam propulsion made rams once again technically feasible, and the ironclad CSS Virginia demonstrated the ram's effectiveness when it sank the USS Housatonic in Hampton Roads in 1862. The French, British, and American navies became even more convinced of the ram's utility following the Battle of Lissa in 1866, when the Austro-Hungarian Erzherzog Ferdinand Max rammed and sank the disabled Italian flagship Re d'Italia in a matter of minutes.

In 1882, Rear Admiral Daniel Ammen proposed a ram intended exclusively for coastal defense against European ironclads. Not all were convinced, and it was more than a decade before funds were appropriated for a single experimental vessel. *Katahdin*'s primary armament was the wrought steel ram itself, although she also carried four quick-firing six-pounder guns for defense against torpedo boats. Her double bottom was subdivided into fourteen compartments that could be flooded to lower the ship about six inches to further reduce her already slight profile. *Katahdin*'s low freeboard made her, in the words of Rear Admiral David Potter, "the most uncomfortable warship ever to fly the American flag." The problem lay not so much with her stability as with the fact that underway her hatches had to be closed against incoming seas. This resulted in temperatures that "attained tropical fervour" — 110 degrees in the officers' mess and 125 degrees in the galley, while "the unfortunates who shovelled coal into the fireboxes beneath the boilers smouldered at a height of Fahrenheit I do not venture to name."

Intended as she was for coastal defense, *Katahdin* spent the Spanish-American War on patrol between Norfolk, Virginia, and New England. Commander George Francis Faxon Wilde lobbied hard for her to be sent to join Admiral William T. Sampson's squadron in Cuba, but no sooner was permission granted than the Spanish fleet was destroyed at the Battle of Santiago. Decommissioned on October 8, 1898, eleven years later, now called Ballistic Experimental Target A, *Katahdin* was sunk by gunfire off Rappahannock Spit, Virginia.

Allen, "USS *Katahdin*." Gardiner & Lambert, eds., *Steam, Steel and Shellfire*.

USS Kearsarge

Mohican-class screw sloop (3m). *L/B/D:* 198.5′ bp × 33.8′ × 15.8′ (60.5m × 10.3m × 4.8m). *Tons:* 1,550 disp.; 1,031 burthen. *Hull:* wood. *Comp.:* 160. *Arm.:* 2 × 11″, 4 × 32pdr. *Mach.:* horizontal back-acting engines, 842 ihp, 1 screw; 11 kts. *Built:* Portsmouth Navy Yard, Kittery, Me.; 1862.

Ordered under the emergency war program of 1861, USS *Kearsarge* (named for a New Hampshire

▲ Crewman standing by the forward superstructure of the low-slung harbor defense ram **Katahdin** in 1898. Note the ladder curving up the turtle-back hull and the low, open bridge. From a stereophoto by J. F. Jarvis, *courtesy U.S. Naval Historical Center, Washington, D.C.*

mountain) had a rather commonplace career in the European Squadron of the U.S. Navy. Under Captain Charles W. Pickering, she departed Portsmouth, New Hampshire, on January 24, 1862, and took part in the blockade of CSS SUMTER at Gibraltar; *Sumter*'s commander, Captain Raphael Semmes, thereupon left the ship. Thereafter *Kearsarge* patrolled the western Atlantic in pursuit of Semmes's new ship, CSS ALABAMA, and other raiders. In June 1864, *Kearsarge* was at Flushing, Holland, under Captain John A. Winslow, when word arrived that the notorious Confederate raider had put into Cherbourg on June 11. Three days later, *Kearsarge* arrived off the French coast. Local officials told him that any attempt to embark U.S. sailors put ashore from *Alabama* would violate French neutrality, so Winslow — a shipmate of Semmes's before the war — put to sea to await *Alabama*'s inevitable departure. On the morning of June 19, *Alabama* stood out of Cherbourg and opened fire on *Kearsarge* at 1057. Fitted with protective chain cables and fighting with better-quality munitions, *Kearsarge* was more than a match for the war-weary *Alabama,* which began to sink after an hour. *Kearsarge* rescued most of *Alabama*'s crew except for Semmes and about forty others, who escaped aboard a British yacht. This single engagement against the Confederacy's most notorious commerce raider made *Kearsarge* one of the best-known ships in the U.S. Navy.

After an unsuccessful effort to locate CSS FLORIDA, *Kearsarge* proceeded to the Caribbean and from there to Boston, where she was decommissioned for repairs. *Kearsarge* continued in service for another thirty years, seeing service in virtually every sphere of U.S. interest around the world: the Mediterranean, South America, the Pacific, and the China Station. She wrecked on Roncador Reef

off Central America while en route from Haiti to Bluefields, Nicaragua, on February 2, 1894, without loss of life. Deemed unsalvageable, she was stricken from the navy list the same year.

Guérout, "Engagement between the C.S.S. *Alabama* and the U.S.S. *Kearsarge*." Leary, "*Alabama* vs. *Kearsarge*."

Kronan

1st rate ship (3m). *L/B/D:* 197′ × 43.5′ × 16′ (60m × 13.3m × 4.9m). *Tons:* 2,140 disp. *Hull:* wood. *Comp.:* 500 crew, 300 soldiers. *Arm.:* 124–28 guns. *Des.:* Francis Sheldon. *Built:* Skeppsholmen, Stockholm; 1672.

The wreck of the seventeenth-century Swedish flagship *Kronan* ("Crown") was discovered in 1980 by Anders Franzén, fourteen years after his discovery of WASA. The ship's loss was well documented, having occurred about four miles off the southeast coast of the island of Öland on June 1, 1676, dur-

ing the Battle of Öland, when the Swedish fleet was defeated by a combined Danish-Dutch force. The battle, the worst naval defeat in Swedish history, also saw the loss of the first-rate ship *Svärdet* ("Sword") and the death of 1,400 of the ships' crews.

Designed by the English shipwright Francis Sheldon, whom Karl X Gustaf recruited from England in 1654, *Kronan* was the first three-decked ship built for the Swedish navy. Laid down and launched in 1668 but not completed until 1672, she became flagship of the Swedish navy in 1675. *Kronan*'s loss was not due to battle damage but rather to improper ship handling. On May 25, the Swedes had allowed a Danish fleet to escape in a battle fought between Bornholm and Rügen. Hoping to gain an advantage by fighting closer to home, the fleet of sixty ships was running northward before a gale with the combined Danish and Dutch fleet in pursuit when a signal was given to turn and close with the enemy. *Kronan* apparently turned without taking in sail. The ship heeled sharply to port. A sudden explosion blew out the starboard side of the hull. She sank quickly, taking with her all but 42 of the crew of 850, including Admiral Baron Lorentz Creutz. One survivor reported that Creutz's last order was: "In the name of Jesus, make sure that the cannon ports are closed and the cannon made fast, so that in turning we don't suffer the same fate as befell the *Wasa*." Archaeological evidence shows that this order was not carried out in time. Eight cannon were found on the seabed about 100 meters from the ship, and the lower deck gunports were open.

The remains of the vessel, found at a depth of twenty-six meters, consist of the aftermost two-thirds of the port side of the hull from the orlop deck to the upper deck. Unlike *Wasa*, which was lost on her maiden voyage in 1628, *Kronan* had been in service for a number of years, and the site has yielded a great range of artifacts from the battle-tested ship and her crew. In the first ten years of excavation, 20,000 separate objects representing 6,518 artifacts were identified. *Kronan* was armed with between 124 and 128 bronze cannon (some of which may have been recovered from *Wasa*), 60 of which were salvaged during the 1680s. Between 1981 and 1990, another 43 were raised, the largest of which were 36-pdrs.; 25 were of Danish origin, 8 Spanish, 6 Danish, and 4 German. The oldest of these was a German gun cast in 1514; the newest was cast in Sweden in 1661. Personal possessions included remains of clothing, eating utensils, musical instruments, and navigational instruments including compasses, sundials, and dividers. Of the coins, some originating from as far away as Egypt and Turkey, the oldest dates from the 1400s. *Kronan* has also yielded a large number of sculptural carvings.

In the course of the modern excavation, divers also made and used a replica seventeenth-century diving bell. This consisted of a weighted platform suspended by iron rods from a bell shaped like a lampshade. The reserve air within the bell allowed the diver to conserve air on the descent to the bottom and to increase his working time on the seafloor.

Einarsson, "Royal Ship *Kronan*." Franzén, "*Kronan:* Remnants of a Mighty Warship."

L

Leontophoros

Galley; "octoreme." *Hull:* wood. *Comp.:* 2,800. *Arm.:* 4 × 6pdr. *Built:* Heracleia Pontica (mod. Eregli, Turkey); 3rd cent. BCE.

Following the death of Alexander the Great in 323 BCE, control of his vast empire fell to a number of his "companions," veterans of his six-year military campaign from Macedonia in northern Greece across Asia Minor and the Middle East to Egypt in the south and India in the east. The strongest of these was Antigonus Monophthalmus ("One-Eyed") in Asia, who, with his son, Demetrius the Besieger, sought to maintain control of Alexander's empire. He was opposed by a coalition of other rulers, notably Lysimachus in Thrace, Ptolemy in Egypt, Cassander in Macedonia, and Seleucus in Babylon. This coalition defeated and killed Antigonus at the Battle of Ipsus in 301.

Demetrius maintained a base of power in Greece, and in 294 he became ruler of Macedonia. A creature of war, he built up a powerful fleet that defeated Ptolemy at the Battle of Salamis on Cyprus in 306, and that attempted a siege of Rhodes the following year. According to Plutarch, Lysimachus became so alarmed at the growth of Demetrius's fleet that he requested permission to watch a naval review and "went off in amazement."

One of the challenges to understanding the construction and manning of ancient Mediterranean warships has been in interpreting the meaning of their numerical classification: the four, the five, the sixes, up to the sixteens, the twenties, and, ultimately, the forty, of which there was probably only one. For a long time it was thought that the numbers referred to the banks of oars, but pictorial and other evidence suggests that there were no vessels with more than three banks of oars. The numbers seem to refer to the number of rowers in a vertical group of rowers. A five, for example, might have two rowers pulling on the topmost and middle oars (thranites and zygians, respectively), and one rower (a thalamian) on the lowest oar; an eight might be configured three/three/two; and so on. Where speed was a primary requirement, fives and eights might also include single-banked vessels with each oar pulled by five or eight oarsmen.

The increase in the number of oarsmen gave rise to three developments. The traditional sitting position for rowers (known from the Venetian term as *a sensile*) gave way to a combination of sitting and standing (*a scaloccio*). More oarsmen on a given oar meant longer oars and wider ships. A ship with five men on each oar would need to be twenty feet wide to accommodate the oarsmen (plus the width of the passage between the port and starboard oars), while an eight would have a beam of at least thirty-two feet. These requirements made for more stable ships, which were thus better platforms for catapults, ballista, firepots, and other implements of destruction.

To counter the threat of Demetrius's intimidating sixteen, Lysimachus built the octoreme *Leontophoros* sometime in the 290s or 280s BCE. Little is known of this ship save the size of the crew, a total of 1,600 oarsmen ("800 in each part") and 1,200 soldiers. Lionel Casson interprets this as a catamaran warship consisting of two hulls (the "parts"), each rowed by 800 men sitting on two banks of fifty oars each, with four men to an oar. The inboard oars may have overlapped, but the space between the hulls would have been bridged by a platform that provided ample space for the 1,200 soldiers, as well as such military machinery as catapults and arrow-shooting ballista.

Whether *Leontophoros* saw action under Lysimachus is unclear, but it is fairly certain that she was part of Ptolemy II's fleet when it defeated Antigonus Gonatas (son of Demetrius) in 280 BCE. The ship may well have survived to be at the Battle of Cos, where Antigonus defeated Ptolemy in 258, thus asserting Macedonian control over the Aegean.

As fantastic as the claim of a ship carrying 2,800 sailors and marines may seem, it is not unique, and the third century saw the development of a number of these "super-galleys" — sometimes designated as twenties, thirties, and culminating in the forty designed for Ptolemy IV. According to Athenaeus's detailed description of this "double prowed" and "double sterned" vessel, it had a complement of 7,250: 4,000 oarsmen, 400 officers and deckhands, and 2,850 marines.

Athenaeus, *Deipnosophistai.* Casson, *Ships and Seamanship in the Ancient World.*

HMS Leopard

Portland-class 4th rate 50 (3m). *L/B/D:* 146′ × 30.5′ × 17.5′ (44.5m × 9.3m × 5.3m). *Tons:* 1,045 tons. *Hull:* wood. *Comp.:* 350. *Arm.:* 22 × 24pdr, 22 × 12pdr, 4 × 6pdr, 2 × 6pdr. *Des.:* Sir John Williams. *Built:* Sheerness Dockyard, Eng.; 1790.

HMS *Leopard* was laid down at Portsmouth Dockyard in 1775, but ten years later, still in frame, she was taken to Sheerness, where she was finally launched in 1790. She saw action in various theaters during the French Revolution and the Napoleonic Wars, including the Mediterranean and North American Stations. She was on duty with the latter in early 1807 when a number of sailors, both British and American citizens, deserted from HMS *Bellisle, Bellona, Triumph, Chichester, Halifax,* and *Zenobia,* then blockading the French 74s *Patriote* and *Eole* in Chesapeake Bay. A number of the sailors joined the crew of the 36-gun frigate

USS CHESAPEAKE, and Vice Admiral Sir George Berkeley, commander-in-chief of the North American Station, dispatched HMS *Leopard* to search the frigate.

On June 22, 1807, Captain Salisbury Pryce Humphreys was stationed off Cape Henry, Virginia, when he hailed USS CHESAPEAKE, outward bound for the Mediterranean under Commodore James Barron. A boat was sent over with a copy of Berkeley's order, but Barron refused a request to search his ship and at the same time ordered the gun deck quietly cleared for battle. The order came too late, for no sooner had the boarding party returned to *Leopard* than the British opened fire. Three broadsides followed, to be answered by only a single cannon shot before Barron surrendered his unready ship. Humphreys refused to accept the surrender but dispatched a boarding party to look for deserters, taking three Americans and the British sailor, who was tried and hanged at Halifax.

Although many subsequently saw in the *Chesapeake-Leopard* affair a prelude to the War of 1812, at the time it did little more than strain diplomatic relations between the United States and Britain. But even as late as 1843, Joseph Allen could regret that,

> as has in too many instances been the case, the spirited conduct of Vice Admiral Berkeley and of Captain Humphreys was disavowed by the British government; the British right of search was given up, and Vice Admiral Berkeley recalled from the North American command.

Leopard remained on the North American Station until 1812, when she was converted to a troopship. On June 28, 1814, she was en route from England to Quebec with 475 men of the Royal Scots Guards when she grounded on Anticosti Island in the Gulf of St. Lawrence in heavy fog. The ship was a total loss, although none of the crew or soldiers were lost.

Hepper, *British Warship Losses.* Strum, "*Leopard-Chesapeake* Incident of 1807." Tucker & Renter, *Injured Honor.*

Lexington

(ex-*Wild Duck*) Brigantine (2m). *L/B/D:* 94′ loa × 24.5′ × 11′ (28.7m × 7.5m × 3.4m). *Tons:* 210 bm. *Hull:* wood. *Comp.:* 110. *Arm.:* 14 × 4pdr, 2 × 6pdr, 12 swivels. *Built:* Philadelphia(?); ca. 1773.

Purchased by Abraham van Bibber for the Maryland Committee of Safety at St. Eustatius, the merchantman *Wild Duck* sailed from the Dutch West Indies to Philadelphia with a cargo of gunpowder in February 1776. Purchased by the Continental Congress's Marine Committee and renamed *Lexington,* in honor of the site of the first battle of the American Revolution on April 19, 1775 — "the shot heard round the world" — she was fitted out as a warship under Joshua Humphreys and put under command of Captain John Barry. According to the report of a British spy, she was distinguished by "two topgallant yards and royals, square tuck, painted yellow and a low round stern painted lead color, black sides and yellow mouldings."

On April 7, *Lexington* captured the tender *Edward,* in the Continental Navy's first victory in a single-ship action. Over the next six months, *Lexington's* crew captured two sloops and helped rescue a cargo of gunpowder from the stranded merchantman *Nancy.* Under Captain William Hallock, *Lexington* was captured by HMS *Pearl* (32 guns) en route from the Caribbean to Philadelphia. Seventy of her crew were confined below decks, but they managed to overwhelm the prize crew and return *Lexington* to Baltimore.

Under Captain Henry Johnson, *Lexington* sailed for France on February 20, 1777, seizing two prizes en route. Together with *Reprisal* and *Dolphin,* she embarked on a cruise during which the three vessels captured thirteen ships in the Irish Sea between June 18 and 25. Two days later, *Lexington* was forced into Morlaix, Brittany, where she remained until ordered out of France on September 13. Becalmed off Ushant on September 19, *Lexington* was brought to battle by HMS *Alert* (14), being forced to surrender when her powder was exhausted.

Millar, *Early American Ships.* U.S. Navy, *DANFS.*

Liberty

Sloop. *L/B:* 64′ × 18′ (19.5m × 5.5m). *Tons:* 85 bm. *Hull:* wood. *Built:* Massachusetts(?); <1768.

On June 10, 1768, Bostonians opposed to the Townshend Acts and intent on preventing customs commissioners from collecting duties on imported goods locked an official in the cabin of John Hancock's merchant sloop, *Liberty,* while the ship's cargo of Madeira wine was being landed. In retaliation, Hancock's ship was towed away from the dock by crew from the HMS *Halifax.* Although the protesting citizens of Boston forced the customs officials to take refuge in Castle William in Boston Harbor, the affair was eventually resolved in favor of the Crown, and *Liberty* was confiscated from Hancock.

The following April, *Liberty* was outfitted in Boston and, under Captain William Reid, patrolled off Rhode Island to inspect colonial vessels for customs violations. When the ship's crew abused Captain Joseph Packwood in Newport on July 19, 1769, the outraged citizens boarded the ship, cut her free, and scuttled her. The ship was later burned at Goat Island in the first open defiance of British authority in the colonies. An account written, but not published, at the time invited Reid to

> determine for the future to enter upon some employment worthy of a man and no longer disgrace and degrade himself by continuing to be an infamous detested tool, pimp and informer to a Board whose imperious arbitrary behavior have rendered them ridiculous and contemptible.

The guilty parties were never caught.

Millar, *Early American Ships.* Sherman, "An Accounting of His Majesty's Armed Sloop *Liberty.*"

HMS Little Belt

(ex-*Lille Belt*) Corvette, 6th rate (3m). *L/B/D:* 116.3′ × 30.3′ × 12.5′ (35.4m × 9.2m × 3.8m). *Tons:* 460 bm. *Hull:* wood. *Comp.:* 121. *Arm.:* 2 × 9pdr, 18 × 32pdr. *Des.:* Hohlenberg. *Built:* Copenhagen; 1801.

Throughout the Napoleonic Wars, when not neutral, Denmark was drawn into alliance with France, which resulted in her being invaded by the Royal Navy twice, first in 1801 and again in September 1807. In that year, a fleet of sixty-five warships under Vice Admiral James Gambier, accompanied by twenty-nine thousand soldiers under General Lord Cathcart, arrived off Copenhagen. After a four-day bombardment, the city surrendered and the British seized sixteen ships of the line, ten frigates, and forty-three other vessels; among these was *Lille Belt,* which was commissioned as HMS *Little Belt.* (The name is that of a strait between Fyn Island and mainland Denmark that connects the Kattegat with the Baltic.)

Put in service on the North American Station, in 1811 she became the focus of an incident between the United States and Great Britain that nearly brought about the War of 1812 a year early. In 1807, the Royal Navy had outraged American opinion when HMS LEOPARD fired on Commodore James Barron's frigate USS CHESAPEAKE and forcibly removed members of her crew, some of whom were former British sailors. Four years later, the frigate HMS GUERRIÈRE impressed an American seaman, and Commodore John Rodgers was ordered to sea with the frigate USS PRESIDENT in mid-May. Although he failed to find the *Guerrière,* on the night of May 17, 1811, the Americans caught up with and engaged *Little Belt* about forty-five miles from the mouth of Chesapeake Bay. Two broadsides were exchanged, and *Little Belt* was all but dismasted, with thirteen dead and nineteen wounded, before Captain Bingham broke off the engagement. Upon her return to Halifax, *Little Belt* was condemned as "almost a wreck" and sold. The vastly superior *President* survived the battle with hardly a mark, prompting Lord Howard Douglass to observe in his *Naval Gunnery:*

> If a vessel meet an enemy of even greatly superior force, it is due to the honor of her flag to try the ef-

fect of a few rounds; but unless in this gallant attempt she leave marks of her skill upon the larger body, while she, the smaller body, is hit at every discharge, she does but salute her enemy's triumph and discredit her own gunnery.

Roosevelt, *Naval War of 1812.*

HMS Little Belt

Sloop. *L/B/D:* 59′ bp × 16′ × 7′ dph (18m × 4.9m × 2.1m). *Tons:* 90 bm. *Hull:* wood. *Comp.:* 18. *Arm.:* 1 × 12pdr, 2 × 6pdr. *Built:* Fort Erie, Ont.; 1812.

Built for Captain Robert H. Barclay's Lake Erie Squadron, the second HMS *Little Belt* was named for the 18-gun sloop of war that had engaged USS PRESIDENT (38 guns) in 1811 in an incident that presaged the outbreak of the War of 1812. On September 10, 1813, *Little Belt* was one of five vessels in Barclay's line when it sailed against the fleet of Master Commandant Oliver Hazard Perry at the Battle of Lake Erie, off Put-In Bay. *Little Belt* was captured by the schooners *Scorpion* and *Chippeway* while trying to flee the scene of the disastrous battle, which spelled the end of British control of the Great Lakes. Following repairs, *Little Belt* joined the American fleet in time to help transport the army of General William Henry Harrison to Buffalo following its victory over the British at the Battle of the Thames on October 5. Blown ashore at Black Rock, New York, in a gale on December 8, *Little Belt* was burned by the British three weeks later.

Hepper, *British Warship Losses.* U.S. Navy, *DANFS.*

HMS London

London-class 2nd rate 90 (3m). *L/B/D:* 176.5′ × 46.5′ × 21′ (53.8m × 14.2m × 6.4m). *Tons:* 1,871 bm. *Hull:* wood. *Comp.:* 750. *Arm.:* 28 × 32pdr, 30 × 18pdr, 30 × 12pdr, 2 × 9pdr. *Built:* Chatham Dockyard, Eng.; 1766.

Built during the long peace between the Seven Years' War and the American Revolution, HMS *London* was the eighth ship of the name. Her chief distinction lies in her role as Rear Admiral Thomas

Graves's flagship during the Battle of the Chesapeake, where the Royal Navy's defeat resulted in the end of the American Revolution. In August 1780, Graves sailed in *London* with six ships of the line as reinforcements for Vice Admiral Marriott Arbuthnot, commander of the North American Station. On March 16, 1781, *London* was present in a skirmish with a French squadron under Chevalier Destouches off Chesapeake Bay. Graves succeeded Arbuthnot in July, and on August 28, he was joined by a fourteen-ship squadron under Rear Admiral Samuel Hood. With only five of his own ships ready for sea, Graves accompanied Hood in turning south for Chesapeake Bay to prevent a French squadron under Rear Admiral Count François Joseph Paul de Grasse from entering Chesapeake Bay and cutting off Major General Charles Cornwallis — then dug in on the Yorktown peninsula — and from landing reinforcements and provisions for General George Washington.

En route from the Caribbean, Hood had reconnoitered Chesapeake Bay on August 25 but found no sign of the French. De Grasse's fleet of twenty-seven ships arrived four days later and anchored off Cape Henry, where Graves and Hood found them on the morning of September 5. Rather than bear down on the French fleet while it was in disarray, Graves ordered his ships in line-ahead formation, as called for in the *Fighting Instructions,* with *London* in the middle of the line, Hood's BARFLEUR (90 guns) fourth in line, and Rear Admiral Francis S. Drake's *Princessa* (70) sixteenth in line. The French got under way at about noon, and at 1405 Graves ordered his captains to wear ship, changing course from west to east so that they paralleled the French on the same tack and putting Princessa in the van and *Barfleur* to the rear. Shortly after 1600, Graves raised the signal "to bear down and engage close," but he neglected to take down the signal for "line ahead," with drastic consequences. The van of the British line took the brunt of the French broadsides, and the middle squadron was closely engaged, but the seven ships in Hood's division barely took part in the battle. According to a published account, a conversation afterward took place between Graves, Hood, and Drake:

Admiral Graves asked Admiral Hood why he did not bear down and engage? The answer was: "You had up the signal for the line." Admiral Graves then turned to Admiral Drake, and asked him how he came to bear down? He replied: "On account of the signal for action." Admiral Graves then said: "What say you to this, Admiral Hood?" Sir Samuel answered: "The signal for the line was enough for me."

The fighting stopped by about 1815. Although both fleets intended to renew the engagement, light airs over the next few days made this impossible, and on the ninth Graves lost sight of the French fleet, which had doubled back toward the Chesapeake. The next evening, De Grasse rendezvoused in the bay with Comte de Barras de Saint-Laurent, who had arrived from Newport, Rhode Island, with eight ships. Graves returned to New York, where, over the next month, he was reinforced by six more ships of the line. On October 19, he sailed for the Chesapeake with twenty-five ships of the line and seven thousand troops. The same day, General Washington accepted Cornwallis's surrender at Yorktown. Graves arrived at the Chesapeake five days later, but upon hearing of the defeat, he returned to New York.

On November 10, *London* sailed for Jamaica but took no part in the British defeat of De Grasse and the capture of his VILLE DE PARIS at the Battle of the Saintes in April 1782. The only other battle for which *London* received battle honors was the action off the Ile de Groix on June 23, 1795. In this engagement, the Channel Fleet Squadron of Vice Admiral Alexander Hood, Viscount Bridport, captured three ships from Rear Admiral Louis Thomas Villaret de Joyeuse in a running battle off Brittany. *London* remained in service until broken up in 1811.

Clowes, *Royal Navy.* Larrabee, *Decision at the Chesapeake.*

Louisiana

Casemate ironclad. *L/B:* 264′ × 62′ (80.5m × 18.9m). *Tons:* 1,400. *Hull:* iron. *Arm.:* 2 × 7″, 3 × 9″, 4 × 8″, 7 × 32pdr. *Armor:* 4″ casemate. *Mach.:* 2 centerline paddlewheels, 2 screws. *Built:* E. C. Murray, New Orleans; 1862.

CSS *Louisiana* was one of two ironclads ordered for the defense of New Orleans (the other was CSS *Mississippi*). She was laid down in October 1861 and launched in February 1862, but inadequate supplies and labor delayed her completion. By April 19, when Flag Officer David G. Farragut began shelling Forts Saint Philip and Jackson at the mouth of the Mississippi, Commander John K. Mitchell ordered the still unfinished ship to the defense of the Mississippi. Although with the sides of her casemate set at a forty-five-degree angle she looked imposing, her arming and iron plating were incomplete. Moreover, the screw propulsion was not hooked up, and she had to be towed the ninety miles to the mouth of the river. Much to the consternation of his subordinates and superiors, Mitchell attempted to complete *Louisiana*'s fitting out upriver of the forts rather than use her with his other ships against the Union mortar boats. On the morning of April 24, 1862, Farragut began his run past the forts. Although *Louisiana* took part in the engagement, Farragut's fleet anchored at New Orleans the next day. On April 28, as the river ports were surrendering, Mitchell set *Louisiana* on fire, and she blew up.

Still, *Iron Afloat.* U.S. Navy, *DANFS.*

HMS Lutine

Frigate (3m). *L/B/D:* 143.2′ × 38.8′ × 12.2′ (43.6m × 11.8m × 3.7m). *Tons:* 951 bm. *Hull:* wood. *Comp.:* 240. *Arm.:* 6 × 24pdr, 26 × 12pdr, 10 × 6pdr. *Des.:* Joseph M. B. Coulombe. *Built:* Toulon, France; 1779.

La Lutine ("The Sprite") was commissioned in the French navy in 1785, just four years before the start of the French Revolution. On December 18, 1793, she was one of sixteen ships handed over to a British fleet under Vice Admiral Samuel Hood by French Royalists at Toulon who preferred that the ships go to their historical enemy rather than the revolutionary Republicans. Later the same year, she was commissioned in the Royal Navy as HMS *Lutine* and stationed on the North Sea.

In the fall of 1799, a consortium of London merchants anxious over the worsening conditions in Europe prevailed upon the Admiralty to allow them to ship a cargo of some £2 million in gold bullion, some of it intended for payment of British soldiers, to the Continent. It was a tense time for merchants and military strategists alike, as the Anglo-Russian coalition against the French in Holland was on the verge of collapse. *Lutine* sailed for Cuxhaven under Captain Lancelot Skynner on October 9. At about midnight that night, she was blown ashore in a gale on the coast of Vlieland, near the Zuider Zee, and lost with all hands but two, both of whom died shortly thereafter. Despite many attempts, little of the ship's cargo has ever been recovered. In 1859, the bell was found, however, and because Lloyds of London, the association of insurance underwriters, had taken an enormous loss when *Lutine* sank, the bell was returned to it. It has hung ever since in the Underwriting Room at Lloyds, where it is rung just before an important announcement. Traditionally, one ring preceded the announcement of the loss of a vessel, and two rings the arrival of a vessel previously reported overdue or missing.

Van der Molen, *"Lutine" Treasure.*

M

HMS Macedonian

Lively-class 5th rate 38 (3m). *L/B/D:* 154′ × 39.4′ × 13.5′ dph (46.9m × 12m × 4.1m). *Tons:* 1,082 bm. *Hull:* wood. *Comp.:* 362. *Arm.:* 14 × 32pdr, 28 × 18pdr, 4 × 9pdr. *Des.:* Sir William Rule. *Built:* Woolwich Dockyard, Eng.; 1810.

HMS *Macedonian* has the distinction of being the only British warship captured and returned to an American port during the War of 1812. On October 25, 1812, she encountered Captain Stephen Decatur's larger and more powerful USS UNITED STATES (44 guns) about 500 miles south of the Azores. The battle opened at about 0920, and by noon, *Macedonian* was shattered both in hull and crew. With 104 dead and wounded (as against only 12 American casualties), Captain John Surman Carden surrendered his vessel. After two weeks of repairs in mid-Atlantic, the two ships were able to proceed to New York, where they arrived in December. Purchased by the government and commissioned as USS *Macedonian,* in May 1813 she slipped out of New York with *United States* and the sloop HORNET; the three ships were forced, however, into New London, where they remained until war's end. In 1815, *Macedonian* joined the ten-ship Mediterranean Squadron sent to stop the harassment of U.S.-flag shipping by Barbary pirates, and on June 17, she helped capture the Algerian frigate *Mashuda.*

In 1819, *Macedonian* became the first ship to serve on the Pacific Station. Under Captain John Downes (first mate of USS ESSEX in 1813), she ranged as far north as Acapulco, protecting U.S. commerce in South America during a period of widespread revolt against Spanish rule led on the naval side by Chile's Scottish-born Admiral Lord Cochrane. Relieved by USS CONSTELLATION (Captain Charles G. Ridgely), *Macedonian* returned to the Atlantic seaboard in 1821. After five years in the West Indies, she returned for another year in the Pacific. In 1828, she was broken up at the Norfolk Navy Yard. As was the custom, some of her timbers were used in a second ship of the same name. This second *Macedonian* continued in service until 1875; some of her timbers eventually ended up in a City Island, New York, restaurant called Macedonia House.

De Kay, *Chronicles of the Frigate "Macedonian."*

Machault

Ship (3m). *L/B/D:* ca. 131.2′ × 36.1′ × 18′ (40m × 11m × 5.5m dph). *Tons:* 500–550 burthen. *Hull:* wood. *Comp.:* 150. *Arm.:* 28 × 12pdr, swivels. *Built:* Bayonne, France; 1758.

The Battle of the Restigouche, June 22 to July 8, 1760, was the last naval engagement between French and British forces in the Seven Years' War (also known as the French and Indian War), their struggle for primacy in North America. Although fought between minor units, the battle was a prelude to the French defeat in the war. In November 1759, *Machault* was sent from Quebec to France with an urgent plea for the relief of Montreal. The government's response was tepid; in lieu of the 4,000 troops requested, 400 were sent, along with as many supplies as could be found. On April 10, 1760, *Machault* sailed from Bourdeaux under Captain Giraudais at the head of a six-ship fleet. Two days out, two ships were captured by Boscawen's blockading fleet, and a third later sank. On May 16–17, Giraudais's ships captured seven merchantmen off the Gaspé Peninsula. Learning that a British force had preceded him up the St. Lawrence, Giraudais sailed, not for the Caribbean or Louisiana, as his orders dictated, but into Chaleur Bay because the area was a gathering place for displaced French Acadian refugees.

In the meantime, two British fleets were looking for the French, one under Captain John Byron in HMS *Fame* (74 guns) from Louisbourg, Nova Scotia, and the other from Quebec. Byron located the French force on June 22, but three days later *Fame* ran aground; the French failed to capitalize on their advantage, however, before she got off again. Over the next week, Byron's men searched for the channel, which they finally secured by July 1. Giraudais retreated upriver, sinking blockships and establishing shore batteries, but by July 8, three ships were within range of *Machault*. Giraudais struck at 1100 and an hour later blew up his ship near what is now Campbelltown. About thirty more sloops and schooners were sunk, burned, or captured.

Between 1969 and 1972, Canadian archaeologists under Walter Zacharchuk excavated the *Machault* site. Although little of the ship survived, large quantities of wineglasses, together with stoneware, cooking implements, personal possessions, ship's fittings, and other artifacts, were recovered.

Beattie & Pothier, "Battle of the Restigouche." Sullivan, *Legacy of the "Machault."*

USS Maine (BB-2/C)

Maine-class second-class armored battleship (2f/2m). *L/B/D:* 324.3′ × 57′ × 21.5′ (98.8m × 17.4m × 6.6m). *Tons:* 6,682 disp. *Hull:* steel. *Comp.:* 374. *Arm.:* 4 × 10″ (2 × 2), 6 × 6″, 7 × 6pdr, 8 × 1pdr; 4 × 18″TT. *Armor:* 11″ belt, 4″ deck. *Mach.:* vertical triple-expansion engine, 9,000 ihp, 2 screws; 17 kts. *Built:* New York Navy Yard, Brooklyn, N.Y.; 1895.

Laid down in 1888 as an armored cruiser and later designated as a second-class battleship, USS *Maine* was originally rigged as a bark, but the mizzen mast was removed in 1892. The ship's completion was delayed owing to a lack of available armor plate. Her primary armament was housed in two turrets, one starboard side forward, the other aft

and to port. Assigned to the North Atlantic Squadron at the end of 1895, she cruised along the East Coast of the United States from Maine to Key West.

In 1897, U.S. attention was focused on Cuban revolutionaries seeking independence from Spain. At the same time, navalists led by Under Secretary of the Navy Theodore Roosevelt sought to remove the threat of an extension of Japanese influence in the Pacific, especially with respect to the Spanish colony of the Philippines. Then, in response to escalating violence between Cuban revolutionaries and the Spanish authorities, President William McKinley ordered the North Atlantic Squadron moved to winter quarters at Key West, while the Mediterranean Squadron shifted to Lisbon, from where it could track any Spanish fleet movements toward the Caribbean. Finally, *Maine* was dispatched to Havana to show the flag and protect American interests.

Sailing from her homeport at Norfolk on December 11, 1897, *Maine* called at Key West four days later and departed there on January 24, 1898, arriving in Havana the following day. Tensions were so high that the crew were not permitted any liberty, and the ship remained at anchor in the center of the harbor off Morro Castle. At about 2140 on February 15, the forward part of the hull was destroyed in a huge explosion that left 252 people dead and missing. Although Captain Charles D. Sigsbee's initial report cautioned that "public opinion should be suspended until further report," Richard Wainwright, director of the Office of Naval Intelligence, put forth the suggestion that the ship had been blown up. A U.S. naval court of inquiry led by Captain William T. Sampson concluded that the explosion was the result of an underwater mine, although it was "unable to obtain evidence fixing responsibility for the destruction of the *Maine* upon any person or persons."

Fueled by a jingoist press in the full bloom of yellow journalism, American popular opinion wanted a war with Spain, and Congress declared war on April 21, 1898. By the end of the Spanish-American War, Spain had lost the Philippines to the United States, and Cuba had gained its independence. Twelve years later, *Maine* was raised, to

▲ The second-class battleship **Maine.** *Photo by Hugh C. Leighton Co., Portland, Maine. Author collection.*

be sunk at sea with full military honors on March 12, 1914.

Debate over the cause of the explosion continued for the next century. A Spanish investigation suggested that an internal explosion destroyed the ship, an opinion supported by, among others, Commodore George W. Melville, chief of the Bureau of Steam Engineering. But when the ship was raised in 1912, a follow-up investigation supported the finding of Sampson's original board of inquiry. However, in 1975, civilian navy researchers prepared a technical examination concluding that "the available evidence is consistent with an internal explosion alone. . . . The most likely source was heat from a fire in the coal bunker adjacent to the 6-inch reserve magazine."

Blow, *Ship to Remember.* Rickover, *How the Battleship "Maine" Was Destroyed.* U.S. Navy, *DANFS.*

Mainz ships

Discovered during construction of a new hotel in the 1980s, the fourth-century Mainz ships consist of nine major hull fragments from five different vessels. They were originally part of a Roman flotilla situated at the fortress of Mogontiacum (Mainz), the capital of the Roman province of Germania Superior on the Rhine River, about halfway between the North Sea and modern Basel, Switzerland. It appears that the site (located in 50°N, 8°16′E) was actually a breaker's yard, and the ships seem to have been stripped of useful fittings. Construction details of the lightly built hulls are similar. The oak strakes are less than one inch thick, excluding mortise-and-tenon joinery. The hulls were apparently built in two stages. First, the thin strakes were fastened by wooden pegs to the "moulding frames" of a temporary skeleton, thus forming a shell into which permanent frames could be inserted in the conventional Mediterranean "shell-first" fashion. The moulding frames were then removed, and the strakes were fastened to the permanent frames by iron nails clenched on the frames' inner surfaces.

Five vessels of two types have been identified. (The numbering is confused because several fragments identified as being separate ships were later found to be part of the same one.) Ships 1, 4, 7, and 9 are slender, open vessels called *lusoriae*, general-purpose cutters used extensively on the Rhine and Danube Rivers. About 21 meters long, 2.5 meters wide, and 1 meter deep (69 feet by 8 feet by 3 feet),

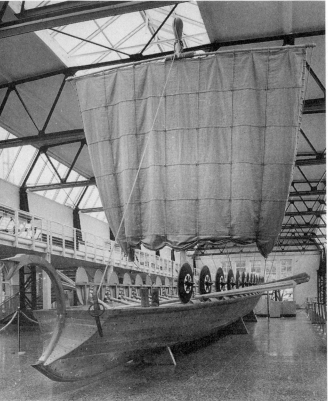

Ancient Shipping) in Mainz, together with reconstructions of the two ship types represented by the finds.

Höckmann, "Late Roman Rhine Vessels from Mainz, Germany"; "Late Roman River Craft from Mainz, Germany."

CSS Manassas

(ex-*Enoch Train*) Ironclad ram (1f). *L/B/D:* 143′ × 33′ × 17′ (43.6m × 10.1m × 5.2m). *Tons:* 387. *Hull:* wood. *Comp.:* 36. *Arm.:* 1 × 32pdr, 1 × 12pdr, 4 × double-shot. *Armor:* 1.5″ belt. *Mach.:* 1 low-pressure and 1 high-pressure engine, 1 screw; 6 kts. *Built:* Paul Curtis & Harrison Loring, Medford, Mass.; 1855.

Built as a river towboat for service on the Mississippi River, in 1861 the single-screw steamer *Enoch Train* was purchased by Captain J. A. Stevenson for use as a privateer. Clad with 1.5-inch iron plate over a concave frame and armed with a 32-pdr gun and an iron ram, *Manassas* (named for the site of a Confederate victory) had a freeboard of only 1.5 inches and presented an extremely low target. Resembling a floating cigar, the "hellish machine" was both unmaneuverable and slow, traits common to most southern ironclads. Shortly after her conversion, she was appropriated by the Confederate Navy for use on the lower Mississippi. Under Lieutenant A. F. Worley, she took part in an attack on the Union blockade at Head of Passes on October 12 and lost her ram in an attack on USS *Richmond*. When Flag Officer David G. Farragut's fleet forced its way past Forts Jackson and St. Philip on April 24, 1862, *Manassas* rammed USS Mississippi and *Brooklyn*, though neither decisively. Trailing Farragut's force upriver, she came under withering fire from *Mississippi*. Run aground and abandoned by her crew, she was set on fire, drifted free, and blew up.

Still, *Iron Afloat.* U.S. Navy, *DANFS.*

they were ideally suited for various types of work, including ramming German dugouts, supplying outposts along the river, and amphibious operations. They had a single mast but were normally propelled by 30 oarsmen at a top speed of 10 knots. The ships were steered by a pair of oars mounted about 2.1 meters forward of the sternpost and held in place by a transverse beam. Ship 3 is a *navis cubiculata* or *iudiciaria* (an inspection boat), shorter and wider (16 meters by 3 meters) and with a small cabin probably intended for visiting officials. Although the vessel probably had a mast, the exact means of propulsion is unknown. One conjecture is that there were outriggers of a sort, and that it was rowed by standing oarsmen.

The vessels were excavated under the supervision of Dr. G. Rupprecht. They are now displayed at the Museum für Antike Seefahrt (Museum of

Mary

Yacht (1m). *L/B/D:* 52′ (keel) × 19.1′ × 7.6′ dph (15.8m × 5.8m × 2.3m). *Tons:* 100 burthen. *Hull:* wood. *Comp.:* 28 crew; 50 pass. *Arm.:* 2 × 4pdr, 6 × 3pdr, 1 × 1.5pdr. *Built:* Amsterdam; < 1660.

Although the British have cultivated yachting to a higher degree than any other nation, the concept of the yacht was originally imported from the Netherlands in the seventeenth century. England's sea-minded Charles II had a ready appreciation for good ships, and when he sailed from Breda to Rotterdam on the first leg of his return from ten years of exile in Europe, he expressed his admiration for the luxuriously appointed Dutch *jacht* that had been put at his disposal. Amsterdam's Burgomeister Van Vlooswick thereupon arranged for his city to give a vessel of similar construction to the King. Named for Charles's sister, who was also the widow of William II of Orange, *Mary* spent a year as the official royal yacht. The word derives from the Dutch word for "hunt."

The one-masted *Mary* drew only five feet (one and a half meters) but was fitted with leeboards that gave her a maximum draft of about ten feet (three meters). This arrangement was typical of the vessels designed for work in the shallow waters off the Dutch coast, but it was not well suited to English sailing. After a year, *Mary* was transferred to the navy for service as a dispatch boat and transport for members of court and other officials. But the idea of pleasure yachts had taken hold, and four yachts of similar design — though of deeper draft and without leeboards — were ordered from the Royal Dockyards in 1662–63. Pepys described *Katherene*, designed by Peter Pett, as "one of the finest things that ever I saw for neatness and room in so small a vessel." Other yachts soon followed, and by 1686, twenty-six had been commissioned. It is interesting to note that the practice of gaudy names is as old as yachting itself: Charles built *The Folly*, Prince Rupert built *Fanfan*, and *Jamie* was named for the Duke of York.

In the meantime, *Mary* was stationed in the Irish Sea, mainly sailing between Holyhead, on the island of Anglesey, and Ireland. During the second (1665–67) and third (1672–74) Anglo-Dutch Wars, she also engaged in antiprivateering duty in the Irish Sea. At about 0200 on March 25, 1675, she was en route from Dublin to Chester when she struck a rock in the Skerries about seven miles from Holyhead and sank, with the loss of thirty-five of her seventy-four passengers and crew. The ship remained undisturbed where she sank (53°25′N, 4°36′W) until July 1971, when two groups of divers from the British Sub Aqua Club independently discovered the wreck site. Among the artifacts recovered were six English and two Dutch bronze guns, coins from the reigns of Elizabeth, Charles I, and Charles II, gold lockets, and various wares in silver and pewter.

Heaton, *Yachting: A History*. McBride, "*Mary*."

Mary Rose

Carrack (4m). *L/B/D:* 105′ (keel) × 38.3′ × 15.1′ (32m × 11.97m × 4.6m). *Tons:* 600 burthen; after 1536, 700. *Hull:* wood. *Comp.:* 415. *Arm.:* 78; after 1536, 91. *Built:* Portsmouth Dockyard, Eng.; 1510.

At the beginning of the sixteenth century, ships were used primarily for moving troops, and sea fights consisted of pitched battles at close quarters in which crew and soldiers fought for the capture of the enemy ship. Even after the development of cannon in the fourteenth century, naval guns were essentially for use against opposing soldiers and sailors massed in preparation for a boarding action. Fighting ships tended to have towering "castles" fore and aft, from which gunners and archers could fire down onto their opponents. The evolution of antiship gunnery became possible with the development of guns of increased range and weight of shot. Because of stability requirements, these could only be mounted low down in the ship, and this only after watertight gunports were developed in the early 1500s.

The oldest extant ship in which these converging technologies is seen is *Mary Rose*, Henry VIII's carvel-built flagship (named for his younger sister), and one of the first English purpose-built warships. Constructed at Portsmouth, she was armed at London with guns manufactured by the

▲ Henry VIII's **Mary Rose**, as depicted in the Anthony Roll — an inventory of the King's ships — prepared by Anthony Anthony in 1546, one year after the **Mary Rose** sank off Portsmouth while sailing out to battle the French. *Courtesy Pepys Library, Magdalene College, Cambridge.*

Belgian Hans Poppenreuter, among others. One indication of the increasing importance of antiship gunnery is the fact that *Mary Rose* carried 200 sailors, 185 soldiers, and 30 gunners, while her predecessors generally carried more soldiers; the larger *Sovereign*, for instance, carried 300 sailors and 400 soldiers. Not only was *Mary Rose* an impressive gun platform, but she also handled well. In 1513, Admiral Sir Edward Howard reported to the King, "Sir, she is the noblest shipp of sayle and grett shipp at this hour that I trow be in Christendom. A shipp of 100 tonne wyl not be soner . . . abowt then she."

In 1511, *Mary Rose* sailed as flagship of Howard's fleet of twenty ships patrolling, with a Spanish fleet, between Brest and the then-English port of Calais. The next year, Henry joined the Holy League of the Papal States and Venice in an effort to contain France's Louis XII. On August 10, 1512, Howard attacked the French fleet at Brest, where he took or destroyed 32 French ships and captured 800 prisoners. The French flagship, LA COR- DELIÈRE, lost all but 6 of her 1,500 crew when she and the English *Regent* caught fire, the latter losing all but 180 of her 700 crew. In April 1513, Howard was killed at the blockade of Brest, and Henry named his older brother Sir Thomas Howard as his replacement. That summer, *Mary Rose* helped bring an English army to Calais (later victorious at the Battle of the Spurs) and then sailed north to Scotland, where Howard took part in the defeat of James IV at the Battle of Flodden Field. *Mary Rose* continued in service until 1536, when Henry embarked on a rebuilding program. She emerged from this armed with 91 guns — some newly made — including bronze culverins, demi-culverins, sakers, and falcons.

In 1544, *Mary Rose* was used in Henry's operations against France. In 1545, Francis I mounted an invasion of Portsmouth with a force of 30,000 troops carried in 235 ships. Henry's defensive fleet consisted of only 60 ships at Portsmouth, with

40 more en route, manned by a total of 12,000 crew. On July 18, the French fleet arrived in the Solent between the Isle of Wight and Portsmouth, and the English fleet weighed anchor. *Mary Rose* came under Vice Admiral Sir George Carew, who had been appointed that same day. Although Admiral Claude d'Annebault's flagship, *La Maîtresse,* sprang a leak and sank off St. Helen's, the French fleet was tactically well positioned. The following morning, French galleys advanced on the English fleet, taking Henry Grace à Dieu under fire. Then the wind sprang up from the north, and the English fleet advanced. Unfortunately, her undisciplined crew — Carew's last known words, to a passing ship: "I have the sort of knaves I cannot rule" — had neither secured the guns nor closed the gunports. Suddenly *Mary Rose* heeled, flooded, and sank, with the loss of all but thirty-five of her complement. Despite the loss, and the fact that the French landed troops both on the Isle of Wight and on the coast of Sussex four days later, the French campaigning was indecisive, and by August 17, d'Annebault's fleet was back at Le Havre. That the French force was equal in determination and superior in execution to the Spanish Armada of 1588 is a fact little known today.

Efforts to salvage *Mary Rose* started immediately but resulted only in the salvage of some guns. In 1836, the pioneering divers John and Charles Deane investigated the wreck. They recovered four bronze and four complete wrought-iron guns (and broken pieces of several others) before they stopped work in 1840. After this, the site of *Mary Rose* was again forgotten. In 1965, military historian Alexander McKee began Project Solent Ships to investigate the wrecks of HMS *Boyne,* Royal George, and *Mary Rose,* the last being the chief object of his search. The ship was positively identified in 1970, lying in 50°45'N, 1°06'W. Twelve years later, after careful excavation and preparation under the guidance of Margaret Rule and with the active participation of Prince Charles, the remaining starboard portion of her hull was raised and housed at Portsmouth Naval Base, where it is on public display.

Among the chief points of archaeological interest is the fact that, in McKee's words,

the *Mary Rose* represents a day in the life of Tudor England. You cannot get that sort of information from libraries; you cannot get it from excavating a land site. . . . What you have in the *Mary Rose* is a four- or five-storey structure complete with everything it contained on that day in 1545.

This includes artifacts used by surgeons, archers, and navigators as well as clothing and other objects in daily use. (Certain organic material, such as linen and horn, does not survive.) The ship is also important to the study of naval architecture, as her construction antedates the use of drawn plans. The surviving pictorial and written record of Tudor-era ships is otherwise scarce.

Bradford, *Story of the "Mary Rose."* McKee, *King Henry VIII's "Mary Rose."* Rule, *"Mary Rose."*

Michael

(also *Great Michael*) Ship. *L/B:* 240' × 36' (73.2m × 11m). *Tons:* ca. 1,000. *Hull:* wood. *Comp.:* 300 crew, 120 gunners, 1,000 soldiers. *Arm.:* 3 basilisks, 12 cannon, 300 mayans, falcons, and quarter falcons. *Des.:* Jacques Terrell. *Built:* Newhaven, Leith, Scotland; 1512.

The early sixteenth century was a revolutionary period in the development of European warships. Until this time, ships served primarily as troop transports; when ships did engage, the battles were decided in boarding actions and hand-to-hand combat. The new ingredient in naval warfare was naval guns capable of damaging ships or land structures at a distance. One of the first monarchs to invest heavily in this technology was James IV. In a series of campaigns that lasted from 1494 to 1506, James employed shipboard guns to force his more independent subjects in the western isles to submit to his authority as King of Scots. Heavy guns require stout ships, and as the size and efficiency of the Scottish fleet grew, so, too, did the size of the individual ships, the biggest of which was the *Michael,* commonly known as *Great Michael.*

Although the earliest written account of the ship is the late-sixteenth-century *Historie* of Robert Lindsay of Pitscottie — "as quotable as it is generally unreliable" — his description squares with the available archival evidence. According to Lindsay, *Michael* was "the greattest scheip and maist of strength that ewer saillit in Ingland or France." As such, she excited the admiration of James's ally, Louis XII, and the envy of the young Henry VIII, the design of whose HENRI GRACE À DIEU of 1514 may well have been influenced by that of *Michael*. One curious bit of evidence for the size of the ship can be found on the site of Tullibardine Castle in Perthshire, where the outline of "the length and breid of hir" was planted in hawthorn trees.

The ship's primary ordnance consisted of three basilisks, two mounted aft and one mounted to five forward, with six smaller cannon on either side of the ship. The ship's guns were probably cast in Flanders, then a center of gun founding in Europe. The gun crews numbered 120, and in addition to these and her 300 crew, *Michael* could carry 1,000 soldiers. The cost of the ship was staggering: £30,000 Scots, or nearly one year's income for the Crown, to build the ship, and a further one-fifth of the treasury to keep her fully manned. Such lavish spending on naval forces was not unheard of, and unlike his contemporaries, James had a fairly coherent naval strategy. Apart from the relative poverty of his kingdom, his biggest concern was Henry VIII of England. To contain his younger brother-in-law, he concluded alliances with Denmark and the Hanseatic League, which held the key to England's Baltic trade, and Louis XII of France.

In 1513, Louis offered James the equivalent of £22,500 Scots and the use of a fleet of galleys under Gaston Prégent de Bidoux in exchange for a guarantee that James would send his fleet to the English Channel should Henry invade France. In June 1513, Henry embarked for Calais, but James's fleet of eleven or more ships did not sail until July 25. When it did, the fleet's commander, James Hamilton, Earl of Arran, sailed northabout Scotland to Ulster, where he burned the English stronghold of Carrickfergus. After landing at Ayr on the Scottish coast, he proceeded to Brest, where the Scottish fleet arrived by early September. The Franco-Scottish fleet was dispersed by a gale, and *Michael* later

ran aground at Honfleur and was not refloated until November. In the meantime, Henry had returned to England from Calais, and James had been killed by the English at the Battle of Flodden, leaving as his heir the infant James V.

Under the circumstances, the Scottish regents had little choice but to downsize their navy, and *Michael* was sold to the French for £18,000 Scots. "La Grande Nef d'Ecosse" proved a valuable substitute in the navy of Francis I, who succeeded Louis XII in 1515. Details of her career under the French flag are scant, although it is known that in October 1521 she led a fleet in the successful siege of the Spanish port of Fuertaventura. Although some have suggested that she participated in the French raid on Portsmouth in 1545 during which Henry VIII's MARY ROSE sank, *Michael*'s ultimate fate is unknown.

Macdougall, "'Greatest Scheip That Ewer Saillit'"; *James IV*. Rodger, *Safeguard of the Sea*.

Mikasa

Pre-dreadnought battleship (2f/2m). *L/B/D:* 432' × 76' × 27' (131.7m × 23.2m × 8.3m). *Tons:* 15,440 disp. *Hull:* steel. *Comp.:* 773. *Arm.:* 4 × 12.2" (2 × 2), 14 × 6.1", 20 × 7.6cm, 12 × 47mm; 5 × 18"TT. *Armor:* 9" belt, 3" deck. *Mach.:* vertical triple expansion, 15,000 ihp, 2 screws; 18 kts. *Built:* Vickers Sons & Maxim, Barrow-in-Furness, Eng.; 1896.

Japan began expanding its navy in the early 1890s, turning first to France and later to England for large warships for which it did not have the industrial capacity. In 1893 and 1894, the Japanese navy ordered six battleships from British yards, the largest of which was *Mikasa*, a ship similar in design to Britain's own *Majestic*-class battleships and, for a few months after her building, the largest warship in the world. Although the original impetus for Japan's military buildup had been friction with China, Japan defeated China at the Battle of the Yalu in 1894 and went on to occupy Korea and, briefly, Port Arthur in Manchuria. Forced to relinquish this naval base by pressure from European countries, Japan was galled when Russia occupied the Liaotung Peninsula and Port Arthur (Lüshun, China) in 1898.

On February 8, 1904, *Mikasa* was Admiral Heihachiro Togo's flagship during the Japanese surprise attack by destroyers on the Russian Far Eastern Fleet at Port Arthur. This was followed the next day by a bombardment of the port, during which *Mikasa* was hit several times. Although only three of eighteen torpedoes hit their targets, the Russians had lost the initiative. On August 10, Rear Admiral Vilgelm Karlovich Vitgeft attempted a breakout to Vladivostok, on the Sea of Japan opposite Hokkaido. Although *Mikasa* was hit twenty-three times and had to undergo extensive repairs, the Battle of the Yellow Sea was a clear defeat for the Russians. Vitgeft was killed when his flagship *Tsarevich* was hit by a twelve-inch shell, and the Russian fleet quickly retired to Port Arthur in disorder. (*Tsarevich* escaped to the German-occupied port of Tsingtao, where she was interned.) In December, the Japanese took Port Arthur from the landward side, and by the end of January 1905, the Russians had lost all seven battleships of the Far Eastern Fleet.

Meanwhile, in September 1904, Admiral Zinovi Petrovich Rozhestvensky had left Kronstadt with the Baltic Fleet at the start of an 18,000-mile voyage around the Cape of Good Hope to Vladivostok. As the fleet steamed through the narrow Korea Strait on May 27, 1905, it was attacked by the Japanese fleet near the island of Tsushima. Rozhestvensky's force included four new and four older battleships, four coast defense ships, and six cruisers (including *Aurora*). Togo had only four battleships, two armored cruisers, and six cruisers. But what the Japanese lacked in numbers they made up for in speed, experience, and morale.

Togo used his battleships' six-knot superiority in speed to outflank the Russian fleet, concentrating first on the flagship. *Kniaz Suvarov* was quickly knocked out of line and eventually sank. Within five hours, the new battleships *Imperator Alexander III* and *Borodino* were also sunk, with the loss of all but one of their 1,692 crew, while *Orel* was captured. Total Russian losses included ten ships sunk (among them six battleships) and four captured; three ships were interned and one escaped. The Japanese lost no ships. *Mikasa* was hit thirty-two times by Russian shells but suffered only eight dead.

On September 12, a magazine explosion killed 114 of *Mikasa*'s crew and left her sunk at her moorings. In August 1906, she was refloated, but her fighting days were over. On September 20, 1923, she was stricken from the list of commissioned ships and preserved as a memorial. At the end of World War II, she was stripped of her fittings in a compromise between the Soviet Union, which wanted her scrapped, and the United States. Fifteen years later, she was restored as a memorial at Yokosuka, thanks in large part to help offered by Admiral Chester Nimitz, USN.

Breyer, *Battleships and Battle Cruisers.* Heine, *Historic Ships of the World.*

USS Mississippi

Mississippi-class sidewheel steamer (1f/3m). *L/B/D:* 229' × 40' (66.5'ew) × 21.8' (69.8m × 12.2m [20.1m] × 6.6m). *Tons:* 3,220 disp. *Hull:* wood. *Comp.:* 257. *Arm.:* 2 × 10", 8 × 8". *Mach.:* sidelever engines, 700 nhp, sidewheels; 11 kts. *Des.:* John Lenthall, Hartt & Humphries. *Built:* Philadelphia Navy Yard; 1841.

One of the first sidewheel steam frigates ordered for the U.S. Navy, USS *Mississippi* was built under the personal supervision of Commodore Matthew Perry, formerly commander of USS *Fulton II* and a strong advocate of steam propulsion. Rigged as a bark, *Mississippi* was used extensively to test the utility of steam for naval operations. As with all paddle frigates, her greatest deficiency was that the placement of her paddles interfered with the guns, and her engines were vulnerable to enemy fire.

In 1845, she sailed as Perry's flagship in the West Indian Squadron during the Mexican War, and she took part in the blockade of Mexican Gulf and Caribbean coast ports, as well as in the capture of Veracruz, Tuxpan, and Tabasco in 1847. With the return of peace, *Mississippi* cruised in the Mediterranean from 1849 to 1851. Calling at Constantinople in 1851, she embarked Hungarian nationalist Lajos Kossuth and fifty fugitives from the Austrian government, then returned to the United States.

Placed once more under Perry's command, in 1852 she sailed for the Far East with his mission, which was charged specifically with opening trade with Japan. His first visit to Edo (Tokyo) in July served to awe the Japanese with his "black ships" (the others were USS POWHATAN and *Susquehanna*) — the first steamships to visit Japan. Perry returned the following year and concluded the Treaty of Kanagawa on March 31, 1854. Except for a visit to the United States in 1855–56, *Mississippi* remained in the Orient until 1860, supporting French and British vessels in the bombardment of Taku on June 25, 1859, and landing marines to protect U.S. interests at Shanghai in August.

Mississippi returned to Boston in 1860 and remained there until assigned to blockade duty off Key West in June 1861. Joining Flag Officer David G. Farragut's fleet for the assault on New Orleans, on April 7, 1863, she became the largest vessel to cross the bar of the river whose name she bore. As the Union fleet ran past Forts Jackson and St. Philip, *Mississippi* destroyed CSS MANASSAS before proceeding to New Orleans, where she remained until 1863. Farragut then ordered her to take part in the run past Port Hudson, the largest Confederate fort below Vicksburg, in company with the screw steamers USS HARTFORD, MONONGAHELA, and *Richmond*. On March 14, 1863, she had just passed Port Hudson when she ran aground. Still within range of the Confederate batteries, she came under devastating fire that killed sixty-four of her crew. Despite efforts of his crew

and officers, including his executive officer George Dewey, Captain Melancthon Smith ordered her set afire and abandoned.

Anderson, *By Sea and by River*. Hagan, *This People's Navy*. Morison, "*Old Bruin*." Perry, *Narrative of the Expedition of an American Squadron to the China Seas and Japan*. U.S. Navy, *DANFS*.

USS Monitor

Monitor. *L/B/D:* 179' × 41.5' × 10.5' (54.6m × 12.6m × 3.2m). *Tons:* 987 disp. *Hull:* iron. *Comp.:* 49. *Arm.:* 2 × 11" (2 × 1). *Armor:* 4.5" belt, 8" turret. *Mach.:* vibrating-lever engines, 320 ihp, 1 screw; 6 kts. *Des.:* John Ericsson. *Built:* Continental Iron Works, Green Point, N.Y. (hull), Novelty Iron Works, New York (turret), and Delamater & Co., New York (engine); 1862.

Shortly after the start of the Civil War, U.S. Navy Secretary Gideon Welles learned of Confederate plans to raise the hull of USS *Merrimack,* which

▼ A Currier and Ives lithograph showing "The Terrific Combat Between the **Monitor** 2 Guns and **Merrimac** 10 Guns: The first between iron clad ships of war, in Hampton Roads, March 9, 1862, in which the little **Monitor** whipped the **Merrimac** and the whole 'school' of rebel steamers." At far left, the **USS Minnesota**; at far right, the Rebel steamers. *Courtesy U.S. Naval Academy, Annapolis, Maryland.*

Federal forces had burned and sunk in their flight from Norfolk's Gosport Navy Yard, and to convert it into an ironclad. To counter the threat posed by such a vessel, he authorized research into the feasibility of an armored steamship clad in either iron or steel. Despite the fact that the French and British had already commissioned La Gloire and HMS Warrior, respectively, most American naval architects of the day considered the project impracticable. "No iron-clad vessel of equal displacement [to a wooden vessel]," they argued, "can be made to obtain the same speed as one not thus encumbered." Welles's advisory board nonetheless proposed that three different designs be tried — two broadside ironclads, which became USS New Ironsides and the poorly armored Galena, and one with a revolving turret.

John Ericsson had designed such a vessel for Napoleon III during the Crimean War. Although the inventor had washed his hands of any involvement with the U.S. Navy following its treatment of him after the tragic explosion aboard USS Princeton in 1844, his colleague Cornelius S.

Bushnell (then building Galena) introduced Ericsson to Welles. Welles then invited Ericsson to Washington to present his model to President Abraham Lincoln and the navy board. On October 4, 1861, he was given a contract for the ship, with the stipulation that all monies be refunded to the navy if construction was not completed in 100 days. In the course of her construction, Ericsson reportedly devised no less than forty patentable inventions. He also chose the name, asserting that "to the Lords of the Admiralty the new craft will be a monitor, suggesting doubts as to the propriety of completing those four steel ships" (harmless blockade-runners) — he was a master of self-promotion — then building for the Confederacy in English yards.

The finished product was revolutionary in the extreme. The iron vessel consisted of two parts, a hull (122 feet by 34 feet) upon which rested an iron "raft" (172 feet by 41 feet), the dual function of which was to protect the hull from ramming and to provide the vessel with stability in a seaway. Within the hull were living spaces for 41 crew, an engine room (where the temperature reportedly reached 178°F/81°C), and storage spaces for coal and ammunition. Visually and technologically, Monitor's most distinguishing feature was the rotating turret, built up of 8 layers of one-inch iron plate and measuring 20 feet in diameter and 9 feet high. Mounted on a steam-powered spindle, the circular turret mounted two 7-ton Dahlgren smoothbore guns. Also protruding from the deck were two ventilation pipes and two funnels aft, and forward a

▼ A general plan of the "iron clad steamer" **USS Monitor** "deduced from the original drawings of Capt. John Ericsson and from actual measurements taken from the actual vessel." The barrels of the eleven-inch guns can be seen in the center turret, which is almost as deep as the hull. The ship was conned from the smaller forward turret, accessed via a ladder. The machinery, aft, led to a single propeller. *Courtesy U.S. Naval Historical Center, Washington, D.C.*

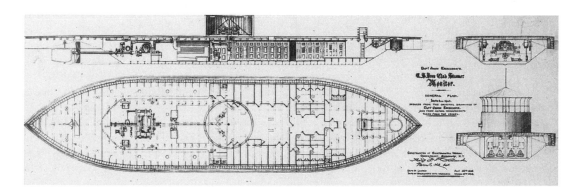

pilot house with 9-inch armor. She was the first warship built without rigging or sails.

Laid down on October 25, 1861, and launched January 30, 1862, USS *Monitor* was commissioned on February 25 under Lieutenant John L. Worden. It was originally intended that *Monitor* join Flag Officer David G. Farragut's West Gulf Blockading Squadron at New Orleans, but Farragut sailed before she was ready. Instead, she was sent to Washington, D.C., leaving New York on March 6 in tow of the screw steamer *Seth Low.* Two days later, she entered Chesapeake Bay just as CSS VIRGINIA — the former *Merrimac* — was attacking the wooden USS CONGRESS and CUMBERLAND in Hampton Roads. That night, Captain Morston, the senior officer at Hampton Roads, ordered *Monitor* to assist the beleaguered USS *Minnesota.*

On the morning of May 9, as *Virginia* approached to finish off the grounded frigate, *Monitor* slipped out of the shadow of the larger ship to challenge the Confederate ironclad. *Monitor* and *Virginia* battled each other for four hours, but neither was able to inflict serious damage on the other. Worden used his ship's superior maneuverability to avoid ramming and shelling by his adversary, but even so, her turret was hit twenty-four times. The two ships were well matched, and although *Virginia* was hard aground for an hour, *Monitor*'s and *Minnesota*'s shot could not penetrate her iron plate. At about 1130, fragments from one of *Virginia*'s shot flew through the eyeslit of *Monitor*'s pilot house. The partially blinded Worden ordered gunnery officer Lieutenant S. D. Greene to take *Monitor* into shallow waters, which he did forty-five minutes later. *Virginia* also broke off the engagement, and so the first battle between ironclad ships ended, and with it the age of the wooden fighting ship.

As long as *Virginia* remained in commission, the Union had no choice but to leave *Monitor* where she was as a deterrent. The Confederates were forced to destroy their ironclad on May 11 when they abandoned Norfolk in the face of General George McClellan's offensive up the Yorktown Peninsula toward Richmond. In company with

USS *Galena* and *Naugatuck, Monitor* then proceeded up the James River to Drury's Bluff, about eight miles below the Confederate capital. Their way stopped by obstructions in the river and heavy Confederate artillery, the ironclads withdrew on May 15. *Monitor* remained in the vicinity through the end of the year, covering the Union retreat after the Seven Days Battle in June and serving on blockade duty at Hampton Roads thereafter.

On December 29, USS *Rhode Island* towed her out of Hampton Roads bound for the blockade off Wilmington, North Carolina. At about 0130 on December 31, 1862, *Monitor* foundered in a storm off Cape Hatteras, taking with her four officers and twelve crew. Her exact location remained unknown until scientists aboard the research ship *Eastward* located her remains on August 27, 1973. Designated a National Marine Sanctuary in 1975, *Monitor* lies in 225 feet of water at about 35°N, 75°23′E, sixteen miles south-southeast of Cape Hatteras Light.

Cox & Jehle, eds., *Ironclad Intruder.* Delgado, *A Symbol of American Ingenuity.* Miller, *USS "Monitor."* Nash, "Civil War Legend Examined." Still, "*Monitor* Companies."

USS Monongahela

Sloop of war (1f/3m). *L/B/D:* 225′ bp × 38′ × 15.1′ (68.6m × 11.6m × 4.6m). *Tons:* 2,078 disp. *Hull:* wood. *Comp.:* 176. *Arm:* 1 × 200pdr, 2 × 11″, 2 × 24pdr, 4 × 12pdr. *Mach.:* horizontal back-acting engines, 532 ihp, 1 screw; 12 kts. *Built:* Merrick & Sons, Philadelphia; 1863.

Commissioned in 1863 with a barkentine rig, the auxiliary screw sloop USS *Monongahela* was named for the Pennsylvania tributary of the Ohio River. After service in the North Atlantic and with Flag Officer David G. Farragut's West Gulf Blockading Squadron off Mobile, Alabama, she began duty on the Mississippi River in March 1863, when she attempted to run past Fort Hudson. In October, she sailed for the Texas coast and took part in the capture of Brazos Santiago and Brownsville at the beginning of November. In the spring of 1864, she resumed blockade duty off Mobile. On August 4, she sailed with Farragut's fleet at the Battle of Mobile Bay. After running past Fort Morgan, she was the first ship to ram CSS TENNESSEE, though she did more damage to herself than to the Confederate ironclad.

Monongahela remained with the West Gulf Squadron through the end of the Civil War, after which she was assigned to the West Indies Squadron. On November 18, 1867, while lying off Frederiksted, St. Croix, she was swept a mile and a half inland on a tsunami. The ship was refloated four months later and towed to New York for repairs. In 1873, she sailed for a three-year tour of duty on the South Atlantic Squadron. After duty as a training ship, she sailed for the West Coast and was converted to an engineless, bark-rigged supply ship in 1883. Seven years later, she returned to the East Coast, where she was converted to a full-rigged training ship. *Monongahela* ended her days as a storeship at Guantánamo Bay, Cuba, from 1904 until her destruction by fire in 1908.

Silverstone, *Warships of the Civil War Navies.* U.S. Navy, *DANFS.*

Mora

Knorr (1m). *Hull:* wood. *Built:* Normandy, France; 1066.

Flagship of one of the most important amphibious invasions in history, *Mora* was a single-masted vessel built in the Viking tradition. A gift from Mathilda to her husband, William, Duke of Normandy — which takes its name from the Norse men who settled there — *Mora* was probably a clinker-built knorr intended for transporting men and animals. The best source of information about the shape and rig of William's ships is the Bayeux Tapestry, a seventy-meter-long, half-meter-wide scroll embroidered by the defeated English. The tapestry recounts the story of the Norman invasion, starting with William's securing an oath of loyalty from Harold (the Earl of Wessex who later succeeded Edward the Confessor as King of England in spite of William's claim to be Edward's heir), William's preparation for the invasion during the summer of 1066, and the invasion itself.

Harold's claim to the throne was weak, and his rivals included the Norwegian Harald Hardraade and William. Although they were not in alliance, it seems that William had knowledge of Harald's plans for an invasion around York, and that this was a factor in the timing of his own expedition across the English Channel. William's forces required an enormous number of ships — estimates of his fleet range from 700 to 1,000 ships — some of them acquired from his Flemish allies. A great number were also built for the invasion. In addition to seamen, the Norman host included about 7,000 soldiers; of these, 2,000 or 3,000 were knights, who would have traveled with a like number of their own warhorses. (In all, a fully equipped knight required four horses for riding and transporting equipment; except for the trained battle steeds, these could be obtained in England.)

In anticipation of an invasion, Harold had stationed the English fleet on the Channel coast, but it was periodically forced to return to London for supplies. William's fleet was apparently ready in July, and although accounts relate that he was delayed by storms, it is likely that he sailed only when he knew both that the English fleet was not on station — it sailed for London on September 8 — and that Harold was preoccupied with containing Harald Hardraade's army, which sailed up the Humber and captured York on September 20. Harold marched an army northward and defeated Harald at the Battle of Stamford Bridge north of York on September 27.

The Norman fleet initially sailed on September 12, but bad weather forced it into St. Valéry. The ships put to sea again on September 27 and reached Pevensey two days later. Learning of William's landing, Harold marched south hoping to catch the Norman army on the peninsula at Hastings and attack with his army and replenished fleet. The army arrived first, and it was up to William to force a battle before the English fleet arrived, which he did on October 14. Harold was killed, struck by an arrow in the eye, the Normans defeated the English, and William the Conqueror was accepted as the legitimate King of England.

The origin of *Mora*'s name is unknown, and it is found in only one nearly contemporary written account. The same document describes the bow as adorned with a gilt statue of a boy holding a trumpet to his lips in his left hand, with his right hand pointing — toward England. In the tapestry, the boy is depicted on the stern.

Rodger, *Safeguard of the Sea*. Wilson, *Bayeux Tapestry*.

CSS Nashville

(later *Thomas L. Bragg,* CSS *Rattlesnake*) Commerce raider (1f/2m). *L/B/D:* 215.5′ × 34.5′ × 21.9′ dph (65.7m × 10.5m × 6.7m). *Tons:* 1,221 tons. *Hull:* wood. *Comp.:* 40. *Arm.:* 2 × 12pdr. *Mach.:* side-lever engine, sidewheels. *Built:* Thomas Collyer, New York; 1853.

The steamship *Nashville* was built for general service between New York and Charleston, South Carolina. On April 12, 1861, she entered the latter port at the end of her last peacetime passage. As she did so, she was fired upon by USS HARRIET LANE, which had come to the relief of Fort Sumter. Seized and commissioned as a commerce raider in October, CSS *Nashville* sank the clipper *Harvey Birch* before putting into Southampton, England, for repairs on November 21, 1861, the first Confederate warship in European waters. Successfully eluding USS *Tuscarora* at Southampton, *Nashville* returned to Beaufort, North Carolina, on February 28, 1862, having captured the schooner *Robert Gilfillan.* Escaping Beaufort, on March 17, 1862, she was sold for use as a blockade-runner, renamed *Thomas L. Bragg,* and ran between South Carolina and the Bahamas before being blockaded in Warsaw Sound, Georgia, for eight months. Recommissioned as the privateer CSS *Rattlesnake,* on February 28, 1863, she was destroyed in the Ogeechee River by the monitor USS *Montauk* as she tried to run the blockade.

Chance et al., *Tangled Machinery and Charred Relics.*

USS Nautilus

Schooner (2m). *L/B/D:* 76.5′ × 23.7′ × 9.8′ dph (23.3m × 7.2m × 3m). *Tons:* 185 disp. *Hull:* wood. *Comp.:* 103. *Arm.:* 12 × 6pdr. *Built:* Henry Spencer, Eastern Shore, Md.; 1799.

Built as a merchant schooner and purchased by the U.S. Navy in 1803, USS *Nautilus*'s first assignment was with the Mediterranean Squadron, then close to war with the corsairs of Algiers, Tunis, and Tripoli. Following the capture of USS PHILADELPHIA in September 1803, *Nautilus* sailed on blockade between Tripoli and Tunis through 1805, using bases at Messina, Syracuse, Malta, and Leghorn (Livorno) for repairs and reprovisioning. In August and September 1804, she took part in attacks on Tripoli, and between April 27 and May 17, 1805, helped in the capture of Derna by the forces of Hamet Caramanli, the Bashaw of Tripoli. The war ended in June of that year, and *Nautilus* remained on station until 1806. Laid up at Washington, she reentered service along the East Coast from 1808 to 1810. She was then rerigged as a brig and given a battery of twelve 18-pdr., short-range carronades before joining Commodore Stephen Decatur's squadron. Shortly after the start of the War of 1812, *Nautilus* sailed from New York, and on July 17, 1812, she was captured by an overwhelming British force consisting of HMS *Africa* (64 guns), *Shannon* (38), and *Aeolus* (32). It is believed that she was taken into service by the Royal Navy, but her subsequent fate is unknown.

U.S. Navy, *DANFS.*

Nautilus

Submersible (1m). *L/B:* 21.3′ × 6.4′ (6.5m × 2m). *Hull:* wood, copper, iron. *Comp.:* 4. *Arm.:* torpedo (mine). *Mach.:* hand crank, screw. *Des.:* Robert Fulton. *Built:* J. C. Périer, Paris; 1801.

Although Robert Fulton is best remembered for his development of the NORTH RIVER STEAM BOAT

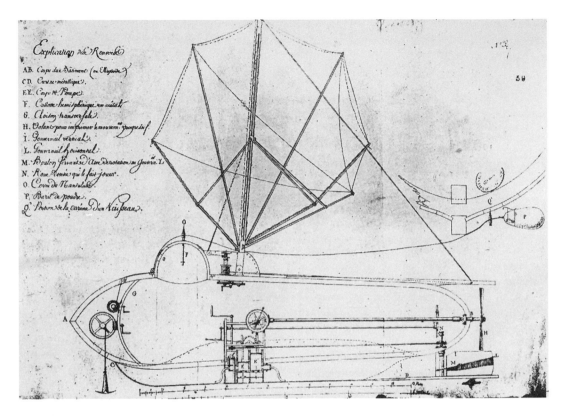

▲ Robert Fulton's original plan for the submarine **Nautilus** shows the metal bottom (CD), conning tower dome (F) and auger (O), transverse bulkhead (G) with cranks to control the anchor and powder keg (P), propeller (M), vertical (I) and horizontal (L) rudders, the means of attaching the powder keg to a ship's hull (P & Q), and a collapsible mast and sail for operating on the surface. Subsequent modifications included the addition of compressed air tanks and a porthole. *Courtesy The Mariners' Museum, Newport News, Virginia.*

in the United States, he first gained international attention with his experiments in submarines. When he began developing his ideas for a submarine is unclear, but on December 13, 1797, he submitted to France's Executive Directory a proposal for a system of submarine warfare. This included a rate schedule for the destruction of English ships: "4000 Livers [livres] per Gun for each British ship over 40 Guns . . . and 2000 Livers per Gun for

All vessels of war under 40 tons [*sic*]." In many respects, *Nautilus* resembled the submarines developed a hundred years later. The hydrodynamic hull was a cylinder with a pointed bow and slightly tapered stern. A conning tower doubled as a hatch, there was a periscope, and thin tubes could be used to admit air when the vessel was just below the surface. As originally designed, the oxygen supply was sufficient for four men to remain submerged with two candles burning for three hours. In 1802, Fulton tried experiments with a compressed air canister, and to do away with the need for candles, he inserted a three-quarter-inch glass porthole that admitted enough light to read a watch at a depth of twenty-five feet. Diving and surfacing was regulated by water in ballast tanks, admitted by valves and expelled with compressed air. Propelled by a hand crank attached to a single, four-bladed propeller, *Nautilus* traveled at two knots. The submarine was steered by means of a vertical rudder and a forward horizontal diving plane. When surfaced, she had an auxiliary sail that could be collapsed on deck.

Fulton's original design had an auger sticking up through the conning tower. This was to have drilled a hole in the hull of a ship, to which an explosive charge would then be fixed. On September 12, 1801, Fulton and three crew departed Le Havre for Cap La Hogue, a distance of seventy miles that *Nautilus* covered in five days. He attempted to close with two English brigs, but both sailed off, though whether by coincidence or because they had seen the curious vessel is unknown. The next year, at Brest, *Nautilus* trailed an explosive charge at a distance of 200 meters that succeeded in destroying a target ship, but the charge could have been set without a submarine. First Consul Napoleon Bonaparte was impressed with the possibilities of such mines, however, and asked if he could see the *Nautilus*. He was informed that Fulton had dismantled it, ostensibly because of rot, but more likely to prevent its design being copied without appropriate compensation.

Fulton eventually made his way to England and managed to interest Prime Minister William Pitt in his ideas, but he never built another submarine. In the optimistic belief that his device would bring an end to naval warfare, Fulton referred to his submarine as "A Curious Machine for Mending Politics." Contemporary French and British naval officers deemed Fulton's devices inappropriately destructive. In the long run, neither view prevailed.

Philip, *Robert Fulton.*

Nemesis

Paddle frigate (1f/2m). *L/B/D:* 184′ × 29′ (41′ew) × 6′ (56.1m × 8.8m (12.5m) × 1.8m). *Tons:* 660 bm. *Hull:* wood. *Comp.:* 60–90. *Arm.:* 2 × 32pdr, 4 × 6pdr. *Mach.:* 2 cyl, 120 nhp, sidewheels; 8 kts. *Built:* Cammell Laird & Co., Ltd., Birkenhead, Eng.; 1839.

Although the first iron-hulled steamship, *Aaron Manby,* was launched in 1821, a number of practi-

cal considerations prevented the widespread adoption of iron hulls. The most important of these was overcome in 1839, when Astronomer Royal Sir George Airey determined how to compensate for the effect of iron on the ship's compass. The same year, the Honourable East India Company ordered the paddle gunboat *Nemesis* for service in China. While wooden ships of the same size drew thirteen feet, *Nemesis* drew only six feet of water fully loaded, which gave her a decided advantage in riverine operations. When under sail, her crew could lower two seven-foot drop keels to improve her ability to sail to windward. Although *Nemesis* carried Airey's compass correctors, these were improperly fitted, and on her maiden voyage she ran aground off St. Ives and stove in several iron plates.

In March 1840, *Nemesis* sailed for India under Captain William Hutcheon Hall. (Although never commissioned in the Royal Navy, *Nemesis* was usually under the command of Royal Navy officers.) The first iron steamship to round the Cape of Good Hope, she was forced into Delagoa Bay for repairs to some plates that fractured when the ship broached off South Africa. Continuing to China, she arrived off the Bogue Forts in November. *Nemesis* played a significant role in the First Opium War and typified the technological advantage that Britain had over the Chinese. In the words of a contemporary British account, she was

> as much admired by our countrymen as dreaded by the Chinese. Well may the latter offer a reward of 50,000 dollars for her, but she will be difficult to take. They call her the devil ship, and say that our shells and rockets could only be invented by the latter. They are more afraid of her than all the Line-of-Battle ships put together.

Nemesis was in the thick of the fighting at the Bogue Forts, Amoy, and Ningpo in 1840 and at Woosung in 1842. Upon her return to Bombay in 1843, it was found that she had suffered much less damage than her wooden counterparts, and Captain Hall's official report to the Admiralty on the ship's performance contributed to its ordering more iron ships. After repairs at Bombay, she began cruising between Bombay, Karachi, and Bassein. She was sold in 1852.

Brown, "*Nemesis:* The First Iron Warship." Hall, *Narrative of the Voyages and Service of the "Nemesis."* Mallard, "Ships of India, 1834–1934."

USS New Ironsides

Ironclad (1f/3m). *L/B/D:* 232′ × 57.5′ × 15.7′ (70.7m × 17.5m × 4.8m). *Tons:* 4,120 disp. *Hull:* wood. *Comp.:* 460. *Arm.:* 2 × 150pdr, 2 × 50pdr, 14 × 11″, 1 × 12pdr, 1 × 12pdr. *Armor:* 4.5″ belt, 1″ deck. *Mach.:* horizontal direct-acting engine, 700 hp, 1 screw; 6 kts. *Des.:* Merrick & Sons. *Built:* William Cramp & Sons Ship and Engine Building Co., Philadelphia; 1862.

Named in honor of USS CONSTITUTION, who earned the nickname "Old Ironsides" during her engagement with HMS GUERRIÈRE, USS *New Ironsides* was one of three ironclads ordered shortly after the start of the Civil War. (The other ships were USS MONITOR and *Galena.*) Modeled on contemporary European designs, she was one of the most powerful ships afloat. Never regarded as sea-kindly, she had a pronounced tumblehome; originally rigged as a ship, her masts were later cut down. *New Ironsides* entered service as flagship of Rear Admiral Samuel du Pont's South Atlantic Blockading Squadron in August 1862. Stationed off Charleston, South Carolina, on April 7 she took part in the bombardment of Forts Moultrie and Sumter; hit 55 times, she suffered no serious damage. Flying the flag of Rear Admiral John A. Dahlgren, *New Ironsides* took part in the bombardment of Morris Island between July and September, receiving 214 hits, again with only negligible effect.

Of more serious concern were attacks by spar torpedo boats. *New Ironsides* avoided the first of these on August 21, but on October 5, 1863, she was attacked by CSS DAVID, which managed to detonate a mine on her starboard quarter. The damage was insignificant, and *New Ironsides* remained on station until May 1864, when she returned to Philadelphia. Joining the North Atlantic Blockading Squadron in October, she took part in the bombardment of Fort Fisher, North Carolina,

on Christmas Eve and again on January 13–15, 1865, when the fort was finally captured. Decommissioned on April 7, 1865, two days before the Confederate surrender at Appomattox, *New Ironsides* was laid up at League Island, Philadelphia. She was destroyed by fire on December 16, 1866.

Anderson, *By Sea and by River.* Silverstone, *Warships of the Civil War Navies.* U.S. Navy, *DANFS.*

USS Niagara

Brig. *L/B/D:* 109.8′ × 30′ × 4.7′ dph (33.5m × 9.1m × 1.4m). *Tons:* 493 bm. *Hull:* wood. *Comp.:* 142. *Arm.:* 2 × 12pdr, 18 × 32pdr. *Built:* Adam & Noah Brown, Presque Isle, Pa.; 1813.

USS *Niagara* was one of two sister ships built under the supervision of Master Commandant Oliver Hazard Perry, who was given responsibility for the all but nonexistent Lake Erie Fleet during the War of 1812. Chief credit for giving shape to this ad hoc fleet fell to the New York shipbuilders Adam and Noah Brown, who would later have a hand in the building of FULTON STEAM FRIGATE and *Walk-in-the-Water,* the first Great Lakes steamboat. Noah Brown had been sent to Lake Erie by the Navy Department. Wood was abundant, but skilled labor, naval stores, and guns all had to come overland. Nonetheless, by July 1813 Brown had built the brigs *Niagara* and *Lawrence,* and the schooners *Ariel* and *Ohio,* and had helped in the building or reconstruction of a handful of other vessels. In the words of Howard Chapelle,

> The amount of work that Brown accomplished with about 200 men, without power tools, and in a wilderness during the worst winter months, makes some of the modern [World War II] wartime production feats something less than impressive.

Perry's function was to contain the British advance along the northern frontier from Canada. His fleet was initially blockaded at Presque Isle (now Erie), Pennsylvania, by Captain Robert Barclay, who lifted the blockade on July 30. Three days later, Perry sailed to the western end of Lake Erie, where he established a base at Put-in Bay in the

Bass Islands north of present-day Sandusky, Ohio. His fleet comprised nine ships: USS *Lawrence, Niagara* (20 guns), *Ariel* (6), *Caledonia* (3), *Somers* (2), *Scorpion, Porcupine, Trippe,* and *Tigress* (1). With his supply lines from Lake Ontario cut, Barclay — a veteran of Trafalgar — was forced to bring the Americans to battle, and on September 10, he sailed from Fort Malden, Ontario, with his fleet of six ships: HMS *Detroit* (20), *Queen Charlotte* (16), *Lady Prevost* (13), *Hunter* (10), *Little Belt* (2), and *Chippeway* (2).

Approaching each other in parallel battle lines — the engagement was the only traditional fleet action of the war — the two squadrons engaged each other at 1145. Perry's flagship was *Lawrence,* named for his good friend Captain James Law-

---

▼ "We have met the enemy and they are ours," wrote Oliver Hazard Perry from his flagship **Niagara** shortly after the stunning American victory over the British at the Battle of Lake Erie in 1813. The ship shown here is a replica commissioned in 1990. *Courtesy Modern-Ad, Butler, Pennsylvania.*

rence, who had died on June 1 in the battle between USS CHESAPEAKE and HMS *Shannon,* and whose dying words — "Don't give up the ship" — were emblazoned on a pennant flying from the masthead. *Lawrence* took the brunt of the fighting from *Detroit* and *Queen Charlotte* and by about 1430 had suffered eighty-four dead and wounded. With nineteen of his crew, Perry transferred his flag to *Niagara,* whose captain, Jesse D. Elliott, had kept her out of the fray. Perry immediately sailed through the center of the British line, crossing the "T" and sending raking broadsides the length of Barclay's two biggest ships. Barclay, who had lost an arm in the battle, was forced to strike, thus becoming the first British commander in history to surrender an entire squadron.

That afternoon, Perry wrote to General William Henry Harrison, "We have met the enemy and they are ours. Two Ships, two Brigs one Schooner & one Sloop." The battle at Put-in Bay was a turning point in the War of 1812, for in securing control of Lake Erie, Perry removed the British threat to the Northwest Territory. On September 23, *Niagara* sailed in support of Harrison's attack on Fort Mal-

den, and then covered the army's recapture of Detroit before going back to Presque Isle for the winter. The following year, she captured four British ships on Lake Erie before returning again to her homeport, where she remained as a receiving ship until 1820. The same year her hull was intentionally sunk in Misery Bay, whose cold, fresh water acted as a preservative.

Raised in 1913, she was restored and put on exhibit at various ports along the middle lakes for the Battle of Lake Erie centennial. Kept on permanent exhibit at Erie, she was restored again in 1939 and 1963. A replica of the brig built by Melbourne Smith for the Pennsylvania Historical and Museum Commission was launched in 1988.

Chapelle, *History of the American Sailing Navy*. Roosevelt, *Naval War of 1812*. U.S. Navy, *DANFS*.

Nordenfelt I

Submarine. *L/B/D:* 64′ × 9′ × 11′ (19.5m × 2.7m × 3.4m). *Tons:* 60 disp. *Hull:* iron. *Comp.:* 3. *Arm.:* 1 × 14″TT; 1 25mm. *Mach.:* compound steam engine, 1 screw, 100 ihp; 9/4 kts. *Des.:* Thorsten Nordenfelt & George Garrett. *Built:* Thorsten Nordenfelt, Stockholm; 1885.

The first armed submarine commissioned for a European navy, *Nordenfelt I* was the product of a collaboration between a Norwegian arms dealer and an English minister–turned–naval architect. Inspired by the near success of a Russian spar torpedo attack on a Turkish ship during the Russo-Turkish War of 1877, the Reverend George Garrett built two experimental submarines, engineless *Resurgam* (1877) and *Resurgam II* (1879), which was powered by a steam engine. The latter vessel sank while being towed to Portsmouth, and the Admiralty's interest in Garrett's ideas sank with it. Garrett was able to introduce his ideas to Thorsten Nordenfelt, and the unlikely pair collaborated on a number of submarine projects over the next decade.

Nordenfelt I's power plant consisted of a steam engine that provided power in the usual way when the vessel was surfaced. When *Nordenfelt I* was submerged, the funnel was lowered and stowed, the furnace was sealed (to prevent the crew from being asphyxiated), and steam was generated from latent heat acting on water kept in storage tanks, the same process Garrett had used in *Resurgam II*. The armament consisted of a single 14-inch Whitehead torpedo fired from an external tube, and a 25-mm machine gun of Nordenfelt's design. Notice of the vessel's trials excited considerable interest among European naval observers, but the vessel's performance was less inspiring. Although the *Nordenfelt I* passed under the spectator boat and remained submerged for up to five minutes at a time, the *London Times* wrote that "It is certain that the Nordenfelt boat will effect no revolution."

If not revolutionary, *Nordenfelt I* did set off a modest arms race. The vessel was purchased by Greece in 1886 and was taken to Piraeus, although it seems that she was never put in service there. Nonetheless, the threat of such a vessel so alarmed the Turks that they commissioned two submarines from Nordenfelt and Garrett, only one of which was completed. Russia also acquired one, the 125-foot *Nordenfelt IV*, which mounted two 14-inch torpedo tubes but had the same mono-source power plant. While in tow to Russia, *Nordenfelt IV* went aground on the coast of Jutland and was wrecked.

Gardiner & Lambert, eds., *Steam, Steel and Shellfire*. Maber, "Nordenfelt Submarines."

Nuestra Señora de Atocha

Galleon (3m). *L/B/D:* 110′ × 33′ × 14′ (33.5m × 10.1m × 4.3m). *Tons:* 550 tons. *Hull:* wood. *Comp.:* 260. *Arm.:* 20–24 guns. *Built:* Alonso Ferrera, Havana, Cuba; 1620.

Nuestra Señora de Atocha was the object of one of the most valuable, and possibly most contentious, treasure wrecks ever found. One of four convoy escorts built in 1619–20 for the Armada de la Guarcha, which carried the royal silver and protected the Spanish treasure fleets that plied between Havana and Spain, *Atocha* was named for the Virgin associated with one of the most revered shrines in Madrid. Reportedly built of less than the best materials, on her first voyage *Atocha* sprung her mainmast en route from Havana to Sanlúcar, and on her return to Cuba she leaked badly in the bows. Sailing to Portobello, Panama, *Atocha* was designated the *almiranta,* or second-in-command, of the treasure fleet returning to Spain. She embarked silver and gold shipped from the mines of Potosí (in Bolivia), Peru, and Colombia, together with forty-eight passengers returning to Spain. Departing Panama on July 22, 1622, the treasure fleet called first at Cartagena for tobacco and emeralds, and then sailed north for Havana, where they arrived on August 22 to load raw copper and indigo. In addition to whatever was smuggled aboard to evade taxes, *Atocha* carried 35 tons of silver (901 ingots and 255,000 coins) and 161 pieces of gold — a cargo valued at one million pesos.

Despite the threat of hurricanes at that time of year, the twenty-eight-ship fleet sailed six weeks later than planned, on September 4. The next morning, a hurricane hit, and the ships were driven north toward the Florida Keys. Twenty-one of the ships passed to the west of the low-lying islands, but *Atocha, Nuestra Señora de Santa Margarita,* and four others did not. Early Tuesday morning, *Atocha* was dashed on a reef off Key West and sank in fifteen feet of water with only her mizzen mast visible. Five survivors from the ship's complement of 260 were rescued by the merchantman *Santa Cruz.* All told, the storm had sunk six ships with their 550 passengers and crew.

Santa Cruz returned directly to Havana, and officials immediately prepared to recover what they could from the ships. Divers discovered that *Atocha*'s hatches were still fastened and could not be forced without explosives, but before they could return, the mizzen mast snapped off in another storm, and the ship was lost. Government efforts to find the ships continued until 1623, without success. In 1626, a Havana merchant named Francisco Núñez Melián obtained a salvage contract, and on June 26, 1623, using a primitive diving bell, one of his divers recovered a silver ingot from *Santa Margarita.* Altogether, the site yielded 313 silver ingots, 100 sheets of copper, 8 bronze guns, and 64,000 coins. Subsequent efforts were not as well rewarded, though Melián continued to search for *Atocha* off and on until 1643.

In 1970, chicken farmer turned treasure hunter Mel Fisher formed a company called Treasure Salvors, Inc., and began looking for *Atocha.* Working with a permit from the State of Florida, in 1971 Treasure Salvors recovered the first artifacts, including an anchor and a gold chain. Employing such crude devices as the "mailbox," which directed prop wash to clear away sand and whatever else overlay the object of their search, over the next four years the company recovered about $6 million worth of gold and silver, as well as a large number of rapiers, muskets and small arms, storage jars, and coins. Of the ship itself, only some rudder pintles and an anchor were found. In 1973, in an attempt to improve its standing with potential investors and the State of Florida, Treasure Salvors hired Duncan Mathewson as staff archaeologist.

On July 13, 1975, Mel's son Dirk located five of the ship's bronze guns lying in thirty-nine feet of water. A week later, diving was suspended when he, his wife, and another member of the crew drowned after their dive boat capsized in a storm. The next five years revealed little new material from *Atocha,* although in 1980 Treasure Salvors divers relocated the remains of *Santa Margarita,* which they salvaged for two years. The search for *Atocha* continued until July 20, 1985, when the salvors found the hull of the ship, piles of silver ingots, and chests of silver. Treasure Salvors made some attempt to excavate the site properly, but the main effort was in the recovery of treasure, as the company name, and its designation of the site as "the motherlode," suggested.

In the meantime, the *Atocha* site had been the object of increasing criticism by nautical archaeologists who considered Treasure Salvors' techniques crude and destructive, and the Florida government moved to take control of the site. The Supreme Court eventually found in favor of Fisher's group on the grounds that its title to the wreck was supported by admiralty law precedent, despite the historical value of the site. Nonetheless, a movement was afoot to protect submerged archaeological sites from treasure hunters in the same way that comparable sites on land are. Concern for these irreplaceable troves of archaeological and anthropological information spread slowly, but aided in part by the outcry over the disastrous handling of the archaeologically priceless but commercially worthless DE BRAAK site in Delaware Bay, preservationists were able to force passage of the Abandoned Shipwreck Act of 1987, which moved historic shipwrecks out of the jurisdiction of standard admiralty law.

Lyon, *"Santa Margarita"; Search for the "Atocha."* Mathewson, *Treasure of the "Atocha."*

Nuestra Señora de la Concepción

Nao (3m). *L:* ca. 140′ (42.7m). *Tons:* 600. *Hull:* wood. *Comp.:* 500. *Arm.:* 40 guns. *Built:* Havana, Cuba; 1620.

Built as a merchantman, the details of the first twenty years of the ship known officially as *Nuestra Señora de la puria y limpia Concepción* are little known. In 1639, the Casa de la Contratación ("House of Trade") in Seville chartered the ship to sail as *capitana* of the twenty Spanish ships bound for Veracruz. Armed with 40 guns and carrying a total complement of 500 men, women, and children, *Concepción* made the westward crossing in 64 days. As was the custom, the ships unloaded at San Juan de Ulúa, the port of Veracruz, and remained there over the winter.

When the return fleet sailed on July 23, 1641, *Concepción* carried between one and four million pesos (35 to 140 tons) of silver, some gold, and 1,200 bales of cochineal and indigo. Although Don Juan de Villavicenio requested permission to have the ship repaired at Havana, he was overruled, even after the fleet was forced back so a leak in *Concepción* could be repaired. The fleet departed again on September 20, a month after the last ships normally sailed for Spain, in order to avoid the hurricane season.

Eight days out, a hurricane hit the fleet off the coast of Florida. All told, nine ships were lost and only two continued to Spain. The storm blew out on October 1, and *Concepción* turned south for Puerto Rico. On October 31, the damaged ship grounded on Abrojos Reef, north of Hispaniola in 20°43′N. She broke up two days later; 33 men in the surviving ship's boat landed on Hispaniola, and about 240 more people reached the island on makeshift rafts constructed from *Concepción's* timbers.

Several expeditions were mounted to find the wreck, but it was not until 1688 that Captain William Phips discovered the site. Between February 7 and April 19, divers recovered 25 tons of silver, 7 guns, and some gold — a treasure worth £250,000. In 1976, American treasure hunter Burt Webber rediscovered the wreck and excavated millions of dollars in silver.

Earle, *Wreck of the Almiranta.*

Nuestra Señora del Rosario

Galleon. *Tons:* 1,150 toneladas. *Hull:* wood. *Comp.:* 443. *Arm.:* 51 guns. *Built:* Ribadeo, Galicia, Spain; 1587.

Built for the *carrera de las indias,* the trade between Spain and the Americas, *Nuestra Señora del Rosario* was fitting out at Cadiz on June 20, 1587, when she was seized in the name of Philip II for use in the Spanish Armada. On November 17, she was designated as flagship of the Andalusian Squadron under the accomplished seaman Don Pedro de Valdés. Thanks to his efforts, when the Armada sailed from Lisbon on May 9, 1588, she was the most heavily armed ship in the fleet, boasting 51 guns. Her complement comprised 117 crew and 300 soldiers, as well as servants, priests, and other supernumeraries, and she carried about 50,000 escudos, one-third of the money earmarked for operations in England. The fleet departed La Coruña on July 22 and seven days later was off the Scilly Islands. Fighting between the English and Spanish fleets began on June 30. Trying to help other ships that had been badly damaged, *Rosario* lost her foremast and bowsprit, and the Spanish fleet pressed on, leaving Valdés to fend for himself. That night, Sir Walter Raleigh approached in *Margaret and John* but sailed off with the rest of the fleet.

The next day, Sir Francis Drake appeared, having left his comrades for the sake of a fat prize. Although *Rosario* was larger and more powerfully armed and manned than REVENGE, rather than risk a fight with England's most celebrated seaman, Valdés accepted Drake's terms and surrendered. So far as Elizabeth's government was concerned, the most valuable aspect of the capture was the money (about half may have been pocketed by Valdés, Drake, or both), followed by *Rosario*'s gunpowder. In 1589, the *Rosario* sailed from Dartmouth to Chatham and then to Deptford. The prisoners were finally freed on November 24, 1590. Whether *Nuestra Señora del Rosario* ever sailed again is unknown, but it seems unlikely. In 1618, still in Deptford, she was cleaned "of all the slubb, ballast and other trash within board, making her swim and removing her near into the mast dock where she was laid and sunk for the defense and preservation of the wharf there."

Martin, *Spanish Armada Prisoners.*

Nydam boat

L/B: 75′ × 10.5′ (22.9m × 3.2m). *Hull:* wood. *Comp.:* 30+. *Built:* Germany; 350–400 CE.

The oak-hulled Nydam boat is one of two vessels discovered in 1863 in a bog off Als Sound in Schleswig-Holstein, about fifty miles north of Kiel, Germany. Dating from the fourth century CE, she represents a transitional phase in the development of northern European shipbuilding toward the end of the period of Roman occupation and influence. In the first century, the Roman historian Tacitus wrote of the Germans:

> The shape of their ships differs from the normal in having a prow at both ends, which is always ready to be put in to shore. They do not rig sails or fasten their oars in banks at the sides. Their oarage is

loose, as one finds on some rivers, and can be shifted, as need requires, from side to side.

The Nydam boat is clearly an extension of this tradition. A very large double-ender, she was clinker-built with five strakes on either side of the keel. Some of the oak planks were as long as forty-five feet, and they were joined to each other by clenched bolts and to the frames by bast ropes; there is also clear evidence of caulking between the planks. There is no indication that the boat carried a mast or rigging for sails, but there were fifteen thole pins on either side of the hull, as well as oars, thwarts, poles, and a nine-foot-long steering oar. Although the evidence is only circumstantial, it is likely that the Nydam boat represents the kind of vessels in which the Anglo-Saxons crossed the North Sea to settle in England, starting in the fifth century. Her lines also seem to anticipate those of the seventh-century SUTTON HOO ship found in England.

Holes had been cut in the bottom of the hull, suggesting that the Nydam boat was intentionally sunk to prevent her cargo from being captured. In and around the boat were hundreds of weapons and other artifacts, including 107 swords, 552 spearheads, 70 knives, bows, arrows, quivers, wooden shields, bronze and iron ornaments, as well as the skulls of several horses and one of a cow, and 34 Roman coins dating from between 69 and 217 CE. The hull and contents of the Nydam boat were initially housed at a museum in Kiel, but today they are displayed at Schloss Gotorp in the town of Hedeby, Schleswig-Holstein. A smaller fir boat found at the same time and thought to be of Scandinavian origin was probably used for firewood by soldiers during the war between Prussia and Denmark in 1865.

Arenhold, "Nydam Boat at Kiel." Tacitus, *On Britain and Germany.* Throckmorton, ed., *Sea Remembers.*

O'Higgins

Frigate (3m). *Hull:* wood. *Comp.:* 600. *Built:* <1817.

In 1817, Thomas Lord Cochrane was invited by General Bernardo O'Higgins, Supreme Director of the Republic of Chile, to assume command of his fledgling country's navy in the struggle against Spanish rule. Something of a maverick within the Royal Navy, Cochrane had recently been implicated in a stock scandal and dismissed from service, and he readily accepted the new assignment. Turning down a comparable offer to serve the Spanish against the Chileans, he assumed the rank of Vice Admiral of Chile, Admiral and Commander-in-Chief of the Naval Forces of the Republic. Arriving at Valparaiso toward the end of 1818, Cochrane hoisted his flag in a captured Spanish ship renamed *O'Higgins.* In January 1819, he took a small squadron comprising his flagship, *Lautaro* (44 guns), *San Martín* (56), and *Chacabuco* (20) to blockade Callao. After his men silenced a shore battery and captured a gunboat, the Spanish dubbed Cochrane "El Diablo." The blockade was lifted in March, and the Chileans captured a number of valuable prizes along the Peruvian coast before returning to Callao in September.

Illness forced the breaking of the blockade for a second time, and the fleet split up, Cochrane taking *O'Higgins* south to the heavily fortified port of Valdivia, Chile, which was still held by the Spanish. After reconnoitering the port, he requisitioned a schooner and a brig to strengthen his force. Returning to Valdivia, *O'Higgins* hit a rock, and the ammunition was ruined by water. Cochrane calmed his men and insisted they carry out their mission with bayonets. On February 3, 1821, they succeeded in capturing eight forts, killing 100 men, capturing another 100, and putting 800 to flight. This victory strengthened the Chileans strategically and so shifted the balance of power that the government was able to raise £1 million in London.

At the end of September, Cochrane returned with seven ships and 4,500 soldiers to Callao, which he blockaded for five weeks. At 2200 on November 5, he led 240 men in fourteen boats to cut out the Spanish frigate *Esmeralda.* Although they failed to achieve complete surprise, in only fifteen minutes the Chilean crew took the ship, together with 210 officers and men; they suffered only 11 dead against 160 Spanish. As an English observer aboard HMS *Conway* wrote,

> The loss was a death-blow to the Spanish naval forces in that quarter of the world; for although there were still two Spanish frigates and some smaller vessels in the Pacific, they never afterwards ventured to show themselves, but left Lord Cochrane undisputed master of the sea.

Cochrane refused to allow the prize to be named for himself, and the captured ship was renamed *Valdivia.* After taking the town of Pisco in March, Cochrane shifted his flag to *San Martin,* which was lost at Callao when General José Francisco de San Martín insisted that she be brought too close to shore to offload a cargo of wheat. Lima capitulated shortly thereafter, and Cochrane returned to Valparaiso in *O'Higgins.*

In 1823, Cochrane was invited to render similar services for Brazil, then seeking independence from Portugal, and he again performed with distinction. Three years later, his erstwhile flagship

▲ The cruiser **USS Olympia** at San Francisco Harbor in 1895. Note her pronounced ram bow, cruiser stern, and mixed armament of 8-inch, 5-inch, 6-pdr., and 1-pdr. guns. The flagship of Commodore George Dewey's victorious squadron at the Battle of Manila Bay in 1898 survives today at Philadelphia. *Courtesy U.S. Naval Historical Center, Washington, D.C.*

O'Higgins was lost at sea en route from Chile to Buenos Aires.

Twitchett, *Life of a Seaman.*

USS Olympia (C-6)

Olympia-class cruiser (2f/2m). *L/B/D:* 344.1′ × 53′ × 21.5′ (104.9m × 16.2m × 6.6m). *Tons:* 5,586 disp. *Hull:* steel. *Comp.:* 411. *Arm.:* 4 × 8″ (2 × 2), 10 × 5″, 4 × 6pdr, 6 × 1pdr; 6 × 18″TT. *Mach.:* triple-expansion, 18,000 hp, 2 screws; 20 kts. *Built:* Union Iron Works, San Francisco; 1895.

Named for the capital of Washington State, USS *Olympia's* first commission was as flagship of the Asiatic Fleet. In 1898, she came under command of Captain Charles V. Gridley and flew the flag of Commodore George Dewey. At the time, Spanish-American relations were strained by Spain's treat-ment of Cuban nationalists, and the loss by explosion of the USS MAINE at Havana Harbor was seen by many as an excellent pretext for a war. In the Far East, such a war would be centered on the Spanish colony of the Philippines, the seizure of which would further enhance America's position as a world power.

War began on April 25, and two days later, Dewey received orders to proceed to Manila. In addition to *Olympia,* he had under his command the cruisers BALTIMORE, *Raleigh,* and *Boston,* and the gunboats *Petrel* and *Concord.* Manila was weakly defended by a poorly maintained, inadequately trained Spanish squadron consisting of Rear Admiral Patricio Montojo's flagship, the cruiser *Reina Christina,* which mounted six 6.2-inch guns and was only half as big as *Olympia,* together with the wooden cruiser *Castilla* and five gunboats. After slipping unseen into Manila Bay on May 1, Dewey's ships came under fire at a range of about 9,000 yards. As he later recalled: "At 5:40 when we were within a distance of 5,000 yards, I turned to Captain Gridley and said, 'You may fire when you are ready Gridley.' . . . The very first gun to speak was an 8-inch . . . of the *Olympia.*" The gunnery was appalling on both sides — in Dewey's fleet, only 2.4 percent of the 5,859 shells expended hit their targets — but after two hours, the two largest Spanish ships had been sunk and most of the rest were either sinking or burning. Dewey resumed shelling at 1100, and Montojo surrendered at 1230. Only one American sailor was killed. Returning to Hong Kong on May 20, *Olympia* sailed for New York by way of the Suez Canal and the Mediterranean and arrived to a hero's welcome on October 10, 1899.

Three years later, *Olympia* became flagship of the Caribbean Division, North Atlantic Squadron, and later alternated between assignments in the Atlantic, Mediterranean, and Caribbean. Withdrawn from service in 1906, except for midshipmen cruises from Annapolis between 1907 and 1909, in 1912 she became a barracks ship at Charleston, South Carolina. As war with Germany threatened, she was recommissioned in 1916 and sailed on convoy duty in the North Atlantic. Following the Brest-Litovsk Treaty between Russia and Germany and the start of the Russian Revolution, *Olympia* was dispatched to Archangel and Murmansk to help garrison those northern ports against Bolshevik intrusion. With the end of World War I, *Olympia* moved to the Mediterranean and between 1918 and 1920 spent most of her time helping to quell disturbances along the Adriatic coast of Yugoslavia, which had come into being with the collapse of the Austro-Hungarian Empire. *Olympia*'s last overseas mission was to carry the remains of World War I's Unknown Soldier from Le Havre to Washington, D.C., for interment at Arlington National Cemetery. Decommissioned and preserved as a historic ship at Philadelphia in 1922, she was taken over by the Cruiser *Olympia* Association in 1957.

Beach, *United States Navy*. Emerson, "USS *Olympia*." U.S. Navy, *DANFS*.

Olympias

Trireme (2m). *L/B/D:* 120.7′ × 17.7′ × 11.8′ dph (36.8m × 5.4m × 3.6m). *Tons:* 45 disp. *Hull:* wood. *Comp.:* 196. *Des.:* John F. Coates, John Morrison. *Built:* Piraeus, Greece; 1987.

Among the largest, and certainly the fastest, warships in classical antiquity was the trireme, a long,

narrow vessel propelled by 170 oars and fitted with a large bow ram with which to punch holes in enemy ships. Triremes — in Greek, *trieres* — evolved from the triacontor and pentecontor, oared ships propelled by 30 and 50 oars, respectively. These smaller vessels probably served chiefly as transports, and when enemy ships engaged each other, the crews would attempt to capture their opponents' ships in a boarding action. However, the most effective way to disable an enemy ship was to ram it. This tactic was one to which the faster and more maneuverable trireme was ideally suited. It is estimated that the trireme was as much as 30 percent faster than a pentecontor, which remained the standard vessel for smaller city-states lacking the resources to build, much less man, triremes. In the years prior to Xerxes' invasion of Greece in 480 BCE, the Athenians built 200 triremes; at the Battle of Salamis, however, they had to draw on their Plataean and Chalcidian allies to man their ships, each of which required 170 oarsmen, a helmsman, and up to 30 auxiliaries, for a total of 40,000 people.

Although large numbers of triremes were built, few details of their design and construction remain. Pictorial and sculptural evidence, though relatively abundant, is inexact, and written descriptions are scant. Archaeological evidence is also slight and likely to remain so. Being unballasted, triremes did not sink; they could be towed away from battle even if badly damaged, and if they were beyond salvage, they would simply drift at sea until they broke up. The primary evidence for the trireme's dimensions comes from the excavation of the trireme sheds at Zea, near Piraeus. These were capable of housing vessels up to 40 meters in length and 5.6 meters in width. The written record also attests to the materials and method of construction. The primary woods employed for planking were fir, pine, and cedar, fir being lighter and therefore preferable, while the keels were of oak, which was better suited to being hauled ashore. The hull was of the shell-first, mortise-and-tenon construction typical of Mediterranean ships of antiquity.

One of the most dedicated students of the trireme is John Morrison, who spent more than half a century researching the evolution, dimensions, manning, and tactical use of triremes. In the 1980s, he and John Coates, retired Chief Naval Architect of the Royal Navy, collaborated on the design of a trireme based on the available evidence. Having determined the basic dimensions, the most complex design issue was the arrangement and size of the oars. Triremes had three banks or files of oars, each pulled by one man. On the uppermost bank were 62 oarsmen, called thranites, 31 on either side, while the lower two tiers held 54 zygians and 54 thalamians, respectively. The thranites' oars pivoted on a short outrigger set out from the hull so that they would not interfere with those of the lower two tiers. The thalamians' oar ports were less than half a meter above the waterline and were covered with leather sleeves to prevent water from entering.

There were two sizes of oars: 9 cubits (4 meters), used by oarsmen at the bow and stern, and 9.5 cubits (4.22 meters), used by oarsmen — who sat on fixed seats — in the middle of the vessel. Although triremes carried two masts, sails were probably not used when the vessel was being rowed because if the wind were coming from anywhere but dead astern, the vessel would heel too much for the oars to work. Even over fairly long periods, rowing could be faster than sailing. Thucydides records one nonstop voyage from Piraeus to Mytilene in 427 BCE in which a trireme was rowed 184 miles in little more than 24 hours (about 7.5 knots) and Xenophon describes the 129-mile run from Byzantium to Heraclea on the Black Sea being covered in about 18 hours (about 7 knots).

In 1982, Coates and David Moss built a mockup of a trireme oar system, and in 1984 the Hellenic Navy expressed its interest in building a full-scale replica, which took two years to complete. Approximately two millennia after her ancestors last plied the Mediterranean, the trireme *Olympias* took to the waters at Piraeus. Manned by volunteer rowers of both sexes from around the world, *Olympias* proved a dramatic success. Although there was much to be learned about the preferred practices in rowing and steering a trireme, *Olympias* attained sprint speeds of 7 knots in the first season. Three years later, after learning a lot about

how to row the ship and modifying the oars, speeds of 8.5 knots were achieved in a short sprint.

The trireme seems never to have been improved upon for speed. Larger vessels were apparently built, such as the Roman quinquireme and later large polyremes, but the root words "three," "four," and "five" apply not to the number of banks of oars but to the number of oarsmen (*remex*) on each side of the ship. In a trireme, there was one oar on each of three levels, and one oarsman to each oar. In a quinquireme, the oars on the top two levels were pulled by two men each, and the smaller oars on the bottom level were pulled by one man, so that there were five files of oarsmen on each side of the ship. In the larger and later polyremes, there were only two levels of oars, with each oar pulled by four men (in an octoreme, or "eight") or five men (in a decareme, or "ten"). It is likely that the oars manned by three or more men were at least partly worked by the "stand-and-sit" stroke of the later medieval galleys. Oared vessels continued to evolve and survived in European navies as late as the eighteenth century. The last naval engagements in which oared ships played a significant role were fought in the Russo-Swedish War of 1788–90.

Casson, *Ships and Seamanship in the Ancient World.* Coates, "Trireme Sails Again." Gardiner & Morrison, eds., *Age of the Galley.* Morrison & Coates, *Athenian Trireme.* Morrison & Williams, *Greek Oared Ships.*

USS Oregon (BB-3)

Battleship (2f/1m). *L/B/D:* 351.2′ × 69.3′ × 24′ (107m × 21.1m × 7.3m). *Tons:* 10,288 disp. *Hull:* steel. *Comp.:* 473. *Arm.:* 4 × 13″, 8 × 8″, 4 × 6″, 20 × 6pdr; 6 × 1pdr; 6 × 18″TT. *Armor:* 18″ belt; 3″ deck. *Mach.:* triple expansion, 9,000 hp, 1 screw; 15 kts. *Built:* Union Iron Works, San Francisco; 1896.

The only battleship assigned to the Pacific Fleet, on February 16, 1898, USS *Oregon* was just coming out of dry dock in Bremerton, Washington, when news reached her of the sinking of the battleship USS MAINE at Havana the day before. Ordered to San Francisco, she arrived there on March 9 and received orders three days later to join Admiral William Sampson's Atlantic Battle Squadron in

 A hero of the Spanish-American War, the battleship **Oregon** was maintained as a museum ship from 1921 until requisitioned for use as a hulk at Guam in 1944. *Author collection.*

Florida. *Oregon* sailed on March 19; she stopped for coal at Callao on April 4, entered the Strait of Magellan on April 17, stopping at Punta Arenas, and arrived at Rio de Janeiro on April 30. There the crew learned that war with Spain had been declared on April 21. Disregarding rumors of a Spanish torpedo boat on the South American coast and of an intercepting squadron en route from the Cape Verde Islands, Captain Charles E. Clark proceeded to Bahia, Barbados, and, finally, Jupiter Inlet, Florida, arriving there on May 24. Despite boiler trouble in the Pacific, adverse winds and currents in the South Atlantic, and a bunker fire that lasted two days between Bahia and Barbados, *Oregon* made the 14,000-mile journey in a record 66 days. Joining Admiral Sampson's fleet on May 28, *Oregon* took part in the destruction of Admiral Pascual Cervera's fleet at Santiago Bay on June 3. *Oregon's*

journey demonstrated both that heavy battleships could stand up to adverse conditions for extended periods and that a canal across the Central American isthmus was vital to U.S. national security. (The Panama Canal opened in 1914.)

After a refit in New York, *Oregon* was assigned to the Asiatic Station, where she took part in the suppression of the Philippine Insurrection. Dispatched to China during the Boxer Rebellion, she did not return stateside until 1906, when she was decommissioned in Puget Sound. In and out of commission through World War I, in 1918 she was briefly attached to the American Siberian Expeditionary Forces sent to aid anti-Bolshevik Czechoslovak forces in Vladivostok. A preservation effort to save *Oregon* began in 1921, but in 1942 she was struck from the navy list and sold for scrap. In 1944, the hull of *Oregon* was requisitioned for use as a hulk at Guam. In 1956, *Oregon's* remains were sold to a Japanese firm, and the ship was scrapped at Kawasaki.

Bradford, "And *Oregon* Rushed Home." Sternlicht, *McKinley's Bulldog.* Webber, *Battleship "Oregon."*

L'Orient

(ex-*Sans Culotte, Dauphin Royal*) 1st rate 120 (3m). *Hull:* wood. *Arm.:* 120 guns. *Built:* Toulon, France; 1791.

Originally named for the heir apparent to the French throne, following the death of Louis XVI in 1792, *Le Dauphin Royal* was renamed *Sans Culotte,* the name given to lower-class extremists during the French Revolution. Stationed at Toulon, in March 1795 she flew the flag of Admiral Martin during his skirmish with Vice Admiral William Hotham's Mediterranean Fleet. Three years later, *L'Orient* sailed as flagship of an armada assembled at Toulon under command of Vice Admiral François Paul Brueys d'Aiguilliers. Bound ultimately for Egypt, where the French intended to establish a bridgehead from which they could invade British India (the ship's new name suggests the tendency of French strategic thinking), some 75 warships, 400 transports, 10,000 sailors, and 36,000 soldiers led by General Napoleon Bonaparte slipped out of port on May 20, 1798. The same day, a blockading force under Rear Admiral Horatio Nelson was blown off station in a gale. On June 10, the French were at Malta, which they captured on the twelfth. Continuing via Crete, they reached Egypt on July 1, seizing the port of Alexandria the next day and Cairo three weeks later. In the meantime, Brueys stationed his fleet off the island of Aboukir in the Nile Delta east of Alexandria. On August 1, his thirteen ships were anchored in line ahead, and many of the crew were getting water ashore when Nelson finally caught up with him in mid-afternoon. Brueys made two miscalculations: that Nelson would not attack until the next morning, and that his own ships did not need to clear for action the shoreward-facing guns because Nelson would attack only from the sea. He was disappointed on both counts.

Five of Nelson's ships passed between the van of the French line and the shore, while another six, led by Nelson's HMS VANGUARD, ranged themselves on the seaward side of the French line. The battle began at 1830, with the 74-gun BELLEROPHON opposite Brueys's *L'Orient.* By 2000, the British ship was forced to disengage, but *L'Orient* was ablaze and Brueys and Captain Louis de Casabianca were mortally wounded. HMS *Swiftsure* and *Alexander* pressed home the attack on the French flagship, and at about 2200, *L'Orient*'s magazine exploded and the ship blew apart. Only about seventy-five of the French crew survived, including Casabianca's ten-year-old son, Jacques, whose steadfast loyalty was commemorated in Felicia Heman's 1829 ballad, which begins, "The boy stood on the burning deck / Whence all but he had fled."

With the loss of *L'Orient,* the six ships in the French van and center quickly surrendered. The British ships had anchored by the stern, and with a favorable wind, they now continued down the French line to capture or destroy all the French ships except *Généreux, Guillaume Tell,* and two frigates, which escaped under Rear Admiral Pierre Charles de Villeneuve. Two other ships of the line were sunk, three were beyond repair, and six were brought into the Royal Navy. The Battle of the Nile was the first decisive defeat of the French in years, and Nelson was lionized throughout Europe, not least by his own officers and crew. Among his many tributes was a casket made from the main mast of *L'Orient* presented to him by *Swiftsure*'s Captain Benjamin Hallowell and in which he was buried after his death aboard HMS VICTORY at the Battle of Trafalgar in 1805.

Culver, *Forty Famous Ships.*

Ormrinn Langi

Dragon ship (1m). *Hull:* wood. *Comp.:* 64 oarsmen; 200 total? *Built:* Torberg Skavhogg, Lade, Norway; ca. 999.

At the end of the tenth century, southern Norway was ruled by Olaf Tryggvason, a Viking who had lived in Gardarik (Russia, in the eastern Baltic), Vendland (modern Poland and Germany), and the British Isles, where he married an Irish princess. He was "the gladdest of all men and very playful," according to the thirteenth-century Icelandic chronicler Snorri Sturluson, who records that Olaf ran on the oars outside the ship when his men were rowing. He was also one of the first Christian kings of Norway, and he baptized Leif the Lucky during one of the latter's visits from Greenland. Olaf ordered several ships built for himself, the most renowned of which was the *Ormrinn Langi* ("Long Serpent"). Available accounts describe a vessel more akin to a massive floating garrison designed to dominate the battle line in home waters than the sort of vessels that carried the Vikings coursing through the seas and rivers of Europe. The ship is described in some detail in Snorri's history of Olaf.

> In the *Long Serpent* there were thirty-four rowing seats. The [dragon] head and the crook at the stern were all gilded and the bulwarks were as high as an ocean-going ship. That was the best fitted and the most costly ship that was ever built in Norway.

The crew consisted of "no men older than sixty or younger than twenty, all especially selected for action and courage."

In the spring of 1000, Olaf sailed with a fleet of sixty ships, including eleven large vessels and "ships with twenty rowing seats and smaller crafts." At Rogaland, Olaf married off his sister Ingebjörg to Ulfson, the Jarl of Gautland. From there he sailed for a meeting with Boleslav I in Vendland, near the mouth of the Oder River, where he stayed the summer. In the meantime, Denmark's Svein Forkbeard (the father of Canute) and Sweden's King Olaf Sköttkonung had joined forces with Erik, Jarl of Lade, whose father Olaf Tryggvason had earlier deposed as King of Norway.

On Olaf's return to Norway, he was tricked into dividing his fleet, so that he was left with only his eleven largest ships. This force met the fleet of his confederated enemies somewhere in the narrow Øresund, not far from Copenhagen, or near an otherwise unknown island of Svold off Rügen. Snorri's account of the Battle of the Svold is a vivid depiction of how battles at sea were fought before the invention of guns. As the combined fleet approached, Olaf lashed his ships together with *Ormrinn Langi, Ormrinn,* and the *Crane* at the center. When the Danish ships closed,

> the forecastle men . . . cast anchors and grappling hooks onto King Swein's ships, and they could bear their weapons down upon them; they cleared all the ships they could hold fast; but King Swein

and those who escaped fled into other ships and at last drew from reach of the shots.

The same happened with the ships and men of Olaf the Swede. When Erik came up, the battle-weary Norwegians began to pull back to their own ships, and as they did so, Erik's men cut the outer ships loose, so that

> the Danes and the Swedes came into shooting range and from all sides they lay against King Olaf's ships. Eric the Jarl continually lay alongside the ships and fought with hand weapons; and as soon as men in his ship fell, Danes and Swedes came up in their stead.

The men in the *Ormrinn Langi* fought almost to the last man, and in the end Olaf and Kolbjörn, his marshal, leaped into the sea, followed by those of his men who were still living. Erik's men searched for Olaf from small boats in an effort to capture him, but his body was never recovered. There were rumors that Olaf managed to escape in a ship belonging to Boleslav's daughter, Astrid, his former sister-in-law. "But in whatsoever wise it was, King Olaf never again came back to his kingdom in Norway," which was divided between his three opponents.

Jones, *A History of the Vikings.* Snorri Sturluson, *Heimskringla.*

HMS Orpheus

Screw corvette (1f/3m). *L/B/D:* 254′ × 41′ × 19′ (77.4m × 9.4m × 5.8m). *Tons:* 1,706 bm. *Arm.:* 16 × 8″, 1 × 7″, 4 × 40pdr. *Mach.:* direct-acting horizontal engines, 400 hp, 1 screw; 12 kts. *Built:* Chatham Dockyard, Eng.; 1861.

Commissioned in 1861, HMS *Orpheus* was a flush-deck warship intended for service as flagship of the Australasian Naval Station. Under Captain William Farquharson Burnett, she sailed for Sydney, where Burnett broke his commodore's pennant. On January 31, 1863, *Orpheus* sailed for Auckland to join HMS *Niger* and *Harrier* at Manukau Harbour. Of immediate military concern was the conduct of the

Second Maori War. Approaching Manukau Harbour under sail and steam on the clear morning of February 7, 1863, *Orpheus*'s officers failed to heed semaphore signals from Manukau Heads indicating the proper approach — across Manukau bar — into Auckland. At about 1230, *Harrier*'s Quartermaster Frederick Butler, who was aboard under arrest for desertion, pleaded to share his local knowledge with the sailing master. He quickly discovered that *Orpheus*'s chart was not current; despite an immediate course change, the ship hit hard two minutes later. With no assistance available to her in the treacherous shoal waters, the ship was quickly battered to a hulk. Of the ship's complement of 258, only 69 survived what remains to this date New Zealand's worst maritime disaster.

Fairburn, *"Orpheus" Disaster.* Hetherington, *Wreck of H.M.S. "Orpheus."*

Oseberg ship

Karvi. *L/B/D:* 70.8' × 16.7' × 5.2' dph (21.6m × 5.1m × 1.6m). *Tons:* 11 disp. *Hull:* wood. *Comp.:* 35. *Built:* Norway; ca. 815–20.

Dating from the beginning of the period of Viking expansion, the Oseberg ship was found in 1904 in a burial mound located on a farm of the same name at Slagen, about seventy miles south of Oslo. The Oseberg ship is a karvi, a large, clinker-built open boat with 12 strakes per side, each riveted to the one below it. The planking was fastened to the 17 ribs by baleen or whale-bone lashings, a technique that made the boat highly elastic. There were 15 oar holes beneath the shield racks on either side of the ship, and the oars themselves measured between 3.7 meters and 4 meters. The rudder, really an enlarged oar, was fitted on the starboard (or steering board) side aft. Evidence suggests that the mast would have stood about 13 meters high and set a single square sail. The ship's one-meter, seven-kilo anchor was made of forged iron with an oak anchor stock. Although the Oseberg ship is estimated to have been about fifteen to twenty years old when it was buried, the ship probably served more as a chieftain's private vessel than as a warship. Its low freeboard also suggests that it was built for coastal rather than offshore sailing.

Despite a long-standing belief that the Oseberg mound was the burial place of Queen Åsa, grandmother of Harald Comely-Hair, the evidence is only conjectural. The mound was probably looted in the Middle Ages, at which time the ship's bow was damaged; many of the ship's timbers had also collapsed under the weight of the rocks placed in and around the ship when it was buried. The excavation and preservation of the burial site was led by Gabriel Gustafson, who oversaw the removal of thousands of wood fragments that were treated with creosote and taken to Oslo, where they were painstakingly reassembled. In 1926, the ship was moved to the Viking Ship Hall at Bygdøy, Oslo, where it is housed together with remains of the GOKSTAD and Tune ships. Thanks to the blue clay of the Slagen area, the Oseberg horde yielded a great many well-preserved wooden artifacts, including, in addition to the items noted above, a bailing bucket, figureheads, beds, tents, and the remains of more than ten horses, oxen, and cows.

Sjøvold, *Oseberg Find and the Other Viking Ship Finds.*

P

HMS Pandora

6th rate 24 (3m). *L/B/D:* 114.5′ × 32′ × 16′ (34.9m × 9.8m × 4.9m). *Tons:* 520 bm. *Hull:* wood. *Comp.:* 160. *Arm.:* 22 × 9pdr, 2 × 3pdr. *Built:* Adams & Barnard, Deptford Dockyard, Eng.; 1779.

HMS *Pandora* was named — some might say aptly — for the woman of Greek myth who let escape from a box all the evils to which mankind is subject, save hope, which lay, inexplicably, at the bottom. On November 7, 1790, she sailed from Portsmouth under Captain Edward Edwards in search of the mutineers from HMS BOUNTY. Calling at Tenerife and Rio de Janeiro, she rounded Cape Horn in January 1791 and arrived at Tahiti on March 23, 1791. Within the week, the fourteen "mutineers" — some of whom had been kept aboard *Bounty* against their will — remaining at Tahiti were arrested. Having also acquired some breadfruit trees (the object of *Bounty*'s voyage) as well as a schooner named *Resolution* built by the mutineers, *Pandora* sailed six weeks later. The prisoners were confined in "Pandora's Box," an eleven-by-eighteen-foot hutch erected on the quarter deck. Sailing westward, the ship searched in vain for *Bounty* and the other mutineers among the islands of Polynesia, losing one boat and four of her crew off Palmerston Island, and then *Resolution*, with nine men, for which she searched the Friendly (Tonga) Islands for almost a month.

Passing within sight of Vanikoro, in the Santa Cruz Islands, where La Pérouse's *Boussole* and *Astrolabe* had wrecked three years before, on August 26 *Pandora* entered Endeavour Strait between New Guinea and Australia. Two nights later, she struck a reef. The following morning, she sank in sixty feet of water; thirty-one crew and four prisoners were drowned. On August 31, the ninety-nine ill-provisioned survivors put to sea in the four ship's boats and sailed for the Dutch settlement at Kupang, Timor, 1,100 miles to the west. They arrived on September 13; three weeks later, they sailed for Batavia in the East Indiaman *Rembang*. At Semarang, they were reunited with the crew of the long-lost *Resolution*, which had arrived a few weeks before without a man lost during its 5,000-mile voyage. A few days later, they arrived at Batavia, where Edwards and company embarked in four Dutch traders. They arrived at Table Bay on March 18, 1792, where they joined HMS *Gorgon*, which finally landed at Spithead on June 20. In the subsequent trial of the nine *Bounty* mutineers who survived the journey, four were acquitted, two pardoned, one reprieved, and three hanged. *Pandora*'s remains were discovered by divers in the 1980s, and excavation began in 1993.

There is an interesting sidebar to the *Pandora* story. While at Timor, Edwards had been forced to take responsibility for eight men, a woman, and her two children. The adults were convicts who had stolen a small boat from the British penal colony at Botany Bay and sailed 3,254 miles in 69 days without the loss of a single life. The woman, Mary Bryant, had been transported in 1786 and gave birth to a girl en route. She later bore a son, who was still at her breast on the voyage to Timor. He died at Batavia, and her daughter died aboard *Gorgon*. Her case came to the attention of James Boswell, who visited her and the four other surviving convicts in Newgate Prison and later secured for them a pardon and bestowed an annuity on Bryant of £10 per year.

McKay & Coleman, *24-Gun Frigate "Pandora," 1779.* Marden, "Wreck of H.M.S. *Pandora*." Rawson, *"Pandora"'s Last Voyage.*

USS Peacock

Sloop of war (3m). *L/B/D:* 117.9' × 31.5' × 16.3' (35.9m × 9.6m × 5m). *Tons:* 509 bm. *Hull:* wood. *Comp.:* 140. *Arm.:* 2 × 12pdr, 20 × 32pdr. *Des.:* William Doughty. *Built:* Adam & Noah Brown, New York; 1813.

Named to commemorate the victory of USS HORNET over HMS *Peacock*, on February 24, 1813, USS *Peacock* departed for the southeastern United States in March 1814. While cruising off Cape Canaveral, Florida, on April 29, she encountered the 18-gun HMS *Epervier* and a merchant ship bound from Havana to Bermuda. She fought the British brig for forty-five minutes before Commander Richard Wade was forced to strike. After putting into Savannah with her prize (which served in the Mediterranean Squadron under the same name until her disappearance in 1815), *Peacock* set out on her second cruise, during which she took fourteen prizes between the Grand Banks, the coasts of Ireland and Spain, and the West Indies. On January 23, 1815, she began her third cruise, to the Indian Ocean, where she captured the East India Company's cruiser *Nautilus* on June 30, only to release her upon learning that the War of 1812 was over.

Peacock sailed with the Mediterranean Squadron from 1816 to 1821. The following year, she began service with Commodore David Porter's antipiracy "Mosquito Fleet" in the West Indies. In 1824, she joined the Pacific Squadron, with which she sailed under Master Commandant Thomas ap Catesby Jones. Over the next three years, she ranged around the Pacific working to protect U.S. commercial interests threatened by revolution in Spain's South American colonies, as well as in the Pacific islands frequented by American whalers. *Peacock* was the first U.S. warship to visit Tahiti, where Jones drew up an agreement for the safety of shipwrecked American sailors. In 1826, he visited the Hawaiian Islands and negotiated a more comprehensive treaty with King Kamehameha III — never ratified by the United States — relating to both the treatment of U.S. sailors and favorable trading rights for American merchants. En route home, *Peacock* was nearly stove by a whale. She was broken up shortly after her return to New York in 1826.

Johnson, *Thence round Cape Horn.* U.S. Navy, *DANFS.*

USS Pennsylvania

Ship of the line 120 (3m). *L/B/D:* 210' lbp × 56.8' × 24.3' dph (64m × 17.3m × 7.4m). *Tons:* 3,105 om. *Hull:* wood. *Comp.:* 1,100. *Arm.:* 16 × 8", 104 × 32pdr. *Des.:* Samuel Humphreys. *Built:* Samuel Humphreys, Philadelphia Navy Yard; 1837.

The first ship to carry the name, USS *Pennsylvania* has the distinction of being the largest sailing ship ever built for the U.S. Navy. One of "nine ships to rate not less than 74 guns each" authorized by Congress in 1816, *Pennsylvania*'s design seems to have been a response to the effects of the British blockade of American ports during the War of 1812. As such she was probably intended less for duty on foreign station than as a coast defense vessel capable of driving off or destroying blockading ships. Rated at 120 guns, *Pennsylvania* was pierced for 132 guns on four decks (lower, middle, upper, and spar), not including bow chasers and stern guns.

As the world settled into a peacetime routine, the need for such powerful ships lessened, and construction was slow. Laid down in 1821, she was not launched for sixteen years. Active duty personnel in all the services numbered only 22,000 in 1840, and with a total complement of 1,100, it was impossible to man the *Pennsylvania* with a full crew at that time. As a result, she was put in ordinary at Norfolk, Virginia, and in 1842 she became a receiving ship. An ordnance report from 1846 shows her armament consisting of ninety 32-pdr., twelve 8-inch shell guns (first adopted by the French navy in 1837), two 9-pdr., and one swivel. *Pennsylvania* remained at Norfolk until the Civil War, and she was one of ten sailing warships burned at the Navy Yard by the U.S. Navy to prevent their capture by Confederate forces.

Chapelle, *History of the American Sailing Navy.* U.S. Navy, *DANFS.*

Philadelphia

Gundalow (1m). *L/B/D:* 53.3' × 15.5' × 3.8' dph (16.3m × 4.7m × 1.2m). *Hull:* wood. *Comp.:* 45. *Arm.:* 1 × 12pdr, 2 × 9pdr. *Built:* Skenesborough, N.Y.; 1776.

During the American Revolution, one of Britain's primary objectives was to sever New England from

▲ A replica of the gundalow **Philadelphia,** one of three such vessels in the fleet cobbled together by Benedict Arnold to stall the British advance down Lake Champlain in 1776. The original vessel was sunk at the Battle of Valcour Bay, but recovered in 1934 and exhibited at the Smithsonian Institution. *Courtesy Lake Champlain Maritime Museum, Vergennes, Vermont.*

the rest of the colonies, by attacking down Lake Champlain, between New York and Vermont, and into the Hudson River Valley. To counter this threat, General Benedict Arnold assembled a small army of soldiers and shipbuilders at Skenes-

borough, New York, and, in the course of a few months, threw together a fleet of three galleys, one cutter, and eight gunboats, one of which was *Philadelphia.* The lightly armed, flat-bottomed gundalows set two square sails on a single mast, although the ships' primary means of propulsion was probably sixteen oars. On October 11, 1776, Arnold's fleet was moored off southwest Valcour Island about fifty-five miles north of Fort Ticonderoga, when Captain Thomas Pringle's fleet — five warships, twenty gunboats, and twenty-eight longboats — rounded the southern end of the island. In the ensuing action, the two-masted galleys Congress and *Washington* were run aground and captured, and *Philadelphia* was sunk by a single round of 24-pdr. shot. The four-day battle was a tactical defeat for the revolutionaries. Nonetheless, with his ammunition depleted, Pringle was forced to postpone his drive south until the following spring. In the meantime, the Continental Army reinforced its position enough to inflict a stunning victory against the British at Saratoga, considered a turning point in the American Revolution.

In 1934, Colonel Lorenzo F. Hagglund, a salvage engineer, found the remains of *Philadelphia* in ten fathoms of water, her mast still standing. Remarkably preserved after 158 years in the cold, fresh water of Lake Champlain, the hull was raised on August 1, 1935, and exhibited in New York until 1961. *Philadelphia* then underwent four years of restorative work before being exhibited at the Smithsonian Museum of American History in Washington, D.C.

Fowler, *Rebels under Sail.* Lundeberg, *Gunboat "Philadelphia."*

USS Philadelphia

Frigate (3m). *L/B/D:* 157′ × 39′ × 13′ (47.9m × 11.9m × 4m). *Tons:* 1,240 bm. *Hull:* wood. *Comp.:* 307. *Arm.:* 26 × 18pdr long, 16 × 32pdr carr. *Des.:* Josiah Fox. *Built:* Samuel Humphreys, Nathaniel Hutton & John Delavue, Philadelphia; 1800.

One of six frigates built with funds provided by merchants during the Quasi-War with France, USS *Philadelphia* was commissioned under Captain

Stephen Decatur, Sr., toward the end of the war. Considered one of the fastest ships of her day, on her first tour of duty off Guadeloupe she captured five French armed vessels and recaptured six U.S. vessels. Returning to the United States in March 1801, *Philadelphia* was prepared for service in the Mediterranean, where U.S. merchant vessels were being harassed because of the government's refusal to pay tribute to the rulers along the Barbary Coast of North Africa. Sailing under command of Captain Samuel Barron in a squadron led by Commodore Richard Hale in USS PRESIDENT, *Philadelphia* sailed on blockade duty off Tripoli for a year before returning to the United States at the end of July 1802. The following spring, she returned to the Mediterranean under Captain William Bainbridge. On August 26, 1803, she captured the Moroccan ship *Mirboka* (24 guns) together with her American prize, the brig *Celia*, and brought them both into Gibraltar.

Proceeding to blockade duty off Tripoli, on October 31 *Philadelphia* hit an uncharted reef in the harbor. Under fire from shore batteries and gunboats, the ship remained fast, and Bainbridge was forced to surrender his ship and crew. Shortly after the new year, Captain Stephen Decatur, Jr. — son of her first commander — proposed to Commodore Edward Preble a plan to destroy the ship where she lay and so prevent the enemy from refloating her for their own use. On February 16, 1804, Decatur slipped past the Tripolitan ships in the gunboat INTREPID. The volunteer crew of sixty boarded *Philadelphia*, overpowered her small crew, and set fire to the ship, all without any American casualties.

Chapelle, *History of the American Sailing Navy.* U.S. Navy, DANFS.

CSS Pioneer

Submarine. *L/B/D:* 30′ × 4′ × 6′ dph (9.1m × 1.2m × 1.8m). *Tons:* 4 tons. *Comp.:* 3′. *Arm.:* clock-work torpedo. *Mach.:* manual screw. *Built:* J. R. McClintock and Baxter Watson, New Orleans; 1862.

Designed and built by New Orleans machinist J. R. McClintock, the cigar-shaped *Pioneer* was the

first of three submarines built in the Confederacy during the Civil War. (Her successors were the five-man *Pioneer II* and the celebrated H. L. HUNLEY.) Commissioned as a privateer in March 1862, J. K. Scott commanding, on trials *Pioneer* reportedly completed several successful dives and sank a schooner and several smaller vessels by means of a clock-work torpedo designed to be screwed into the enemy ship's hull. Before she could see action against the enemy, *Pioneer* was scuttled in Bayou St. John to avoid capture by Flag Officer David Farragut's forces after the fall of New Orleans on April 25, 1862. She was subsequently raised and surveyed by Union engineers. In 1868, she was sold for scrap. Ten years later a smaller, similar vessel was raised and displayed at the Louisiana Home for Confederate Soldiers. In 1954, this vessel (long identified as the *Pioneer*) was moved to the Louisiana State Museum in New Orleans.

Ragan, "Union and Confederate Submarine Warfare."

USS Powhatan

Sidewheel steamer (3m). *L/B/D:* 253.8′ × 45′ × 18.5′ (53.3m × 13.5m × 4m). *Tons:* 3,479 disp. *Hull:* wood. *Comp.:* 289. *Arm.:* 1 × 11″, 10 × 9″, 5 × 12pdr. *Mach.:* inclined engine, 1,500 ihp, sidewheels; 11 kts. *Built:* Gosport Navy Yard, Portsmouth, Va.; 1852.

Named for the Indian chief who ruled the coastal area of eastern Virginia in which the English colony of Jamestown was settled in 1607, the bark-rigged USS *Powhatan* was the largest and one of the last of the U.S. Navy's paddle frigates. After two years as flagship of the navy's Home Squadron, in 1853 she joined the East India Squadron. Commodore Matthew C. Perry had arrived in the Orient the year before with instructions to effect a treaty to open Japan to American trade and to guarantee the protection of shipwrecked American sailors. Perry's first visit to Edo (Tokyo) Bay with the steamers MISSISSIPPI and *Susquehanna* preceded the arrival of *Powhatan*, but during his second visit, the Treaty of Kanagawa was signed on her decks on March 31, 1854. En route back to the United States, in the summer of 1855, she joined

Lexington　Susquehannah　Powhattan　Macedonian　Mississippi　Vandalia　Saratoga　Southampton　Supply

▲ One of the last sidewheel steamers built for service with the navy, **USS Powhatan** served as flagship of Commodore Perry's famous mission to "open" Japan in 1854. This primitive painting shows the ships' boats — American flags flying — approaching the shore, with the fleet anchored offshore. **Powhatan** is flying the Commodore's pennant. *Courtesy The Mariners' Museum, Newport News, Virginia.*

the Royal Navy screw frigate HMS RATTLER in freeing a number of ships being held by pirates at Kulan, China.

Two years later, *Powhatan* joined the West Indies Squadron, and she remained in active service through the Civil War. Under Lieutenant David Dixon Porter, in 1861 she took part in the relief of Fort Pickens, Florida, and helped establish blockades off Mobile and the Mississippi. From 1863 to 1864, she operated off Charleston and with the West Indies Squadron, and in the winter of 1864–65, she took part in the reduction of Fort Fisher, North Carolina. After the war, she was Rear Admiral John A. Dahlgren's flagship in the South Pacific. Returning to the Home Squadron in 1869, she remained in Atlantic waters until decommissioned

in 1886. She was broken up the following year in Meriden, Connecticut.

Canney, *Old Steam Navy.* U.S. Navy, *DANFS.*

USS President

Frigate (3m). *L/B/D:* 175′ × 44.3′ × 13.1′ (53.3m × 13.5m × 4m). *Tons:* 1,576 bm. *Hull:* wood. *Comp:* 450. *Arm.:* 32 × 24pdr, 22 × 42pdr, 1 × 19pdr. *Des.:* Joshua Humphreys, Josiah Fox, William Doughty. *Built:* Christian Bergh, New York; 1800.

One of the U.S. Navy's original six frigates, USS *President* was authorized by Congress to combat the Barbary corsairs of North Africa. Although she was laid down in 1795, work on *President* was suspended following the peace with Algiers, only to be resumed at the start of the Quasi-War with France three years later. Completed in 1800 under the direction of Naval Constructor William Doughty, *President* was considered the fastest ship of her class in the world. The frigate put to sea in August 1800 under Commander Thomas Truxton, but hostilities with France ended the next month. In 1801, she sailed as flagship of Commodore Richard

▲ Portrait of the frigate **USS President** riding out a gale at anchor off the coast of Marseilles. Note how her topmasts and yards have been sent down to reduce windage. *Courtesy U.S. Naval Historical Center, Washington, D.C.*

Dale's "Squadron of Evolution" (which included UNITED STATES, PHILADELPHIA, and ESSEX) sent to the Mediterranean to protect American merchantmen from renewed attacks by corsairs. *President* remained in the Mediterranean until the following year, returning again in 1804–5. Put in ordinary upon her return, she was reactivated in 1809 as the British continued impressing American seamen into the Royal Navy.

Following the impressment of one such sailor on May 1, 1811, by HMS GUERRIÈRE, *President* was ordered to sea on the twelfth under Commodore John Rodgers, and after a long chase, five days later she engaged HMS LITTLE BELT (18 guns) about forty-five miles off the Chesapeake. The night action broke off after fifteen minutes; *President* had one man injured and suffered slight damage to the rigging, as against thirteen killed and nineteen wounded on *Little Belt,* which was con-

demned as "almost a wreck" upon her return to Halifax. In many respects, the incident resembled the CHESAPEAKE-LEOPARD affair, and it might have brought on the start of an Anglo-American war a year early but for Rodgers's restrained handling of the incident.

The United States declared war on June 18, 1812, and three days later, *President* sailed as flagship of a squadron that included *United States, Congress,* HORNET, and ARGUS on a North Atlantic cruise. Two days later, *President* fell in with HMS *Belvedira,* but after an eight-hour chase, the British ship escaped after one of *President*'s bow chasers blew up, killing and wounding several of the crew, including Rodgers, whose leg was broken. *President* made three more cruises to European waters and the Caribbean, but with lackluster results. Returning to New York on February 18, 1814, she was forced to remain there by the British blockade for almost a year.

At the end of 1814, she came under command of Captain Stephen Decatur. Although the Treaty of Ghent had been signed on December 24, the news had not yet arrived, and on January 14, 1815, Decatur tried to slip the blockade. *President* grounded on a sandbar several hours later, breaking her keel and straining her hull. The next day, HMS *Endymion* (50) gave chase until Decatur turned for a broadside action. *President* had the advantage until HMS *Pomone* and *Tenedos* arrived on the scene. Vastly outgunned and with fifty of his crew dead or wounded, Decatur struck. *President* was taken to Bermuda and seized as a war prize. Too damaged for further work, she was broken up at Portsmouth in 1817, but not before her lines were taken off and used for a new Royal Navy ship of the same name and reputation for speed.

Roosevelt, *Naval War of 1812*. U.S. Navy, *DANFS*.

Princess Mary

(also known as *Mary Imperial* and *Great Galley*) Galleass (4m). *L/B/D:* ca. 180′ (gundeck) × 34′ × 15′ dph (54.9m × 10.4m × 4.6m). *Tons:* 800. *Hull:* wood. *Comp.:* 800–1,200. *Arm.:* 70 brass guns, 147 iron guns. *Built:* Greenwich, Eng.; 1515.

One of the largest English ships of her day, and one of England's last oared warships, *Princess Mary* (often referred to as *Great Galley*) was built during the reign of Henry VIII, five years after the launch of MARY ROSE. As described by Venetian ambassadors, whose letters form the first written account of the ship, she was as large as one of their first-rate galleys, with 120 oars (60 to a side) and four masts, three with topmasts and topsails, and the main with a topgallant mast and sail. Her complement was considerable by modern standards. The Venetians credit her with 60 gunners and 1,200 fighting men, while French accounts credit her with 800 fighting men. The number of *Princess Mary*'s brass and iron guns varied over the years. She seems to have been launched with 217 guns, 14 of them big guns mounted aft. In 1540, she carried 87 guns, while eight years later, she carried 97. The inventory of 1540 demonstrates the variety of armament. Her brass guns included five cannons, two demi-culverins, four sakers, and two falcons, while iron guns numbered twelve port pieces, two single slings, fifty double bases, and ten single (or small) bases.

Princess Mary remained in the Thames until war with France was renewed in 1522. Assigned to a fleet commanded by Sir William Fitzwilliam, she was not a success and was given a rebuild at Portsmouth that resulted in what was virtually a new ship. The next year, Fitzwilliam wrote that Clerk of the Ships Robert "Brigandine intends to break her up and make her carvel" planked, rather than clenched, "for she was the dangeroust ship under water that ever man sailed in." The ship underwent a second rebuild in the late 1530s, after which she may have been called *Great Bark*. (There is some confusion because of the tendency for different names to be applied to the same vessel, and the same name to different vessels.) This vessel probably took part in an expedition to Scotland in 1544. Her name appears on a number of ship lists until 1562, and she was probably broken up sometime between then and 1565.

Anderson, "Henry VIII's *Great Galley*." Loades, *Tudor Navy*.

USS Princeton

Sloop of war (1f/3m). *L/B/D:* 164′ × 31.5′ × 17′ (50m × 9.3m × 5.2m). *Tons:* 954 disp. *Hull:* iron. *Comp.:* 166. *Arm.:* 2 × 12″, 12 × 42pdr. *Mach.:* semicylindrical reciprocating engines, 220 hp, 1 screw; 10 kts. *Built:* John Lenthall, Philadelphia Navy Yard; 1843.

A warship of innovative design and armament, USS *Princeton* was built "under the patronage of Captain Robert F. Stockton and the superintendence of [John] Ericsson." The two had previously collaborated in the building of *Robert F. Stockton*, the first ship to carry a direct-acting screw engine, the primary advantage of which was that the engines could be placed below the waterline and out of the line of fire. Built by Merrick and Towne of Philadelphia, *Princeton*'s propulsion consisted of a semicylindrical reciprocating steam engine driving a single helicoidal screw — that is, one with a single blade that spiraled around the shaft. Arriving at New York, on October 19, 1843, *Princeton* beat Brunel's side-wheeler *Great Western* over a twenty-one-mile course.

The following January, she received her two 12-inch shell guns, the British-built "Oregon," de-

▲ One of the U.S. Navy's worst peacetime tragedies was the explosion of **USS Princeton**'s 12-in. gun, the "Peacemaker," during an official cruise on the Potomac River, February 29, 1844. President John Tyler was below when the explosion occurred, but Secretary of State Abel P. Upshur and Secretary of the Navy Thomas Gilmer — one third of his cabinet — were killed. *Courtesy U.S. Naval Historical Center, Washington, D.C.*

the congressional resolution annexing Texas. After service in the Mediterranean in 1848–49, where she was admired by European observers, she returned to Boston Navy Yard in 1849 and was broken up. Some of her timbers and Ericsson's engine were used in the construction of USS *Princeton* of 1851, the second of five vessels so named.

Baxter, *Introduction of the Ironclad Warship*. Tucker, "U.S. Navy Steam Sloop *Princeton*."

Providence

(ex-*Katy*) Topsail sloop (1m). *L/B/D:* 67′ × 20′ × 9′ (20.4m × 6.1m × 2.7m). *Tons:* 95 bm. *Hull:* wood. *Comp.:* 52–90. *Arm.:* 12 × 6pdr, 10 swivels. *Built:* Providence, R.I.; <1768.

Originally owned by Providence merchant John Brown, the merchant sloop *Katy* was one of two chartered by the Rhode Island General Assembly in June 1775 to protect Rhode Island shipping from British warships, in particular HMS Rose. Abraham Whipple, *Katy*'s first captain, captured the sloop *Diana* during the summer and was then ordered to capture a store of gunpowder at Bermuda, an unsuccessful operation. Purchased by the General Assembly on her return, *Katy* sailed for Philadelphia and, renamed *Providence*, entered the Continental Navy under Captain John Hazard.

On February 17, 1776, *Providence* sailed for the Bahamas, again in search of gunpowder, as part of a squadron commanded by Esek Hopkins in Alfred. The Americans occupied Nassau in early March but failed to capture the gunpowder. Hopkins's ships returned to New London, where *Providence* became John Paul Jones's first command. After carrying soldiers from New London to New York and escorting a convoy of colliers to Philadelphia, *Providence* sailed on an independent cruise on August 1. Jones quickly captured a whaleship and a merchant ship and dispatched his prizes to Philadelphia. He then turned for Nova Scotia, where he burned or captured eight fishing schooners and recruited new crew to replace those he had put aboard his prizes.

Returning to Rhode Island on October 9, Jones took command of *Alfred*. The two ships, with *Prov-*

signed by Ericsson, and the New York–built "Peacemaker," modeled on Ericsson's gun but designed by Stockton. In February 1844, the ship sailed to Washington, D.C., with a view to persuading Congress to approve the fitting out of more ships with more heavy guns, a measure endorsed by President John Tyler. Her third Potomac cruise, on February 29, was attended by 300–400 people, including officials and their families and, for the second time, Tyler. During the demonstration of the Peacemaker, the gun exploded, killing eight people. Among them were Secretary of State Abel P. Upshur and Secretary of the Navy Thomas Gilmer; nine were wounded, including Stockton and Senator Thomas Hart Benson.

Following repairs, *Princeton* was deployed with the Home Squadron in 1845, serving on blockade duty in the Mexican War and carrying to Galveston *idence* now under Captain Hoysted Hacker, took the merchantmen *Active* and *Kitty* and the armed transport HMS *Mellish,* before *Providence* was forced back to Newport for repairs. In February 1777, *Providence* ran the British blockade off Narragansett Bay and captured another transport off Cape Breton, Nova Scotia. Put under Captain John P. Rathbun, *Providence* made two more coastal cruises before sailing again for the Bahamas in early 1778. Through a series of brilliant stratagems, Rathbun took and held the town for three days (January 27–30), during which time he spiked the guns of Fort Nassau, seized 1,600 pounds of gunpowder (at last), took 6 British prizes, and freed 30 American prisoners, all without bloodshed. The Americans returned to Rhode Island unscathed on January 30, 1779.

Providence followed up this action with the capture of HM Brig *Diligent* (12 guns) off New York on May 7. The latter was taken into the Continental Navy and repaired in time to take part in the disastrous Penobscot expedition under Commodore Dudley Saltonstall in Warren, together with *Providence* and thirty-seven other ships. On August 13, *Providence* and all but two of the American ships were run aground and burned to avoid capture by a superior British fleet that had appeared in Penobscot Bay.

In 1976, a fiberglass replica of *Providence* was built to commemorate the U.S. Bicentennial. Based at Newport, Rhode Island, she was used for sail training through the 1990s.

Miller, *Sea of Glory.* Morison, *John Paul Jones.* Rider, *Valour Fore and Aft.*

PT-109

Patrol torpedo boat. *L/B/D:* 80′ × 20.8′ × 5′ (24.4m × 6.3m × 1.5m). *Tons:* 45 tons. *Comp.:* 13. *Arm.:* 1 × 40mm; 2 × 20mm; 4 × 21″TT. *Hull:* wood. *Mach.:* Packard marine engines, 4,050 bph; 40 kts. *Built:* Elco Naval Division, Electric Boat Co., Bayonne, N.J.; 1942.

One of the more than 500 lightweight, fast torpedo boats built during World War II, *PT-109* entered service in the Pacific on July 10, 1942. Transferred to Motor Torpedo Boat Squadron 5 in Septem-

ber 1942, she came under command of Lieutenant John F. Kennedy. Active throughout the Solomons campaign, on the night of August 1–2, 1943, *PT-109* was one of fifteen PT boats patrolling the Blackett Strait south of Kolombangara Island. In the words of Samuel Eliot Morison, the action was "unsuccessful in a military sense, but important to a future President of the United States." At about 0230, *PT-109* was cut in half by the *Amagiri,* a *Fubuki*-class destroyer under Commander Hanami, and sank in about 8°03′S, 156°58′E. After the war, the story of Lieutenant Kennedy's efforts to rescue the injured and bring about the rescue of his crew (two of the thirteen died in the collision) were magnificently exploited to further his political career. It is interesting to note that one of the authors of the official report on Kennedy's conduct was Lieutenant Byron S. White, whom Kennedy would later appoint to the Supreme Court of the United States.

Bulkley, *At Close Quarters.*

Punic (Marsala) ship

Liburnian. *L/B:* ca. 110′ × 16′ (33.5m × 4.9m). *Hull:* wood. *Comp.:* ca. 75. *Built:* Tunisia(?); <241 BCE.

In 1969, a commercial dredger working in the harbor of Marsala in western Sicily uncovered the remains of several shipwrecks. The following summer, Honor Frost led a team of underwater archaeologists to the site, which over four seasons yielded a pile of ballast stones, a forty-foot length of keel, together with about one-third of the original port side of the hull and fragments of the starboard side. Most significant was the recovery of a portion of the sternpost, from which archaeologists were able to determine the shape of the hull. The fact that the stern had been driven into the relatively hard bottom of seaweed and sand indicated that the ship had sunk stern first, probably after being rammed. This, combined with the presence of ballast stone and the absence of amphorae, suggested that she was a warship.

Those crew who could get off took with them their personal weapons — the ship's primary armament was the bow ram — but they left ample evidence of what they ate. Food remains show that the crew had an excellent diet that included deer, goat, horse, ox, pig, and sheep, as well as olives, nuts, and fruit. Most unexpected was the recovery of the stems of plant material, which botanical testing showed to be hops, nettles, or cannabis. Circumstances suggest the last; possibly it was chewed during long-distance rowing or before going into battle, just as the Royal Navy later issued rum to its crews. Mixed in with the ballast stones were the bones of a dog and a human, possibly an injured crewman trapped by the shifting ballast.

The vessel is believed to have been a "long ship" known as a liburnian, an oared vessel with seventeen sweeps on either side, each pulled by two oarsmen. Small and swift, Liburnians were employed for carrying messages and for scouting. All other known wrecks of the period have been of "round" cargo ships. The presence of this wreck at Marsala is historically significant, because it was near this port — then known as Lilybaeum — that Rome defeated Carthage in the Battle of the Aegates (Egadi) Islands, sinking about 50 ships and capturing another 70 from a fleet of 220 ships. This battle concluded the first Punic War and forced the Carthaginians to give up their hold in western Sicily. In the first millennium BCE, Mediterranean trade was dominated by three great powers in turn. First were the Phoenicians, whose chief ports were

Sidon and Tyre in what is now Lebanon, from the eleventh to the eighth century. They were succeeded by their colonial offspring, Carthage, in what is now Tunisia, which lost to Rome after a succession of three Punic Wars, fought 264–241 BCE, 218–201 BCE, and, finally, 149–146 BCE.

One of the most fascinating discoveries about Carthaginian shipbuilding was the high degree of literacy and organization associated with it. Careful examination of the Punic ship showed that the builders had written on the various members to mark their placement in relation to one another. Archaeologists and historians of shipbuilding concur that "the findings on the Punic ship show a degree of planning and organization that is without parallel until the Industrial Revolution."

Tragically, despite the enormous historical, archaeological, and cultural value of this find, the Punic Marsala ship has been all but abandoned. In 1992, after several years of neglect, the Sicilian parliament voted to designate funds for repair and conservation of the ship's remains, which had been raised and housed in Marsala. Three years later, before any money had been spent, the parliament annulled the grant.

Delgado, ed., *Encyclopedia of Maritime and Underwater Archaeology*. Frost, "How Carthage Lost the Sea"; "Marsala Punic Ship." Frost et al., *Punic Ship*.

HMS Queen Charlotte

Umpire-class 1st rate (3m). *L/B:* 190′ × 52.3′ × 22.3′ (57.9m × 15.9m × 6.8m). *Tons:* 2,279 bm. *Hull:* wood. *Comp.:* 850. *Arm.:* 30 × 32pdr, 28 × 24pdr, 42 × 12pdr. *Des.:* Edward Hunt. *Built:* Chatham Dockyard, Eng.; 1790.

Named for the consort of George III, HMS *Queen Charlotte* was built during a period when Britain was not actively at war with her traditional enemies. But an uneasy peace ruled and the navy was on a war footing. *Queen Charlotte* spent several years as flagship of Admiral Richard Howe during the Nootka Sound Controversy with Spain in 1790, and again during the French Revolutionary Wars

starting in 1793. In May 1794, she sailed from Portsmouth with thirty-two ships of the line to intercept a grain fleet bound from North America to France. A French fleet under Rear Admiral Villaret de Joyeuse sailed from Brest to provide protection

---

▼ Philippe-Jacques de Loutherbourg's depiction of the "Battle of the Glorious First of June 1794," showing Admiral Lord Howe's **HMS Queen Charlotte** with her topmast by the boards, closely engaged by Rear Admiral Villaret de Joyeuse's **Montagne**. Though the French fleet lost six ships, the grain fleet under their protection reached France, giving Villaret de Joyeuse a strategic victory. *Courtesy National Maritime Museum, Greenwich.*

for the convoy, and on May 28, the two fleets made their first contact. A partial action resulted in the dismasting of the French *Révolutionnaire,* which lost about 400 men dead and wounded but escaped capture that night. HMS *Audacious* was also dismasted and forced home. The next day, Howe nearly captured three French ships before Villaret de Joyeuse ceded the weather gauge advantage to rescue them. Two days of fog prevented a further engagement. But on June 1, Howe ranged his fleet to windward of the French and signaled for each of his ships to steer for her French counterpart, pass under her stern, and engage her on the lee side. A few minutes before 1000, *Queen Charlotte* passed below Villaret de Joyeuse's *Montagne* and poured in a succession of broadsides. Engaged by both *Montagne* and *Jacobin, Queen Charlotte* lost her fore topmast, but *Montagne* escaped with her stern stove in and 300 of her crew dead or wounded. Howe's tactic was so successful that the battle was over by noon and six prizes were taken. Howe was too enervated to follow up his tactical victory with a strategic one, and the French grain fleet continued unscathed to Brest. Nonetheless, the battle was known as the Glorious First of June.

On June 23, 1795, *Queen Charlotte* flew the flag of Admiral Alexander Hood, Viscount Bridport, when he engaged another fleet under Villaret de Joyeuse in the Battle of Groix, during which the French lost three ships in a general chase off Brest. Two years later, the men of *Queen Charlotte* took part in the Nore mutiny, which was resolved thanks in large part to the intervention of Viscount Keith, who hoisted his flag in her as second-in-command of the Channel Fleet. She was Keith's flagship in the Mediterranean three years later when, on March 17, 1800, she caught fire about twelve miles off Livorno. Keith was ashore at the time, but his ship sank with 690 of her crew.

Clowes, *Royal Navy.* Hepper, *British Warship Losses.*

R

HMS Ramillies

(ex-*Royal Katherine*) 2nd rate 90 (3m). *L/B:* 153′ × 40′ (46.6m × 12.2m). *Tons:* 1,086 bm. *Hull:* wood. *Comp.:* 888. *Arm.:* 90 guns. *Built:* Woolwich Dockyard, Eng.; 1664.

The name *Royal Katherine* was first given to an 84-gun ship built in 1664 that saw considerable action in the Second and Third Anglo-Dutch Wars. She took part in the English victory at the Battle of Lowestoft (June 3, 1665), the English defeat in the Four Days' Battle (June 1–4), and their subsequent victory at Orfordness (July 25, 1666). When war with the Dutch was renewed a few years later, *Royal Katherine* (sometimes spelled *Catherine*) was part of the Anglo-French fleet defeated by the Dutch at Solebay on May 28, 1672, and again at the two battles of Schooneveldt on May 28 and June 4 the next year. During the War of the League of Augsburg, *Royal Katherine* was part of the Anglo-Dutch fleet that defeated the French at the three-day Battle of Barfleur, on May 19–22, 1692.

In the age of sail, in order to obtain funding for new ships from a parsimonious Parliament, the Admiralty would request funding to "rebuild" an old one. Despite appearances to the contrary, the result was in essence the same. So it was that the "rebuilt" *Royal Katherine* emerged from the yard in 1702. During the War of the Spanish Succession, she was present at the siege of Gibraltar on July 24, 1704, and at the siege of Vélez Málaga, Spain, on August 13, she flew the flag of Admiral of the Fleet Sir George Rooke. Two years later, the ship was renamed for the site of the Duke of Marlborough's victory over the French in Belgium. The next half-century was relatively uneventful for the *Ramillies*.

At the start of the Seven Years' War between England and France, the Marquis de la Galissonière captured Minorca, in the western Mediterranean, in April 1756. Ordered to the relief of the besieged garrison at Port Mahon, Vice Admiral the Honourable John Byng was dispatched from Portsmouth with thirteen ships of the line and three frigates. On May 20, 1757, he engaged La Galissonière's fleet about thirty miles from Port Mahon. When the French withdrew, Byng failed either to pursue the fleet or to relieve Port Mahon, which soon surrendered. Instead, he retired to Gibraltar to await reinforcements. Vice Admiral Sir Edward Hawke was sent out to try to recapture Minorca, but the English had lost the island for good.

Although there was widespread condemnation of Byng for failing in his mission, as his court-martial progressed aboard HMS St. George, it became clear that he was being made the scapegoat for a failure of government policy. Sentenced to a firing squad, Byng was executed on the deck of HMS *Monarch* on March 14, 1757. Condemnation of the punishment was widespread. In England, it was said that "the unfortunate Admiral was shot because Newcastle [the Prime Minister] deserved to be hanged." But the French had the last word. When Voltaire's fictional Candide visits Portsmouth, he asks why an admiral has been sentenced to die. "In this country," he is told, "it's considered a good idea to kill an admiral from time to time, to encourage the others."

Ramillies did not long survive Byng. In 1760, she was returning to Plymouth before an approaching gale when a combination of poor piloting and inadequate ship handling led to the ship's piling up on the rocks off Bolt Head on the evening of February 15. Only 26 of the 725 crew survived.

Clowes, *Royal Navy*. Hepper, *British Warship Losses*. Pope, *At Twelve Mr. Byng Was Shot.*

Randolph

Frigate (3m). *L/B/D:* 132.8′ × 34.5′ × 18′ (40.5m × 10.5m × 5.5m). *Tons:* ca. 690. Hull: wood. *Comp.:* ca. 200. *Arm.:* 32 guns. *Des.:* Joshua Humphreys. *Built:* John Wharton & Joshua Humphreys, Philadelphia; 1776.

Named for Peyton Randolph, a prominent Virginia delegate to the First Continental Congress, USS *Randolph* was one of the first frigates ordered by Congress for the fledgling Continental Navy. As his ship was launched during an acute manning shortage, Captain Nicholas Biddle recruited a large number of his crew from among imprisoned British seamen. During her first cruise, she lost her mainmast and a large number of crew died of fever before she put into Charleston on March 11. She lost two more masts to lightning before departing on September 1. Two days later, she captured four rich prizes, which were taken into Charleston. While there, John Rutledge, President of the South Carolina General Assembly, suggested that *Randolph* lead a flotilla of South Carolina Navy ships to escort a number of merchant ships through the British blockade. The ships sailed on February 14, 1778, and got away unscathed. The colonial warships sailed for the Caribbean but captured no significant prizes. On the evening of March 7, *Randolph* engaged HMS *Yarmouth* (64 guns) off Barbados. The battle was going well for Biddle's ship when its magazine blew up, destroying the ship and killing all but four of her complement.

Jamieson, "American Privateers in the Leeward Islands." McCusker, "American Invasion of Nassau in the Bahamas." U.S. Navy, *DANFS.*

Ranger

Ship sloop (3m). *L/B/D:* 131.4′ (berth deck) × 28′ × 11′ dph (40.1m × 8.5m × 3.4m). *Tons:* 697 bm. Hull: wood. *Comp.:* 140. *Arm.:* 18 × 6pdr. *Built:* James K. Hackett, Portsmouth, N.H.; 1777.

The Continental Congress appointed John Paul Jones as master of the newly built ship *Ranger* on June 14, 1777. (On the same date, coincidentally, Congress also resolved "that the flag of the thirteen United States be thirteen stripes, alternate red and white; that the union be thirteen stars, white in a blue field, representing a new constellation.") *Ranger* sailed for France on November 1 and arrived at Nantes on December 2, having taken two English prizes en route. On February 14, 1778, Admiral LaMotte Piquet's flagship *Robuste* became the first foreign ship to salute the Stars and Stripes after *Ranger* rendered honors to the French fleet at Quiberon Bay.

Ranger departed Brest on April 11 and took or burned four vessels in the Irish Sea. On the night of April 22, Jones entered Solway Firth and the next morning took forty men in two boats to raid Whitehaven, from which Jones had sailed to America at the age of thirteen. The rebels spiked the guns of the English fort and set fire to a collier. Jones then crossed the bay to Scotland with a view to capturing the Earl of Selkirk to help effect a prisoner exchange. Selkirk was away, and the shore party contented itself with stealing some silver from Lady Selkirk. Jones was appalled and later purchased it from his crew and returned it, with apologies. On April 25, *Ranger* fought HMS *Drake* (20 guns) off Carrickfergus, Ireland, in an engagement described by Jones as "warm, close and obstinate." The poorly manned *Drake* lost five killed (including Captain George Burdon) and twenty injured. A prize crew was put aboard, and the two ships returned to Brest, capturing a storeship en route. *Ranger* returned to the United States under Lieutenant Thomas Simpson in company with *Boston* and *Providence,* arriving at Portsmouth with three prizes on October 15, 1778.

Between February and November 1779, *Ranger* sailed with *Queen of France* and, variously,

WARREN or *Providence,* capturing eighteen prizes (three were later retaken) valued at more than $1 million. On November 23, 1779, *Ranger* joined Commodore Abraham Whipple's squadron bound for Charleston, South Carolina. On January 24, 1780, *Ranger* and *Providence* captured three supply transports off Tybee Island before returning to the defense of the port. When Charleston fell on May 11, 1780, *Ranger, Providence,* and *Boston* were captured and commissioned into the Royal Navy. HMS *Halifax* (ex-*Ranger*) was sold the next year.

Miller, *Sea of Glory.* Morison, *John Paul Jones.* Sawtelle, ed., *John Paul Jones and the "Ranger."*

USS Ranger

(later USS *Rockport, Nantucket, Bay State, Emery Rice*) Screw steamer (1f/3m). *L/B/D:* 177.3′ × 32′ × 12.8′ (54m × 9.8m × 3.9m). *Tons:* 1,120 disp. *Hull:* iron. *Arm.:* 1 × 11″, 2 × 9″, 1 × 60pdr. *Mach.:* compound engine, 560 ihp, 1 screw; 10 kts. *Built:* Harland & Hollingsworth, Wilmington, Del.; 1876.

First deployed with the Asiatic Fleet, after two years at Hong Kong USS *Ranger* began a twenty-two-year career as a hydrographic survey vessel and as a protector of the American seal fisheries. From 1905 to 1908, she sailed as a schoolship with the Philippine Nautical School, and in 1909, she was loaned to the Massachusetts Maritime Academy. She remained under its control until 1940, except for the years 1917–20, when (renamed first USS *Rockport* and then *Nantucket*) she was used as a gunboat and a training ship. In 1940, *Nantucket* was transferred to the Maritime Administration's new U.S. Merchant Marine Academy at Kings Point, New York. Renamed *Emery Rice,* for the master of the merchant ship *Mongolia* — the first U.S. vessel to fire on a U-boat in 1917 — she was withdrawn from sea duty in 1944. Fourteen years later, she was broken up for scrap. Although it was impossible to preserve the ship, the San Francisco Maritime Museum's Karl Kortum saved the sixty-one-ton horizontal back-acting compound-condensing main propulsion steam engine (known in England as a return connecting-rod engine). After a quarter-century in storage, this engine was put on display at the American Merchant Marine Museum in Kings Point.

McCready, "*Emery Rice* Engine." U.S. Navy, *DANFS.*

CSS Rappahannock

(ex-HMS *Victor, Scylla*) Commerce raider (2f/3m). *L/B/D:* 201′ (lbp) × 30.3′ × 14.5′ (61.3m × 9.2m × 4.4m). *Tons:* 1,042 tons. *Hull:* wood. *Comp.:* 100. *Arm.:* 2 × 9″. *Mach.:* reciprocating engines, 350 nhp, 1 screw; 11 kts. *Built:* Mare & Co., Blackwall, Eng.; 1856.

Laid down and launched as a screw gunship, HMS *Victor* saw service in the Royal Navy during the Crimean War but was put in ordinary after only two years in commission. Sold to a Confederate naval agent who claimed to want her for the China trade, British authorities seized the renamed *Scylla* when it became clear she was intended for service in the Confederate Navy as a replacement for CSS

◄ The barkentine-rigged screw steamer **USS Ranger** drying sails, probably off the Mare Island Navy Yard, California, in December 1899, toward the end of her two-decade tour of duty as a fisheries protection vessel. *Courtesy U.S. Naval Historical Center, Washington, D.C.*

GEORGIA. With her refit still incomplete, on November 24, 1863, her crew took her out of Sheerness with riggers and machinists still aboard. Commissioned at sea and named for the Virginia river, her engines burned out, and she put into Calais for repairs. In February 1864, the French government, afraid of compromising its neutrality, refused to allow her departure, and she spent the balance of the war as a supply vessel. Following the war, she was turned over to the U.S. government.

Spencer, *Confederate Navy in Europe.*

HMS Rattler

Screw sloop (1f/3m). *L/B/D:* 176.5′ × 32.7′ × 11.8′ (53.8m × 10m × 3.6m). *Tons:* 1,112 disp. *Hull:* wood. *Arm.:* 1 × 68pdr, 4 × 32pdr carr. *Mach.:* vertical "Siamese" engine, 519 ihp, 1 screw; 9.1 kts. *Des.:* Isambard Kingdom Brunel & Francis Petit Smith. *Built:* Sheerness Dockyard, Eng.; 1843.

Following a series of demonstrations of the feasibility of screw propulsion by John Ericsson (with the 45-foot launch *Frances B. Ogden*), Francis Petit Smith (with the 34-launch *Francis Smith* and the 237-ton *Archimedes*), and others in the late 1830s, the Admiralty Board ordered the construction of its first screw steamer in 1840. With machinery designed by Isambard Kingdom Brunel (who had changed the propulsion of *Great Britain* on the strength of the *Archimedes* trials) and Smith, *Rattler* easily attained 83/4 knots and proved herself in races with her paddle-driven half-sister *Polyphemus.* Between February 1844 and January 1845, the designers experimented with 32 different propellers of two, three, and four blades. The most successful of these was a Smith two-blade propeller with a diameter of 10 feet 1 inch, a pitch of 11 feet, and a length of 1 foot 3 inches.

The ultimate contest between screw and paddle propulsion was actually a series of races between *Rattler* and ALECTO, another paddle half-sister. Starting on March 30, 1845, the two ships raced each other in a variety of conditions and using various combinations of propulsion: steam or sail only, or both together. The most celebrated contest

fell on April 4, when *Rattler* and *Alecto* engaged in a tug-of-war. *Alecto* was given a significant advantage by towing *Rattler* stern-to at 2 knots before *Rattler*'s engines were engaged. Five minutes later, *Rattler* had pulled *Alecto* to a standstill and was soon pulling the paddle-driven vessel at 2.8 knots. Although this is frequently cited as the turning point in the Admiralty's thinking about screw propulsion, it had already ordered seven screw frigates, as well as other smaller ships, and the first screw battleship, HMS *Ajax,* was about to be laid down.

HMS *Rattler* was finally commissioned in 1849, when she joined the antislavery patrol off Africa under Commander Arthur Cumming. Two years later, she was dispatched to the East Indies Station, where the Royal Navy was active in the suppression of piracy along the coasts of China and Malaysia. In July 1855, under Commander William Fellowes, she was joined by HMS *Eaglet* and crew from the USS POWHATAN in freeing four ships taken by pirates at Kulan, China. An estimated 500 pirates were killed and another 1,000 taken prisoner, with the loss of only six British and four American lives. *Rattler* returned to Britain shortly thereafter and was broken up at Woolwich in 1856.

Brown, "Introduction of the Screw Propeller into the Royal Navy." Gardiner & Lambert, eds., *Steam, Steel and Shellfire.* Phillips, *Royal Navy.*

Reale

Galley (3m). *L/B/D:* ca. 131′ × 18′ × 4.5′ (40m × 5.5m × 1.5m). *Tons:* 170 disp. *Hull:* wood. *Comp.:* 700. *Arm.:* 1 × 36pdr, 2 × 9pdr, 8 × 4.5pdr. *Built:* <1571.

Reale, or Royal, is the name given to Don Juan of Austria's flagship at the Battle of Lepanto in 1571. The last great battle between oared ships, Lepanto pitted a combined fleet of Venetian, Papal, and Spanish galleys against a unitary Turkish fleet. In 1570, the Turks demanded that Venice cede control of Cyprus, and when the Venetians refused, they besieged the port of Nicosia. Venice appealed to other Christian powers for help and found allies in

Pope Pius V, who ignored the Papacy's traditional rivalry with Venice in northern Italy, and Spain's Philip II, who was indifferent to Venetian troubles in the east but irritated by Muslim pirates in the western Mediterranean. Fleets from the three unlikely allies sailed to Crete at the end of August, but by the end of September, they had split up and returned home. Meanwhile, the Turks captured Nicosia and besieged Famagusta. Though prospects for joint action were dim, Venice, Spain, and the Papacy hammered out a Treaty of Alliance in May 1571. Don Juan of Austria, son of Emperor Charles V and half-brother of Philip II, was designated Captain General, while Sebastiano Veniero, Venice's general at sea, and Marc Antonio Colonna, the Papal commander-in-chief, reported to him.

In September 1571, the fleets assembled at Messina, Sicily, and sailed from there on September 16. Skirting the coast of Italy, they crossed the Adriatic to arrive ten days later at Corfu, opposite the Gulf of Patras. The Turkish fleet had been raiding Venetian outposts along the Dalmatian coast of the Adriatic, and with the fall of Famagusta in August, Ali Pasha was ordered to find and destroy the Christian fleet. On the day the enemy left Messina, he sailed for Lepanto (in Greek, Navpaktos) on the strait between the Gulfs of Patras and Corinth. Reconnaissance missions by both the Christians and the Turks underestimated each other's strength, and by October 7, 1571, both sides were eager for battle.

To ensure that the Christian fleet would fight as one, ships of all nationalities were mixed through the different squadrons, and Don Juan, Veniero, and Colonna sailed side by side at the head of the 62 galleys in the center squadron. Juan de Cardona sailed with 7 galleys in the van, Agostino Barbarigo of Venice on the left flank with 53 galleys, Andrea Doria of Genoa with 50 galleys on the right, and, in reserve, the Marquis of Santuz with 30 galleys. Six Venetian galleasses commanded by Antonio Duodo sailed ahead of the main squadrons. The Christians had about 44,000 men and 30,000 soldiers, most of the latter relying on guns rather than bows and arrows as their chief weapon.

Opposing the Christians was a slightly larger Turkish force under Ali Pasha in the center with 90 galleys, Uluch Ali with 61 galleys and 32 galliots on the left wing, and Mohammed Scirocco with 55 galleys on the right. In addition, there were about 30 vessels in reserve; total Turkish manpower was about 75,000. Although the Turks had a numerical superiority in ships and their line was a mile longer than the allied one, Turkish galleys tended to be more lightly built; nor did they have anything equivalent to the heavy firepower of the Venetian galleasses, which mounted a heavier broadside armament than galleys, carried on a deck above the rowers.

The power of these hybrid ships told early, and they sank a galley of Scirocco's squadron at about 1030 and disrupted the Turkish line as it passed and veered toward the shore. Ali Pasha's division attacked the Christian center and had the advantage until a Papal galley attacked the Turkish flagship. By 1300, the Turkish standard was captured, Ali Pasha was dead, and the Turkish center was disintegrating. The course of battle on the southern flank was the subject of much discussion. Uluch Ali tried to outflank Doria, but the Genoese moved south to prevent him from doing so, until Uluch Ali wheeled and attacked the center again. Venetian resentment of the Genoese Doria was so great that he was later accused of trying to flee the battle. In fact, he acquitted himself bravely.

By the end of the battle, the Turks had lost 80 ships sunk or damaged beyond repair and another 130 captured. Casualties totaled 30,000 dead and wounded, about 7,000 taken prisoner, and about 10,000 Christian galley slaves freed. Against these, the Christians had lost 12 ships and about 7,700 men, with another 14,000 wounded. Although defeat could have spelled disaster for Christian Europe, the victory was most important as proof that the Turks were not invincible. The Christian allies pursued a tiring campaign in 1572 during which they captured a single Turkish ship, and that winter Venice signed a treaty under which its merchants were allowed to resume their trade to Alexandria. It mattered little, for the old spice route to the East (upon which Venetian prosperity rested) was going the way of the oared galley, replaced by Portuguese carracks trading directly with the Indies via the Cape of Good Hope.

Rodgers, *Naval Warfare under Oars.*

Rear-Admiral Popov

Circular battleship (2f). *L/D:* 120.0′ × 14.8′ (36.6m dia. × 4.5m). *Tons:* 3,550 disp. *Hull:* steel. *Comp.:* 206. *Arm.:* 2 × 12.2″. *Armor:* 1.8″ belt. *Mach.:* compound engines, 4,500 ihp, 6 screws; 8 kts. *Des.:* Andrei Aleksandrovich Popov. *Built:* New Admiralty Yard, St. Petersburg, Russia; 1874.

The larger and better known of two circular battleships built by the Russian Imperial Navy in the 1870s, *Rear-Admiral Popov* was laid down as *Kiev* but later renamed in honor of her designer, Rear-

---

▼ The curiously designed Russian circular iron-clad **Rear-Admiral Popov** lying in the Nikolaiev Depositing Dock, South Russia. The design concept was an interesting one, but it fell short of expectations. *Courtesy Peabody Essex Museum, Salem, Massachusetts.*

Admiral Andrei Aleksandrovich Popov. Popov's idea was to create a stable platform for large-caliber guns to guard the shallow coastal waters around the Black Sea ports of Odessa, Nikolayev, and Ochakov. The ships mounted two 11-inch guns (they may have been fitted ultimately with 12-inch guns) mounted on a revolving turntable that could turn in an arc of thirty-five degrees on either side of the centerline. *Novgorod,* the first of the two ships, was constructed at St. Petersburg in 1872 and then taken apart and put on trains for reassembly at Nikolayev, where she was completed in 1874. *Kiev* was built from the keel up at Nikolayev. After reviewing the results of *Novgorod's* trials, Popov recommended that the second ship's diameter be enlarged by almost six meters. *Kiev* was renamed in honor of Popov before her launch, and by imperial decree both ships were designated as Popovkas, as was *Livadia,* a yacht of similar design. Both *Rear-Admiral Popov* and *Novgorod* performed well in their assigned roles, and during the Russo-Turkish War, the two ships served with the Danube Flotilla. Designated Coastal Defense Armor-Clad Ships in 1892, they later served as storeships until

stricken from the naval lists in 1903. They were not scrapped until 1912.

Martelle, "*Novgorod* and *Rear-Admiral Popov.*"

Re d'Italia

Re d'Italia–class broadside ship (1f/3m). *L/B/D:* 294′ × 54.4′ × 23.8′ (89.6m × 16.6m × 7.2m). *Tons:* 5,700 disp. *Hull:* wood. *Comp.:* 550. *Arm.:* 6 × 8″, 30 × 6.5″, 4 × 72pdr. *Armor:* 4.5″ belt. *Mach.:* single expansion, 1,800 ihp, 1 screw; 12 kts. *Built:* William H. Webb, New York; 1864.

The Italian navy came into being with the unification of Italy in 1860. Owing to its limited shipbuilding capacity, a number of its earliest ships were built abroad, in France, England, and the United States. Modeled on the French ironclad GLOIRE, the ironclad sister ships *Re d'Italia* and *Re di Portogallo* were named in honor of Italy's Victor Emmanuel II and his son-in-law, Luis II, King of Portugal. In 1866, Prussia's Chancellor Otto von Bismarck encouraged Italy to declare war on Austria-Hungary with the objective of extending Italian hegemony over Venetia, Trieste, Istria, and the Dalmatian coast of what is now Croatia. As Italy's Minister of the Marine Agostino Depretis told Admiral Count Carlo Bellion di Persano, "The Adriatic is an Italian Sea, and the Austrian flag must disappear from it. Do as you think best, but this end must be attained."

By any measure, Italy possessed an overwhelming advantage against the Austro-Hungarian navy. Overall the Italian fleet numbered 37 ships with 645 guns; the 27 Austrian ships mounted 532 guns. More telling, Italy possessed 12 ironclads to Austria's 7. An Italian victory at sea appeared to be a foregone conclusion, but Persano was hesitant and refused to meet the inferior Austrian force when it appeared off Ancona at the end of June. When Vice Admiral Baron Wilhelm von Tegetthoff returned to his base at Pola, Persano finally put to sea. Convinced that it needed a naval victory to strengthen its hand at the forthcoming peace talks, the Italian government ordered Persano to seize the island of Lissa (Vis) on the Dalmatian coast.

The invasion force set sail on July 15 with 800 troops embarked in Vice Admiral Giovanbattista Conte Albini's wooden Second Squadron, protected by Persano's First Squadron of ironclads led by *Re d'Italia*. Landings began on the eighteenth, but Persano failed to press home his advantage, even after the arrival of the *Affondatore* on the nineteenth. This new turret ram, fresh from the builder's yard in England, mounted two 10-inch guns, and English observers thought her powerful enough to sink the entire Austrian fleet on her own. From the start, however, Persano's behavior was a confusing mix of hesitation and bravado. When told of the approaching Austro-Hungarian fleet on the morning of the twentieth, he is said to have remarked: "Ecco I pescatori!" (Here come the fishermen).

At 1045, with Tegetthoff's fleet approaching in a triple chevron formation, the Italians opened fire. As the Italian fleet steamed out to cross the bows of the Austrian ships, Persano inexplicably decided to transfer from *Re d'Italia* to *Affondatore*. He neglected to tell anyone in his fleet, however, and as *Affondatore* had no admiral's pennant to indicate his presence on board, he effectively relinquished all command and control for the duration of the battle.

Despite their overwhelming firepower, the Italians seemed unsure of how to deal with the Austrian fleet. The wooden ship of the line *Kaiser* rammed *Re di Portogallo* and then limped off to San Giorgio, pursued halfheartedly by *Affondatore*. Persano refused to ram her, possibly afraid that she might fall over on his low-slung turret ship. At about 1120, *Re d'Italia* crossed in front of Tegetthoff's flagship, ERZHERZOG FERDINAND MAX. With his steering gear damaged, and reluctant to ram an Austrian ship lying in his way, Captain Faà di Bruno put his engines in reverse. As the Italian flagship came to a stop, *Erzherzog Ferdinand Max* rammed, punching a 300-square-foot hole in her port side. As the Austrian ship pulled away, the Italian ship heeled over and sank, taking with her 383 of her officers and crew. At this point, the battle was almost over, although Persano did not realize he had lost his flagship until 1600. Despite the loss of *Re d'Italia* and the ironclad *Palestro,* when he returned to Ancona, Persano declared himself victorious, and even foreign journalists took several days to be persuaded that the Austrians had not only won the battle but won it decisively. Persano was subsequently court-martialed and cashiered from the service.

Chesneau & Kolesink, ed., *Conway's All the World's Fighting Ships 1860–1905.* Sokol, *Imperial and Royal Austro-Hungarian Navy.*

Revenge

Ship (3m). *L/B/D:* 92′ (keel) × 32′ × 16′ dph (28m × 9.8m × 4.9m). *Tons:* 441 burthen. *Hull:* wood. *Comp.:* 250. *Arm.:* 2 demi-cannon, 4 cannon-periers, 10 culverins, 6 demi-culverins, 10 sakers, 2 falcons, 2 portpieces, 4 fowlers, or 6 bases. *Built:* Deptford Dockyard(?), Eng.; 1577.

Revenge was one of the first galleons, built to a new model recommended by Sir John Hawkins and Matthew Baker and characterized by a narrow length-to-beam ratio, a lower freeboard, and a square stern. These so-called race-built ships were faster and more maneuverable than the high-charged ships, with towering fore- and sterncastles, that then predominated in European navies. Depicted as having three masts — though she may have carried a bonaventure mizzen on occasion — her upperworks were painted in a green-and-white harlequin pattern. Commanded by some of the greatest captains of the Elizabethan navy, *Revenge* is perhaps the most famous of the ships to fight in the Spanish wars.

In September 1580, she was part of the English fleet dispatched to root out a combined Papal-Spanish force that had landed in Munster, Ireland, and taken refuge on Smerwick Bay. In the winter of 1587, *Revenge* became the flagship of a squadron commanded by Sir Francis Drake and organized in anticipation of the Spanish Armada. Although Drake attempted to sail against the Spanish fleet after its first departure from Spain in the spring of 1588, he was frustrated in this effort by contrary winds in June and July.

After returning to Plymouth, Drake finally got his chance on July 31, when *Revenge* took part in the first action between the English and Spanish fleets. With Hawkins's *Victory* and Frobisher's *Triumph, Revenge* engaged Juan Martínez de Recalde's *San Juan de Portugal,* the largest of the Spanish galleons, between Fowey and Plymouth. With their longer-range culverins, the English ships were able to hit their opponent from a distance of about 300 yards, out of range of the Spanish guns, until the appearance of *El Gran Grin,* when the English retired. That night, *Revenge* was the lead ship in the English squadron as it trailed the Spanish fleet, but Drake doused his stern light and sailed off in pursuit of some unidentified ships, leaving ARK ROYAL and some others trailing what turned out to be the bulk of the Spanish fleet. The next morning, Drake captured Don Pedro de Valdés's NUESTRA SEÑORA DEL ROSARIO, which had been damaged the previous day in a collision with another ship. This turned out to be the biggest prize of the campaign.

On August 3, *Revenge* and other ships fell on Juan Gómez de Medina's GRAN GRIFÓN, which had fallen behind the rest of the fleet. Though the English surrounded their prey, the Spanish fleet managed to rescue their comrade, which was taken in tow by a galleass. Drake continued the pursuit of the Spanish fleet to their anchorage at Calais, where the English fireships forced them into disorder. On August 8, Drake briefly engaged Medina Sidonia's flagship SAN MARTÍN before sailing after the bulk of the Spanish fleet as it headed into the North Sea. The English continued after the Spanish until leaving them to their fate to put into the Firth of Forth for badly needed supplies on August 12.

The next year, *Revenge* was again Drake's flagship in the so-called counter-armada, with which the English hoped to destroy whatever Spanish ships had survived the return from England, establish the pretender Don Antonio on the throne of Portugal at Lisbon, and then seize the Azores as a base from which to intercept the all-important Spanish treasure fleet from the Americas. The ill-conceived expedition was not a success, and the English fleet returned much the worse for wear after two months, with only about 2,000 of the 10,000 soldiers originally embarked fit for duty. In 1590, *Revenge* sailed as Sir Martin Frobisher's flagship in his unsuccessful attempt to intercept the Spanish treasure fleet near the Iberian Peninsula.

In August 1591, Lord Thomas Howard (in *Defiance*) led a similar expedition comprising about a dozen other Queen's ships and armed merchantmen, including *Revenge,* now flying the flag of Vice Admiral Sir Richard Grenville. Unbeknownst to the English, the Spanish had dispatched a fleet of fifty-five ships under Don Alonso de Bazan to rendezvous with the *flota,* which had left Havana with about seventy ships of all kinds. On September 7, Don Alonso learned that Howard's fleet was anchored north of Flores in the Azores. On the morning of the eighth, he divided his fleet to encircle the island and come at the English pincer fashion. Taken by surprise and vastly outnumbered, Howard ordered his fleet northeast. Grenville preferred to fight and weighed anchor only after embarking some men who had been sent ashore for water.

At about 1700, *Revenge* was boarded by the 37-gun *San Felipe* and *San Bernabé,* followed by *San Cristobál, Asunción,* and *La Serena.* The grappled ships fought through the night, and both *Asunción* and *La Serena* eventually sank. Mortally wounded by musket fire, Grenville ordered his ship blown up, in the words of a contemporary account, "that the Spaniards should never glory to have taken a ship of her majesty's." But after fourteen hours of battle — only three fought in daylight — and repeated boardings, the captain and master surrendered, and the Spanish put a prize crew aboard the devastated ship. According to Sir Richard Hawkins, *Revenge* wallowed

> like a logge on the seas . . . the masts all beaten over board, all her tackle cut asunder, her upper worke altogether rased, and in effect evened she was with the water, but the very foundation or bottom of a ship, nothing left over head either for flight or defence.

The surviving English crew were taken prisoner and transferred out of the ship, and Grenville died a few days later. The treasure fleet rendezvoused with Don Alonso's fleet soon after, and the combined fleet of some 120 ships sailed for Spain. En route, they were overtaken by a week-long storm during which *Revenge,* about fifteen Spanish warships, and scores of merchant ships were lost.

Earle, *Last Fight of the "Revenge."* Rowse, *Sir Richard Grenville of the "Revenge."* Tennyson, *"Revenge."*

Roccaforte

Buss (3m?). *L/B/D:* 125.3′ × 46.7′ × 30.7′ dph (38.2m × 14.2m × 9.4m). *Tons:* ca. 500 burthen. *Hull:* wood. *Comp.:* 100. *Built:* Venice; <1264.

At the start of the thirteenth century, Venice agreed to provide the ships and provisions necessary for 20,000 infantry, 4,500 knights, and 9,000 squires for conveying the Fourth Crusade to the Levant. The cost, including the loan of fifty ships for a year, came to the princely sum of 85,000 Cologne marks. It soon transpired that the Crusaders did not have the money required, so the Venetians hired them for an expedition to take the Dalmatian port of Zara from the Hungarians in 1203 and, in 1204, to attack Constantinople, the capital of the Byzantine Empire. The sack of Constantinople, the "Crusade against the Christians," helped consolidate Venice's trading power in the eastern Mediterranean, but it also excited the jealousy of rivals such as Genoa, with which Venice would be at war — mainly at sea — off and on for the next two centuries.

The ships of the Mediterranean could be broadly divided between round ships, powered by sail and used as freighters for goods and people, and oared galleys, used primarily for fighting. Built for capacity and economy, the round ships were easy prey to pirates and enemies of the state, but in the Middle Ages, the larger ones were built with fore- and sterncastles from which archers and soldiers could defend the ship against a boarding action. Ordinarily, Venetian merchant fleets bound for the Levant would be escorted by galleys. In 1264, a fleet of fifty-five galleys was sent ahead to Syria, to be followed by a convoy of merchantmen consisting of the *Roccaforte,* a large state-owned buss built for combat and commerce, and a number of smaller merchant tarettes. The Venetian galleys failed to find a Genoese force of sixteen galleys under Admiral Simone Grillo, who ambushed the *Roccaforte* and her consorts off Saseno. The Venetians transshipped the precious goods from the tarettes to the *Roccaforte,* scuttled three of the smaller vessels, and set the rest adrift to be plundered of their oil, honey, and other bulk goods. After looting the tarettes, Admiral Grillo offered the Venetians in the *Roccaforte* safe quarter. The Venetian buss was all but impregnable to an assault from the low-slung Genoese galleys, and the convoy commander Michele Daru offered the taunting reply

> that if [the Genoese] were stout fellows, let them come on, and that the ship was all loaded both with gold and the richest merchandise in the world. And afterwards, . . . the Admiral and the other galleys circled about. And then they went off and carried victory from this fight and took the tarettes to Genoa, and the *Roccaforte* turned back to Ragusa.

Roccaforte's invulnerability was due to her great height — nearly forty feet from the keel to the top of the castles and probably four times higher than the Genoese galleys. Her hull had three decks, and she probably carried three masts setting lateen sails, which had replaced the square sails of the ancient Mediterranean. The cumbersome lateen rig required a large crew. To tack, the long yards — the largest could be as long as the hull — had to be lowered and worked around to the leeward side of the mast. Lateen sails could not be reefed, and the only way to shorten sail in heavy weather was to lower the yard and bend on a smaller sail; normally ships carried three or four sails of different size. Venetian statutes indicate that in the thirteenth century, a buss of 240 tons required a crew of 50,

whereas a square-rigged cog of the same size in the fourteenth and fifteenth centuries required only 20 sailors 20 years of age or older, and 8 apprentices.

In 1268, Venice offered the *Roccaforte,* among other ships, to Louis IX of France for his proposed crusade to convert the Emir of Tunis. (The future St. Louis died on this, his last crusade, in 1271.) The ship's dimensions were recorded in documents bearing on these negotiations, and they show that she was an exceptionally large vessel for her day. By the end of the century, the large round ships such as *Roccaforte* had been superceded in Venice by great galleys used as freighters; in the 1300s, the northern European cog would be adopted as a standard freighter.

Gardiner & Unger, *Cogs, Caravels and Galleons.* Lane, *Venetian Ships and Shipbuilders.*

HMS Rose

Seaford-class 6th rate 20 (3m). *L/B/D:* 108′ × 30.1′ × 9.5′ (32.9m × 9.2m × 2.9m). *Tons:* 430 tons. *Hull:* wood. *Comp.:* 160. *Arm.:* 20 × 9pdr. *Built:* Hugh Blades, Hull, Eng.; 1757.

Bearing one of the most common names in the Royal Navy (first used as early as 1322), HMS *Rose* was one of a class of the Royal Navy's smallest-rated vessels. Built at the outset of the Seven Years' (French and Indian) War, *Rose* served on patrol along the coast of France and in the Caribbean. In 1768, the Admiralty Board considered the ship for Captain James Cook's first South Seas expedition, but as she could not be made ready in time, he sailed in *Endeavour* instead. Later that year, *Rose* was dispatched to the coast of North America, where she was active in impressing sailors from merchant ships for the Royal Navy. In 1774, *Rose* was dispatched to Narragansett Bay to suppress the very active and lucrative smuggling trade that had helped make Newport the fourth wealthiest city in the colonies.

Captain James Wallace was so successful that the merchants of Newport were forced to appeal to

Rhode Island's colonial legislature for the formation of a navy to combat the frigate. At the same time, they fitted out the merchant sloop *Katy* — which they renamed PROVIDENCE — to patrol their waters. Rhode Island, in turn, asked the Continental Congress for the creation of a Continental Navy. In July of 1776, *Rose* took part in the British campaign to expel General George Washington's Continental Army from New York and saw action against shore batteries along the Hudson. Three years later, *Rose* took part in the defense of Savannah, which the British had just captured and which was under threat of attack from a French fleet commanded by Comte Jean-Baptiste d'Estaing. On September 9, 1779, *Rose* was scuttled in the Savannah River to prevent the French fleet from advancing upriver. The city remained in British hands until the end of the American Revolution in 1782, when the hulk was broken up so that regular commerce could be resumed.

In 1970, John Fitzhugh Millar built a replica of the ship in anticipation of the U.S. Bicentennial. The ship is used as a sail-training vessel and dockside attraction, sailing to ports from the Great Lakes to Europe from her homeport of Bridgeport, Connecticut.

Bailey, *Manual for Sailing aboard the American Tall Ship "Rose."* Lyon, *Sailing Navy List.*

Royal Caroline

(later *Royal Charlotte*) Royal yacht (3m). *L/B/D:* 90.1′ × 24′ × 12.1′ (27.4m × 7.3m × 3.7m). *Tons:* 232 bm. *Hull:* wood. *Comp.:* 70 crew. *Arm.:* 24 guns. *Des.:* Joshua Allin. *Built:* Deptford Dockyard, Eng.; 1750.

Royal Caroline was a royal yacht built for the use of George II and his wife, Queen Caroline. She was sailed for pleasure cruises by the royal family, and as a transport for members of court traveling between England and Holland. On the latter assignments, she was usually escorted by as many as four frigates and, when the King was aboard, accompanied by the First Lord of the Admiralty. Her distinguished captains included Sir William Cornwallis

and Sir Hyde Parker, both of whom rose to flag rank. In 1761, the vessel was renamed *Charlotte* (later *Royal Charlotte*) for George III's prospective bride and Queen, Princess Sophie Charlotte of Mecklenburg-Strelitz. Little used by the royal family after 1806, she was broken up in 1821.

Royal Caroline's design was based on that of a ship built in 1700 as *Peregrine Galley* and later named *Carolina* and *Royal Caroline*. Ordered by William III, this vessel was designed by Peregrine, Lord Danby, an admiral who had designed several vessels for Peter the Great, but whose efforts were not initially appreciated by the Admiralty. His success is seen not only in the similarity of the second *Royal Caroline*'s design but in the fact that the later ship was, in turn, the prototype for a long line of 20-gun and 32-gun ships, including the *Richmond*-class frigates, the last of which were ordered in 1804.

Bellabarba & Osculati, *Royal Yacht "Caroline" 1749.*

HMS Royal Charles

(ex-*Naseby*) 1st rate 80 (3m). *L/B/D:* 162′ × 42.5′ × 11′ (49.4m × 13m × 3.4m). *Tons:* 1,230 bm. *Hull:* wood. *Arm.:* 80 guns. *Des.:* Peter Pett. *Built:* Woolwich Dockyard, Eng.; 1655.

Two years after he assumed the title of Lord Protector of England, Oliver Cromwell authorized the construction of three "great ships" for the navy: the 80-gun *Naseby* (so named for his victory over the Royalists in 1645), and the 64-gun *London* and *Dunbar* (subsequently renamed *Henry*). *Naseby*'s original adornments included a figurehead portraying, according to Samuel Pepys,

> Oliver on horseback trampling 6 nations under foote, a Scott, Irishman, Dutch, French, Spaniard and English as was easily made out by their several habits: A Fame held a laurell over his insulting head, & the word God with us.

When Charles II returned from exile in the *Naseby*, he ordered the ship named for himself as well as a new figurehead of Neptune, an act that irritated the parsimonious Pepys, who complained, "God knows, it is even the flinging away of £100 out of the King's purse."

Commercial rivalry between England and the Dutch Republic led to the start of the Second Anglo-Dutch War in 1665. At the Battle of Lowestoft, *Royal Charles* was flagship of the Duke of York (later James II), Lord High Admiral. The two fleets — each numbered more than 100 ships — met before dawn on June 13. Although the English had superior organization and more powerful guns, the Dutch fought well. By mid-afternoon, *Royal Charles* was in danger of being sunk or surrendered to *Eendracht* when the Dutch flagship exploded, killing all but 5 of her 400 crew, including the Dutch Admiral Wassenaer van Obdam. *Royal Charles* was so damaged that the Duke of York shifted his flag to the *St. Michael* and later still the *James.* Nonetheless, Lowestoft was a clear English victory, with only 250 dead compared with 4,000 Dutch dead. For his failure to pursue the retreating Dutch fleet, the Duke of York was obliged to pull down his flag after the battle, which was the last of the year.

In the spring of 1666, command of the fleet was divided between Prince Rupert and George Monck, Duke of Albemarle, in *Royal Charles.* At the end of May, with the Dutch fleet still in port, Charles unwisely divided his force and sent Rupert west to prevent a French force from joining Admiral Michiel Adriaanszoon de Ruyter. Monck was left with only fifty-six ships to oppose the eighty-five Dutch ships under de Ruyter. Nonetheless, Monck attacked the Dutch force as soon as it appeared on June 11. The English attack was impressive, and he renewed battle the next day. Early on the second day, he profited from a tactical error by Lieutenant Admiral Cornelis Tromp, until de Ruyter came to his countryman's assistance. Each side lost three ships. On June 13, Monck retreated to the west in hopes of joining Rupert, but in so doing the *Royal Prince* (90 guns) ran aground on Galloper Shoal and was burned by the Dutch. Battle was joined again on June 14, but by the end of the day, with the wind rising and supplies exhausted (to say nothing of the crews), both sides

retired. The Four Days' Battle remains one of the longest fleet engagements on record. Although the English losses were more than double those of the Dutch — 20 ships lost, 5,000 crew killed, and 2,000 taken prisoner — the English regrouped fast, and the fleet put to sea again in July.

On August 4, the two fleets met in the North Sea off North Foreland, both Rupert and Monck flying their flags in *Royal Charles.* The battle proved disastrous for the Dutch, as usual because of the lack of discipline, although de Ruyter fought long and well. Dutch losses amounted to 20 ships, 4,000 dead, and 3,000 prisoners; the English lost three ships. (This battle was also known as the St. James' Day Fight because it took place on the Feast of St. James, July 24 in the Julian calendar, by which England still reckoned dates.)

In the spring of 1667, the English treasury was exhausted by a combination of Charles's extravagance and the lasting effects of both the Great Plague of 1665 and the London fire of September 1666. Charles decided to economize by laying up his fleet. Seeing their opportunity, the Dutch fleet attacked the fort at Sheerness on June 10 and advanced up the Medway. The English scuttled a number of ships in an effort to block the channel, and an iron chain was strung across the river between Upnor and Gillingham. Over the course of three days, twenty-three ships were lost, most intentionally sunk by the English and then burned by the Dutch. The losses included two first rates, three second rates, two third rates, six fourth rates, and one sixth rate. Orders were given to burn the *Royal Charles*, but at the approach of a Dutch boat from the *Bescherming*, the crew fled. As Pepys recounted,

> The Dutch did take her with a boat of nine men, who found not a man aboard her, and . . . presently a man went up and struck her flag and jack. . . . They did carry her down at a time when both for wind and tide, when the best pilot in Chatham would not have undertaken it, they heeling her on one side to make her draw little water.

Incompatible with the needs of the Dutch fleet, *Royal Charles* never fought again, and the Dutch displayed her at Rotterdam as a war trophy. She was auctioned and broken up in 1673, during the Third Anglo-Dutch War.

Clowes, *Royal Navy*. Fox, *Great Ships*. Hainsworth & Churches, *Anglo-Dutch Naval Wars*. Pepys, *The Shorter Pepys*.

HMS Royal George

(ex-*Royal Anne*) *Royal George*–class 1st rate 100 (3m). *L/B/D:* 178′ × 51.8′ × 21.5′ (54.3m × 15.8m × 6.6m). *Tons:* 2,047 bm. *Hull:* wood. *Comp.:* 850. *Arm.:* 28 × 42pdr, 28 × 24pdr, 28 × 12pdr, 16 × 6pdr. *Built:* Woolwich Dockyard, Eng.; 1756.

The first-rate ship HMS *Royal George* was laid down as *Royal Anne* in 1746 but renamed in honor of the reigning monarch, George II, before her launch ten years later. The first warship to exceed 2,000 tons burthen, *Royal George* was commissioned at the start of the Seven Years' War with France and joined the Western Squadron in blockading the port of Brest and Quiberon Bay. On November 9, 1759, the British fleet was blown off station, and Vice Admiral Hubert de Brienne, Comte de Conflans, seized the opportunity to sortie from Brest with twenty-one ships of the line. This he did the same day that Admiral Sir Edward Hawke left Torbay, beating against the westerlies to regain his station. On the afternoon of November 20, 1759, the two fleets spotted each other off Brest, and Hawke ordered his ships to "form as you chase." Conflans decided to return to Brest, and despite the treacherous shoals and reefs of Quiberon Bay, Hawke ordered his ships to follow the French. As Conflans later wrote, "I had no reason to believe that if I went in first with my ships the enemy would dare follow, in spite of his superiority [of two ships] which must anyway restrict his movements."

The ensuing destruction of the French fleet was decisive. *Thésée* foundered when water rushed in through her lower gun ports, and *Héros* struck to HMS *Magnanime* (a French prize of 1748). As *Royal George* came up with Conflans's flagship *Soleil Royal* (80 guns), the French *Superbe* inter-

posed herself but sank after one broadside from Hawke's flagship. The French *Formidable* also struck before darkness fell, and Hawke ordered his fleet to anchor. The next morning revealed HMS *Resolution* and *Essex* driven ashore on Le Four shoal, but *Soleil Royal* was lost on Rouelle shoal and three other French ships were damaged beyond repair.

Hawke was knighted for his action, and *Royal George* spent the rest of the war on blockade duty off Brest. Peace came in 1763, and between that year and 1778, the Royal Navy laid up ninety-seven ships of the line, *Royal George* among them. When France threw in her lot with the American colonists and allied with Spain, *Royal George* was recommissioned. In July 1778, she was under command of Sir Charles Hardy in his ignominious withdrawal before the combined Franco-Spanish fleet as it advanced up the channel. (Sailors in *Royal George* are said to have blindfolded the figureheads, popularly believed to represent the former king, so that "George II should never see an English Fleet chased up their own channel.") In the event, Admiral Louis Guillouet, Comte d'Orvilliers, withdrew of his own accord, and England was spared further anxiety about the biggest invasion to threaten since the Spanish Armada in 1588.

At the end of 1779, *Royal George* sailed with Admiral Sir George Rodney's fleet to relieve Gibraltar and took part in the capture of two Spanish convoys, one guarded by nine ships under Admiral Don Juan de Langara; seven of these were captured or sunk. In 1782, she was part of another fleet, under Admiral Lord Howe, assembled for the permanent relief of Gibraltar. The ships were anchored at Spithead, taking on supplies, when on August 29 *Royal George* was being heeled at a slight angle to make some minor repairs below the waterline. At the same time, casks of rum were being loaded aboard and the lower deck gunports were not properly secured. At about 0920, the ship suddenly rolled over on her beam ends, filled with water, and sank, taking with her 800 people, including as many as 300 women and 60 children who were visiting the ship. A subsequent court-martial acquitted the ship's officers and crew (most of whom were dead) of any wrongdoing and blamed the accident on the "general state of decay of her timbers."

Several attempts were made to salvage the ship. In 1783, William Tracey succeeded in moving the ship slightly before the Admiralty decided to abandon the project. In 1834, the pioneering diver Charles Deane recovered thirty guns before his work was interrupted to investigate a nearby wreck that turned out to be MARY ROSE. The remains of *Royal George* were eventually blown up by Royal Engineers in the early 1840s.

Hepper, *British Warship Losses.* Johnson, *"Royal George."*

HMS Royal Sovereign

1st rate 100 (3m). *L/B/D:* 184′ × 52′ (56.1m × 15.8m). *Tons:* 2,175 bm. *Hull:* wood. *Comp.:* 850. *Arm.:* 100 guns. *Built:* Devonport Dockyard, Plymouth, Eng.; 1787.

Launched in 1787, more than twelve and a half years after her laying down, the third HMS *Royal Sovereign* was a dull sailer known to her crews as "the West Country Wagon." Completed at the height of the Nootka Sound controversy, when Britain and Spain were poised for war over possession of the harbor on Vancouver Island, Canada, from 1790 to 1794 she was flagship of Vice Admiral Thomas Graves in the Channel Fleet. In 1794, she was part of Lord Howe's fleet against Admiral Louis-Thomas Villaret de Joyeuse's Brest Squadron at the Glorious First of June, during which she was hotly engaged by the French *Impetueux* and *Terrible* and suffered fifty-eight crew killed and wounded. *Royal Sovereign* remained with the Channel Fleet through 1803 and was caught up in the Spithead mutiny of 1797, for which two of her crew were hanged.

In 1804 *Royal Sovereign* joined the blockade of Toulon, and the following year she became flagship of Vice Admiral Cuthbert Collingwood and Captain Edward Rotherham. She remained with Vice Admiral Lord Nelson's squadron in the long chase of Admiral Pierre de Villeneuve's Combined Fleet from the Mediterranean to the West Indies and back. At the Battle of Trafalgar on October 21, 1805, she led the lee column and was the first British ship to close with the Combined Fleet. Undermanned, her gun crews could only fire broadsides from one side of the ship at a time. After raking first Admiral Alava y Navarrete's flagship *Santa Ana* (112 guns) and then the French *Fougueux* (74), she came under the combined fire of *San Leandro* (64), *San Justo* (74), and *Indomptable* (80). The latter four ships moved on, leaving *Royal Sovereign* to grapple with *Santa Ana* alone, which struck to her at 1415 with casualties numbering 340 dead and wounded. *Royal Sovereign* lost her mizzen and mainmasts during the engagement and suffered 141 killed and wounded. Collingwood, who had succeeded to command of the fleet with the death of Nelson, had to shift his flag to the frigate *Euryalus,* and *Royal Sovereign* was towed to Gibraltar by HMS *Neptune.*

Royal Sovereign returned to duty in the Mediterranean the next year and remained on the blockade of Toulon until 1812, when she transferred to the Channel Fleet. Made a receiving ship at Plymouth in 1816, she was renamed *Captain* in 1825, and broken up at Pembroke Dockyard in 1849.

Mackenzie, *Trafalgar Roll.* Schom, *Trafalgar.*

S

HMS St. George

Duke-class 2nd rate 90 (3m). *L/B/D:* 177.5' × 50' × 21.1' (54.1m × 15.2m × 6.4m). *Tons:* 1,932 bm. *Hull:* wood. *Comp.:* 750. *Arm.:* 28 × 32pdr, 30 × 18pdr, 30 × 12pdr, 2 × 6pdr. *Des.:* Sir John Williams. *Built:* Portsmouth Dockyard, Eng.; 1785.

The fourth Royal Navy ship of the name, HMS *St. George* was named for the patron saint of England. She participated in the action at Genoa following the French closure of that port to British shipping. In 1801, she was Rear Admiral Horatio Nelson's flagship prior to the Battle of Copenhagen. He transferred his flag to HMS ELEPHANT, whose lighter draft enabled him to sail closer inshore for the bombardment of the Danish capital on April 2. In 1811, *St. George* was the flagship of Rear Admiral Robert Reynolds's Baltic Fleet. On November 1, she sailed with a number of other ships from Hano Bay in southeast Sweden to England. A merchant ship collided with her, and she was driven aground on Låland Island, sustaining extensive damage. After major repairs, she got under way again with a jury rig on December 17, in company with HMS *Cressy* and DEFENCE. On Christmas Eve, the ships were in the North Sea off Jutland when a gale struck. Captain Daniel Guion attempted to anchor near Ringkøbing, Denmark, to await a favorable wind, but *St. George* ran aground before the anchors could be let go. Despite efforts to lighten the ship, she was pounded by the heavy seas and sank with the loss of all but eleven of her company. *Defence* was lost the same night.

Hepper, *British Warship Losses.*

USS St. Mary's

Sloop of war (3m). *L/B/D:* 149.3' × 37.3' × 18' (45.5m × 11.4m × 5.5m). *Tons:* 958 bm. *Hull:* wood. *Comp.:* 195. *Arm.:* 16 × 32pdr, 6 × 8". *Built:* Washington Navy Yard, Washington, D.C.; 1844.

Named for the Maryland county, the U.S. Navy's second *St. Mary's* was originally slated for duty with the Mediterranean Squadron. Immediately before her departure, U.S. relations with Mexico began to deteriorate over the annexation of Texas, which Congress and President John Tyler had just approved. In March 1845, *St. Mary's* sailed in Commodore Robert Stockton's squadron to bolster U.S. forces in the Gulf of Mexico. In November, she carried John Slidell, the new minister to Mexico, to Veracruz, and she remained in the gulf through the winter. When the Mexican-American War began in May 1846, she was assigned to blockade duty off Tampico and remained there intermittently through May 1847.

The following year, *St. Mary's* was assigned to the Pacific Squadron, with which she cruised between California, Chile, and the Far East for five years. After a refit at Philadelphia, she returned to the Pacific for a further two years. In 1856, Commander Charles Davis took command of the ship at Panama City. His first assignment was to negotiate the surrender of William Walker, a U.S.-born buccaneer who had tried to establish a personal empire in Nicaragua. Davis succeeded, but in 1860, when Walker attempted a similar intrigue in Honduras, he was captured and shot. *St. Mary's* remained on the West Coast through the Civil War. After a cruise to Australia and New Zealand in 1870, she returned to Norfolk in 1872.

Two years later, Congress transferred *St. Mary's*

to the New York Nautical School. This, the first federally assisted merchant marine officer-training program, later evolved into the New York (State) Merchant Marine Academy and formed the model for all other state merchant marine academies and the U.S. Merchant Marine Academy at Kings Point, New York. *St. Mary's* served as a schoolship until 1908, when she was sold and broken up at Boston.

Mitchell, *We'll Deliver*. U.S. Navy, *DANFS*.

USS San Jacinto

Screw frigate (3m). *L/B/D:* 237' × 37.8' × 17.3' (72.2m × 11.5m × 5.3m). *Tons:* 2,150 disp. *Hull:* wood. *Comp.:* 235. *Arm.:* 6 × 8". *Mach.:* horizontal condensing engines, 500 hp, 1 screw; 11 kts. *Des.:* Samuel Hartt. *Built:* New York Navy Yard, Brooklyn, N.Y.; 1852.

The U.S. Navy's second screw frigate was named for the site of Sam Houston's victory over the Mexican army in 1836. Built to an experimental design, USS *San Jacinto* was fitted with an off-center propeller shaft. Her greatest defect was her engines, which were replaced after only one year of faulty service. Recommissioned in 1854, she sailed in European and Caribbean waters for a year before assignment as flagship of the East India Squadron. Sailing via the Cape of Good Hope as flagship of Commodore James Armstrong, in April 1852, *San Jacinto* conveyed Townsend Harris to Siam (Thailand) to negotiate the first U.S. treaty with that country. From there she proceeded to Shimoda, where in August Harris established the first foreign consulate in Japan. *San Jacinto* remained in the Far East for two years, protecting U.S. merchant interests and landing marines to fight Chinese troops at Whampoa and Canton during the Second Opium War, which ended with the Treaties of Tientsin between China, Britain, the United States, France, and Russia in 1858.

Returning to the United States that same year, *San Jacinto* next joined the Africa Squadron, and on August 8, 1860, she captured the brig *Storm King*, from which 616 slaves were freed at Mon-

rovia, Liberia. She remained on station until August 27, 1861, when she sailed for the United States under Captain Charles Wilkes, returning via the Caribbean, where she searched unsuccessfully for Captain Raphael Semmes's CSS SUMTER. On November 8, Wilkes intercepted the Royal Mail steamer *Trent* about 230 miles east of Havana and arrested the Southern diplomats James Mason and John Slidell, who were en route to their posts in England. The *Trent* Affair strained relations between the United States and Britain until the Southerners' release in 1862.

In March 1862, *San Jacinto* took part in naval operations of the Peninsular Campaign in Virginia before proceeding to the East Gulf Blockading Squadron at Key West. From then on, her duties varied between blockade duty in the gulf and off North Carolina, and the pursuit of the Confederate raiders ALABAMA (from October 1862 to January 1863), FLORIDA, and TALLAHASSEE. In the interim, she spent most of her time on blockade off Mobile, Alabama, where she captured four prizes. *San Jacinto* was lost on New Year's Day 1865 after hitting a reef near Great Abaco Island, Bahamas.

U.S. Navy, *DANFS*. Warren, *Fountain of Discontent*.

San Juan de Sicilia

Galleon. *Tons:* 800. *Hull:* wood. *Comp.:* 350–400. *Arm.:* 26 guns. *Built:* Dubrovnik(?); <1586.

Long known simply as the Tobermory Galleon, *San Juan de Sicilia* was originally a merchantman from Ragusa (Dubrovnik) on the Dalmatian coast. This Adriatic port, whose name is the origin of the word *argosy*, meaning a large ship, accounted for at least three ships in the Spanish Armada: *Sveti Nikola* (known in Spanish as *San Nicolas Prodaneli*), *Annuncijata* (*La Annunciata*), and *Brod Martolosi*, which was entered on the lists as *San Juan de Sicilia*. Owned by Petrov Jug and Jaketa Martolosic, in 1586 *Brod Martolosi* apparently carried a cargo of wool from England bound for the eastern Mediterranean. When she put into Termini, Sicily, the

Spanish viceroy requisitioned the ship, unloaded the cargo, and embarked a Sicilian regiment of 300 soldiers for Cartagena. Her captain, Luka Ivanov Kinkovic, was known in Spanish as Lucas de Juan.

In January 1588, *San Juan de Sicilia* sailed for Lisbon via Gibraltar, where she was armed with 26 guns and attached to Martín de Bertendona's Squadron of the Levant. In July, her captain, Don Diego de Enriquez, brought her into Laredo after a severe gale. While there, the *Casa de Paz*, which carried medical supplies for the Armada, was condemned and her stores were transferred to *San Juan de Sicilia* and *Santa Maria del Vision*. During the encounter with the English fleet, *San Juan de Sicilia* saw little action until August 4, when she supported galleasses under attack from Lord Howard's ARK ROYAL. Three days later, she bore the brunt of the fighting at the Battle of Calais, together with SAN MARTÍN, *San Marcos*, and *Santa Anna*. Great efforts were made to keep her afloat, and she sailed in company with the main fleet as far as Edinburgh during its retreat to Spain.

The galleon continued on her own around the north of Scotland but was finally forced to put into Tobermory Bay on the north coast of the Isle of Mull. Short of provisions, Don Diego de Enriquez obtained food and supplies in exchange for the services of about a hundred infantrymen. These fought for Lachlan McLean of Duart in his reduction of the islands of Canna, Rum, Eigg, and Muck and his siege of Arnamurchan Castle on the mainland. About a month later, the ship mysteriously exploded and sank in sixty fathoms. The survivors probably numbered no more than fifty men, most of whom apparently returned to Spain and Ragusa via Edinburgh and Flanders.

Title of the ship fell to the seventh Earl of Argyll. Over the years, there were persistent rumors of treasures in the sunken ship — which was long misidentified variously as *Florencia* and *Florida* — and several Stuart kings attempted to gain control of the wreck. Starting in the 1650s and for a century thereafter, a succession of individuals and syndicates worked the site. The most experienced of these was Hans Albricht von Treilaben, who with Andreas Peckell had excavated more than fifty guns from the Swedish warship *Vasa*. In the 1730s, James Rowe dynamited the hull, but he gave up in frustration.

Interest in the Tobermory wreck resumed in the early twentieth century. An adventurer named Lieutenant Kenneth Mackenzie Foss dove on the site for twenty-three years, with little to show for his efforts. In the 1950s, the eleventh Duke of Argyll invited the participation of the Royal Navy, and the legendary Lieutenant Commander Lionel Crabb worked on the site. In 1965, Dr. Harold Egerton located the ship using his newly developed high-power output, short-pulse-length sonar to view the remains of the hull beneath the seabed without disturbing it. Nonetheless, few artifacts have been recovered from the site.

McLeay, *Tobermory Treasure.*

San Martín

Galleon (3m). *Tons:* 1,000 tons. *Hull:* wood. *Comp.:* 650. *Arm.:* 48 guns. *Built:* Portugal(?); <1588.

Best known as the Duke of Medina Sidonia's *capitana general,* or flagship, in the Spanish Armada in 1588, the galleon *San Martín* was originally built as a Portuguese warship. Brought into the Spanish navy following Philip II's annexation of Portugal in 1580, she sailed as *capitana* of Don Alonzo Bazan, Marqués of Santa Cruz, when the Spanish defeated a French fleet of 75 ships at the Battle of Terceiro in the Azores on July 25, 1582. Sometime thereafter, Philip began formulating his ambitious plan for an amphibious invasion of England using troops gathered under the Duke of Parma at Nieuport and Dunkirk in the Spanish Netherlands. To accomplish this, Medina Sidonia assembled a fleet of 130 ships. These included his own Squadron of Portugal with 12 ships and those of Biscay (14), Castile (16), Andalusia (11), Guipuzcoa (14), and Levant (10). Other warships included four Neapolitan galleasses and four Portuguese galleys. In addition, the Spanish chartered from Hanseatic merchants in the Baltic 23 hulks (or *urcas*) as storeships, and they had 22 pinnaces — *zabras* and *pataches* — that served as dispatch boats and scouts. Of the 30,000 people in the Armada ships, more than 19,000 were soldiers intended to fight with Parma's forces. Ranged against this formidable assemblage, the English had about 197 ships: 34 royal ships belonging to the Crown, 105 merchant ships, and 58 victuallers and coasters, with a combined complement of just under 16,000 men.

La Felicissima Armada — "the most blessed fleet" — assembled at Lisbon in the spring of 1588, and on May 30, it sailed. Plagued by inadequate supplies of food and water (some had been poorly stowed, some had simply rotted over the winter), most of the fleet put into La Coruña. From there the fleet set out again on July 22. A week later, the Spanish were off Plymouth, minus the four galleys, which fled to port in the face of the Atlantic gales, and the Biscayan galleon *Santa Ana*. Medina Sidonia was intent on maintaining his ships in a defensive formation as they stood up the channel, but they could not entirely avoid confrontations with the English. Although the more numerous English ships were in general smaller and more lightly armed than their opponents, their guns had greater range and they could engage the Spanish without coming under fire or risking a boarding action, in which case the Spanish would certainly have had the upper hand.

On Sunday, July 31, the English ships made their first attack on the Spanish, but as it was evident from their actions that the English wanted to avoid a boarding action at all costs, Medina Sidonia ordered his ships to advance up the channel. The English pursued them through the night, and although there were no significant engagements on August 1, Sir Francis Drake, in Revenge, captured Nuestra Señora del Rosario. The next day saw major engagements off Portland Bill. The first, between Spanish and English galleons, was initiated by the Spanish, who had the weather gauge, but when the Spanish sought to close with Lord Howard of Effingham's Ark Royal, he stood out to sea to avoid a boarding action. The Mediterranean galleasses had meanwhile tried to cut out six

English ships, including Martin Frobisher's *Triumph*. In the ensuing melee, *San Martín* herself was cut off for more than an hour and engaged closely by *Ark Royal*. By August 4, the Armada was south of the Isle of Wight when *San Martín* was again isolated and engaged by Frobisher. Damaged below the waterline, the Spanish flagship was eventually rescued by other ships in the squadron.

At this point, both fleets had spent a lot of gunpowder and ammunition, though to relatively little effect, and there were no ship actions for the next few days. By August 6, the Spanish had crossed the channel to anchor in the exposed roadstead at Calais. The English fleet — now numbering about 140 ships, with the arrival of Lord Henry Seymour's fleet — gathered to the southeast and at a council of war determined to launch a fire-ship attack. On the night of August 7–8, eight ships of between 90 and 200 tons were commandeered; the ships were loaded with combustibles and, with guns double-shotted, set on fire to sail downwind of the Spanish ships. Good seamanship enabled the Spanish to avoid the fire ships in some order, and they lost only one ship to grounding — the galleass *San Lorenzo* — though many ships lost their anchors in their haste to get under way. More important, Medina Sidonia had lost an anchorage, and there was nowhere his ships could go between Calais and Parma's (still unready) transports at Dunkirk.

The last and most hotly contested battle between the two fleets was fought off Gravelines on August 8. The initial focus of the battle was *San Martín*, which fought a rearguard action at the edge of the sandbanks that run from Calais up the Dutch coast. More units of both fleets joined the battle, fought at close range, and at least four Spanish ships were lost. When the battle was over, the Spanish fleet was kept off the coast by the shallows and the adverse wind and tide. By August 9, it was clear that there was little choice for the once "invincible" armada but to sail into the North Sea, around Scotland and Ireland, for home. Little did anyone imagine that only sixty-seven Spanish ships would return to Spanish ports, nearly fifty having been lost at sea or wrecked on the rocky coasts that ring the British Isles. "Thus," as it is recorded in Hakluyt,

> the magnificent, huge, and mighty fleet of the Spaniards (which themselves termed in all places invincible) such as sayled not upon the Ocean sea many hundreth years before, in the yeere 1588 vanished into smoke; to the great confusion and discouragement of its authors.

San Martín returned to Santander on September 23, though 180 of her crew soldiers and crew who had survived the fighting succumbed to disease and privation. *San Martín*'s subsequent fate is unknown.

Hakluyt, *Principal Navigations.* Mattingly, *Armada.* Rodríguez-Salgado, et al., *Armada: 1588–1988.*

Santísima Trinidad

Galleon (3m). *L/B/D:* 167.5′ (gundeck) × 50′ × 33′ (51.1m × 15.2m × 10.1m). *Tons:* 2,000. *Hull:* wood. *Comp.:* 400–800. *Arm.:* 54 guns. *Des.:* Don Domingo Nebra. *Built:* Bagatao, Manila, Philippines; 1750.

Officially named *Santísima Trinidad y Nuestra Señora del Buen Fin* ("Most Holy Trinity and Our Lady of the Good End") and optimistically nicknamed El Poderoso — "the powerful one" — *Santísima Trinidad* was the largest "Manila galleon" built for trade between the Philippines and Mexico. Modeled on the Spanish specification for a 60-gun ship, she was pierced for only 54 broadside guns but never mounted a full battery. Despite ordinances limiting the size of the Manila galleons, authorities routinely overlooked most irregularities, but with her enormous draft, oversized top hamper, and pronounced sheer, her size was too great to be ignored. The Crown ordered her replaced or cut down, and in 1757 she had her bulwarks and upper decks reduced, further limiting the number of guns she mounted. These alterations did not affect her gargantuan hold, nor did they much improve her poor sailing qualities.

On August 1, 1762, *Santísima Trinidad* departed Cavite for Acapulco. It was late in the season, and contrary winds kept her from exiting the San Bernardino Strait until late September. On the night of October 2–3, a typhoon brought down her fore- and mainmasts, and she turned back for the Philippines under a jury rig. Unbeknownst to the ship's company, Spain and England were at war and Manila had fallen. As the ship passed through the strait, she was met by HMS *Panther* (60 guns) under Captain Hyde Parker (who had sailed in Commodore Anson's CENTURION during the capture of *Nuestra Señora de la Covadonga* in 1743) and the frigate *Argo* (28), under Captain Richard King. Although "the *Panther*'s shot was not able to penetrate" the galleon's hardwood hull, the crew of the overcrowded ship (she carried 800 people) was dispirited and soon surrendered, despite the loss of only 18 killed and 10 wounded to the 35 British dead and 37 wounded. *Santísima Trinidad* remained in her captors' possession until their return to England in June 1764. She was sold at Plymouth the next year, and proceeds amounted to about £30,000 for the two captains — an enormous amount of money in those years — with smaller shares for the other officers and crew. The ship herself was probably broken up for her wood.

Marley, "Last Manila Galleon." Schurz, *Manila Galleon.*

USS Saratoga

Corvette (3m). *L/B/D:* 143′ bp × 36.5′ × 12.5′ (43.6m × 11.1m × 0.3m). *Tons:* 734 bm. *Hull:* wood. *Comp.:* 212. *Arm.:* 8 × 24pdr, 6 × 42pdr, 12 × 32pdr. *Des.:* Henry Eckford. *Built:* Noah Brown, Vergennes, Vt.; 1814.

During the American Revolution, the British were twice frustrated in their attempt to march from Canada down the Lake Champlain–Hudson River Valley to New York. In October 1776, General Benedict Arnold's autumn victory at the Battle of Valcour Bay had forced the postponement of the invasion, and in the following year General Horatio Gates won a crucial victory at the Battle of Saratoga. Late in the War of 1812, the British under General Sir George Prevost were ready to attempt the same strategy. Standing in his way was Master Commandant Thomas Macdonough, who, aided by the New York shipbuilder Noah Brown, had built his flagship, the aptly named corvette USS *Saratoga*, in the remarkably fast time of only thirty-five days. After blockading the mouth of the Richelieu River during the summer, Macdonough was forced to drop down the lake as the British army began its advance in August. The army was accompanied by a naval force that included the 36-gun HMS Confiance, the largest warship ever built on Lake Champlain. American forces withdrew to Plattsburg Bay, where Macdonough deployed his fleet of fourteen vessels across the mouth of Cumberland Bay, with kedge anchors and spring lines set so that each ship could turn on its own axis. Battle was joined when the British fleet rounded Cumberland Point on September 11. HMS *Linnet* opened fire first, followed by *Confiance*, which let loose her first broadside against *Saratoga* at point-blank range. After two hours, Macdonough brought his ship around to present a fresh broadside to *Confiance*, which was soon forced to strike; forty-one of her crew were killed, Captain George Downie among them, and a like number wounded. *Linnet* surrendered soon thereafter, as had *Finch* and *Chubb* earlier. The victory was decisive in ending the threat to the United States from Canada, and news of the victory influenced negotiations at the Treaty of Ghent, which was concluded on December 24.

Roosevelt, *Naval War of 1812*. U.S. Navy, *DANFS*.

USS Scourge

(ex-*Lord Nelson*) Schooner (2m). *L/B:* 57′ × 20′ (17.4m × 6.1m). *Tons:* 110. *Hull:* wood. *Comp.:* 50. *Arm.:* 1 × 32 pdr, 8 × 12 pdr. *Built:* Asa Stanard, Niagara, N.Y., 1811.

Built for William and James Crooks, the Lake Ontario merchant schooner *Lord Nelson* was seized on June 5, 1812, by Lieutenant Melancthon Woolsey in *Oneida*, for violating the recently imposed Embargo Act. Thirteen days later, the War of 1812 broke out, and Lieutenant Woolsey purchased *Lord Nelson* for the U.S. Navy at auction for $2,999.25. Renamed USS *Scourge*, the vessel was incorporated into Captain Isaac Chauncey's Lake Ontario

Squadron under Lieutenant H. McPherson. She took part in attacks on York (now Toronto) on April 27, 1813, and Fort George, on the Niagara River, on May 27. On the night of August 8, while off the Niagara River, *Scourge* was overwhelmed in a line squall and lost all but nine of her crew. The schooner USS Hamilton was also lost.

In 1930, the U.S. government paid an indemnity to Crooks's descendants. In 1971, the Hamilton and Scourge Project was formed to locate the sunken ships. Two years later, they were located lying at a depth of 300 feet, both in a remarkable state of preservation.

Cain, *Ghost Ships "Hamilton" and "Scourge."* Nelson, "*Hamilton* and *Scourge.*" Roosevelt, *Naval War of 1812*.

CSS Shenandoah

(ex-*Sea King*, later *El Majidi*) Commerce raider. *L/B/D:* 220′ × 36′ × 20′ (67.1m × 11m × 6.1m). *Tons:* 1,018 grt. *Hull:* steel. *Comp.:* 73. *Arm.:* 4 × 8″, 2 × 32pdr, 2 × 12pdr. *Mach.:* direct-acting engines, 1 screw; 9 kts. *Built:* Alexander Stephen & Sons, Ltd., Govan, Scotland; 1864.

The first ship designed solely as a troop transport, the composite-built auxiliary screw steamship *Sea King* made one voyage under the British flag before being purchased in September 1864 by Confederate agents in England. Sailing from London on October 8, *Shenandoah* met the supply vessel *Laurel* off Funchal on October 19 and was commissioned under Lieutenant J. I. Waddell. *Shenandoah* proceeded to Australia by way of the Cape of Good Hope, taking five prizes in the Atlantic and one in the Indian Ocean. Departing Melbourne on February 19, 1865, *Shenandoah* had spectacular luck against the American whaling fleet, burning five ships before sailing into the Bering Sea. On June 23, Waddell learned that the Civil War was over, but he continued his cruise and took twenty-one more prizes, eight of which were sunk. On August 2, a British ship informed Waddell of the war's end, at which point he converted *Shenandoah* to look as much like a merchantman as possible. *Shenandoah* arrived at Liverpool on November 6, 1865, having captured thirty-eight prizes. Seized by the U.S. government, she was sold to the Sultan of Zanzibar and renamed *El Majidi.* She foundered at sea en route from Zanzibar to Bombay.

Horan, ed., *C.S.S. "Shenandoah."* Silverstone, *Warships of the Civil War Navies.* Waddell, *CSS "Shenandoah."*

Shtandart

Frigate (3m). *L/B/D:* 100.1′ × 23′ × 8.2′ (30.5m × 7m × 2.5m). *Tons:* 186 disp. *Hull:* wood. *Comp.:* 120. *Arm.:* 28 guns. *Des.:* Peter I. *Built:* Vibe Gerense and Ivan Nemtsov, Voronezh Shipyard, St. Petersburg, Russia; 1703.

When Peter I ("the Great") ascended the throne in 1682, Russia was an enormous but virtually land-locked country. Its only coast was on the White Sea, and its only seaport was Archangel. Access to saltwater became a primary objective of Peter's foreign policy, which he pursued with vigor and imagination for his entire reign. Looking first to the south, in 1695 he led an army against the Crimean Tatars in order to reach the Sea of Azov. This campaign initially failed, but the next year Peter built a fleet on the Don River at Voronezh and with it captured Azov. He capitalized on this success by constructing a naval shipyard at Taganrog.

Peter had long been interested in maritime affairs, and after the Azov campaign, he organized and accompanied the "Grand Embassy" to study a variety of industries and institutions in western Europe. Peter himself spent four months in a Dutch shipyard at Zaandam and another four months at the Royal Navy Dockyard in Deptford. Although keen to enlist the support of European powers against the Turks in an effort to continue his drive to the Black Sea, they were embroiled in the controversies that led to the War of the Spanish Succession. Returning to Russia, Peter decided to gain a sea coast on the Baltic at the expense of the Swedish empire, whose coast ran from Stockholm to Riga and included modern Finland, Latvia, Lithuania, and Estonia.

The Northern War lasted from 1700 to 1721 and resulted in Russia's winning the territory of the eastern Baltic States. Peter built a fleet on the Svir

River and after crossing Lake Ladoga captured a string of forts on the Neva River in 1702. The Baltic was now within reach, and Peter issued contracts for sixteen vessels of various sizes, six to be built on the Syas River and the remainder to be built at the Olonets Shipyard on the Svir. On September 8, 1703, less than six months after the contract was issued, the frigate *Shtandart* ("standard," for Peter's new royal standard) was launched. Peter had designed and helped oversee construction of *Shtandart,* and in September, he sailed as her captain en route from Olonets to the newly founded city of St. Petersburg.

Over the next few years, Sweden tried several times to retake St. Petersburg but was turned back in large part thanks to the strength of Peter's fleet, which operated along the Neva between St. Petersburg and the fortress at Kronstadt. In 1709, the Russians won a stunning victory on land at the Battle of Poltava, and for the next few years Peter's attention was focused on Turkey. Under the Treaty of Edirne, he was forced to surrender Azov, and his designs in the Baltic assumed even greater importance than before. The Swedes were preoccupied with the Danish fleet in the western Baltic and neglected the rapid growth of the Russian fleet, which included sailing ships and a preponderance of galleys. Despite terrific losses, the galleys achieved some important victories, the first at the Battle of Gangut Head (Hangø) in the Gulf of Finland on August 6, 1714.

In 1716, *Shtandart* was withdrawn from service, and the following year Peter ordered the ship laid up in the Kronverk Canal behind Peter and Paul Fortress. Here, he declared, "she must stay forever as a monument to the Russian art of shipbuilding." She remained on view for eleven years, but in 1727, she was found to be beyond repair, whereupon Catherine I (Peter's widow) decreed that "therefore she is to be dismantled. . . . And for the memory of her name . . . which was given her by His Highness . . . she is to be built anew." This last order was not carried out.

Although not the first large naval ship built for the Russian fleet, because of her close connection with Peter the Great and his capital, *Shtandart* has always had a special place in the traditions of the Russian navy, and there were ships of that name in the Russian navy until the death of the last czar. In 1994, shortly after the dissolution of the Soviet Union, a group of naval historians in St. Petersburg began the reconstruction of a replica of *Shtandart.*

Martous & Palmer, "Reconstruction of Russian Maritime History."

Skuldelev ships

The Skuldelev find consists of the remains of five clinker-built Viking-era ships. These ships were loaded with rocks and sunk in the Peberrende narrows of Roskilde Fjord in an effort to prevent an enemy fleet from sailing up the fjord and attacking the town of Roskilde, Denmark. Long known as "Queen Margrethe's ship," in the belief that they were a single vessel sunk on orders of the Queen in about 1400, this dating proved wrong, although the purpose was not. Roskilde was a major trading center in the tenth and eleventh centuries, and its protection from seaborne raiders would have been of major importance, especially in the period of unrest between about 1040 and 1070.

Excavation of the site began in 1957 under Olaf Olsen and Ole Crumlin-Pedersen of the Danish National Museum. Two ships were identified in the first season, and in the second year a third ship was excavated together with what was initially called Wreck 4. These remains turned out to be part of Wreck 2, but because this was not discovered until 1959, the fourth and fifth ships have always been known as Wrecks 5 and 6. After excavation, labeling, and conservation, the fragmentary remains of the five vessels were erected on delicate metal frames that show the general shape of the complete ship. These are housed in the Viking Ship Museum in Roskilde, built on a site overlooking Roskilde Fjord. The five clinker-built ships include two warships (Wrecks 2 and 5), two knorrs (Wrecks 1 and 3), and a fishing boat (Wreck 6).

Skuldelev 1

Trading vessel; knorr. *L/B/D:* 53.5′ × 14.8′ × 6.9′ (16.3m × 4.5m × 2.1m). *Hull:* deal, oak, lime. *Built:* 1010.

The larger of the two trading vessels found at Roskilde was in all likelihood built not in Denmark but in Norway, a theory supported by differences in detail and the fact that the pine planking used in building was probably unobtainable in Denmark during the period in question. In addition, the hull is of heavier construction and not suited to being driven ashore on the beaches of Denmark, as were the other vessels. With a capacity of fifteen to twenty tons, this is the sort of ship that would have been used for long-distance trading to the British Isles, Iceland, Greenland, and beyond.

Skuldelev 2

Longship. *L/B:* 95.1′ × 13.1′ (29m × 4m). *Comp.:* 50–100 men. *Hull:* wood. *Built:* ca. 930.

Wreck 2 is the least well-preserved of the Roskilde ships, with only about one-quarter of the original fabric surviving. Although her original length can only be approximated, this is the longest Viking ship yet found. According to the sagas, ships that carried between thirteen and twenty-three pairs of oars were considered longships — of which this was probably one — while those that carried more than twenty-five pairs were called great ships. Built with thin oak planking (those that survive are only two to two and a half centimeters thick), the bottom planks have been worn down from being repeatedly run up on beaches to discharge the ship's crews.

Skuldelev 3

Trading vessel; knorr. *L/B/D:* 45.3′ × 11.2′ × 4.6′ (13.8m × 3.4m × 1.4m). *Hull:* wood. *Comp.:* 5–9. *Built:* 1030.

The best-preserved ship of the five ships at Roskilde, with approximately three-quarters of the original wood having survived, this vessel is the first Viking ship in which the whole stem has been

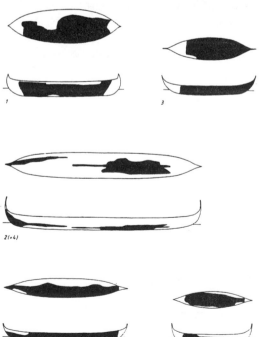

preserved. It is similar in construction to Wreck 5, the chief differences being a broader length-to-beam ratio than that of the small warship, and a gunwale with only seven oar holes, five forward (three to port and two to starboard) and two aft. In addition, the vessel had a half deck and a four-meter-long hold amidships with a total cargo capacity of about five tons.

Skuldelev 5

Warship. *L/B/D:* 57.1' × 8.5' × 3.6' (17.4m × 2.6m × 1.1m). *Hull:* oak and ash. *Comp.:* 25–30. *Built:* 960.

Known as the small warship, this ship is similar in form to the Ladby ship. Of particular note is the comparatively narrow length-to-beam ratio, a feature that had been considered an anomaly in the Ladby ship. However, it is now accepted that Danish ships of the period were generally narrower than their Norwegian counterparts. The hull is pierced for twelve pairs of oars, and as with Wreck 2, it shows signs of repeated beaching. Vessels of this design seem to have been copied both in the Baltic and in Normandy, where descendants of the type are amply illustrated in the Bayeux Tapestry showing William the Conqueror's Norman invasion of England in 1066.

Skuldelev 6

Fishing boat. *L/B/D:* 38.0′ × 8.2′ × 3.9′ (11.6m × 2.5m × 1.2m). *Hull:* pine.

The smallest of the five ships found at Roskilde, this vessel is often regarded as a fishing boat. She carried a mast and could probably be propelled by oars, although there are no oar holes in the remains of the ship.

Crumlin-Pedersen, "Skuldelev Ships." Olsen & Crumlin-Pedersen, *Five Viking Ships from Roskilde Fjord.*

Le Soleil Royal

Vaisseau (1st rate) (3m). *Hull:* wood. *Arm.:* 104 guns. *Built:* Brest, France; 1669.

Named in honor of the Sun King, Louis XIV, *Le Soleil Royal* was one of the most powerful ships of her day. As flagship of the revitalized French navy brought into being by Minister of Marine Jean-Baptiste Colbert, she was sumptuously decorated with wooden carvings depicting a variety of motifs emblematic of the French monarch. The taffrail was embellished with a rendering of the sun god drawn across the sky by a team of horses, while the ornate figurehead showed a seahorse flanked by winged maidens. The hull was painted a royal blue highlighted by the wales, strakes, and additional embellishments in gold. As the sculptures recovered from the Swedish warship WASA prove,

such lavish ornament was not uncommon in seventeenth-century warships. Charles Le Brun's drawings of the statuary for *Le Soleil Royal* are in the Louvre.

Details of the first decade of *Le Soleil Royal's* service are obscure, but after her refit in 1689, she flew the flag of Vice Admiral Anne-Hilarion de Cotentin, Comte de Tourville, Admiral of the French fleet. The year before, England's Catholic King James II had been overthrown in favor of the Dutch Protestant William III of Orange in the Glorious Revolution. In March 1689, a French fleet helped James II land in Ireland in the first of several failed efforts to regain his throne. In July 1690, Tourville led a fleet of seventy ships out of Brest, and on July 10, he met a combined English and Dutch force of fifty-seven ships off Beachy Head. Ordered to engage the enemy against the larger fleet, Admiral Arthur Herbert, Lord Torrington, lost eight ships while the French lost none in a victory they called Béveziers.

Two years later, the position was reversed as Tourville, with a fleet of only forty-four ships — the remainder were with Vice Admiral Jean d'Estrées in the Mediterranean — was ordered to sail from Brest on May 12, 1692, to clear the English Channel for Louis XIV's invasion force of 30,000 men assembled near Cherbourg. On May 20, Tourville met an Anglo-Dutch fleet of eighty-eight ships off Pointe de Barfleur. By increasing the distance between his ships sailing in line ahead, Tourville prevented his fleet from being encircled or outflanked by the English and Dutch ships, under command of Admiral Edward Herbert, Earl of Orford, in HMS *Britannia*. But *Le Soleil Royal* was so badly damaged that Tourville was forced to transfer his flag to *Ambiteux* the next day. Ten French ships slipped away, but *Le Soleil Royal*, *Admirable*, and *Conquerant* were forced into Cherbourg, where they ran aground and were destroyed by English fire ships. Another twenty ships made for Brest, and Tourville ordered the remaining twelve to the shallow roads off La Hogue. There, on June 2, Tourville's brilliant handling of the fleet at Barfleur was obliterated, and as the French army and James II (audibly proud of his disloyal subjects, to the chagrin of his allies) looked on from shore, the English fleet burned or sank a dozen ships.

Clowes, *Royal Navy.* Culver, *Forty Famous Ships.*

USS Somers

Brig (2m). *L/B/D:* 103′ × 25′ × 11′ dph (31.4m × 7.6m × 3.4m). *Tons:* 259 bm. *Hull:* wood. *Comp.:* 120. *Arm.:* 10 × 32pdr. *Built:* New York Navy Yard, Brooklyn, N.Y.; 1842.

USS *Somers,* the second ship of the name, was named for Richard Somers, who died while commanding the bomb ketch INTREPID at Tripoli in 1804. A small, swift vessel, one of *Somer*'s primary missions was to train young naval ratings and officers for careers at sea, an idea fostered especially by Commodore Oliver Hazard Perry. Although designed to carry 90 officers and crew, on her second voyage the brig carried a complement of 120. Three-quarters of them were still teenagers, but they included the scions of some distinguished families: two sons of Matthew Calbraith Perry, the son of Commodore John Rodgers, and Philip Spencer, the son of President John Tyler's Secretary of War, John Canfield Spencer.

Under command of Captain Alexander Slidell Mackenzie, *Somers* sailed from New York on September 12, 1842, bound for Monrovia with dispatches for the slave patrol frigate USS *Vandalia.* After calling at Madeira and the Canary Islands, the ship arrived at Cape Mesurado, the site chosen by Matthew Perry for the African-American colony of Liberia in 1822, only to find *Vandalia* had left. After only two days in port, *Somers* sailed for St. Thomas, Danish West Indies, on November 12. Two weeks later, on the strength of a report of a shipmate, Midshipman Philip Spencer, together with the boatswain's mate and another seaman, were placed under arrest for plotting a mutiny. Further investigation by Mackenzie and his officers revealed that Spencer intended to seize the ship and kill the officers and any who sided with them. For their crime, they were hanged, while still at sea, on December 1. Mackenzie was later court-martialed and, despite the standing of Spencer's fa-

ther, acquitted of charges of illegal punishment, oppression, and murder.

Somers subsequently remained with the Home Squadron, cruising along the Atlantic and Gulf coasts. During the Mexican-American War, she took up blockade duty off Veracruz, under command of Lieutenant Raphael Semmes, later captain of CSS ALABAMA. On December 8, 1846, while chasing a blockade-runner, *Somers* capsized in a squall and sank with the loss of 32 of her 76 crew. In 1986, her remains were found in 110 feet of water about a mile off Isla Verde.

Delgado, "Rediscovering the *Somers.*" McFarland, *Sea Dangers.*

HMS Sovereign of the Seas

(later HMS *Sovereign,* HMS *Royal Sovereign*) 1st rate 102 (3m). *L/B:* 232′ loa (128′ keel) × 48′ (70.7m (39.8m) × 14.6m). *Tons:* 1,141 bm. *Hull:* wood. *Arm.:* 102 guns. *Des.:* Phineas Pett. *Built:* Peter Pett, Woolwich Dockyard, Eng.; 1637.

In 1634, the ill-fated monarch Charles I informed the great English shipbuilder Phineas Pett of his "princely resolution for the building of a great new ship" as part of his overall effort to improve and expand the navy of England, whose enemies and concerns included the Dutch — her most serious rival in overseas trade — France and Spain, and North African corsairs preying on vessels west of the English Channel. Though critics warned that "the art or wit of man cannot build a ship fit for service with three tier of ordnance," neither Charles nor Pett was to be dissuaded. Built at a cost of £65,586 — about ten 40-gun ships could have been built for the same amount — *Sovereign of the Seas* was intended as an instrument of propaganda as well as war. The Royal Navy's most lavishly ornamented vessel, her decorations were carved by the brothers John and Mathias Christmas and described in a booklet prepared by Thomas Heywood, who also managed to include a description of the ship itself:

> She hath three flush Deckes, and a Fore-Castle, an halfe Decke, a quarter Decke, and a round-house.

Her lower Tyre [tier] hath thirty ports, which are to be furnished with Demy-Cannon [30-pdr.] and whole Cannon through out, (being able to beare them). Her middle Tyre hath also thirty ports for Demi-Culverin [10-pdr.], and whole Culverin: Her third Tyre hath Twentie sixe Ports for other Ordnance, her fore-Castle hath twelve ports, and her halfe Decke hath foureteene ports; She hath thirteene or fourteene ports more within Board for murdering peeces, besides a great many Loope holes out of the Cabins for Musket shot. She carrieth moreover ten peeces of chase Ordnance in her, right forward; and ten right aff, that is according to Land-service in the front and the reare. She carrieth eleaven Anchors, one of them weighing foure thousand foure hundred, &c. and according to these are her Cables, Mastes, Sayles, Cordage; which considered together, seeing his Majesty is at this infinite charge, both for the honor of this Nation, and the security of his Kingdome, it should bee a great spur and incouragement to all his faithful and loving Subjects to bee liberall and willing Contributaries towards the *Ship-money.*

In fact, the ship-money tax levied by Charles for his naval program was much resented by his "faithful and loving subjects," and in *Sovereign of the Seas* can be seen some of the excess that contributed to his overthrow and execution in 1649. Under Oliver Cromwell's Commonwealth, the ship was renamed *Sovereign;* following the restoration of Charles II in 1660, she was rebuilt and renamed *Royal Sovereign.* Despite her vast size, the ship was slow and of limited value in actual combat as she could not keep company with other ships. Nonetheless, during the three Anglo-Dutch Wars, she saw action at the Battle of Kentish Knock in 1652, Orfordness (1666), Solebay (1672), Schooneveldt (1673), and the Texel (1673). Following another rebuild in 1685, in the War of the League of Augsburg, she was at Beachy Head (1690) and Barfleur (1692). Eleven years later, a misplaced candle set the ship on fire, and she burned at Chatham.

Heywood, *His Majesty's Royal Ship.*

HMS Speedy

Brig (14). *L/B:* 78' × 26' (23.8m × 7.9m). *Tons:* 208 bm. *Hull:* wood. *Comp.:* 90. *Arm.:* 14 × 4pdr. *Built:* King, Dover, Eng.; 1782.

European navies did not employ brig-rigged vessels in significant numbers until after the Seven Years' War. The Royal Navy introduced a new class of brig — the prototype was HMS *Childers* — in 1778. Fast and nimble, the two-masted square-riggers were used as dispatch boats and for convoy protection. Probably the most famous Royal Navy brig is HMS *Speedy,* which is remembered as the vessel in which Lieutenant Thomas Lord Cochrane acquired his reputation as one of the most enterprising officers of his day. Her early career, however, is illustrative of the variety of duties to which these vessels were assigned.

At the start of the French Revolutionary Wars in 1793, *Speedy* was dispatched to Gibraltar under Charles Cunningham. She undertook a variety of assignments around the Iberian Peninsula and in the western Mediterranean for the next year. On June 9, 1794, she was looking for a British squadron off the coast of Nice when she closed with three French frigates that Commander George Eyre assumed to be British. He realized his mistake too late, and *Speedy* struck to the *Sérieuse* (36 guns). Taken into the French navy, she was recaptured the following March by HMS *Inconstant* (36). *Speedy* remained in the Mediterranean, cruising with Commodore Horatio Nelson's squadron off the coast of Italy, and she took part in the capture of six vessels carrying arms for the siege of Padua.

On October 3, 1799, under command of Jahleel Brenton, *Speedy* attacked a convoy of eight merchantmen and two escorts. Though none were taken, six were forced ashore near Cape Trafalgar and destroyed. On November 6, *Speedy* fought off a flotilla of twelve Spanish gunboats while escorting a transport bound for Livorno with wine for the fleet. The Spaniards were driven off, but *Speedy* suffered extensive damage to her hull and rigging. Shortly thereafter, Brenton was assigned to command the recently captured *Généreux,* and Lieutenant Cochrane assumed command of *Speedy* on March 28, 1800.

Speedy cruised off the Spanish coast with great success. In thirteen months under Cochrane's command, she captured upward of 50 vessels, together with 122 guns and 534 prisoners. On December 21, 1801, Cochrane evaded a Spanish frigate detailed to capture her by flying the Danish flag and the quarantine flag and having a Danish-speaking officer explain that the ship had been at a North African port riddled with the plague. On May 6, 1802, *Speedy* fell in with the Spanish frigate *El Gamo* (32) off Barcelona. Although Cochrane had described *Speedy* as "crowded rather than manned" with a crew of 90 officers and men when he took command, nearly 40 of these had been put aboard various prizes to be taken into port, and *Speedy*'s complement numbered only 54. Nonetheless, Cochrane commenced an attack of unrivaled daring. Running alongside the larger ship, Cochrane fired a series of treble-shotted broadsides into *El Gamo,* whose twenty-two 12-pdr., eight 9-pdr., and two carronades were mounted too high to damage the smaller brig. Cochrane then led a boarding party and captured the frigate and her crew of 319. Spanish losses were 15 killed (including Captain Don Francisco de Torris) and 41 wounded, as against 3 British dead and 8 wounded. Although outnumbered six to one, the British took *El Gamo* into Port Mahon, Minorca. To keep the Spanish crew below decks, their captors loaded *El Gamo*'s main-deck guns with canister and pointed them down the hatchways.

Instead of the honors he so richly deserved for such an unparalleled feat of arms, Cochrane was all but ignored. Although he was promoted to the rank of post-captain, his recommendation that Lieutenant Parker be promoted was overruled by Lord St. Vincent, First Lord of the Admiralty, on the grounds that "the small number of men killed on board the *Speedy* did not warrant the application." Cochrane imprudently observed that she had suffered more casualties than had HMS VICTORY at the Battle of Cape St. Vincent, for which Admiral Sir John Jervis had been made Earl St. Vincent and his first captain a knight.

Cochrane received more respect from his enemies. Ordered back to the Mediterranean, on July 3 *Speedy* was escorting a slow transport when she was set upon by three French frigates. After several hours of combat, Cochrane was forced to haul down his flag. The French captain of the *Dessaix* was so impressed by his enemy that he declined to accept Cochrane's sword in surrender. *Speedy*'s subsequent career is unknown, but it is doubtful that she entered French service.

Cochrane was soon exchanged and went on to further fame in the frigates *Pallas* and *Impérieuse*. His brazen and tireless campaigning against corruption in the service kept him out of favor with his superiors, and in 1814 he was disgraced because of his apparent complicity in a stock swindle perpetrated by a French refugee under his command. In 1816, Cochrane accepted an offer to command the Chilean navy against the Spanish, and he sailed in the O'HIGGINS. He went on to serve in the Brazilian and Greek navies before his reinstatement as a rear admiral in the Royal Navy in 1832.

Clowes, *Royal Navy.* Cochrane, *Autobiography of a Seaman.* Phillips, *Royal Navy.*

Star of the West

(later *Saint Philip*) Sidewheel steamship (2m/1f). *L/B/D:* 228.3′ × 32.7′ × 24.5′ dph (69.6m × 10m × 7.5m). *Tons:* 1,172 grt. *Hull:* wood. *Arm.:* 2 × 68pdr; 4 × 32pdr. *Mach.:* 2 vertical beam engines; 11.5 kts. *Built:* Jeremiah Simonson, Greenpoint, N.Y.; 1852.

Laid down as *San Juan* but launched as *Star of the West,* this brigantine-rigged sidewheel steamship was built for the passenger trade between New York and California. In December 1860, the Buchanan administration chartered her to carry arms and men to Major Robert Anderson's garrison at Fort Sumter in Charleston, South Carolina, and on January 5, 1861, she left New York. Although Secretary of the Interior Jacob Thomson alerted authorities in Charleston of her impending arrival, President James Buchanan neglected to advise Anderson, and when *Star of the West* entered Charleston Harbor four days later, she came under fire. Receiving no support from Anderson, the captain of

Star returned to New York. Anderson and South Carolina Governor Francis W. Pickens exchanged accusations of having committed acts of war, and Pickens began preparations to attack Fort Sumter.

Three months later, the Federal government again chartered *Star of the West,* to carry troops from Texas to New York. On April 17 — five days after the bombing of Fort Sumter and the outbreak of the Civil War — she was captured off Texas by the Confederate Army steamer *General Rusk.* Renamed *Saint Philip,* she sailed for two years under the Confederate flag. During Union operations to take Vicksburg in March 1863, she was scuttled in the Tallahatchie River to protect the approaches to Fort Pemberton, Mississippi.

Silverstone, *Warships of the Civil War Navies.* U.S. Navy, *DANFS.*

CSS Sumter

(ex-*Habana,* later *Gibraltar*) Commerce raider (1f/3m). *L/B/D:* 184′ × 30′ × 12′ (56.1m × 9.1m × 3.7m). *Tons:* 437 grt. *Hull:* wood. *Comp.:* 18. *Arm.:* 1 × 8″, 4 × 32pdr. *Mach.:* direct-acting engine, 1 screw; 10 kts. *Built:* Vaughn & Lynn, Philadelphia; 1859.

Built for the New Orleans & Havana Line, the auxiliary merchant bark *Habana* was purchased at New Orleans and commissioned as the auxiliary cruiser CSS *Sumter* on June 30, 1861. The first command of Captain Raphael Semmes, she captured eighteen prizes in a cruise that took her through the Caribbean and Atlantic as far south as Maranhão, Brazil, and which also tied up a considerable number of Union warships. While coaling at Martinique in December, she was discovered by USS *Iroquois,* but she eluded the blockade and escaped to Cadiz on January 4, 1862. The Spanish government allowed her only to make necessary repairs, and *Sumter* sailed for Gibraltar without refueling. Unable to escape, she was sold at auction to the Liverpool-based Fraser, Trenholm and Company, which served as financial agent for the Confederacy. (Semmes meanwhile preceded her to Liverpool to take command of CSS ALABAMA.)

Renamed *Gibraltar,* the ship sailed to Liverpool under the British flag. Sold back to the Confederate government, she sailed for Wilmington with a cargo of munitions including two Blakeley cannon. She arrived there in April 1863. Her subsequent service record is unknown. She was reported at Birkenhead in July 1864, and it is believed that in 1867 "she went down in a gale near the spot where the *Alabama* was sunk off Calais, France."

U.S. Navy, *DANFS.* Wise, *Lifeline of the Confederacy.*

Sutton Hoo ship

L/B/D: 88.6′ × 14.8′ × 4.9′ dph (27m × 4.5m × 1.5m). *Hull:* wood. *Comp.:* 41+. *Built:* England(?); ca. 625.

Sutton Hoo is the name of a gravesite in East Anglia about eighty-six miles northeast of London near the town of Woodbridge. The area contains fifteen burial mounds dating from the early Anglo-Saxon period and is located a mile north of the River Deben about eight miles from the North Sea. In 1938, the owner of the land on which the site lies, Edith Pretty, commissioned archaeologist Basil Brown to excavate some of the mounds. While excavating mound 1 the following year, Brown discovered the remains of a ship that had been buried with the effects of an important chieftain, circumstantially identified as Raedwald, who ruled the East Angles from 599 to 625 and who was the acknowledged overlord of the other kings of England.

One interesting aspect of the ship is that at the time of its discovery, it no longer existed. In reacting with the soil, the ship's timbers and iron fastenings had dissolved, leaving very clear casts, traces and impressions of their actual form and placement. In outline, the Sutton Hoo ship is similar to, though longer than, the Norse OSEBERG and GOKSTAD ships, which date from the ninth century. The central keel was scarfed to long stem and stern posts that curved gracefully upward, increasing in thickness as they reached their ends. The hull consisted of nine strakes on either side of the keel, fastened to each other with iron rivets and strengthened by twenty-six transverse frames.

There are traces of twenty-eight rowlocks in four groups, seven on either side of the hull forward and aft of amidships (a similar midships break in rowing positions can be seen in ships depicted in the Bayeux Tapestry), and the helmsman probably steered the ship with an oar lashed to the starboard side of the hull about two meters forward of the sternpost. Although there is no evidence that the Sutton Hoo ship carried a sail, the hull shape and certain construction details suggest she could have sailed. *Sæ Wylfing,* a half-scale model built in 1993, demonstrated excellent sailing ability, achieving speeds of ten knots or better in Force 4 conditions. The ship was probably dragged from the river over rollers and then slid into the trench, during which process some of the stern planks appeared to have sprung. Evidence of repairs to the hull suggest that the ship saw many years of service prior to interment.

It is likely that the site was a burial mound whose inhumed body simply dissolved in the acidic soil. Alternatively, the mound may have served only as a cenotaph to the dead chieftain. Buried with the ship were the personal effects of a male warrior of some significance. Personal belongings included beautifully fashioned gold and garnet buckles and clasps, silver and brass buckles, an iron helmet and face mask, an otter skin hat, two pairs of leather shoes, bone combs, and a lyre wrapped in a beaver skin bag. Fighting implements included an iron sword and its scabbard, six spears, four iron knives, a mail shirt, an ax-hammer, three throwing spears, and a shield. In addition, there was a curious object that has been identified as a scepter; it consists of a long four-sided whetstone with four carved faces at either end, surmounted by a ring atop which stands a stag modeled in bronze.

While the Angles were Germanic in origin, other artifacts found with the warrior's personal possessions show that seventh-century England was by no means cut off from European trade. In addition to a variety of wood and horn drinking vessels, caldrons, and other containers of local provenance, there were sixteen silver artifacts of eastern Mediterranean origin. The largest of these is a seventy-two-centimeter-wide dish with maker's marks dating from the reign of the Byzantine Emperor Anastasius I (491–528). There was also a bronze bowl of a type known as "Coptic" because the principal site of manufacture for such vessels (twenty of which have been found in England) was in Egypt's Nile Delta, though the same type of bowl was made elsewhere in the eastern Mediterranean. Two silver spoons inscribed with the names Saul and Paul in Greek letters, to which has been attributed a Christian significance, were also found. (Raedwald is thought to have converted briefly to Christianity but reverted to paganism.) There were also thirty-seven gold coins from Merovingian Gaul, the earliest of which has been dated to 575 and the latest to 625, the year of Raedwald's death and, presumably, the erection of the burial mound.

Evans, *Sutton Hoo Ship Burial.* Gifford, "Sailing Performance of Anglo-Saxon Ships."

T

CSS Tallahassee

(ex-*Atalanta*; later CSS *Olustee*, CSS *Chameleon*, *Amelia*, *Haya Maru*) Steamship (2f/1m). *L/B/D:* 250′ × 23.5′ × 13.3′ (76.2m × 7.2m × 4.1m). *Tons:* 546 disp. *Hull:* iron. *Comp.:* 120. *Arm.:* 1 × 84pdr, 2 × 24pdr, 2 × 32pdr. *Mach.:* direct-acting engines, 1,220 ihp, 2 screws, 14 kts. *Built:* John & William Dudgeon, Millwall, London; 1863.

Later known as the ship with seven names, the *Atalanta* was built for Stringer, Pembroke and Company, as a cross-Channel steamer. In July 1864, after successfully running the Union blockade eight times, *Atalanta* was purchased and commissioned as a commerce raider in the Confederate Navy. Renamed CSS *Tallahassee* and later *Olustee,* starting in August she made two cruises off the New England and mid-Atlantic coasts during which she captured thirty-seven prizes. Later that fall, she was converted back to a merchantman and renamed *Chameleon*. She ran the blockade outbound but was frustrated in her attempts to return. Sailing for England, she was given back her first name and then registered as *Amelia*. Before she could reenter civilian service, she was handed over to the U.S. government as reparations. Subsequently auctioned to Japanese interests, she ended her career as *Haya Maru*. She was wrecked between Kobe and Yokohama on June 17, 1868.

O'Driscoll, "Ship with Seven Names." U.S. Navy, *DANFS*.

HMS Téméraire

Dreadnought/Neptune-class 2nd rate 98 (3m). *L/B:* 185′ × 51′ × 21.5′ (56.4m × 15.5m × 6.6m). *Tons:* 2,121 bm. *Hull:* wood. *Comp.:* 750. *Arm.:* 28 × 32pdr, 60 × 18pdr, 10 × 12pdr. *Des.:* John Henslow. *Built:* Chatham Dockyard, Eng.; 1798.

The second ship of the name, HMS *Téméraire* spent her first three years as flagship of the Channel Fleet and the Western Squadron during the War of the Second Coalition against France. At the end of 1801, she had called at Bantry Bay, Ireland, bound for her new station in the Caribbean, when the crew mutinied. Twenty were arrested, and the ship returned to Spithead, where eighteen were hanged at the yardarm. In 1803, *Téméraire* was assigned to blockade duty off western France. In 1805, she was one of eighteen ships detached from the Channel Fleet to a squadron under Admiral Sir Robert Calder in order to follow the Franco-Spanish Combined Fleet (Vice Admiral Pierre Villeneuve) to Spain. Vice Admiral Lord Nelson relieved Calder on September 28 and with his fleet stalked the Combined Fleet until it sailed from Cadiz on October 19–20.

The following day, *Téméraire* was next astern of HMS VICTORY in Nelson's weather column at the Battle of Trafalgar. *Téméraire* relieved pressure on *Victory* by raking *Redoutable*'s starboard side. She was being mauled by the French 74 and *Neptune* (80 guns) when she was approached by *Fougueux* (80), against which she unleashed two devastating broadsides. The French ship drifted onto *Téméraire* and was swiftly captured by a British prize crew. With losses totaling 121 killed and wounded and her masts and rigging a shambles, *Téméraire* was unfit for further sea duty. She was employed as a prison ship from 1813 to 1815, and thereafter as a receiving ship at Devonport and Sheerness. In 1836, she was briefly recommissioned under Captain Thomas Fortescue Kennedy, who as her first lieutenant led in the capture of *Fougueux* at Trafalgar. Two years later, she was en route to be broken up at Rotherhithe when J. M. W. Turner was inspired to paint "The *Téméraire* towed to her last berth." Turner's rendering of the *Téméraire* occasioned much discussion, both when it was painted and later. In a letter to John Ruskin in 1886, Robert Leslie wrote of Turner's placement of "the black funnel of the tug — abaft her mast or flagpole — his first, strong, almost prophetic idea of smoke, soot, iron, and steam, coming to the front in all naval matters." There remained, however, some question as to the accuracy of Turner's depiction, which was cleared up in a letter from W. Hale White of the Admiralty to Leslie and Ruskin:

It has been objected that the masts and yards in the picture are too light for a ninety-eight gun ship; but the truth is that when the vessel was sold she was jury-rigged as a receiving ship, and Turner therefore was strictly accurate. He might have seemed more accurate by putting heavier masts and yards in her; but he painted her as he saw her. This is very important, as it gets rid of the difficulty which I myself have felt and expressed, that it was very improbable that she was sold all standing in sea-going trim, as I imagined Turner intended us to believe she was sold, and answers also the criticism just mentioned as to the disproportion between the weight of the masts and yards and the size of the hull.

Mackenzie, *Trafalgar Roll*. Schom, *Trafalgar*. Uden, *Fighting "Temeraire."*

CSS Tennessee

Casemate ironclad (1f/2m). *L/B/D:* 217′ × 48′ × 14′ (66.1m × 14.6m × 4.3m). *Tons:* 1,273 disp. *Hull:* wood. *Comp.:* 133. *Arm.:* 2 × 7″R, 4 × 6.4″R. *Armor:* 4–6″ casemate. *Mach.:* high-pressure engines, 1 screw; 6 kts. *Des.:* J. L. Porter. *Built:* Henry D. Bassett, Selma, Ala.; 1864.

Built at Selma, on the Alabama River, the ironclad ram CSS *Tennessee* was fitted out at Mobile. Her construction was hampered by shortages of material and manpower, and Admiral Franklin Buchanan had to conscript the civilians at Mobile in order to complete her fitting out. Her casemate was sheathed in layers of two-inch-thick iron. In addition to six rifled guns and a ram, she had "a hot water attachment to her boilers for repelling boarders,

throwing one stream [of water] from forward of the casemate and one abaft." *Tennessee's* engines were taken from a sidewheel steamer, and she had no living accommodations.

Tennessee became the flagship of Admiral Franklin Buchanan, and in June 1864, she was stationed at the approaches to Mobile Bay, ninety miles south of the port. At 0530 on August 5, Flag Officer David G. Farragut's long-anticipated force of four ironclad steamers and fourteen gunboats ran past Forts Morgan and Gaines. In addition to *Tennessee*, Buchanan's fleet included the wooden gunboats CSS *Gaines, Morgan,* and *Selma. Tennessee* attempted to ram USS HARTFORD and ran down the Union line until abreast of Fort Morgan. At 0900, Buchanan turned for Farragut's ships, now anchored four miles into the bay. As the ironclad approached, she was rammed by USS MONONGAHELA, *Lackawanna* (twice), and *Hartford.* The worst damage was inflicted at close range by the fifteen-inch guns of the monitor *Manhattan* and eleven-inch guns of *Chickasaw.* With two crew killed and fourteen wounded, her exposed rudder chains shot away, and no means of escape, *Tennessee* surrendered. *Selma* did likewise, *Gaines* had sunk, and *Morgan* escaped. Union losses included the monitor *Tecumseh* and a supply vessel. Commissioned into the U.S. Navy the next day, USS *Tennessee* took part in the siege of Fort Morgan, which surrendered on August 28. After service on the Mississippi River, in 1867 she was sold for scrap.

Still, *Iron Afloat.* U.S. Navy, *DANFS.*

USS Texas

Second-class battleship (1f/2m). *L/B/D:* 308.8′ × 61.1′ × 24.5′ (94.1m × 18.6m × 7.5m). *Tons:* 6,315 disp. *Hull:* steel. *Comp.:* 392. *Arm.:* 2 × 12″, 6 × 6″, 12 × 6pdr; 4 × 18″TT. *Armor:* 12″ belt, 3″ deck. *Mach.:* triple expansion, 8,600 ihp, 2 screws; 17.8 kts. *Built:* Norfolk Navy Yard, Portsmouth, Va.; 1895.

One of the first two armored cruisers built for the "New Navy," the primary armament of the first USS *Texas* consisted of two 12-inch guns mounted

▲ The complex array of guns carried by capital ships at the end of the nineteenth century is clearly seen in this photograph of the second-class battleship **USS Texas.** Amidships is the turret for one of her two 12-inch guns. Just forward of that is a 6-inch gun, and then two 6-pounder guns. *Courtesy U.S. Naval Historical Center, Washington, D.C.*

en echelon — that is, one to starboard and the other to port, but not on the same athwartships axis. Shortly after the sinking of her near sister ship MAINE at Havana on February 15, 1898, *Texas* was detached from the North Atlantic Squadron to join Commodore Winfield Scott Schley's Flying Squadron to guard the coast against a possible attack by Spanish ships. The Spanish-American War began on April 24, and on May 27, *Texas*, Captain John W. Philip commanding, began blockade duty along the coast of Cuba between Santiago de Cuba and Guantánamo Bay. There, she and *Marblehead* reduced the Spanish fort on June 16. On July 3, she was with the Flying Squadron off Santiago when Admiral Pascual Cervera y Topete was ordered to

sortie with his fleet. Under withering fire from *Texas*, BROOKLYN, OREGON, and other ships, Cervera's four cruisers were run aground and two torpedo boats were sunk; 323 Spaniards died and 151 were wounded. After service as a station ship at Charleston, *Texas* was renamed *San Marcos* and converted to a target ship in 1911. She was sunk off Tangier Island, Maryland.

Trask, *War with Spain in 1898.* U.S. Navy, *DANFS.*

HMS Tonnant

3rd rate 80 (3m). *L/B/D:* 194.2' bp × 51.8' × 23.2' (59.2m × 15.8m × 7.1m). *Tons:* 2,281 bm. *Hull:* wood. *Comp.:* 700. *Arm.:* 32 × 32pdr, 34 × 18pdr, 18 × 32pdr carr. *Built:* Toulon, France; 1792.

Launched in the first year of the French Republic, *Tonnant* ("Thundering") was commissioned as part of the Mediterranean Fleet of Vice Admiral Comte Martin. Her first engagement was against Vice Admiral William Hotham's fleet off Genoa on March 14, 1795. Three years later, during Napoleon's Egyptian Campaign, she flew the flag of Commodore A. A. du Petit-Thouars at the Battle of the Nile on August 1, 1798. Directly astern of the flagship L'ORIENT, though completely dismasted, she was captured only after a protracted struggle, exemplified by the conduct of her captain, who, despite the loss of both arms and a leg, continued to exhort his crew until he died from loss of blood.

One of six French ships captured that day, *Tonnant* was taken into the Royal Navy and in 1803 became flagship of Commodore Sir Edward Pellew. In March 1805, she was detached from the Channel Squadron off Brest for blockade duty at El Ferrol, Spain. Vice Admiral Lord Nelson assumed command of her squadron in September, and at the Battle of Trafalgar, *Tonnant* sailed in the lee squadron led by Admiral Cornwallis's ROYAL SOVEREIGN. Going to the relief of HMS *Mars*, she engaged the Spanish *Monarca* and *San Juan Nepomuceno* and the French *Fougueux* and *Pluton* (all 74 guns). Captain Charles Tyler ran his ship into *Algesiras* (74), whose crew attempted to board *Tonnant*. They were repulsed, and at 1430 the French ship struck her colors. *Tonnant's* casualties numbered seventy-six killed and wounded.

Assigned to the Channel Fleet from 1806 to 1809 under Rear Admiral Eliab Harvey (captain of *Royal Sovereign* at Trafalgar), she later sailed on blockade off Cadiz. During the War of 1812, she was in Rear Admiral George Cockburn's squadron at the capture of Washington, D.C. In December, she was with Vice Admiral Sir Alexander Cochrane's squadron during the attack on New Orleans. She ended her career on the Irish Station based at Cork from 1815 to 1818. Three years later, she was broken up at Plymouth.

Longridge, *Anatomy of Nelson's Ships*. Mackenzie, *Trafalgar Roll*. Schom, *Trafalgar*.

HMS Trincomalee

(ex-*Foudroyant*, *Trincomalee*) *Leda*-class 5th rate 46 (3m). *L/B/D:* 150.1′ × 39.8′ × 13.8 dph (45.8m × 12.1m × 4.2m). *Tons:* 1,052 disp. *Hull:* wood. *Comp.:* 284. *Arm.:* 28 × 18pdr, 8 × 32pdr, 10 × 9pdr. *Des.:* Sir Robert Seppings. *Built:* Wadia Shipyard, Bombay, India; 1817.

The oldest Royal Navy ship still afloat, *Trincomalee* was named for a port on the east coast of Ceylon (Sri Lanka) captured from the French in 1795. A *Leda*-class frigate built in response to the heavily built American frigates CONSTITUTION, PRESIDENT, and UNITED STATES, she had a hull constructed of Malabar teak. With the advent of the Pax Britannica in the wake of the Napoleonic Wars, *Trincomalee* saw limited service before being laid up in England in 1819. Recommissioned as a sixth-rate, 26-gun sloop in 1847, she served for three years on antislaving duty in the West Indies and off West Africa. After a refit, in 1852 she transferred to the Royal Navy base at Esquimault, Vancouver Island, and remained in the Pacific for four years.

In 1857, she returned to England and became a training ship, stationed first at Sunderland and from 1861 as a reserve training ship at West Hartlepool and then Southampton. In 1897, the Royal Navy Reserve sold *Trincomalee* to G. Wheatley Cobb, a philanthropist who had earlier restored the second *Foudroyant*, which was lost in a storm in

▼ The 5th-rate ship **HMS Trincomalee** as she looked in 1979 when she was cut down as a floating school, with windows fitted in the gunports. Note her Indian figurehead and the painted cathead — the beam along which the anchor chain was run in order to keep the anchor away from the hull when "catting" it (raising it) or letting it go. *Courtesy Norman Brouwer.*

1893. Cobb renamed *Trincomalee* in honor of that ship, and she continued as a training ship for boys and girls as young as eleven years old. Cobb's widow donated the ship to the Society for Nautical Research upon his death, and the new *Foudroyant* continued work as a sail-training ship until 1986. Handed over to the Trincomalee Restoration and given back her old name, *Trincomalee* is undergoing restoration to her 1817 appearance for use as a museum ship at Hartlepool.

Horton, *HMS "Trincomalee."* Marsh, *Story of a Frigate.*

Trinidad Valencera

Tons: 1,100. *Hull:* wood. *Comp.:* 360. *Arm.:* 32 guns. *Built:* Venice(?); <1587.

Trinidad Valencera was one of five Venetian traders requisitioned by Spanish authorities in Sicily for use as an armed transport with the Spanish Armada. Over the objections of her merchant captain Horatio Donai, she was fitted with 28 bronze guns. When the fleet sailed, she was the most heavily armed ship in Martin de Bertendona's Levant Squadron, which included 10 converted merchant ships from the Mediterranean. In addition to her own armament, she carried four of the King's guns, and a complement of 79 seaman, 281 Neapolitan soldiers, and a cadre of officers. During the Armada campaign, *Trinidad Valencera* (a Spanish corruption of her Venetian name, *Balanzara*) saw action off Portland Bill (August 1–2), the Isle of Wight (August 2–3), and in the crucial rearguard action fought at the Battle of Gravelines on August 7–9, just before the Armada sailed into the North Sea for the brutal return to Spain.

On about August 20, *Trinidad Valencera*, GRAN GRIFÓN, and two other hulks separated from the main fleet off northern Scotland; none would return to Spain. On September 12, *Trinidad Valencera* was caught in a storm off the north coast of Ireland and, leaking badly, came to anchor in Kinnagoe Bay on the fourteenth. Two days later, she split in two and sank. Most of the ship's company seem to have made it safely to shore, but several days later they were tricked into laying down their weapons. Stripped of their clothes and other possessions by a nominally inferior force, 300 of the soldiers and sailors were slaughtered by an Anglo-Irish force. Thirty-two of the surviving crew eventually made it to Scotland and, with safe passage from James VI, on to France. The officers were marched to Dublin, where all but two were murdered on orders from the Lord Deputy, Sir William Fitzwilliam.

Sport divers discovered the *Trinidad Valencera* wreck site in 1971. As the crew had removed what they could from the ship, there are few substantial artifacts. Chief among them are the ship's guns, which have added considerably to the knowledge of naval gunnery in the sixteenth century. In addition, there are ship's fittings, a few dislocated structural timbers, and pieces of rigging and other cordage.

Martin, *Full Fathom Five;* "*La Trinidad Valencera.*"

Trumbull

Frigate (3m). *L/B/D:* 151′ × 34′ × 18′ (46m × 10.4m × 5.5m). *Tons:* 682 bm. *Hull:* wood. *Comp.:* 199. *Arm.:* 24 × 12pdr, 6 × 6pdr. *Built:* John Cotton, Chatham, Conn.; 1776.

Named for Governor Jonathan Trumbull of Connecticut, *Trumbull* was one of the thirteen original frigates ordered by the Continental Congress in 1775. Under command of Captain Dudley Saltonstall, she was found, following her launch, to draw too much water to get over the bar at the mouth of the Connecticut River. It was not until Captain Elisha Hinman assumed command and girdled her with empty barrels to float her over the bar that she was moved to New London for fitting out. In late May 1780, *Trumbull* left New London, and on June 1, 1780, she ran into the Liverpool privateer *Watt* (36 guns). In one of the bloodiest naval engagements of the war, the two ships fought to a draw, *Trumbull* losing her main and mizzenmasts, suffering eight crew dead and thirty-one wounded; *Watt* was set on fire and lost thirteen killed and seventy-nine wounded. Repairs and lack of funds kept

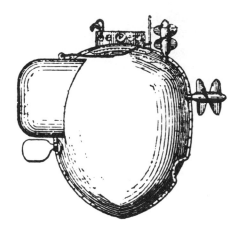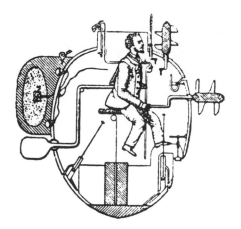

▲ David Bushnell's submarine **Turtle** of 1776 came very close to destroying a British warship in New York Harbor. This 1885 drawing by F. M. Barber is based on Bushnell's written description of the vessel. *Courtesy U.S. Naval Historical Center, Washington, D.C.*

Trumbull at Philadelphia until August 8, 1781, when she sailed as escort for a merchant convoy. On the night of August 28, she lost her foretop and topgallant masts in a storm, and the next morning she was set upon by HMS *Iris* (32) and *General Monk* (20). (*Iris* was Trumbull's sister ship, the former HANCOCK.) Although three-quarters of the crew refused to fight (many of them were originally British prisoners, as was common in the Continental Navy), Nicholson engaged the enemy for an hour and a half before striking. The last of the original frigates was towed to New York and broken up.

Fowler, *Rebels under Sail.* U.S. Navy, *DANFS.*

Turtle

Submarine. *L/D:* 7.5′ × 6′ dph (2.3m × 1.8m). *Tons:* ca. 2,000 lb. *Hull:* wood. *Comp.:* 1. *Arm.:* detachable mine. *Mach.:* 2 screws; 2–3 kts. *Des.:* David Bushnell. *Built:* David & Ezra Bushnell, Saybrook, Conn.; 1776.

Designed by David Bushnell and built by him and his brother Ezra at the latter's farm, *Turtle* took her name from her resemblance to "two upper tortoise shells of equal size, joined together." Conceived by Bushnell as a way of attacking the British fleet at Boston, Massachusetts, *Turtle* combined the four essential abilities of a true submersible. She could be propelled independently, dive below the surface of the water, provide thirty minutes of air for the one-man crew, and operate offensively against an enemy ship.

Diving was achieved by admitting water to the bilge; the water could be expelled by a foot-operated bellows. Light was admitted through watertight windows in the truncated conning tower; when submerged the interior was illuminated by a phosphorescent wood called foxfire. *Turtle* was powered by two manual screw-like devices, one for forward movement and the other for ascending and descending. She held 700 pounds of ballast, 200 pounds of which could be jettisoned in an emergency. Air was supplied through a pair of crude snorkel-like devices fitted with check valves. In addition to a tiller-handled rudder, the operator was provided with a compass and a depth gauge. *Turtle*'s offensive capability was in the form of a detachable torpedo, or mine, of Bushnell's. This mine consisted of a casing filled with 150 pounds of gunpowder, which was to be attached to an auger that was bored into the underside of a ship's hull. The mine had a timer set to detonate an hour after the mine's release from *Turtle*.

When the British evacuated Boston, Bushnell

offered his ingenious craft to General George Washington, who was desperate for something that might dislodge the British from New York and who agreed to provide funds to bring *Turtle* to the city. David Bushnell was too frail to operate the craft himself, and it was intended that his brother take her into battle, but he fell ill. In his place, Sergeant Ezra Lee, a Connecticut volunteer, was hastily trained.

Turtle's first target was the 64-gun HMS *Eagle,* flagship of Vice Admiral Richard "Black Dick" Howe, lying with the British squadron off Staten Island. At 2230 on the night of September 5, 1776, Lee and *Turtle* were towed as close to the fleet as possible before they were cast off on their own. Against the current, it took Lee two hours to maneuver *Turtle* alongside *Eagle.* Everything went according to plan, but for some reason Lee was un-able to bore the auger into *Eagle*'s hull before he briefly lost control of *Turtle* and shot to the surface. Afraid of being detected, he decided to abandon the attempt and headed back to shore. As he passed Governors Island, a British cutter put out to investigate. As the boat approached, Lee detached the mine, upon which the British returned the way they came. An hour later, the mine exploded in the British anchorage, throwing up a huge geyser of water that persuaded the British to slip their cables and flee. Two more attempts to use *Turtle* against the British were unsuccessful. The submarine's ultimate fate is not known, though it is believed that, after the British took New York, she was destroyed to prevent her falling into enemy hands.

Miller, *Sea of Glory.* U.S. Navy, *DANFS.*

U

HMS Unicorn

(ex-*Unicorn II, Cressy, Unicorn*) *Leda*-class 5th rate 46 (3m). *L/B/D:* 150.1′ × 39.8′ × 13.8 dph (45.8m × 12.1m × 4.2m). *Tons:* 1,052 disp. *Hull:* wood. *Comp.:* 284. *Arm.:* 28 × 18pdr, 8 × 32pdr, 10 × 9pdr. *Des.:* Sir Robert Seppings. *Built:* Chatham Dockyard, Eng.; 1824.

A member of one of the Royal Navy's most successful classes of heavy frigates, HMS *Unicorn* has the curious distinction of being one of the oldest, least used, and best preserved wooden ships in the world. Laid down in 1822 and launched two years later, the Royal Navy realized immediately that it had little use for another 46-gun frigate of the same class as HMS *Shannon* and Trincomalee, and she was immediately put in ordinary, unrigged and disarmed. She was employed as a powder hulk at Woolwich from 1857 to 1862, when she was moved to Sheerness and laid up. Ten years later, she was towed to Dundee for use as a drillship. She would remain in this line of work until 1967; during both world wars, she served also as the Area Headquarters of the Senior Naval Officer, Dundee. In 1939, she was renamed *Unicorn II* to free the name for a new aircraft carrier, and in 1941 she became *Cressy*. When the carrier was scrapped in 1959, she took back her old name. The frigate was herself headed to the ship breakers in 1967 when former Captain J. C. L. Anderson initiated an effort to save the ship and have her restored and rigged in the manner originally intended.

Stewart, "Seppings Survivor"; *Welcome aboard the Frigate "Unicorn."*

USS United States

Frigate (3m). *L/B/D:* 175′ × 43.5′ × 14.3′ (53.3m × 13.3m × 4.3m). *Tons:* 2,200 tons. *Hull:* wood. *Comp.:* 364. *Des.:* Joshua Humphreys, Josiah Fox, William Doughty. *Built:* Joshua Humphreys, Philadelphia; 1797.

One of the U.S. Navy's original six frigates, authorized by Congress specifically to combat the Barbary corsairs in the western Mediterranean, USS *United States* was launched in 1797, followed shortly by Constellation and Constitution. Heavily built with a flush spar deck above the gundeck, *United States, Constitution,* and President were rated as 44s and designed to carry thirty 24-pdr. and twenty to twenty-two 12-pdr. long guns; the latter were eventually superseded by the more powerful, short-range 42-pdr. carronades. (The 38s, including Chesapeake and *Congress,* were designed to carry twenty-eight 24-pdrs and eighteen to twenty 12-pdrs.)

Commissioned under Captain John Barry, during the Quasi-War with France, in July 1798 *United States* sailed with USS *Delaware* for the Caribbean in search of French prizes. She captured two privateers on her first cruise, and three in the second, during which the West Indies Squadron grew to two frigates, three ships, and four revenue cutters. With the conclusion of the war, the American navy was all but disbanded, and *United States* was laid up at the Washington Navy Yard with four of her sister ships; *Constitution* was at Boston.

In June 1810, the recommissioned *United States* put to sea under Captain Stephen Decatur. Two years later, the United States declared war on Great Britain, and Decatur's ship joined Commodore John Rodgers's North Atlantic Squadron. Their

▲ Painting of the action between the **USS United States** and **HMS Macedonian** on October 25, 1812, by Arthur N. Disney, Sr. The British frigate was dismasted and so badly damaged that repairs took two weeks at sea. *Courtesy U.S. Naval Historical Center, Washington, D.C.*

second cruise began on October 8, 1812; three days later, *United States* split off from the squadron. On October 25, about 500 miles south of the Azores, *United States* engaged HMS MACEDONIAN (38 guns) under Captain John Surman Carden. Battle was joined at about 0920, and Decatur positioned his ship on *Macedonian's* quarter. By noon the British frigate was a dismasted hulk with 104 of her crew dead or wounded; American casualties were 12 dead and wounded. Mid-ocean repairs to the British prize took two weeks, and it was not until December that *United States* returned to New York, where *Macedonian* was brought into the U.S. Navy. In May 1813, the ships slipped out of New York with the sloop HORNET, but they were forced into New London, where they were blockaded for the duration of the war.

No sooner was the War of 1812 over than Congress declared war on Algiers, and *United States* was sent to the Mediterranean. Although peace was quickly made, *United States* was kept on station until 1819. Laid up for five years, her subsequent career reflected the widening scope of American merchant and naval interests. She sailed variously with the Pacific Squadron (1824–27, 1841–42), Mediterranean Squadron (1833–38, 1847–48), Home Squadron (1839–40), and African Squadron (1846–47). It was on her second patrol in the Pacific that she was joined by ordinary seaman Herman Melville, who translated his fourteen-month experience into the novel *White-Jacket, or The World in a Man-of-War*, in which his ship is called the USS *Neversink*.

Decommissioned in 1849, *United States* was captured (with the rest of the Norfolk Navy Yard) and commissioned as the Confederate receiving ship CSS *United States* (or sometimes *Confederate States*). Sunk as a blockship in the Elizabeth River, she was raised and broken up at Norfolk in 1865.

Chapelle, *History of the American Sailing Navy.* U.S. Navy, *DANFS.*

HMS Vanguard

3rd rate 74 (3m). *L/B:* 168′ × 47′ (51.2m × 14.3m). *Tons:* 1,664 bm. *Hull:* wood. *Comp.:* 530. *Arm.:* 28 × 32pdr, 30 × 24pdr, 16 × 9pdr. *Built:* Deptford Dockyard, Eng.; 1787.

When France under the Directory declared war on Great Britain in 1793, the Kingdom of Naples allied itself with Britain, which was forced thereby to commit major resources to the Mediterranean. The British presence there intensified even more after Napoleon invaded Italy in 1796. The next year, HMS *Vanguard* became the flagship of Rear Admiral Horatio Nelson, his first command after having his right arm amputated because of injuries incurred during an attempted landing at Santa Cruz de Tenerife, in the Canary Islands. He was immediately sent to cruise off Toulon to determine the intentions of the huge French fleet mustering there under Vice Admiral François Paul Brueys d'Aiguïlliers. On May 20, 1798, *Vanguard* was dismasted in a gale; repairs were made at Sardinia, and she returned to Toulon to find that the French had sailed, also on the twentieth. Earl St. Vincent then appointed Nelson — over two more senior officers — to search for and destroy the French armada, numbering some 75 warships, 400 transports, 10,000 sailors, and 36,000 soldiers.

By June 7, Nelson had a fleet of fourteen ships of the line but, through a confusion of orders, no frigates, a situation that led him to declare, "Frigates! Were I to die this moment, *want of frigates* would be found engraved on my heart!" Lacking these "eyes of the fleet," he was unable to locate the French armada until after it had captured Malta, at which point he supposed it to be headed for Egypt to establish a bridgehead for the capture of British India. Finding no French in Alexandria, Nelson put back to Sicily for water and provisions. Setting to

sea again, on July 28 he learned that the French had been seen bound for Egypt, to which he now returned. On August 1, the British were off Alexandria and that same afternoon found the French fleet of thirteen ships of the line and four frigates anchored in line ahead in Aboukir Bay. Many of the crews were ashore watering ship, and though they were recalled immediately, Admiral Brueys seems to have believed that Nelson would attack the following morning and that he had a night to prepare.

Nelson felt that when the French cleared for battle, they would assume that his attack would come from the sea and not bother with the guns facing the shore. At 1630, five of Nelson's ships passed between the French van and the shore while *Vanguard* and five other ships anchored to seaward. Seven French ships were pummeled by thirteen British (*Culloden* had run aground, and *Swiftsure* and *Alexander* did not arrive off Aboukir until 2000), while the rest of the French fleet remained out of action to leeward. Nelson described the action briefly in a letter to Lord Howe:

I had the happiness to command a band of brothers; therefore, night was to my advantage. Each knew his duty, and I was sure each would feel for a French ship. By attacking the enemy's van and centre, the wind blowing directly along their line, I was able to throw what force I pleased on a few ships. This plan my friends readily conceived by the signals, . . . and we always kept a superior force to the enemy. At twenty-eight minutes past six, the sun in the horizon, the firing commenced. At five minutes past ten, when the *Orient* blew up, having burnt seventy minutes, the six van ships surrendered. I then pressed further towards the rear; and had it pleased God that I had not been wounded and stone blind [from a piece of scrap iron that hit

▲ The experimental gunboat **USS Vesuvius** in 1891. The barrels of the three pneumatic guns, just forward of the mast, pass through the deck to the bottom of the hull. *Courtesy U.S. Naval Historical Center, Washington, D.C.*

him in the forehead], there cannot be a doubt but that every ship would have been in our possession.

In the event, the Nile proved the most decisive victory of its day, and Rear Admiral Comte de Villeneuve escaped with only *Généreux, Guillaume Tell,* and two frigates. Two ships of the line were sunk, three were beyond repair, and six were taken into the Royal Navy. Nelson was honored with a peerage (Baron Nelson of the Nile and Burnham-Thorpe) and with gifts from Czar Paul of Russia, Ottoman Sultan Selim III, and the East India Company, among others.

France's army in Egypt remained cut off in the Middle East until 1802, although Napoleon returned to Europe in October 1799. In the meantime, French continental armies advanced through Italy with little resistance from the fragmented re-

publics. In December 1798, the Neapolitan royal family sailed to exile in Sicily aboard *Vanguard.* Shortly thereafter, Nelson commenced a blockade of Malta, which held out for two years. Nelson later shifted his flag to HMS *Foudroyant,* and in 1800 *Vanguard* returned to home waters. Though she remained in active service, she was not present at the other major battles of the Napoleonic Wars. Reduced to a prison ship in 1812 and a powder hulk in 1814, *Vanguard* was broken up in 1821.

Bennett, *Nelson the Commander.*

USS Vesuvius

Dynamite gun cruiser (1f/2m). *L/B/D:* 252.3′ × 26.4′ × 9′ (76.9m × 8.1m × 2.7m). *Tons:* 930 disp. *Hull:* steel. *Comp.:* 70. *Arm.:* 3 × 15″, 3 × 3pdr. *Mach.:* steam, 2 screws; 21 kts. *Built:* William Cramp & Son Ships and Engine Building Co., Philadelphia; 1890.

Named for the Italian volcano, the third USS *Vesuvius* was a unique vessel developed during the transition from muzzle-loading guns to recoil-controlled breech-loaders. Her three 15-inch "pneumatic dynamite" guns were designed by U.S.

Army Lieutenant E. L. Zalinski and used compressed air to propel the nitrocellulose/nitroglycerin shells. Mounted in parallel, the barrels led from just forward of the massive compressed air tanks on the lower deck amidships up through the foredeck. The range — up to one and a half miles — varied according to the amount of compressed air admitted to the firing chamber. The direction of fire could be changed only by turning the ship, and aiming the guns was crude.

Vesuvius operated with the North Atlantic Squadron from 1890 to 1895, when she was decommissioned for a refit. During the Spanish-American War, on June 13, 1898, Vesuvius's guns were engaged in a night bombardment of Santiago. While they inflicted few casualties, the huge shells were nonetheless terrifying because the pneumatic propellant was barely audible ashore. Decommissioned at the end of the war, she exchanged her gun

barrels for torpedo tubes in 1904 and was used as a torpedo vessel for two more years. From 1910 to 1921, Vesuvius served as a station ship at Newport. She was broken up in 1922.

Allen, "Story of the USS Vesuvius and the Dynamite Gun." U.S. Navy, DANFS.

HMS Victoria

Sans Pareil–class battleship (1f/2m). L/B/D: 340' × 70' × 29' (103.6m × 21.3m × 8.8m). Tons: 11,020 disp. Comp.: 430–583. Arm.: 2 × 16.25", 1 × 10", 12 × 6", 12 × 6pdr; 6 × 14"TT. Armor: 18" belt, 3" deck. Hull: steel. Mach.: triple-expansion steam, 7,500 ihp, 2 screws; 15.3 kts. Built: Sir W. G. Armstrong, Whitworth & Co., Ltd., Newcastle-on-Tyne, Eng.; 1890.

The Sans Pareil class was the first class of battleships built after the Admiral-class barbette ships, which included HMS CAMPERDOWN. The last single-turret ships built for the Royal Navy — and as such representing a step backward from the earlier class — they were the first to be driven by triple-expansion engines. Victoria was commissioned as flagship of the Mediterranean Fleet, to replace Camperdown, and remained on that station the

▼ Flagship of the Mediterranean Fleet, **HMS Victoria** was lost in one of the Royal Navy's most inexplicable and unsettling peacetime accidents. *Courtesy National Maritime Museum, Greenwich.*

whole of her brief career. On June 22, 1893, en route from Beirut to Tripoli, the fleet was steaming north-northeast in parallel columns six cables (1,200 yards) apart. For reasons never adequately explained, Vice Admiral Sir George Tryon ordered the two divisions to turn 16 points toward each other. Although there seemed to be some concern over the outcome of the maneuver — which sent the ships toward each other at a combined speed of 10 to 12 knots — no one questioned the order. *Camperdown*'s ram struck *Victoria* just abaft the anchors 12 feet below the waterline, making a breach nearly 28 feet long. *Victoria* was turned toward shore in an attempt to reach shallow water, but the inrush of water was too great, and she quickly went down by the bows, taking with her 22 officers and 336 men. Because of the speed with which *Victoria* sank, the apparent effectiveness of the ram was confirmed in the minds of many naval planners, and rams remained a feature of warship design until the early 1900s.

Mead, "Loss of the *Victoria*." Parkes, *British Battleships*.

HMS Victory

1st rate 100 (3m). *L/B/D:* 226.5′ × 52′ × 21.5′ dph (69m × 15.8m × 6.6m). *Tons:* 2,162 bm. *Hull:* wood. *Comp.:* 850. *Arm.:* 2 × 68pdr, 28 × 42pdr, 28 × 24pdr, 28 × 12pdr, 16 × 6pdr. *Des.:* Sir Thomas Slade. *Built:* Chatham Dockyard, Eng.; 1765.

The seventh ship of the name, and the third first-rate ship so called, HMS *Victory* was launched in 1765, two years after the conclusion of the Seven Years' War, but she was not commissioned until 1778. When France signed a treaty of cooperation with the American colonies, *Victory* was made flagship of Admiral Sir Augustus Keppel's Channel Fleet and, on July 23, took part in an indecisive battle off Ushant (or Ile d'Ouessant, off the western tip of Brittany), where she lost thirty-five killed and wounded. She remained in the Channel Fleet for the next two years and was briefly assigned to Vice Admiral Hyde Parker's North Sea Convoy Squadron designated to protect English shipping from the Dutch, now allied with the French. On

December 12, flying the flag of Admiral Richard Kempenfelt, she captured a French convoy off Ushant bound for America. In 1782, *Victory* was Lord Howe's flagship in the relief of Gibraltar. Paid off at Portsmouth the following year, *Victory* remained in ordinary for eight years.

In 1792, *Victory* became flagship of Vice Admiral Sir Samuel Hood's Mediterranean Fleet, which occupied Toulon (surrendered to the English by Loyalist troops) and captured Bastia and Calvi, Corsica, which Hood sought to use as a British base in 1794. The next year, Admiral Sir John Jervis broke his flag in *Victory*. With only half as many ships of the line as the French and Spanish combined fleets, Jervis consolidated his force at Gibraltar. On February 14, 1797, he sailed with fifteen British ships to intercept a large Spanish convoy guarded by twenty-seven ships of the line. In the ensuing engagement off Cape St. Vincent, the British broke the Spanish line and inflicted terrible damage on the Spanish flagship, *Principe de Asturias* (112 guns) before forcing *Salvador del Mundo* (112) to strike. *Victory* lost only nine killed and wounded in the battle. The British also captured the first-rate *San Josef* and the two-deckers *San Nicolás* and *San Ysidro*. Their success was due in no small part to Commodore Horatio Nelson, then in HMS CAPTAIN. In 1798, *Victory* returned to Portsmouth, where she was considered fit only for a prison hospital ship at Chatham.

In 1800, it was decided to rebuild *Victory*, a process that took three years. On May 16, 1803, she became flagship of Lord Nelson's Mediterranean Fleet, Captain Thomas Masterman Hardy commanding. At this time, Napoleon had begun formulating elaborate plans for the invasion of England, and Nelson was ordered to contain Vice Admiral Pierre Villeneuve's squadron at Toulon. Flying his flag in *Bucentaure*, Villeneuve slipped out in January 1805, returned to port, and sailed again on March 30. After picking up Admiral Federico Carlos Gravina's Spanish fleet at Cadiz, Villeneuve sailed for a rendezvous with other French forces at Martinique. Learning of his move, Nelson set off in hot pursuit across the Atlantic. In June, Villeneuve learned that Nelson had followed him to the Caribbean, and he returned to Europe almost immediately. Nelson followed close behind, arriving off southern Spain four days before the Combined Fleet skirmished with Admiral Sir Robert Calder's fleet off El Ferrol.

Villeneuve arrived at Cadiz on August 21, and remained there, blockaded first by Vice Admiral Sir Cuthbert Collingwood and then, in October, by Nelson, fresh from meetings in London with Prime Minister William Pitt and First Lord of the Admiralty Lord Barham. Daunted by the prospect of an engagement with the British fleet, Villeneuve stayed put until he learned that Napoleon was relieving him of his command. At 0600 on October 19, the Combined Fleet — eighteen French and fifteen Spanish ships of the line — weighed anchor, and within two and a half hours, the news had been signaled to Nelson, fifty miles to the southwest. The fleet took two days to straggle out of Cadiz, and at first it seemed as though Villeneuve was going to make a run for the Mediterranean. But at 0800 on October 21, he turned back to face Nelson. Twelve days before, Nelson had outlined his plan of attack, "the Nelson Touch," as he called it in a letter to Emma Hamilton:

> The whole impression of the British Fleet must be to overpower from two or three ships ahead of their Commander-in-Chief, supposed to be in the Centre, to the Rear of their Fleet. . . . I look with confidence to a Victory before the Van of the Enemy could succour their Rear.

On the eve of the battle, he concluded his remarks to his officers with the encouraging observation, "No Captain can do very wrong if he places his ship alongside that of an enemy."

In a move that might well have failed under any other commander, Nelson divided his fleet into two divisions, the weather division headed by *Victory* and the lee by Collingwood in HMS ROYAL SOVEREIGN. As the British lines approached the Combined Fleet, at 1125 Nelson ordered his most famous signal run up *Victory*'s masts: "England expects that every man will do his duty." *Victory* failed to cut off *Bucentaure,* and she came under all but unchallenged broadsides from *Redoutable* for

forty-five minutes. Finally, at 1230, *Victory* let off a broadside into the stern gallery of the French flagship, though she was soon enfiladed by *Bucentaure, Redoutable,* under Jean-Jacques Lucas, and the French *Neptune.* (The Roman sea god was impartial at Trafalgar, which also saw the participation of HMS *Neptune* and the Spanish *Neptuno.*) Nelson had insisted on wearing his full allotment of medals and decorations, and at 1325, he was wounded by a French sharpshooter as he paced the quarterdeck with Hardy. In the meantime, *Redoutable* and *Victory* lay side by side, exchanging murderous volleys until *Redoutable* drifted into HMS TÉMÉRAIRE. Stuck fast between the unrelenting broadsides of the two British ships, *Redoutable* finally surrendered, and *Victory* was out of the battle by 1430. Her mizzen topmast was shot away, many of the other masts were severely weakened, and her bulwarks and hull were considerably shot up. Nelson had been taken below, and at 1630 — having first been informed of the capture of fifteen of the enemy ships — the hero of the Nile, Copenhagen, and now Trafalgar, died.

British prizes numbered more than nine French and ten Spanish ships, including *Bucentaure.* Of these, two escaped, four were scuttled, and eight sank in a storm that hit after the battle. Casualties in the Combined Fleet totaled 6,953, as against 448 British dead and 1,241 wounded; *Victory* lost 57 dead and 102 wounded. Towed to Gibraltar by HMS *Neptune, Victory* sailed for England, reaching Sheerness on December 22, from where Nelson's body was carried to St. Paul's Cathedral for a state funeral. His death was not in vain, for with Trafalgar he had destroyed the French battle fleet and any threat of a Napoleonic invasion of Britain. England would rule the seas uncontested for a century. Defeated at sea Napoleon may have been, but six weeks later his armies won a crushing victory at Austerlitz. Napoleon would try the fate of Europe for another decade.

After a refit at Chatham, in 1808 *Victory* reentered service as the flagship of Sir James Saumarez's Baltic Fleet, which blockaded the Russian fleet and kept open the supply of naval stores from Sweden. Except for a brief spell escorting a

▲ Thomas Whitcombe's depiction of Admiral de Grasse's surrender of his flagship **Ville de Paris** to a fleet under Rear Admiral Sir George B. Rodney at the Battle of the Saintes, off the island of Dominica (April 12, 1782). Only seven months earlier, de Grasse's fleet had ensured a colonial victory in the American war of independence. *Courtesy National Maritime Museum, Greenwich.*

troop convoy for the relief of the Duke of Wellington's forces in the Peninsular Campaign, she remained in the Baltic until paid off in 1812. Since 1824, *Victory* has served as flagship of the commander-in-chief at Portsmouth. In 1922, she was dry-docked and opened as a museum. She received her last battle wound in World War II, when a German bomb exploded in her dry dock.

Bennett, *Nelson the Commander.* Bugler, *HMS "Victory."* Fraser, *"H.M.S. Victory."* Longridge, *Anatomy of Nelson's Ships.* McKay, *100-Gun Ship "Victory."* Mackenzie, *Trafalgar Roll.* Schom, *Trafalgar.*

Ville de Paris

1st rate 104 (3m). *L/B/D:* 177' × 48.5' × 23' (57.9m × 16.4m × 7.5m). *Tons:* 2,347. *Hull:* wood. *Arm.:* 90–104 guns. *Built:* Rochefort, France; 1764.

Following the French defeat in the Seven Years' War, Louis XV's Minister of the Marine Etienne-François de Choiseul set about to rebuild the French navy. Between 1763 and 1771, the number of French ships of the line rose from about thirty-five to sixty-four, and in 1771 there were also fifty frigates operational. One of the first of the new ships was *Ville de Paris,* which had been laid down in 1757 but was not completed until after the war. Originally rated as a 90-gun ship, she was subsequently enlarged to carry 104 guns (some authorities say 120 guns) during the reign of Louis XVI.

Hostilities with Great Britain resumed in 1778, when France decided to support actively the aspirations of Britain's American colonies in their war of independence. The naval war was truly global, and there were major campaigns in North America, the West Indies, the Indian Ocean, and European waters. On July 23, 1778, a French fleet under

Comte d'Orvilliers sailed from Brest for a month-long cruise to watch the British. Two days later, the French came in contact with a British fleet under Admiral the Honorable Augustus Keppel, flying his flag in HMS VICTORY. For two days, d'Orvilliers tried to avoid battle, but the two fleets met in a bloody though inconclusive engagement on July 27. The French lost 161 dead and 513 wounded to 133 British killed and 373 wounded before the two fleets returned to their respective homeports.

In March 1781, *Ville de Paris* sailed from Brest as flagship of a convoy led by Admiral François Joseph Paul Comte de Grasse bound for the island of Martinique. On April 28, land was sighted, as was a British fleet under Rear Admiral Samuel Hood. A skirmish developed between the British and French fleets, but the French convoy reached Fort de France unscathed. De Grasse later attempted to land 1,200 troops on St. Lucia, immediately south of Martinique, but he was repulsed by the British. He had more luck at Tobago, which capitulated on June 2. On July 26, the French fleet arrived at Cap François, Haiti, to rendezvous with four ships under Rear Admiral Comte de Guichen (who had commanded *Ville de Paris* at Ushant) and to receive intelligence on the situation unfolding in North America.

The British army under Major General Charles Cornwallis had been ordered into a defensive position on the Yorktown Peninsula of Virginia in Chesapeake Bay. Moving with dispatch, de Grasse sailed from Haiti on August 2 with 28 ships of the line, and at the end of the month, 3,300 French troops landed near the mouth of the James River. Four ships were detailed to guard the York and James Rivers and to prevent Cornwallis from fleeing south. On September 5, an English fleet of 19 ships under Rear Admiral Thomas Graves arrived from New York. The French fleet stood out of the bay in some disorder, but Graves was unable to bring his ships to bear, and the French led the British fleet away from the bay. Although they suffered more casualties — about 200 French dead to 94 British — light airs over the following few days prevented a renewal of the battle, and by September 10, de Grasse was back in the Chesapeake.

Caught between the French fleet and the Continental Army, on October 19 Cornwallis surrendered. The independence declared by the United States five years before was now secure.

On November 5, de Grasse sailed for the Caribbean. Adverse winds twice kept him from an assault on Barbados, and he had to content himself with taking the islands of St. Kitts and Nevis at the end of January 1782. On January 25, Admiral Sir Samuel Hood (flying his flag in the 90-gun HMS BARFLEUR) seized the anchorage at Basse Terre from de Grasse, although the English garrison on St. Kitts was forced to surrender on February 12. De Grasse's ultimate aim was to join a Spanish fleet at Cap François and invade Jamaica.

This plan was frustrated by a British fleet under Admiral George Brydges Rodney in HMS *Formidable* (98 guns), with Hood as second-in-command. On April 12, the British and French fleets met just south of the Iles de Saintes in the channel between Dominica and Guadeloupe. Failure of the French to avoid battle with a superior force, or to engage it on more equal terms, stemmed from de Grasse's decision to rescue the *Zélé* (74), which had been dismasted a few days before in collision with *Ville de Paris*. Battle was joined at about 0830. The British quickly broke the ragged French line and isolated a number of French ships. The battle continued until 1829, when *Ville de Paris*, her ammunition spent, surrendered, the last of five ships to do so. Hood complained that had Rodney given the signal for a general chase, "I am very confident we should have had twenty sail of the enemy's ships before dark." Although the remainder of the French fleet retired to Haiti in reasonably good order, plans for more campaigns in the West Indies were abandoned.

Ironically, the only French ships to reach Jamaica were those captured at the Battle of the Saintes, including *Ville de Paris*. On August 15, she sailed as part of a large convoy bound for England under Admiral Graves. From September 16 to 19, the fleet was overtaken by a hurricane in which a number of transports and fighting ships were lost, the latter including *Ville de Paris* (from which there was only one survivor), the French prizes *Glorieux*,

▲ Often attributed to Captain Charles Wilkes, this engraving of the **USS Vincennes** in Disappointment Bay, Antarctica, was probably based on a sketch by the commander of the U.S. South Sea Surveying and Exploring Expedition of 1838–42. *Courtesy Peabody Essex Museum, Salem, Massachusetts.*

Centaur, and *Hector,* Graves's flagship *Ramillies* (all 74-gun ships), and the storeship *Cornwallis.*

Clowes, *Royal Navy.* Gardiner and Lavery, eds., *Line of Battle.* Hepper, *British Warship Losses.* Larrabee, *Decision at the Chesapeake.*

USS Vincennes

Sloop of war (3m). *L/B/D:* 127′ × 33.8′ × 16.5′ (38.7m × 10.3m × 5m). *Tons:* 780 reg. *Hull:* wood. *Comp.:* 80. *Arm.:* 20 × 32pdr. *Built:* New York Navy Yard, Brooklyn, N.Y.; 1826.

Named for the Indiana fort twice captured by American forces under George Rogers Clark during the American Revolution, the first USS *Vincennes* had one of the most extraordinary careers

of any ship in the U.S. Navy. Dispatched to the Pacific Squadron under Master Commandant William Bolton Finch one week after her commissioning, in 1828 she was ordered to look after American merchant and whaling interests in the Marquesas, Tahiti, and Sandwich Islands (Hawaii). From Hawaii she sailed east, stopping at Macao, Manila, Cape Town, and St. Helena before returning to New York on June 8, 1830, the first U.S. Navy ship to circumnavigate the globe. The following year found her on patrol in the Caribbean under Commander Edward R. Shubrick. In 1833–34, she made a second circumnavigation, under Commander Alexander S. Wadsworth, calling at Guam and Sumatra, among other places, en route.

In 1838, *Vincennes* was chosen as flagship of Lieutenant Charles Wilkes's United States South Sea Surveying and Exploring Expedition, also known as the Great United States Exploring Expedition. The origins of the Wilkes expedition can be traced to John Cleves Symmes, Jr., who believed that "the earth is hollow and habitable within . . . and that it is open at the poles twelve or sixteen degrees." This theory attained widespread currency, but Congress declined to sponsor a voyage of exploration. Symmes and his theory eventually passed into memory, but the cause of a polar expedition was taken up by his erstwhile disciple, Jeremiah Reynolds. In 1836, Congress reversed itself, and Commodore Thomas ap Catesby Jones was appointed to lead the expedition. Exhausted by the endless politics of the preparations, Jones resigned, and command eventually fell to Wilkes.

On August 18, 1838, the expedition sailed with six vessels, *Vincennes, Peacock* (under Lieutenant William Hudson), *Porpoise* (Lieutenant Cadwallader Ringgold), *Relief,* and schooners *Flying Fish* and *Sea Gull.* Calling at Madeira, Cape Verde, Rio de Janeiro, and Rio Negro, they rounded Cape Horn and put in at Orange Harbor on Tierra del Fuego. *Vincennes* remained there while *Relief* surveyed the Strait of Magellan and the four remaining ships sailed south on February 25, 1839. *Porpoise* and *Sea Gull* skirted the (unseen) southeast coast of the Palmer Peninsula as far as 63°10'S on March 15. *Flying Fish* knocked its way south through the ice to 70°S, 101°11'W on March 22, and *Peacock* attained 68°08'S, 97°58'W. *Sea Gull* was later lost in a storm, but the other ships rendezvoused at Valparaiso in May, before continuing to Callao.

The ships reached the Tuamotus group in mid-August and worked their way west toward Tahiti, arriving on September 11. A month later, they continued to Samoa and from there to Sydney, Australia. *Relief* was sent home, and the other ships were readied for their second voyage south. On January 11, 1840, they encountered an ice barrier, and five days later, in 65°18'S, 157°36'E, Henry Eld and William Reynolds in *Peacock* sighted two mountains (named for them), which confirmed the existence of a continental landmass. On January 28, land was also sighted from *Vincennes,* then in 66°35'S, 140°30'E. Wilkes wrote that "it could be seen extending to the east and west of our position, and now that all were convinced of its existence, I gave the land the name of the Antarctic Continent." By the next year, the region had appeared on German maps as Wilkes Land.

After regrouping in New Zealand, the expedition sailed for Hawaii, spending six months en route surveying the Fiji Islands before arriving at Honolulu on September 23, 1841. In December, *Peacock* and *Flying Fish* left to reconnoiter islands in the central Pacific before proceeding to a rendezvous at the Columbia River. In April 1842, *Vincennes* and *Porpoise* sailed for the Pacific Northwest and surveyed the waters around Vancouver Island and the Strait of Juan de Fuca. Returning to the Columbia River in August, Wilkes learned that *Peacock* had wrecked on the bar on July 17, though without loss of life. *Vincennes* was sent to San Francisco while a party of nine men, including geologist James Dwight Dana, botanist William Dunlop Brackenridge, and naturalist-painter Titian Peale, marched overland to San Francisco. *Peacock*'s crew were put aboard a purchased vessel renamed *Oregon.* The squadron sailed for Hawaii in November, and from there the ships made their way west via Wake (where the islands of Wilkes and Peale were named), Manila, Singapore, Cape Town, and eventually New York, where they arrived on June 10, 1842.

Much of the expedition's collections had preceded the ships home, having been sent to Philadelphia from various ports en route. The task of conservation and display fell to the fledgling Smithsonian Institution, established with a half-million-dollar bequest from an Englishman, James Smithson. At first, the scientific achievements paled in comparison with the public enthusiasm for the various courts-martial that began shortly after the ship's return, all centering on the conduct of Lieutenant Wilkes. The choice of the relatively junior officer as expedition leader had been questioned early on, for despite his industry and scientific attainments, he was a poor commander whose conduct, in the words of William Stanton, "in one incident after another created a bond of unity [among his subordinates] that could hardly have existed under a more popular commander."

Little the worse for wear, *Vincennes* was soon assigned to the Home Squadron, and under Commander Franklin Buchanan, she cruised the West Indies and Caribbean until 1844. The next year, *Vincennes* and USS *Columbus* were sent to the

Orient with orders to open trade with Japan. The squadron arrived at Edo (Tokyo) on July 21, 1846, but they were denied permission even to land, much less negotiate, and Commodore James Biddle was obliged to leave after ten days. *Vincennes* was laid up at New York from 1847 to 1849, when she sailed again for a two-year stint with the Pacific Squadron. The following year, she was named the flagship of the United States Surveying Expedition to the North Pacific Ocean. Under Commander John Rodgers, she sailed with *Porpoise* via the Cape of Good Hope to chart parts of the Indian Ocean, the Bonins, and Ladrones in the South China Sea, and the Ryukyu and Kurile Islands (south and north of Japan). In 1855, the expedition sailed through the Bering Strait and 400 miles west to 176°E, farther into the Bering Sea than any ships before them.

In 1857, *Vincennes* joined the antislavery patrol on the African Station, and from June 1861 to the end of the Civil War, she served with the Gulf Coast Blockading Squadron between Pensacola and the Mississippi River. She was sold at Boston in 1867.

Bartlett, "Commodore James Biddle and the First Naval Mission to Japan." Johnson, *Thence round Cape Horn.* Lundeberg & Wegner, "Not for Conquest but Discovery." Reynolds, *Voyage to the Southern Ocean.* Stanton, *Great U.S. Exploring Expedition.* U.S. Navy, *DANFS.*

CSS Virginia

(ex-USS *Merrimack*) Casemate ironclad (1f). *L/B/D:* 262.8′ × 38.5′ × 22′ (80.1m × 11.7m × 6.7m). *Tons:* 3,200 burthen. *Hull:* wood. *Comp.:* 320. *Arm.:* 2 × 7″, 2 × 6.4″, 6 × 9″, 2 × 12pdr howitzers. *Armor:* 4″ casemate. *Mach.:* horizontal back-acting, 1,200 ihp, 1 screw; 7 kts. *Des.:* John M. Brooke. *Built:* Gosport Navy Yard, Norfolk, Va.; 1862.

One of the first screw-propelled warships in the U.S. Navy, the ship-rigged screw frigate USS *Merrimack* (named for a New England river) was built at the Boston Navy Yard and commissioned in 1855. After service in the Caribbean and Europe, she served as flagship of the Pacific Squadron from 1857 to 1859, when she returned to Norfolk and was laid up. On April 17, 1861, one day after Virginia seceded from the Union, engineers were able to light off *Merrimack*'s engines; however, blockships in the channel prevented her moving from Norfolk. As the Gosport Navy Yard was prepared for evacuation on April 20, *Merrimack* was put to the torch and scuttled to prevent her capture by the Confederacy.

Northerners and Southerners alike knew that success rested in their ability to either close or keep open Confederate ports, and that to do either required ships. Recognizing the South's deficiency in this regard, Confederate Navy Secretary Stephen Mallory wrote, on May 9,

> I regard the possession of an iron armoured ship as a matter of the first necessity . . . inequality of numbers may be compensated for by invulnerability; and thus not only does economy but naval success dictate the wisdom and expediency of fighting with iron against wood.

On July 11, he formally authorized that *Merrimack* be raised and converted. Working to plans prepared by Lieutenant John M. Brooke, and under the direction of Lieutenant Catesby ap Roger Jones, an army of workers was put to work to salvage the hull (which had burned to the waterline) and machinery, and to create the central battery frigate CSS *Virginia.* The 170-foot-long casemate consisted of a shell of oak and pine 24 inches thick, sheathed by two layers of 2-inch-thick rolled iron, one layer laid horizontally, the other vertically. Rising at an angle of about 36 degrees, the sides were pierced for 4 guns on either side and 3 at either end (though she mounted only 12 guns) and were rounded fore and aft. The slightly submerged hull was also fitted with an iron ram. Her greatest defects were her deep draft — which made her as impractical for shallow waters as her lack of freeboard made her unfit for the open sea — and her engines, which had been inadequate even in the unarmored *Merrimack.*

On February 24, 1862, the flag officer, Captain Franklin Buchanan, assumed command of *Virginia,* which had been commissioned on the seventeenth. Work was still not complete when she got under way for the first time on March 8 on what should have been a trial run. Instead, escorted by the steam tugs *Beaufort* and *Raleigh, Virginia* stood down the Elizabeth River for Hampton Roads. Six miles away lay the Yorktown Peninsula, the lower half of which was occupied by the Union army. Five ships of the North Atlantic Blockading Squadron stood at anchor between Newport News and Hampton. *Virginia*'s first victim was the 24-gun USS CUMBERLAND, which opened fire at 1400 at a range of 1,500 yards. *Virginia* poured broadsides into the wooden sloop of war, then rammed and sank her at 1530. *Virginia* next engaged USS CONGRESS (44 guns), which had grounded stern to and could bring only two guns to bear. She was set on fire with incendiary shells and blew up later that night. In the meantime, the captains of the other Union vessels were making for Newport News. *Merrimack*'s sister ship USS *Minnesota* grounded and came under fire from *Virginia,* though the water was too shallow for her to close, and she disengaged at about 1700.

The Confederate ironclad was not undamaged. The sinking *Cumberland* had snapped off her ram, two guns were knocked out, her funnel was riddled with shot, and Buchanan had been wounded, leaving Jones in command. Anchoring for the night off Sewell's Point, Jones planned to finish off *Minnesota* the next morning. Unknown to him, the ironclad USS MONITOR had arrived at Newport News during the night. As *Virginia* closed with the stranded frigate at 0800 on the morning of March 9, the "cheesebox on a raft" steamed out to meet her. For four hours the ships exchanged fire, but neither could inflict serious damage on the other. *Virginia* attempted to ram the more maneuverable *Monitor,* but she delivered only a glancing blow. Although she maintained her structural integrity, two of her crew were killed and nineteen wounded. The Battle of Hampton Roads finally broke off at about 1215 when *Monitor* was ordered into shallow water by Lieutenant John L. Worden, who was temporarily blinded by shell fragments. Jones also retired, and so the first battle between ironclads ended, and with it the age of wooden ships.

Virginia underwent repairs at Norfolk for about a month, during which time Flag Officer Josiah Tattnall made her flagship of the Confederate States Navy. On April 11, she escorted CSS *Jamestown* and *Raleigh* on a mission to capture three troop transports destined for General George McClellan's Yorktown campaign. There was no other engagement between *Virginia* and *Monitor,* as the former was charged with protecting the James River, and the latter the York. As McClellan advanced up the Yorktown Peninsula, Confederate General Joseph P. Johnson ordered the evacuation of Yorktown and Norfolk. *Virginia*'s deep draft precluded her moving up the James, and she was blown up on May 11, 1862.

Gardiner & Lambert, eds., *Steam, Steel and Shellfire.* Still, *Iron Afloat.* U.S. Navy, *DANFS.*

W

USS Wachusett

Iroquois-class screw sloop (3m). *L/B/D:* 201.3′ × 33.8′ × 13′ (61.4m × 10.3m × 4m). *Tons:* 1,488 disp. *Hull:* wood. *Comp.:* 123. *Arm.:* 3 × 100pdr, 4 × 32pdr, 2 × 30pdr, 1 × 12pdr. *Mach.:* horizontal steeple engines, 1 screw; 11.5 kts. *Built:* Boston Navy Yard, Boston, Mass.; 1862.

Named for the Massachusetts mountain, USS *Wachusett* was assigned to the Atlantic Blockading Squadron in 1862. After service in the James River during the Peninsular Campaign, in 1863 she was made flagship of a "Flying Squadron" assigned to hunt the Confederate raiders ALABAMA and FLORIDA. Following a six-month refit, *Wachusett*, under Commander Napoleon Collins, was dispatched to the Brazil Station. On September 26, 1864, she sailed into Bahia. A few days later, CSS *Florida* entered port. In an effort to prevent an incident, the Brazilians stationed their fleet between the two antagonists. At 0300 on October 7, *Wachusett* weighed anchor and slipped through the Brazilian fleet to ram *Florida*. The ship did not sink, but in the face of cannon fire, the outnumbered crew surrendered their ship, which Collins towed from Bahia to Hampton Roads. The flagrant violation of Brazilian neutrality was endorsed by everyone from Secretary of State William H. Seward to U.S. Minister to Brazil J. Watson Ebb, who had encouraged the taking of Confederate cruisers in Brazilian ports for more than a year. Later deployed to the Orient to search for CSS SHENANDOAH, *Wachusett* remained in the Pacific until 1867. Thereafter she saw service in a variety of distant stations until 1885; she was sold out of service to W. T. Garrett & Company in 1887.

Owsley, CSS *"Florida."* U.S. Navy, *DANFS*.

Warren

Frigate (3m). *L/B/D:* 152′ × 34.4′ × 17′ (46.3m × 10.5m × 5.2m). *Tons:* 690 bm. *Hull:* wood. *Comp.:* 200. *Arm.:* 12 × 18pdr, 14 × 12pdr, 8 × 9pdr. *Built:* Sylvester Bowers, Providence, R.I.; 1775.

One of thirteen frigates ordered by the Continental Congress in December 1775, and one of five built along the same lines as John Wharton and Joshua Humphreys's RANDOLPH, *Warren* was named for Joseph Warren, a patriot killed at the Battle of Breed's Hill, Boston, in June 1775. Command of *Warren* — with 18-pdr. guns, the most powerful of the new frigates — was given to John B. Hopkins, son of Esek Hopkins, commander-in-chief of the Continental Navy. (The elder Hopkins also flew his commodore's pennant in *Warren* until his dismissal in February 1778.)

Warren finally sailed on March 8, 1778, quickly taking two British supply ships before returning to Boston on the twenty-third. With the possible exception of a cruise with the Massachusetts State Navy brig *Tyrannicide,* she did not sail again until March 13, 1779, in company with *Queen of France* and RANGER. The three ships captured the armed schooner *Jason* and seven of a ten-ship convoy under her guard. Nonetheless, Congress dismissed Captain Hopkins because he ended his cruise too soon, thus allowing his men to jump ship; crew shortages were one of the worst problems facing the Continental Navy.

Warren's next commander was Captain Dudley Saltonstall. While the ship was fitting out at Boston, the British established a base on the Bagaduce Peninsula in Penobscot Bay, 175 miles northeast of Boston. Congress named Saltonstall to command a huge amphibious force consisting of 39 ships and about 300 marines. Arriving below Castine on July 25, the Americans seized Nautilus Island and three cannon the next day. On the twenty-eighth, the Americans landed on the mainland, but following their initial victory, cooperation between the navy and army collapsed, and there was no follow-up. While the commanders temporized, a British force consisting of HMS *Raisonnable* (64 guns) and *Blonde* and *Virginia* (32s) arrived from Boston on August 13. In the face of this intimidating British force, Saltonstall panicked and his undisciplined fleet scattered upriver. The Americans lost their 39 ships, all burned by their own crews save two that were captured, and more than 500 soldiers and sailors were killed or captured. The Penobscot Bay expedition, for which Saltonstall was court-martialed and dismissed, was one of the single worst defeats of the Revolution.

Millar, *Early American Ships*. Miller, *Sea of Glory*. U.S. Navy, *DANFS*.

HMS Warrior

(ex-Oil Hulk C77, *Warrior, Vernon III, Warrior*). Frigate (2f/3m). *L/B/D:* 418′ × 58.4″ × 26′ (128m × 17.8m × 7.9m). *Tons:* 9,137 disp. *Hull:* iron. *Comp.:* 700–709. *Arm.:* 26 × 68pdr, 4 × 40pdr, 10 × 110pdr, 2 × 20pdr, 1 × 12pdr, 1 × 6pdr. *Armor:* 4.5″ hull. *Mach.:* Penn double-acting, single-expansion horizontal-trunk engine, 1,250 nhp/5,267 ihp, 1 screw; 14.1 kts. *Des.:* Isaac Watts, Thomas Lloyd. *Built:* Thames Iron Works, Blackwall, Eng.; 1861.

Often called the world's first battleship and the first ironclad, the revolutionary HMS *Warrior* was a superlative ship — but she was neither the first battleship nor the first ironclad. In 1858, the French navy had ordered six iron-hulled ships; however, her limited industrial base required that the first three — including LA GLOIRE — have wooden hulls sheathed in iron. The British response was decisive. On the initiative of First Sea Lord Sir John Pakington, Surveyor of the Navy Admiral Sir Baldwin Wake Walker developed plans for what would be the most powerful and heavily armored ship afloat.

Although she was not the first iron-hulled warship — that distinction belongs to the GUADE-

LOUPE of 1842 — *Warrior* was the largest warship of her day: 140 feet longer than the 120-gun three-decker HMS *Howe* (1860), and 82 feet longer than HMS *Orlando* (1858), she was the longest single-deck wooden frigate (40 guns) ever built. *Gloire* and her sisters were a mere 256 feet. Perhaps more distinctive was *Warrior*'s graceful 6.5:1 length-to-breadth ratio; even *Orlando* achieved a ratio of only 5.8:1. Despite her extreme size, *Warrior*'s primary armament consisted of twenty-six 68-pdr. breech-loading guns. Twenty-two of these — eleven per broadside — were on the main deck within a central citadel, essentially an armor-protected box in the middle of the ship. Also within the citadel were four 110-pdr. breech-loaders. Just forward of the citadel were two 110-pdr. and just abaft, two 110-pdr. and four more 68-pdr. Upper deck armament included single 110-pdr. bow and stern chasers and, working aft, one 6-pdr. and one 12-pdr., two 20-pdr., and four 40-pdr. On the basis of the heaviest guns alone, *Warrior* was classified as a 40-gun ship.

Warrior was not intended as a line of battleship. Rather, her superior speed enabled her to outdistance and outmaneuver any steam battleship she might encounter. At this stage in its development, mechanical propulsion was unreliable and engines were too inefficient to allow coaling for long-range cruising. Although designed to fight under steam, *Warrior* was rigged as a three-masted ship, and her ten-ton, two-bladed propeller was designed to be lifted free of the water, to reduce drag when cruising under sail. Located between the fore and main masts, her funnels could also be lowered to reduce wind resistance.

HMS *Warrior* was commissioned as part of the Channel Fleet on August 1, 1861, by Captain A. A. Cochrane. During her trials, she received the accolade that defined her threat to the existing naval order: "She looks like a black snake among the rabbits" — the rabbits being the stubbier, high-sided ships of the line that still symbolized the might of the Royal Navy. *Warrior*'s active-duty service was confined to the Channel Fleet, where she could best face the French threat based at Cherbourg. During her first commission, she sailed as far as

Lisbon and Gibraltar and made a tour around Britain.

Warrior's first refit took place between 1864 and 1867, after which she was commissioned again with the Channel Fleet, Captain Henry Boys commanding. By this time, *Warrior* had already been eclipsed by the next generation of British ironclads — including the four-masted *Achilles* and five-masted *Minotaur*-class broadside ships. Her most remarkable accomplishment was in 1869, when she was assigned to help tow the floating dry-dock HMS *Bermuda* to the Royal Navy base at Bermuda, together with her sister ship *Black Prince*. Decommissioned in 1871, she underwent a further four-year refit during which a poop deck was added, she received new boilers, and her bowsprit was short-ened. Commissioned into the First Reserve Fleet for eight years, *Warrior* made eight summer cruises, usually in home waters or to Gibraltar and the western Mediterranean.

Paid off and reclassed as an armored cruiser in 1883, *Warrior*'s star quickly faded. In 1900, she was stricken from the lists and became a hulk, seeing duty as a torpedo depot ship. In 1904, she was renamed *Vernon III* to free her original name for an armored cruiser. This ship sank on June 1, 1916, following damage sustained at the Battle of Jutland, and in 1923 *Vernon III* again became *Warrior*. An attempt to sell the ship in 1925 was unsuccessful, and in 1929 she became a floating oil jetty at Llanion Cove, Pembroke Dock. In World War II, she was briefly used as a depot ship for minesweepers, and in 1942, her name was appropriated for a light aircraft carrier, and she became Oil Hulk C77.

Interest in preserving and restoring *Warrior* began in the 1960s, but the navy held on to the ship until 1978. The following year, she was towed to Hartlepool and placed under the aegis of the Maritime Trust (and later the Warrior Preservation Trust). Initial financing for the restoration came from John Smith's Manifold Trust. A large number of the workers and artisans employed in cleaning and restoring the ship to her 1861 condition were provided through the government-run Manpower Services Commission. In 1987, HMS *Warrior 1860*, as she is officially known, was towed to Portsmouth and put on permanent public display at the Portsmouth Naval Base.

Brownlee, *"Warrior."* Lambert, *"Warrior."* Wells, *Immortal "Warrior."* Winton, *"Warrior."*

Wasa

Royal ship (3m). *L/B/D:* 180' × 38.3' × 15.4' (54.9m × 11.7m × 4.9m). *Tons:* 1,300 disp. *Hull:* wood. *Comp.:* 145 crew; 300 soldiers. *Arm.:* 48 × 24pdr, 8 × 3pdr, 2 × 1pdr, 1 × 16pdr, 2 × 62pdr, 3 × 35pdr. *Des.:* Henrik Hybertson de Groot & Henrik Jacobson. *Built:* Royal Dockyard, Stockholm; 1628.

When she set sail on her maiden voyage, the ship of the line *Wasa* was the most impressive ship in the Swedish navy. She sank within minutes, not a mile from land, and it would be 333 years before her salvage amazed the world and ushered in a new age of nautical archaeology and historic preservation. Named for the royal house of Wasa, the *Wasa* was built for the navy of Gustavus Adolphus (Gustav II Adolf), then the dominant military force in the Baltic, at the height of the Thirty Years' War. Sweden was at war with Poland because the latter's emperor, Sigismund III, an older cousin of Gustavus, was a pretender to the Swedish throne. The campaign in the southern Baltic began early in 1628, and by May, there were thirty-four ships blockading Danzig to prevent the anticipated reinforcement of the city by Austrian General Albrecht Wallenstein's ships — should they appear.

Wasa was scheduled to join the thirty-four as soon as she was ready, and on April 10, 1628, she sailed from Stockholm with about 250 people aboard. Orders of the day read, "If anyone wishes to have his wife with him, he is free to do so here in Strömmen [part of the Stockholm channel] or in the Skärgård but not on a voyage where the objective is the enemy." In the light airs, the crew had to warp the ship out of the harbor — carrying an anchor ahead of the ship in a longboat, dropping it, and then pulling the ship up to the anchor. They continued the process until they reached Slussen, when the fore and main topsails and courses were set to the faint wind. *Wasa* had gone no more than 1,500 yards when a sudden gust laid the ship on her beam ends. Water rushed in through the open gunports, and she sank immediately. The exact death toll is not known, but contemporary estimates put it at about fifty people. Captain Söfring Hansson was among those saved, and during his subsequent court-martial the navy tried to assign blame to the Dutch master builder, Henrik Hybertson de Groot. Although blame was not firmly assigned, construction of Swedish warships subsequently came under more direct control of the navy.

Salvage of the wreck began soon after the sinking, and the Englishman Ian Bulmer succeeded in putting *Wasa* on an even — if still submerged — keel. Although many were willing, the technical apparatus for raising *Wasa* was too primitive to raise a ship of that size from a depth of 35 meters (115 feet). The most successful salvage operations came in 1663–64, when Hans Albrecht von Treileben and Andreas Peckell raised 53 of the bronze guns, most weighing 1.5 tons, all of which were exported to Lübeck in the following year. Having yielded its most valuable cargo, interest in the ship waned until the publication in the 1920s of an article about the ship's loss. *Wasa* remained undiscovered until 1956, when, working from a surface vessel, amateur archaeologist Anders Franzén succeeded in extracting a core sample of the hull. Swedish naval divers quickly confirmed the find, and efforts were soon begun to raise the ship.

Navy divers dug six tunnels between the hull and the mud into which it had settled. Slings were passed beneath the ship and attached to the pontoon vessels *Oden* and *Frigg*. On August 20, 1959, *Wasa* was pulled from the mud, and four weeks later, the ship was transferred — still submerged — to an area where the water was only 15 meters (50 feet) deep. Over the next eighteen months, holes in the hull were patched. These included the gunports and the 5,000 holes through which iron bolts had been passed to secure the hull and which had rusted away. On April 24, 1960, *Wasa* broke the surface, and two weeks later, she floated into a dry dock on her own hull. In preparation for conservation and display, ballast and artifacts were removed from the hull, and by autumn she was safely housed in a museum building, where she remained under continuous water spray to prevent her timbers from disintegrating.

Wasa had three masts, square rigged on fore and main, with a lateen mizzen. Among her most obvious and unusual features were the sharp aft rake of the mainmast (about 8 or 9 degrees) and her steeply sloping decks. Both features were known from contemporary illustrations and models, but historians and naval architects generally believed that these were inaccurate exaggerations. The quarterdeck was 20 meters (65 feet) above the keel, and her mainmast probably 55 meters (165 feet) high.

As *Wasa*'s was the first recovery of its kind, virtually everything that was done was precedent-setting. The wood and all artifacts were permeated with polyethylene glycol, a preservative. Leather was treated in a similar fashion, while six sails had to be painstakingly unfurled in a shallow pool. Divers also rescued an additional 3,000 artifacts of various kinds from the wreck site. These included sculptural pieces that had fallen off as the iron fittings rusted. The need for such elaborate decoration was articulated by Jean-Baptiste Colbert, Louis XIV's pro-navy Minister of Finance: "Nothing can be more impressive, nor more likely to exalt the majesty of the King, than that his ships should have more magnificent ornamentation than has ever before been seen at sea."

Wasa's more than 1,000 sculptures and fragments constitute one of the largest collections of mannerist-style seventeenth-century wooden sculpture in the world. Individual pieces include the magnificent stern decoration showing two lions rampant — originally gilt, and regilded upon their recovery. In addition to the House of Wasa's coat of arms on the stern, the carvings include renderings of biblical and classical themes: a series of figures from the Book of Judges, a representation of Gideon's victory over the Midianites, an image of Hercules, and, lining the bulkhead, two rows of Roman emperors, ten on either side of the bow. The bowsprit portrays a forward-leaping gilded lion.

Among the other artifacts were ship's stores and sailors' personal effects, which give a clear picture of daily life aboard ship. These include wooden plates for the sailors and pewter dishes for the officers, ceramic bowls, leather and felt clothing in sea chests, and more than 4,000 square copper coins called *klippingar*. Among the human remains found on the site were those of women and children, members of the crew's families who had joined the ship for the brief passage. One of the most popular attractions in Sweden since her recovery, *Wasa* is the centerpiece of the Statens Sjöhistoriska Museum on the Stockholm waterfront.

Kvarning & Ohrelius, *Swedish Warship "Wasa."* Naish, *"Wasa."*

Wasp

(ex-*Scorpion*) Schooner (2m). *Hull:* wood. *Comp.:* 49. *Arm.:* 8 × 2pdr, 6 swivels. *Built:* Baltimore(?); <1775.

Built as a merchant schooner for Baltimore owners, the schooner *Scorpion* was purchased by the Continental Congress and commissioned in 1775 under Captain William Hallock. On January 16, she and HORNET became the first two ships of the Continental Navy to put to sea, sailing from Baltimore to join a squadron under Commodore Esek Hopkins in ALFRED. During an expedition to the Bahamas, *Wasp* took part in the capture of Nassau, which Hopkins held for two weeks. The squadron sailed on March 17, and *Wasp* returned to Philadelphia. Operating from that port for the remainder of the year, she patrolled in and around the Delaware Capes, capturing five prizes and recapturing the American *Success* from a British prize crew.

Following the fall of Philadelphia and the collapse of American resistance on the Delaware on November 20, 1777, *Wasp* was probably burned — together with ANDREW DORIA and *Hornet* — to prevent capture by the British.

Miller, *Sea of Glory*. U.S. Navy, *DANFS*.

USS Wasp

Sloop of war (3m). *L/B/D:* 105.6′ × 30.1′ × 14.2′ (32.2m × 9.2m × 4.3m). *Tons:* 450 bm. *Hull:* wood. *Comp.:* 140. *Arm.:* 2 × 12pdr, 16 × 32pdr. *Built:* Washington Navy Yard, Washington, D.C.; 1806.

The U.S. Navy's second *Wasp* was commissioned in 1806 under Master Commandant John Smith. The record of her first years is obscure, but by 1808, she was certainly operating along the East Coast, and in 1810 she cruised out of Savannah and Charleston. The following year, *Wasp* joined Commodore Stephen Decatur's squadron — USS UNITED STATES, *Congress,* and the brig NAUTILUS — and at the beginning of the War of 1812, she was stationed with these ships at Hampton Roads. On October 18, off the entrance of Delaware Bay, she gave chase, under Master Commandant Jacob Jones, to a British convoy of six merchantmen escorted by the brig-sloop HMS *Frolic* (22 guns). The two ships engaged at about 1130, and in a hot engagement, *Frolic*'s crew boarded. The British ship was saved only by the arrival of the third-rate HMS *Poictiers* (74). *Wasp* was taken into the Royal Navy as HMS *Peacock* and was lost at sea off South Carolina in July 1814.

U.S. Navy, *DANFS*.

USS Wasp

Sloop of war (3m). *L/B/D:* 117.9′ × 31.5′ × 14.5′ (35.9m × 9.6m × 4.4m). *Tons:* 509 bm. *Hull:* wood. *Comp.:* 173. *Arm.:* 2 × 12pdr, 20 × 32pdr. *Built:* Cross & Merrill, Newburyport, Mass.; 1814.

The fifth ship of the name, and the fourth to see service in the War of 1812, USS *Wasp* was a ship-rigged sloop of war commissioned under Master Commandant Johnston Blakeley, in 1814. Putting to sea on May 1, she sailed for the English Channel on a commerce-destroying mission. En route, she captured five ships, sinking four and dispatching one as a cartel ship. On June 28, she engaged the sloop of war HMS *Reindeer* (21 guns), capturing her in a short, sharp action during which she sustained heavy damage herself. En route to L'Orient, France, for repairs, she managed to capture and sink two more prizes.

Resuming her cruise on August 27, she captured three prizes by September 1, including one taken from under the guns of the third-rate HMS *Armada* (74). That night, *Wasp* fought the 18-gun brig *Avon,* off southern Ireland, but she was prevented from boarding the sinking ship by the arrival on the scene of three British ships. Between September 12 and 21, she engaged three more ships, sinking two and dispatching the brig *Atalanta* (8) to the United States. All trace of *Wasp* disappeared after October 9, when she spoke a Swedish ship.

U.S. Navy, *DANFS*.

USS Water Witch

Sidewheel sloop (1f/2m). *L/B/D:* 150′ × 23′ × 9′ (45.7m × 7m × 2.7m). *Tons:* 378 burthen. *Hull:* wood. *Comp.:* 77. *Arm.:* 4 × 32pdr, 1 × 24pdr. *Mach.:* inclined condensing engine, 180 hp, 2 sidewheels; 11.5 kts. *Des.:* John Lenthall. *Built:* Washington Navy Yard, Washington, D.C.; 1853.

The first assignment for the gunboat *Water Witch* was to undertake an extensive survey of the region around the River Plate, and in particular the Paraná River in Argentina and Paraguay. The ship sailed under command of Lieutenant Thomas Jefferson Page on February 8, 1853, and after several stops, she arrived at Buenos Aires in May. After ensuring the safety of the Argentine Confederation's General Justo Urquiza following the siege of Buenos Aires, Page began his official assignment. *Water Witch* was the first steam vessel to ascend the Paraná, Paraguay, and Salado Rivers, and her three years of surveys showed that these rivers were navigable by large, powered vessels, a fact that had great implications for the growth of Argentina, Paraguay, and Brazil. Though the expedition was a success, on February 1, 1855, Page ignored a Paraguayan decree forbidding him to ascend the Paraná River, and one sailor was killed when the fort at Itapirú fired on the ship. *Water Witch* was back in the United States in 1856. In 1858, she returned to the Plate as part of Flag Officer W. B. Shubrick's Paraguay Expedition, one aim of which was to negotiate a treaty and compensation for the dead man's family.

At the start of the Civil War, *Water Witch* was assigned to the Gulf Blockading Squadron and operated between Pensacola, Florida, and the Mississippi River. Transferred to the South Atlantic Blockading Squadron, she operated mostly around Ossabaw Island off mainland Georgia until June 3, 1864, when she was captured near Bradley's River. Taken into the Confederate Navy, on December 19, 1864, she was burned to prevent her capture by Federal forces.

Silverstone, *Warships of the Civil War Navies*. Wood, *Voyage of the "Water Witch."*

USS Wyoming

Wyoming-class screw sloop (1f/3m). *L/B/D:* 198.5′ × 33.2′ × 14.8′ (60.5m × 10.1m × 4.5m). *Tons:* 1,457 disp. *Hull:* wood. *Comp.:* 198. *Arm.:* 2 × 11″, 1 × 60pdr, 3 × 32pdr. *Mach.:* horizontal direct-acting engine, 793 ihp, 1 screw; 11 kts. *Built:* Merrick & Sons, Philadelphia; 1859.

Named for a Pennsylvania valley, the first USS *Wyoming* began service with the Pacific Squadron at San Francisco in 1860. With the start of the Civil War, she was assigned to guard the mail ships, and their gold, running between San Francisco and Panama. In June 1862, she was ordered to the eastern Pacific to search for Confederate raiders. Although *Wyoming* crossed the track of CSS ALABAMA, the two ships failed to meet.

In addition to Confederate raiders, the United States also had to contend with the isolationist Mikado of Japan, who had ordered all foreigners expelled on June 25, 1863. Following an attack on the American merchantman *Pembroke* the next day, *Wyoming* sailed from Yokohama to Shimonoseki, and in an hour-long engagement on July 16, she bombarded Japanese shore positions and sank a Japanese steamer. After repairs at Philadelphia in 1864, *Wyoming* returned to the East Indies and in 1866 took part in a punitive expedition against Formosan pirates.

She returned to the United States in 1868 and remained in home waters for the next decade. After a two-year stint on the European Station, *Wyoming* was transferred to the Naval Academy, where she spent another ten years as a training ship. She was sold in 1892.

U.S. Navy, *DANFS*.

Z

Zeven Provinciën

Ship (3m). *L/B/D:* 146.7′ × 38.7′ × 14.4′ (44.7m × 11.8m × 4.4m). *Hull:* wood. *Comp.:* 450. *Arm.:* 80 guns. *Built:* Admiraliteit van de Maze, Delftshaven, Netherlands; 1664.

The commercial rivalry between English and Dutch merchants that led to the Anglo-Dutch War of 1652–54 reemerged in the early 1660s. In anticipation of renewed hostilities, the Dutch undertook a major building program; one of the largest vessels launched was the *Zeven Provinciën.* Admiral Michiel Adrienszoon de Ruyter was in the Mediterranean and then the Caribbean when war began, but upon his return to the Netherlands in late 1665, he was appointed commander-in-chief to succeed the late Admiral Jacob van Wassenaer van Obdam. Shifting his flag to *Zeven Provinciën* in May, de Ruyter led the Dutch fleet for the first time in what became known as the Four Days' Battle. The Dutch had a slight numerical advantage in ships and men, though this was offset by the larger size of the English ships and their guns of greater caliber. The fleets' parity was upset when Charles II ordered Prince Rupert's squadron to prevent a junction of a French fleet with de Ruyter. (France had declared war on England in January but proved an indifferent ally.) Early in the morning of June 11, the Dutch arrived off the Downs with about eighty-five ships. They were met by an English force of about fifty-six ships under George Monck, Duke of Albemarle. The battle was marked by a lack of coordination on the part of the Dutch and stubborn determination by Monck, who after the second day's fighting turned west to link up with Rupert. *Zeven Provinciën*'s rigging was shot up, and de Ruyter was unable to pursue. *Royal Prince* (90 guns) ran aground and was burned by

the Dutch on the twelfth, and Monck's ships were roughly handled by the Dutch on the thirteenth, but deteriorating weather and the imminent arrival of Rupert's squadron prevented further action.

The Dutch failure to achieve a decisive victory enabled the English to put to sea in force in mid-July, thus frustrating Dutch plans for a landing on the English coast. On July 25, the Dutch and English fleets met off North Foreland. As in the Four Days' Battle, Lieutenant Admiral Cornelis Tromp found himself cut off from the body of the Dutch fleet, and he was eventually forced to fly before a smaller English squadron. The heaviest fighting took place in the center and van of the opposing fleets; three Dutch flag officers were killed and *Zeven Provinciën* was completely dismasted. The English attempted to renew the battle in the evening, but de Ruyter managed a masterful withdrawal. All told, the Dutch lost 20 ships, 4,000 dead, and 3,000 prisoners.

The next spring, Charles decided to economize by laying up his fleet. In so doing, he underestimated the determination of the Dutch. On June 14, they sailed into the Medway and Thames, where they burned more than twenty ships and captured the ROYAL CHARLES (90), which they sailed back to Rotterdam. This was the last action of the war — which had been fought entirely at sea — and the Peace of Breda was signed on July 31.

Although the English and Dutch people would have preferred peace, France's Louis XIV had designs on Dutch territory and bribed Charles II to join an alliance against the United Provinces. With war imminent, the Dutch put seventy-five ships of the line into commission. Against this the French

▲ The Dutch Admiral de Ruyter's favorite flagship in the Anglo-Dutch Wars, **Zeven Provinciën** is "a vessel that deserves to rank with Nelson's **Victory,** according to British naval historian William Laird Clowes. A replica of **Zeven Provinciën** is under construction in the Netherlands. *Painting by the preeminent Dutch marine artist Willem van de Velde the Elder; courtesy Rijksmuseum, Amsterdam.*

levied twenty-two and the English sixty-five ships. On June 7, 1672, de Ruyter followed the combined fleet to the English coast near Southwold Bay (or Solebay), ninety miles north of the Thames estuary. In the ensuing fight, the Dutch lost only two ships to three English; more important, they prevented the combined fleet from supporting the French army then infesting the Netherlands. The victory is also credited with helping to precipitate the overthrow of the United Provinces' ruling party and the accession of William of Orange. In England, passage of the Test Act barring Catholics

from positions of trust or profit under the Crown forced the Duke of York (later James II) to resign from the Admiralty.

A year later, on June 7, 1673, and again on the fourteenth, the combined Anglo-French fleet tried to bring the Dutch fleet to battle in the shallows of the Schooneveldt at the mouth of the Scheldt River, but they were beaten back by de Ruyter. In late July, the combined fleet put to sea again, and de Ruyter sailed north to join William at Scheveningen. On August 20, he met the combined fleet off the Texel in the Frisian Islands. The allies had the advantage of the wind, so de Ruyter hugged the shore until the next morning, when he "made all sail and stood down boldly into action." The Battle of the Texel had two major components. Lieutenant Admiral Adriaen Banckers, in the van, cut off a superior French squadron and then returned to help de Ruyter's center, which broke the English line in several places. In the rear, Admiral Sir Edward Spragge and the Dutch Tromp — "men of kindred kidney, brave, rash, and insubordinate" — fought an independent action in which Spragge was killed. Although neither side suffered heavy damage, the English were equally tired of war with the Dutch and of their alliance with Louis XIV, and the Treaty of Westminster was concluded in February 1674. (Three years later, William of Orange married Princess Mary, daughter of the Duke of York; the couple acceded to the English throne in 1688.)

Zeven Provinciën's final naval action came during the War of the League of Augsburg, which pitted an Anglo-Dutch alliance against France. On May 29, 1692, she was heavily damaged at the Battle of La Hogue — in which the French fleet was shattered — and returned to Rotterdam. She was broken up two years later. A replica is currently under construction in the Netherlands.

Clowes, *Royal Navy*. Hainsworth & Churches, *Anglo-Dutch Naval Wars*. Mahan, *Influence of Sea Power upon History*.

Zhenyuan

(later *Chin Yen*) Battleship (2f/2m). *L/B/D:* 308′ × 59′ × 20′ (93.9m × 18m × 6.1m). *Tons:* 7,670 disp. *Hull:* steel. *Comp.:* 350. *Arm.:* 4 × 30.5cm (2x2), 2 × 150mm; 3 × 380mm TT. *Armor:* 14″ belt; 3″ deck. *Mach.:* compound engines, 6,200 ihp, 2 screws; 14.5 kts. *Built:* Maschinenbau Actien Gesellschaft "Vulcan," Stettin Bredow, Germany; 1883.

In the mid-nineteenth century, China's navy still consisted mainly of wooden junks. These were no match for the ships of steam and steel with which European powers had forced open the Chinese markets in the Opium Wars of the 1840s and 1850s, or for the French fleet employed in the Sino-French war for French Indochina. Yet the impetus for the development of a modern navy came as a reaction not to Western intrusion but to Japan's expansionism and rearmament. In 1874, Japan occupied Formosa to quell pirate activities there, and the next year it ordered three ironclads from British shipyards. In response, China attempted to put its provincial fleets under central command and to modernize its fleet. An attempt to purchase

some ships from Britain was rebuffed in deference to Russian objections, so China placed an order with Germany's Vulcan yard for two battleships, *Zhenyuan* (*Chen Yüan*, "Striking Far Away") and *Dingyuan* (*Ting yuan*, or "Eternal Peace").

As Japan modernized, it began to consider acquiring territory on the Korean Peninsula, which had long been within the Chinese sphere of influence. On July 25, 1894, a Japanese squadron attacked a Chinese force off Yashan, Korea, and on August 11, 1894, Japan declared war. Fearing the loss of Pyongyang, the Chinese convoyed 4,000 soldiers to the Yalu River, where they landed on September 16 under the protection of a covering force of 14 ships commanded by Admiral Ding Ruchang. The next morning, a Japanese fleet under Vice Admiral Yuko Ito attacked the Chinese near the mouth of the Yalu. Although the Japanese navy had no battleships, its crews were disciplined and well trained, and Ito's 12 cruisers worked as a cohesive unit. Bearing down on the Chinese in line-ahead formation, they crossed the bows of the Chinese fleet, which straggled into battle in a ragged crescent formation. They then circled behind the Chinese ships, which became ever more disorganized as they turned 180 degrees to meet their attackers. The Chinese fleet's lack of discipline was compounded by a lack of proper ordnance, which included armor-piercing rather than common shells, shells of the wrong size, and shells packed with sand.

After four hours of fighting, the Chinese lost five ships and more than 600 sailors; the Japanese lost no ships and only 78 crew. Admiral Ding ordered his fleet to withdraw first to Port Arthur (Lushun) at the end of the Liaodong Peninsula for temporary repairs, and then across the Gulf of Chilhi to Weihaiwei on the Shantung Peninsula. The Japanese blockaded the Chinese fleet at Weihai through January 1895, when the Japanese army landed on the Shantung Peninsula. In early February, Weihai fell to a joint forces attack during which *Dingyuan* was sunk by torpedo boats, and *Zhenyuan* was heavily damaged. Ordered not to surrender any of his ships, but fearful of what the Japanese would do if he scuttled them, Admiral

Ding committed suicide, followed by the captains of the battleships and the commanders of the Weihai forts.

On February 17, the Japanese seized *Zhenyuan* and took her to Port Arthur, where she was renamed *Chin Yen,* thus becoming Japan's first battleship. Thanks to the rapid expansion of Japan's fleet, she was soon downgraded to a second-class battleship and eventually to a coast defense ship. During the Boxer Rebellion in 1901, *Chin Yen* operated with Japanese forces in lifting the siege of the western enclave at Tianjin. Four years later, in the Russo-Japanese War, she took part in several attacks on Port Arthur — which Japan had been forced to return to China, only to see it snapped up by Russia in 1898 — and she was present at the Battle of the Yellow Sea. After the war, *Chin Yen* was used as a training ship and then as a target ship. In 1912, the ship that had served as the first battleship in two Asian navies was sold for breaking up.

Mach, "Chinese Battleships." Swanson, *Eighth Voyage of the Dragon.*

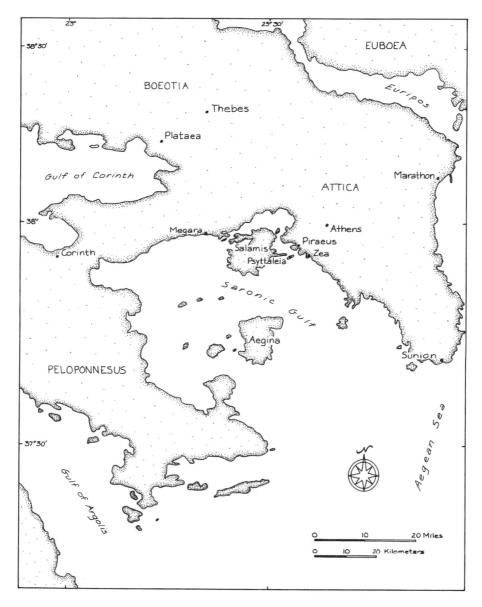

Battle of Salamis

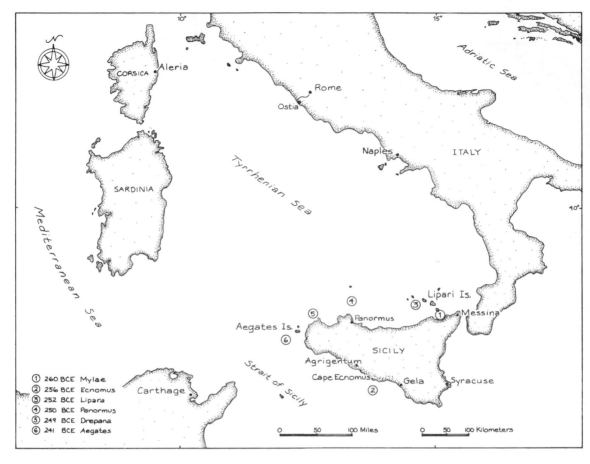

CORSICA · Aleria

Rome
Ostia

Naples

Tyrrhenian Sea

ITALY

SARDINIA

Mediterranean Sea

Adriatic Sea

Lipari Is.
③
④
⑤
① Messina
Panormus

Aegates Is.
⑥

SICILY

Strait of Sicily

Agrigentum
Cape Ecnomus
②
Gela
Syracuse

Carthage

① 260 BCE Mylae
② 256 BCE Ecnomus
③ 252 BCE Lipara
④ 250 BCE Panormus
⑤ 249 BCE Drepana
⑥ 241 BCE Aegates

0   50   100 Miles
0   50   100 Kilometers

Naval Battles of the Punic Wars

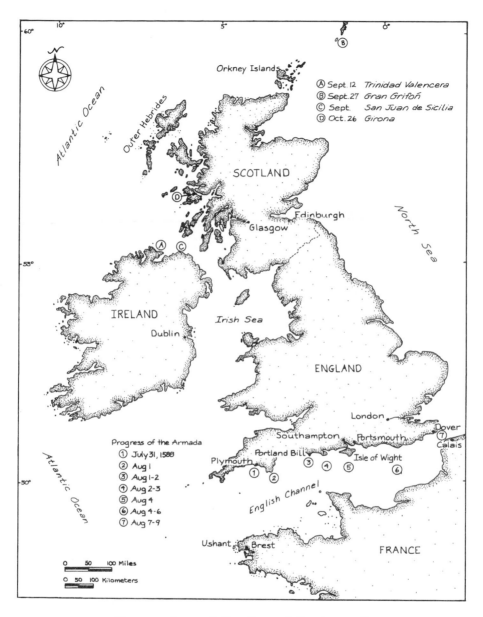

Campaign of the Spanish Armada

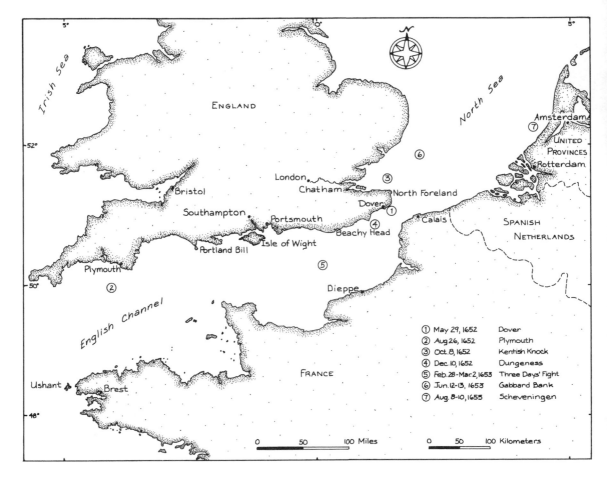

①	May 29, 1652	Dover
②	Aug 26, 1652	Plymouth
③	Oct. 8, 1652	Kentish Knock
④	Dec. 10, 1652	Dungeness
⑤	Feb. 28-Mar. 2, 1653	Three Days' Fight
⑥	Jun. 12-13, 1653	Gabbard Bank
⑦	Aug. 8-10, 1653	Scheveningen

First Anglo-Dutch War

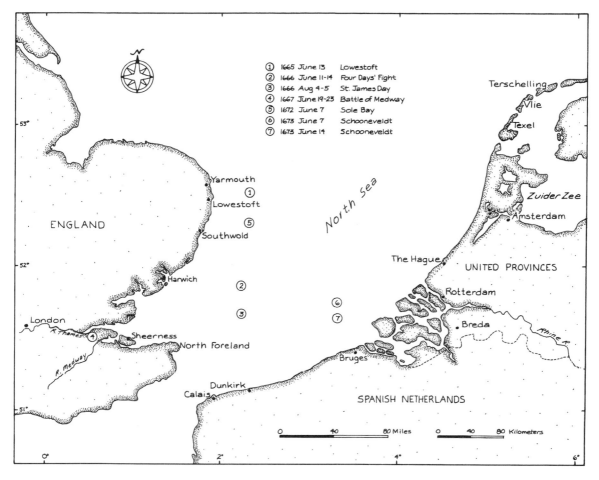

①	1665 June 13	Lowestoft
②	1666 June 11-14	Four Days' Fight
③	1666 Aug 4-5	St. James Day
④	1667 June 19-23	Battle of Medway
⑤	1672 June 7	Sole Bay
⑥	1673 June 7	Schooneveldt
⑦	1673 June 14	Schooneveldt

Second and Third Anglo-Dutch Wars

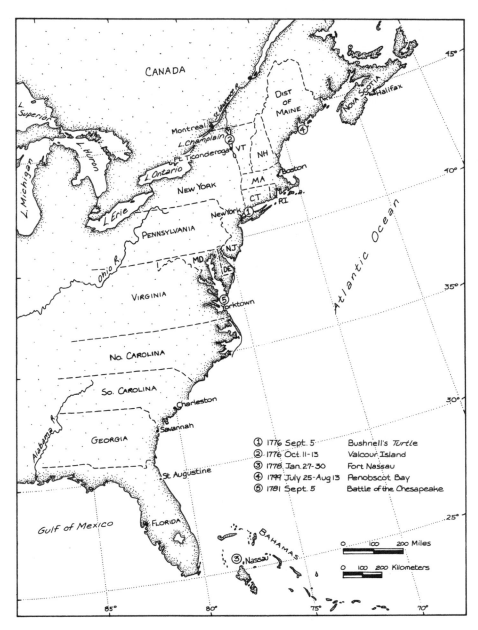

①	1776 Sept. 5	Bushnell's *Turtle*
②	1776 Oct. 11-13	Valcour Island
③	1778 Jan. 27-30	Fort Nassau
④	1799 July 25-Aug 13	Penobscot Bay
⑤	1781 Sept. 5	Battle of the Chesapeake

American Revolution

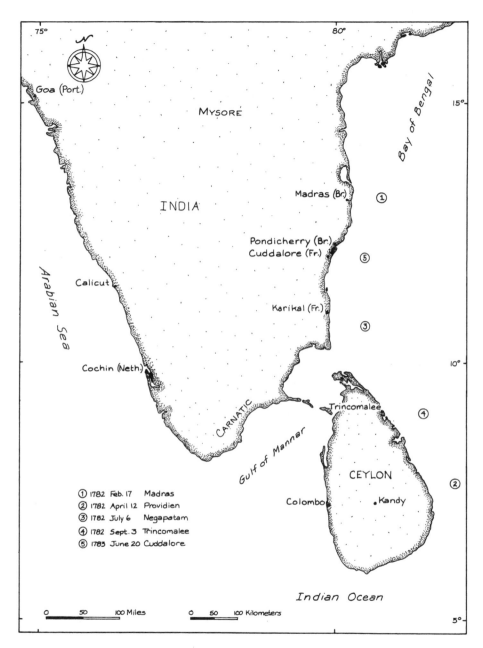

Goa (Port.)

MYSORE

INDIA

Madras (Br.) ①

Pondicherry (Br.) ⑤
Cuddalore (Fr.)

Calicut

Karikal (Fr.) ③

Arabian Sea

Cochin (Neth.)

CARNATIC

Trincomalee ④

Gulf of Mannar

CEYLON

Colombo · Kandy ②

① 1782 Feb. 17 Madras
② 1782 April 12 Providien
③ 1782 July 6 Negapatam
④ 1782 Sept. 3 Trincomalee
⑤ 1783 June 20 Cuddalore

Bay of Bengal

Indian Ocean

0   50   100 Miles
0   50   100 Kilometers

American Revolution: Campaign in India

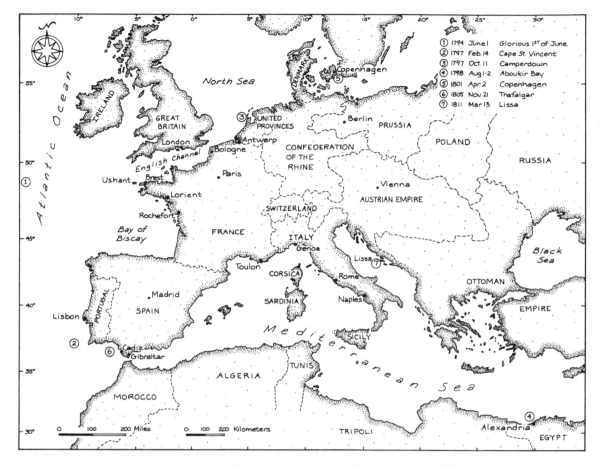

North Sea

Copenhagen ⑤

DENMARK

Berlin • PRUSSIA

POLAND

RUSSIA

GREAT
BRITAIN

IRELAND

London •

③ UNITED
PROVINCES

Antwerp •
Bologne •

CONFEDERATION
OF THE
RHINE

Vienna •

AUSTRIAN EMPIRE

Black
Sea

English channel

• Paris

Ushant •
Brest •
Lorient •

Rochefort •

Bay of
Biscay

FRANCE

SWITZERLAND

ITALY
Genoa •

Lissa • ⑦

OTTOMAN

EMPIRE

Toulon •

CORSICA

SARDINIA

Rome •

Naples •

① ①

PORTUGAL

Lisbon •

② ②

⑥ Cadiz •
Gibraltar •

SPAIN

• Madrid

M e d i t e r r a n e a n

S e a

SICILY

MOROCCO

ALGERIA

TUNIS

TRIPOLI

④

Alexandria •

EGYPT

0   100   200 Miles   0   100   200 Kilometers

Atlantic Ocean

① 1794 June 1   Glorious 1ˢᵀ of June
② 1797 Feb. 14 Cape St. Vincent
③ 1797 Oct. 11 Camperdown
④ 1798 Aug 1-2 Aboukir Bay
⑤ 1801 Apr. 2   Copenhagen
⑥ 1805 Nov. 21 Trafalgar
⑦ 1811 Mar 13   Lissa

French Revolutionary and Napoleonic Wars

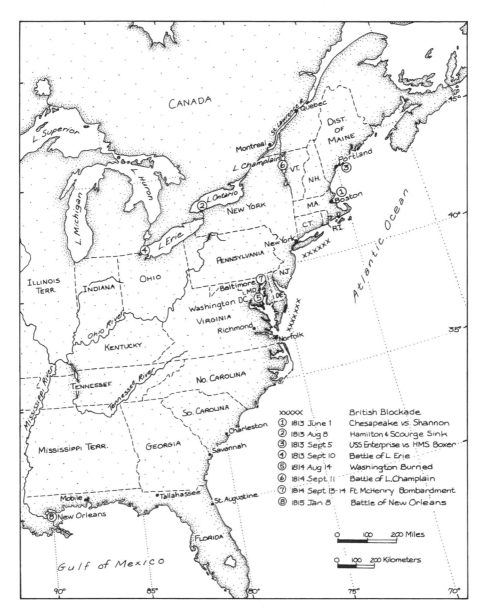

Map labels:

CANADA

L. Superior
L. Michigan
L. Huron
L. Ontario
L. Erie

St. Lawrence R.
Quebec
Montreal
L. Champlain
②
⑥ VT.
NH.
MA.
CT.
RI

DIST. OF MAINE
Portland ③
Boston ①

New York
NEW YORK
PENNSYLVANIA
NJ
⑦ Baltimore
MD ⑤
DE
Washington DC
VIRGINIA
Richmond
Norfolk

Atlantic Ocean

ILLINOIS TERR.
INDIANA
OHIO
Ohio River
KENTUCKY
TENNESSEE
Tennessee River
Mississippi River

No. CAROLINA
So. CAROLINA
Charleston
GEORGIA
Savannah
St. Augustine

MISSISSIPPI TERR.
Mobile
Tallahassee
⑧ New Orleans
FLORIDA

Gulf of Mexico

45°
40°
35°

90° 85° 80° 75° 70°

Legend:

xxxxx		British Blockade
①	1813 June 1	Chesapeake vs. Shannon
②	1813 Aug 8	Hamilton & Scourge Sink
③	1813 Sept 5	USS Enterprise vs HMS Boxer
④	1813 Sept 10	Battle of L. Erie
⑤	1814 Aug 14	Washington Burned
⑥	1814 Sept 11	Battle of L. Champlain
⑦	1814 Sept 13-14	Ft. McHenry Bombardment
⑧	1815 Jan 8	Battle of New Orleans

0   100   200 Miles

0   100   200 Kilometers

War of 1812

American Civil War

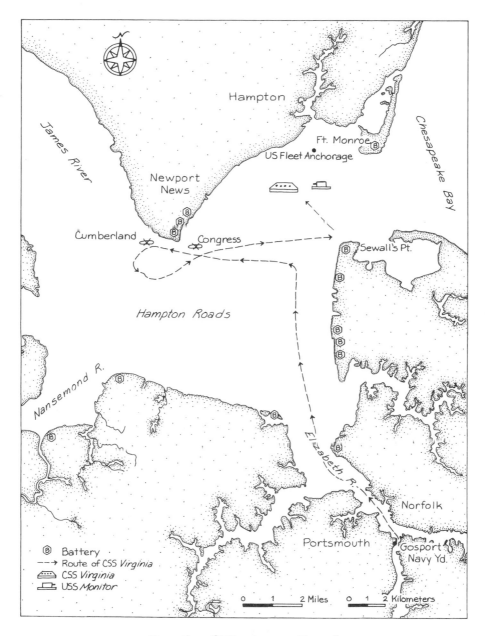

Battle of Hampton Roads

Literary Warships

HMS Achates (64) Richard Bolitho's flagship during the brief Peace of Amiens of 1803 in Alexander Kent's *Success to the Brave* (1983).

Arabella Buccaneer Peter Blood's command in Rafael Sabatini's "Captain Blood" novels, *Captain Blood* (1922), *The Chronicles of Captain Blood* (1931), and *The Fortunes of Captain Blood* (1933).

HMS Argonaute (74) Richard Bolitho's flagship in the Mediterranean in Alexander Kent's *Colors Aloft* (1986).

HMS Ariel Sloop of war in which Jack Aubrey conveys Stephen Maturin to the Baltic in Patrick O'Brian's *The Surgeon's Mate* (1980).

HMS Atropos (22) Napoleonic-era sloop of war in C. S. Forester's *Hornblower and the Atropos* (1953).

HMS Bellipotent (74) Ship under Captain Edward Fairfax Vere into which the American Billy Budd is impressed in Herman Melville's posthumously published *Billy Budd* (1924).

Black Swan Thomas Leach's 40-gun ship in Rafael Sabatini's novel *The Black Swan* (1932).

HMS Boadicea (38) Frigate in which Commodore Jack Aubrey must seize Mauritius Island from the French in Patrick O'Brian's *The Mauritius Command* (1977).

HMS Calypso (36) Nicholas Ramage's ship in a number of Dudley Pope novels starting with *Ramage's Mutiny* (1977), in which the British cut out a captured frigate from a Spanish stronghold — a story based on the fate of *HMS Hermione*.

Clorinda Ship from which the Bas-Thornton children are kidnapped by pirates in Richard Hughes's *High Wind in Jamaica* (1929).

USS Delaware War of 1812–era frigate, similar to the *USS Constitution,* in C. S. Forester's *The Captain from Connecticut* (1941).

HMS Diane (36) Ship cut out of the French port of St. Martin, France, by Jack Aubrey in Patrick O'Brian's *The Letter of Marque* (1988). Aubrey and Steven Maturin later sail for the Indies in the *Diane* in *The Thirteen Gun Salute* (1989), though the ship is wrecked there in *Nutmeg of Consolation* (1991).

HMS Dido (74) Nicholas Ramage's command in the West Indies in Dudley Pope's *Ramage and the Dido* (1989).

HMS Diomede In Frederick Marryat's *Peter Simple* (1834), a frigate commanded by Captain Savage, a character based on Lord Cochrane, under whom Marryat served on the French coast in HMS *Impérieuse* from 1806 to 1809.

HMS Euryalus (100) Richard Bolitho's command in the western Mediterranean in Alexander Kent's *The Flag Captain* (1971).

HMS Harpy Sloop of war on which Mr. Midshipman Easy serves in Frederick Marryat's novel (published in 1836) of the same name. Easy's adventures are based on those of Lord Cochrane, under whom Marryat served in the frigate HMS *Impérieuse* from 1806 to 1809.

Hotspur (20) Horatio Hornblower's 6th-rate in C. S. Forester's *Hornblower and the Hotspur* (1962).

HMS Hyperion (74) Richard Bolitho's Napoleonic-era command in Alexander Kent's *Form Line of Battle!* (1969), *Enemy in Sight!* (1970), and *Honour This Day* (1987).

HMS Indomitable Napoleonic-era warship into which Billy Budd is impressed in Herman Melville's *Billy Budd.* Benjamin Britten later wrote an opera based on the posthumously published novel.

Judea Ship of about 400 tons, whose motto is "Do or Die," in Joseph Conrad's short story "Youth" (1898).

HMS Juno (32) Frigate in which Nicholas Ramage attacks a French convoy off Martinique in Dudley Pope's *Ramage's Diamond* (1976).

HMC Kathleen (8) Cutter in which Nicholas Ramage has a series of adventures — including the capture and recapture of his command — near the Spanish coast prior to the Battle of Cape St. Vincent in Dudley Pope's *Ramage and the Drumbeat* (1968).

HMS Lydia (36) Frigate in which Horatio Hornblower defeats the Spanish *Natividad* (50) on the Pacific coast of Central America in C. S. Forester's *The Happy Return* (also published as *Beat to Quarters*, 1938).

Natividad Old Spanish 50-gun two-decker captured on the west coast of Central America in the early 1800s by HMS *Lydia* in C. S. Forester's *The Happy Return* (or *Beat to Quarters*, 1938).

USS Neversink American frigate in which the title character of Herman Melville's *White Jacket, or, the World in a Man-of-War* (1850) sails from Callao to Norfolk. The novel is based on Melville's own experiences aboard the *USS United States* on a passage from Honolulu to Boston in 1843–44.

HMS Phalarope (36) Richard Bolitho's command during the American Revolution in Alexander Kent's *To Glory We Steer* (1968).

HMS Pinafore Capain Corcoran's "saucy ship" in the 1878 operetta of the same name by W. S. Gilbert and Arthur Sullivan.

HMS Polychrest (24) Jack Aubrey's brig to which the Spanish Captain Azema surrenders in Patrick O'Brian's *Post Captain* (1972).

HM Brig Sophie (14) Jack Aubrey's first command in Patrick O'Brian's *Master and Commander* (1970). *Aubrey*'s exploits in the western Mediterranean are based on those of Lord Cochrane in HM Brig *Speedy*.

HMS Sparrow (20) Richard Bolitho's command in Alexander Kent's *Sloop of War* (1972), which takes place during the American Revolution.

HMS Sunderland (74) Horatio Hornblower's ship in C. S. Forester's *Ship of the Line* (1938).

HMS Surprise (28) Jack Aubrey's command on a voyage to India during which he fights the French *Marengo* (74) in Patrick O'Brian's *H. M. S. Surprise* (1973). Aubrey returns to command of the *Surprise* in *The Far Side of the World* (1984), *The Reverse of the Medal* (1986), *Letter of Marque* (1988), *The Thirteen-Gun Salute* (1989), *The Truelove* (1992), and *The Wine-Dark Sea* (1994).

HMS Tempest (38) Richard Bolitho's command while searching the South Pacific for the *Bounty* mutineers in Alexander Kent's *Passage to Mutiny* (1976).

HMS Undine (32) Richard Bolitho's East Indies command in Alexander Kent's *Command a King's Ship* (1973).

Witch of Endor British cutter captured by the French, then recaptured by escaped prisoner-of-war Horatio Hornblower, in C. S. Forester's *Flying Colours* (1938).

HMS Worcester (74) Ship of the line under Jack Aubrey's command in Patrick O'Brian's *Ionian Mission* (1981).

Naval History: A Chronology

Antiquity to the Early Modern Period

3000 BCE Oared galleys employing "shell-first" hull construction method appear in eastern Mediterranean. Galleys continue to be used for nearly 5,000 years.

9th–8th cent. BCE Ships with two tiers of oars and ships with rams appear in eastern Mediterranean.

5th cent. BCE Trieres — galleys with three banks of oars — introduced in eastern Mediterranean.

480 BCE Battle of Salamis: Greek fleet led by Athenians defeats Persian invasion.

258 BCE Battle of Cos: Antigonus Gonatas of Macedonia defeats Ptolemy II for control of Aegean.

241 BCE March Battle of Mylae: Romans defeat Carthaginians.

241 BCE Battle of the Aegates Islands: Roman fleet wins decisive victory over Carthaginians to end First Punic War.

31 BCE Sept. 2 Battle of Actium: Antony defeated by fleet under Octavian (later Augustus); date marks Rome's transition from republic to empire.

4th cent. CE Lateen (fore-and-aft) sails begin to predominate over square sails in Mediterranean.

7th–14th cent. Cog develops in northern Europe: flat-bottomed, high-sided, with edge-to-edge and clinker-laid planking.

9th cent. Shell-first, clinker-built Viking ships in Scandinavia.

838 Vikings capture Dublin.

11th cent. Frame-first hull construction predominates in Mediterranean.

1000 Battle of Øresund: Olaf Tryggvason is killed; control of southern Norway passes to Eirik.

1066 Norman Conquest: William of Normandy launches invasion across the English Channel (September 27–29) and defeats Harald at Battle of Hastings (October 14).

12th cent. Rudimentary compasses in Europe.

1204 Venice diverts Fourth Crusade to sack of Constantinople.

1274 Nov. 21 Chinese fleet invading Japan is destroyed in typhoon.

1281 Aug. 15–16 Second Chinese naval fleet invading Japan is destroyed in typhoon. Khubilai Khan also sends expedition to Champa (Vietnam).

1292 Khubilai Khan mounts punitive expedition from China to Java.

13th–15th cent. Caravels evolve in southern Europe. Two-masted, lateen-rigged vessels of frame-first construction, they are used extensively in the Portuguese voyages of exploration.

13th cent. Vertical hinged, rudder first appears in northern Europe, eventually to replace side-mounted steering oar. Cross staff for measuring altitudes of celestial bodies invented by Jacob ben Makir in southern France.

14th cent. Naval guns first appear on ships.

14th–15th cent. Mediterranean nao, or carrack, merges Mediterranean and northern European shipbuilding practices. These forerunners of the full-rigged ship combine frame-first construction, high sides, center-line rudder, and rigs of mixed square and lateen sails.

1340 June 24 Battle of Sluys: English win control of the English Channel from French at start of Hundred Years' War.

15th cent. Quadrant is used by Portuguese navigators for measuring altitudes of celestial bodies.

1512 Sept. 19 English defeat French in battle off Brest; *La Cordelière* sunk.

1544 July 19 *Mary Rose* sunk at Portsmouth during French invasion.

mid-16th–17th cent. Galleon — similar to a carrack, but with a lower forecastle that makes it more weatherly — evolves in northern Europe.

1568 Sept. 23 *Jesus of Lübeck* and other English ships under John Hawkins are sunk by Spanish at San Juan de Ulóa, Mexico.

1571 Oct. 7 Battle of Lepanto: Christian coalition defeats Turks at mouth of the Gulf of Corinth, Greece.

1588 July 31–Aug. 8 Spanish Armada against England ends in failure.

1591 Sept. 8 Last fight of the *Revenge* against superior Spanish force in the Azores.

1628 Apr. 10 Swedish flagship *Wasa* sinks at Stockholm on maiden voyage.

1651 Oct. 9 Navigation Act restricts English trade to English ships and requires salute to flag from ships in the English Channel.

1652 May 29 Battle of Dover (Downs): Tromp versus Blake (prelude). First Anglo-Dutch War officially begins July 8.

1652 Aug. 26 Action off Plymouth: De Ruyter versus Ayscue.

1652 Oct. 8 British fleet under Blake defeats Dutch under Witte de With at Battle of Kentish Knock.

1652 Dec. 10 Dutch fleet under Tromp defeats British under Blake at Battle of Dungeness.

1653 Feb. 28–Mar. 2 English under Blake and Monck defeat Dutch under Tromp at Three Days' Battle (or Battle of Portland).

1653 June 12–13 English fleet under Monck and Deane defeats Dutch under Tromp at Battle of North Foreland (Gabbard Bank).

1653 Aug. 8–10 English under Monck defeat Dutch at Battle of Scheveningen (or the Texel); Tromp is killed.

1653 Dec. 16 Cromwell made Lord Protector of the Commonwealth.

1654 Apr. 5 Treaty of Westminster ends war between England and the Netherlands.

1660 May 1 Charles II proclaimed King of England.

1665 Mar. 14 Second Anglo-Dutch War begins.

1665 April Great Plague in London.

1665 June 13 Battle of Lowestoft: English fleet under Duke of York defeats Dutch under van Obdam, who is killed.

1666 June 11–14 Four Days' Battle in the channel: Dutch under de Ruyter defeat the English.

1666 Aug. 4–5 St. James' Day Fight (North Foreland): English defeat Dutch.

1666 Sept. 11 Great London fire.

1667 June 19–23 Dutch fleet sails into the Thames and up the Medway, capturing *HMS Royal Charles.*

1667 July 21 Treaty of Breda ends war between England and the Netherlands.

1672 Mar. 17 Third Anglo-Dutch War begins.

1672 June 7 Battle of Solebay: Dutch defeat English.

1673 June 7 and 14 Battles of Schooneveldt: Dutch gain strategic victories over English fleet.

1673 Aug. 21 Battle of Camperdown: Dutch victory over combined French and English fleet.

1674 Feb. 9 Treaty of Westminster ends war between England and the Netherlands.

1676 June 1 Battle of Öland: Danish-Dutch fleet defeats Swedes; *Kronan* sunk.

1689 Feb. 13 William III and Mary proclaimed king and queen.

1689 May 7 War of the League of Augsburg makes England and France adversaries.

1690 July 10 Battle of Beachy Head: French fleet defeats English in War of the League of Augsburg.

1692 May 28–June 2 Battle of La Hogue (Barfleur): French fleet nearly destroyed by English.

1695–1712 Working independently, Denis Papin, Thomas Savery, and Thomas Newcomen develop low-pressure steam pump, or atmospheric engine.

1702 May 4 War of the Spanish Succession makes England and France adversaries.

1702 Oct. 23 English defeat French fleet at Vigo, Spain.

1704 Aug. 4 English seize Gibraltar.

1707 Oct. 22 *HMS Association* and other ships lost off Scilly Islands.

1756 May 20 Battle of Minorca: Byng fails to press home English attack on Port Mahon in first action of Seven Years' War; he is later hanged.

1757 Sextant invented in England; it is capable of measuring angles of up to 120 degrees.

1759 John Harrison builds first marine chronometer, enabling mariners to determine longitude at sea.

1759 **Aug. 18–19** Battle of Lagos Bay: Violating Portuguese neutrality, English destroy French squadron.

1759 **Nov. 20** Battle of Quiberon Bay: British best French fleet in home waters.

1763 **Feb. 10** Treaty of Paris ends Seven Years' War.

Era of the American Revolution

1769 **July 19** Merchants of Newport, Rhode Island, burn British customs boat *Liberty.*

1770 Grand Trunk Canal links England's industrial heartland to sea.

1773 **Dec. 16** Unknown parties stage the Boston Tea Party aboard the merchant ship *Dartmouth* to protest import duties.

1775 **Apr. 19** American Revolution starts with the "Shot heard round the world" at Battles of Lexington and Concord.

1775 **Sept. 5** Schooner *Hannah* embarks on what is possibly the first naval mission paid for by the Continental Congress.

1776 James Watt develops steam engine, followed by double-acting expansion engine in 1782. Commercial success begins with partnership with Matthew Boulton in 1785.

1776 **Apr. 7** *Lexington* captures *Edward,* the first victory of the Continental Navy in single-ship action.

1776 **March** Hopkins, with *Alfred, Providence, Hornet, Wasp,* and others, occupies Nassau, Bahamas, for two weeks.

1776 **July 4** Declaration of Independence.

1776 **Sept. 5** Bushnell's submersible *Turtle* attempts to sink HMS *Eagle* in New York Harbor.

1776 **Oct. 11–13** Americans gain strategic victory at Battle of Valcour Island, Lake Champlain, but lose *Congress, Philadelphia,* and other vessels.

1776 **Nov. 16** Dutch in St. Eustatius are first to salute a ship — *Andrew Doria* — flying an American flag.

1777 **Nov. 20** American ships burned on Delaware to prevent their capture by British.

1777 **Sept. 19** *Lexington* captured by HMS *Alert* off France.

1777 **Sept. 20** British seize Philadelphia.

1778 Scottish Carron Company develops large-caliber, short-range, "ship-smashing" gun known as carronade.

1778 **Jan. 27–30** Crew of *Providence* seize Fort Nassau, Bahamas.

1778 **Feb. 6** France signs Treaties of Commerce and Alliance with United States.

1778 **Feb. 14** *Ranger* is the first American warship saluted by a foreign vessel — LaMotte Piquet's *Robuste* — in Quiberon Bay, France.

1778 **Mar. 29** *Alfred* captured by HMS *Ariadne* and *Ceres* in West Indies.

1778 **Apr. 25** *Ranger* captures HMS *Drake* off Carrickfergus, Ireland.

1778 **July 27** Battle of Ushant: Inconclusive action between French under d'Orvilliers and British under Keppel.

1779 **July 25–Aug. 13** American expeditionary force against British stronghold on Penobscot Bay ends in failure; *Defence* and *Warren* among forty ships lost.

1779 **Aug. 14–Sept. 22** *Bonhomme Richard, Alliance,* and others raid British shipping in the Irish Sea.

1779 **Sept. 9** HMS *Rose* scuttled in Savannah River.

1779 **Sept. 23** *Bonhomme Richard* captures HMS *Serapis* off Flamborough Head, England. Jones sails in *Serapis* to the Netherlands, where his ship sinks.

1779 **Nov. 24** HMS *Hussar* sinks off Hell Gate, New York.

1780 **Jan. 16** Battle of Cape St. Vincent: British under Rodney defeat Spanish under Langara.

1780 **May 11** *Providence, Ranger,* and others captured at fall of Charleston, South Carolina.

1781 **May 28** *Alliance* captures HMS *Trepassy* and *Atalanta.*

1781 **Apr. 16** Suffren attacks English fleet anchored at Port Praya, Azores.

1781 **Sept. 5** French fleet prevents British from relieving Cornwallis at Yorktown, Virginia, in Battle of the Chesapeake.

1781 **Oct. 19** Cornwallis surrenders British army to Washington at Yorktown.

1782 **Feb. 17** French fleet under Suffren (in *Héros*)

engages British fleet under Hughes at Madras, India.

1782 **Apr. 12** British under Rodney defeat French under de Grasse at Battle of the Saintes. Suffren seriously damages English fleet off Providien, India.

1782 **July 6** Suffren fails to dislodge English fleet from Negapatam, India.

1782 **Sept. 3** Battle of Trincomalee off Ceylon is strategically indecisive; Suffren withdraws to Sumatra for repairs.

1783 **July 15** Marquis de Jouffroy d'Abbans's steamboat *Pyroscaphe* operates on Saone River, France, for fifteen minutes.

1783 **Mar. 11** *Alliance* fights off HMS *Alarm, Sybil,* and *Tobago.*

1783 **July 20** Suffren breaks English blockade of Cuddalore, India, in last of five engagements with English fleet.

1783 **Sept. 3** Peace of Paris ends hostilities between Britain, United States, France, and Spain.

1787–90 John Fitch's unnamed steamboat operates, albeit unprofitably, along the Delaware River.

The French Revolution to the War of 1812

1792 **Sept. 21** France proclaims a republic.

1793 Claude Chappe develops semaphore signaling system in France.

1793 **Jan. 21** Execution of Louis XVI.

1793 **Feb. 1** French Revolutionary Wars start with French declaration of war with Great Britain.

1794 **Mar. 27** U.S. Congress authorizes construction of six frigates: *Chesapeake, Congress, Constellation, Constitution, President, United States.*

1794 **May 28–June 1** French win strategic victory at Battle of the Glorious First of June off France.

1797 **Feb. 14** British defeat Spanish fleet in Battle of Cape St. Vincent.

1797 **Apr. 15** British sailors at the Spithead mutiny for better treatment; many demands are met.

1797 **June 30** Second British mutiny at the Nore put down by force.

1797 **Oct. 11** Battle of Camperdown: British defeat Dutch fleet intending to assist French landing in Ireland.

1798 **Aug. 1–2** Battle of the Nile (Aboukir Bay): Nelson defeats Brueys.

1799 **Feb. 9** USS *Constellation* captures *L'Insurgente* off Nevis during Quasi-War with France.

1801 **Mar.** William Symington's *Charlotte Dundas* tows two barges twenty miles on Forth and Clyde Canal, Scotland.

1801 **Apr. 2** Battle of Copenhagen: British fleet under Hyde Parker and Nelson defeats Danish.

1802 **Mar. 27** Peace of Amiens between Great Britain and France.

1803 Robert Fulton builds early submarine *Nautilus* in France.

1803–5 American fleet blockades North African coast between Tripoli and Tunis in effort to stop tribute payments to North African states.

1803 **Oct. 31** *USS Philadelphia* runs aground off Tripoli and is captured.

1804 **Feb. 16** Captured USS *Philadelphia* burned at Tripoli by American force under Decatur.

1804 **May 18** Napoleon proclaimed emperor of France.

1804 **Sept. 4** Packed with gunpowder, *USS Intrepid* explodes prematurely at Tripoli, killing American crew.

1805 **Apr. 10–July 27** Villeneuve's fleet sails from Spain to West Indies and back, pursued by Nelson.

1805 **May 17** American marines and sailors capture Derna, Tripoli.

1805 **July 22** Battle of Cape Finisterre: Calder fails to press advantage against Villeneuve's returning fleet.

1805 **Oct. 21** Battle of Trafalgar: British fleet demolishes Franco-Spanish fleet off Spain; Nelson killed.

1805 **Nov. 4** Action off Cape Ortegal: British capture four French ships of the line; twenty-two of thirty-three French and Spanish ships captured or sunk at Trafalgar and after.

1805 **Dec. 2** Napoleon wins decisive victory over Austrian and Russian armies at Battle of Austerlitz.

1807 **June 22** USS *Chesapeake* surrenders to *HMS Leopard* following unprovoked attack by British during search for deserters.

1807 **Aug. 17** Fulton's *North River Steam Boat*, first commercially successful steamer, makes maiden voyage on Hudson River.

1808 June 10–23 *Phoenix* makes first sea passage of any steamship along coast of New Jersey.

1811–12 *New Orleans* first steamboat on the Mississippi.

1811 May 17 USS *President* engages HMS *Little Belt* off the Chesapeake in retaliation for British impressment of American seamen.

1812 June–Dec. French army shattered during disastrous invasion of Russia.

The War of 1812 to the Crimean War

1812 June 18 United States declares war on Great Britain.

1812 July 17–20 USS *Constitution* narrowly escapes British squadron after prolonged chase.

1812 Aug. 19 USS *Constitution* defeats HMS Guerrière, which is sunk the next day.

1812 Oct. 18 *USS Wasp* captures HMS *Frolic* east of the Chesapeake.

1812 Oct. 25 USS *United States* captures *HMS Macedonian* south of the Azores.

1812 Dec. 13–Jan. 23, 1813 *USS Hornet* blockades *Bonne Citoyen* at San Salvador, Brazil.

1812 Dec. 29 USS *Constitution* defeats HMS *Java* off coast of Brazil.

1813–14 British maintain tight blockade of American coast, especially off Connecticut and in Chesapeake Bay.

1813 Feb. 14 USS *Hornet* captures brig *Resolution*, with $24,000 in specie.

1813 Feb. 24 USS *Hornet* sinks HMS *Peacock* off Demarara River.

1813 Mar. 13 *USS Essex* anchors at Valparaiso, Chile, at start of commerce-raiding expedition in Pacific.

1813 June 1 HMS *Shannon* captures USS *Chesapeake* off Boston.

1813 July 14–Aug. 14 USS *Argus* embarks on month-long spree against British commerce in Irish Sea until captured by HMS *Pelican*.

1813 Aug. 8 Schooners *Hamilton* and *Scourge* sunk in squall off Niagara River.

1813 Sept. 5 USS *Enterprise* defeats HMS *Boxer* off Portland, Maine.

1813 Sept. 10 Americans under Perry defeat British at Battle of Lake Erie (Put-In Bay).

1813 Oct. 5 Americans under Harrison defeat Tecumseh and Procter at Battle of the Thames (Upper Canada).

1814 Mar. 28 HMS *Phoebe* and *Cherub* defeat USS *Essex* at Valparaiso.

1814 Mar. 31 European allies enter Paris. Napoleon abdicates April 11; retires to Elba May 4.

1814 Apr. 29 USS *Peacock* captures HMS *Epervier*.

1814 June 28 USS *Wasp* defeats HMS *Reindeer*, which is later sunk, off France.

1814 July 25 Americans defeat British at Battle of Lundy's Lane (Upper Canada).

1814 Aug. 14 British burn Washington, D.C.

1814 Sept. 1 USS *Wasp* sinks HMS *Avon* off France.

1814 Sept. 14–15 Siege of Fort McHenry, Baltimore: Francis Scott Key writes national anthem.

1814 Sept. 11 Macdonough defeats Downie at Battle of Lake Champlain, "the greatest naval battle of the war" and a major American victory.

1814 Sept. 27 Privateer *General Armstrong* scuttled at Fayal after spirited defense against British attack.

1814 Dec. 24 Treaty of Ghent signed; ratified at Washington, D.C., February 18, 1815.

1815 Jan. 8 Jackson defeats British at Battle of New Orleans.

1815 Jan. 15 USS *President* captured after running battle with HMS *Majestic, Endymion, Pomone,* and *Tenedos.*

1815 Feb. 20 USS *Constitution* captures HMS *Cyane* and *Levant* near Madeira.

1815 Feb. 26 American privateer *Chasseur* captures schooner *St. Lawrence* off Cuba.

1815 Mar. 23 USS *Hornet* captures HMS *Penguin* off Tristan da Cunha.

1815 June 18 French defeated decisively at Waterloo; Napoleon abdicates a second time June 22.

1815 June 20 USS *Peacock* captures East India Company ship *Nautilus* near Anjer.

1819 *Savannah* is the first steamship to cross the Atlantic.

1821 *Aaron Manby* is the first seagoing iron-hulled ship.

1824 Henri J. Paixhans experiments with shell guns; adopted by France in 1837.

1825 Erie Canal links Hudson River and Great Lakes. First railway built in England.

1832 Apr. 22–23 *Sirius* and then *Great Western* arrive at New York, completing first transatlantic passages under sustained steam power.

1833–36 Working independently, Robert Wilson, Francis Pettit Smith, Frédéric Sauvage, and John Ericsson develop screw propellers.

1836 *Beaver* is the first steamship in the Pacific Northwest.

1837 Samuel F. B. Morse invents telegraphic system and develops Morse code.

1839 John Ericsson's *Robert F. Stockton* is the first screw vessel in the United States.

1840 *Nemesis* is the first iron ship to round Cape of Good Hope, en route to India.

1840s–1850s Clippers developed for fast transport, especially between East Coast and San Francisco.

1843 Isambard Kingdom Brunel launches *Great Britain,* first ocean-going, iron, screw-propeller ship.

1845 Tug-of-war between HMS *Rattler* and *Alecto* demonstrates superiority of screw over side-wheel propulsion.

1852 HMS *Agamemnon,* first warship built with screw propulsion, is commissioned.

1853–56 Crimean War: Russians defeat Turks at Battle of Sinope (November 30, 1853); British and French naval forces operate in Baltic and off Crimea; steam, screws, and shells are used extensively for the first time.

1853 John Ericsson's "caloric ship" *Ericsson* proves unsuccessful.

1854 William Armstrong designs first breech-loading, rifled gun; Royal Navy first adopts them for ship-board batteries in 1860.

1859 France launches first iron-clad warship, *La Gloire.*

1860s High-pressure compound steam engine developed.

1860 Britain launches HMS *Warrior,* first iron-hulled warship.

The American Civil War

1860 Nov. 6 Abraham Lincoln elected president of the United States.

1860 Dec. 20 South Carolina secedes from Union.

1861 Jan. 5 Steamer *Star of the West* comes under fire while bringing arms and supplies to Fort Sumter at Charleston, South Carolina.

1861 Feb. 8 Jefferson Davis elected president of the Confederate States of America.

1861 Apr. 12 USS *Harriet Lane* fires first shot of the Civil War trying to stop an inbound ship at Charleston, South Carolina, before the bombardment of Fort Sumter, which starts later that day.

1861 Apr. 17 *Star of the West* captured off Texas and taken into Confederate Navy as *Saint Philip.*

1861 Apr. 19 Union declares blockade of southern ports; blockading squadrons include North Atlantic (Virginia to North Carolina), South Atlantic (South Carolina to Key West, Florida), East Gulf (Key West to Pensacola, Florida), and West Gulf (Pensacola to Texas).

1861 Apr. 20 Union soldiers burn ships — including *Cumberland, Congress, Merrimack,* and *United States* — in Gosport Navy Yard (Norfolk, Virginia) to prevent their capture by Confederate forces.

1861 July 11 Confederate Navy secretary authorizes conversion of burned hulk of USS *Merrimack* to central battery ship CSS *Virginia.*

1861 July 21 Union army routed at Battle of Manassas, Maryland.

1861 Aug. 29 Federal forces capture Forts Clark and Hatteras at Hatteras Inlet, North Carolina.

1861 Oct. 25 USS *Monitor* laid down.

1861 Nov. 8–Jan. 1, 1862 *Trent* Affair: Tensions between the United States and Britain over arrest of Confederate agents on high seas.

1862 January Semmes's CSS *Sumter* detained at Gibraltar after taking eighteen prizes in six months.

1862 February Western Gunboat Flotilla helps capture Forts Henry (February 6) and Donelson (February 16) on the Cumberland River in Tennessee.

1862 Feb. 25 USS *Monitor* commissioned at New York.

1862 Mar. 8 CSS *Virginia* sinks USS *Cumberland* and *Congress* and engages USS *Minnesota* off Yorktown Peninsula, Virginia. USS *Monitor* arrives two days out of New York.

1862 Mar. 9 Battle of Hampton Roads: First iron-clad battle, between USS *Monitor* and CSS *Virginia,* ushers in new era in naval warfare.

1862 Apr. 6–7 Confederates defeated at Battle of Shiloh, Tennessee.

1862 Apr. 24 West Gulf Blockading Squadron ascends Mississippi River and enters New Orleans August 25.

1862 May 11 CSS *Virginia* blown up in James River, Virginia, to prevent capture by Union forces.

1862 June 6 Memphis, Tennessee, falls to Union forces.

1862 Aug. 24 Confederate raider CSS *Alabama* commissioned off Azores by Semmes. Over the next twenty-three months, she will capture fifty-five ships.

1862 Sept. 17 Confederates defeated at Battle of Antietam.

1862 Sept. 22 Lincoln frees slaves with Emancipation Proclamation.

1862 October Western Gunboat Flotilla command transferred from army to navy.

1862 Oct. 4 West Gulf Blockading Squadron captures Galveston, Texas.

1862 Dec. 12 USS *Cairo* near Baines Bluff, Mississippi, on December 12, 1862.

1862 Dec. 13 Union army defeated at Battle of Fredericksburg, Virginia.

1862 Dec. 31 USS *Monitor* founders off Cape Hatteras, North Carolina, in tow of USS *Rhode Island*.

1863 Jan. 1 Confederates retake Galveston; USS *Harriet Lane* captured.

1863 Jan. 11 Confederate raider CSS *Alabama* sinks auxiliary schooner USS *Hatteras* south of Galveston.

1863 Jan. 16 *Florida* leaves Mobile for seven-month raiding cruise during which she takes thirty-three prizes.

1863 Apr. 9 CSS *Georgia* starts six-month raiding cruise during which she takes nine prizes.

1863 May 1–4 Confederates victorious at Battle of Chancellorsville, Virginia; "Stonewall" Jackson fatally wounded.

1863 June 25 Mikado of Japan orders expulsion of all foreigners from Japan.

1863 June 27 Confederates working from captured schooner *Archer* seize revenue cutter *Caleb Cushing* in Casco Bay, Maine; vessel burned and crew captured the next day.

1863 July 1–3 Union victory at Battle of Gettysburg, Pennsylvania.

1863 July 16 USS Wyoming engages Japanese forts at Shimonoseki, Japan.

1863 Oct. 5 CSS *David* attacks USS *New Ironsides* at Charleston, South Carolina.

1863 Nov. 25 Confederates defeated at Battle of Chattanooga, Tennessee.

1863 Dec. 26 British seize raider CSS *Tuscaloosa* in Simon's Bay, South Africa.

1864 Robert Whitehead develops self-propelled torpedo.

1864 Feb. 17 Submarine *H. L. Hunley* attacks USS *Housatonic* with spar torpedo; both vessels sink.

1864 June Grant begins ten-month siege of Petersburg, Virginia.

1864 June 19 Off Cherbourg, USS *Kearsarge* sinks Confederate raider CSS *Alabama,* which had captured fifty-five ships.

1864 July Commerce raider CSS *Tallahassee* commissioned.

1864 July 9 Union takes control of Mississippi River after fall of Vicksburg, Mississippi (July 4), and Port Hudson, Louisiana.

1864 Aug. 5 Battle of Mobile Bay: Union forces capture CSS *Tennessee.*

1864 Sept. 2 Union army captures Atlanta, Georgia.

1864 Oct. 7 USS *Wachusett* seizes CSS *Florida* at Bahía, Brazil.

1864 Oct. 31 Commerce raider CSS *Shenandoah* begins eleven-month cruise.

1864 Dec. 21 Union army captures Savannah, Georgia.

1865 Jan. 15 Fort Fisher, North Carolina, captured by North Atlantic Blockading Squadron.

1865 Apr. 9 Lee surrenders at Appomattox Court House, Virginia.

1865 Apr. 14 Lincoln assassinated by John Wilkes Booth.

1865 Nov. 6 Commerce raider CSS *Shenandoah* ends cruise at Liverpool.

Pax Britannica to the Sino-Russian War

1869 Suez Canal opens linking Mediterranean and Red Seas.

1870s Triple-expansion steam engine developed.

1871 Aug. 25 "*Alabama* claims" settled by international tribunal.

1877 May 29 During Peruvian insurrection, *Huascar* engaged by HMS *Shah* and *Amethyst* off Ilo, Peru.

1879 **May 21** War of the Pacific: *Huascar* rams and sinks Chilean screw corvette *Esmeralda* off Iquique, Chile.

1879 **Oct. 8** *Huascar* captured after battle with *Cochrane* and *Blanco Encalada* off Antofagasta, Chile.

1891–92 *Baltimore* Affair strains relations between the United States and Chile.

1897 **Sept. 17** Sino-Japanese War: Japanese fleet defeats Chinese at Battle of Yalu River.

1898 **Feb. 15** USS *Maine* blows up at Havana, Cuba

1898 **Apr. 24** United States declares war on Spain.

1898 **May 1** Battle of Manila Bay: U.S. fleet destroys Spain's Philippines fleet.

1898 **Mar. 19–May 24** USS *Oregon* steams 14,000 miles from San Francisco to Florida in record 66 days.

1898 **July 3** Battle of Santiago: United States destroys Spain's Cuban fleet.

1898 **Dec. 10** Treaty of Paris ends Spanish-American War.

Glossary

armor Extra iron or steel plate used to protect a ship from gunfire. The thickness of iron varied according to the part of the ship around which it was placed, vital areas including crew and engine spaces, magazines, and gun turrets.

bark A three-masted vessel square rigged on fore and main, and fore-and-aft rigged on the mizzen.

barkentine A vessel of three to six masts, square rigged on the foremast, and fore-and-aft rigged on the others.

battleship A ship fit to lie in the line of battle; the most heavily armed and stoutly built ships of their day. The battleship concept lasted from the seventeenth century until after World War II, when the development of torpedoes, naval aviation, and missiles rendered them obsolete.

Bermuda rig A fore-and-aft rig in which the mainsail is triangular in shape; also called Marconi rig. (*See also* "gaff rig.")

brig A two-masted vessel, square rigged on both masts.

brigantine A two-masted vessel, square rigged on the foremast, and fore-and-aft rigged on the main.

capital ship The most important class of warship in a given era. The term originally referred to ships fit to sail in the line of battle, or battleships.

caravel A relatively small Portuguese vessel of the fifteenth and sixteenth centuries setting lateen sails on two or three masts and sometimes a square sail on the foremast. Highly maneuverable, caravels helped make possible the voyages of the early Portuguese and Spanish discoverers.

carrack A large seagoing vessel of the fourteenth century that combined northern European and Mediterranean shipbuilding techniques. Carracks resembled the northern cog, but they were constructed frame first and carried more than one mast. By the sixteenth century, they carried three masts and high stern- and forecastles. Carracks were forerunners of galleons.

carronade A short-barreled ship's gun developed by the Carron Company in Scotland. Though of limited range, it was enormously destructive against ships' timbers and was originally known as a "smasher." Within two years, 429 ships of the Royal Navy — "where a short range is ever the distance chosen" — carried carronades. The addition of carronades was not reflected in the nominal rate of a ship: a 54-gun ship mounting 10 carronades was still designated a "44."

carvel construction A method of hull construction in which the longitudinal strakes forming the skin of the hull are flush at the edges. In carvel construction, the planks are fastened to a pre-erected frame. (*See also* "clinker construction," "frame-first construction," and "shell-first construction.")

clinker (or lapstrake) construction A method of hull construction in which the longitudinal strakes forming the hull overlap each other and are "clenched" to each other with iron nails. In clinker construction, the hull is built first; frames were sometimes inserted afterward. (*See also* "carvel construction," "frame-first construction," and "shell-first construction.")

cog A type of capacious merchant vessel that originated in Germany and gradually spread throughout the Baltic and to the Mediterranean. It is characterized by high sides, a relatively flat bottom, and a single square sail.

composite construction A type of hull construction consisting of an iron or steel frame and wooden planking.

compound engine A steam engine in which the steam expands first in a high-pressure cylinder, and then in a low-pressure cylinder.

cruiser A type of warship falling between a battleship

and a destroyer in size, armament, and speed. It was designed primarily for reconnaissance while with the fleet, or for commerce protection, commerce raiding, and patrolling on overseas stations.

cutter A small ship's boat; a single-masted vessel similar to a sloop but usually setting double headsails. Patrol vessels of the U.S. Coast Guard are also called cutters.

destroyer Relatively small warships, torpedo boat destroyers originated as small, fast ships whose primary function was to protect larger ships from torpedo attack. Their roles later included antisubmarine and antiaircraft warfare and convoy protection.

displacement tonnage The standard method of measuring warships. Displacement tonnage is the volume of water displaced by a vessel, the weight of the water so displaced being equal to the weight of the object displacing it.

en echelon An arrangement of gun turrets in which one is mounted on either the starboard or port side of the hull, and the other is mounted astern on the other side of the hull. Most turreted ships in the twentieth century had the primary guns mounted on the centerline.

fore-and-aft sail A sail set parallel to the centerline of a vessel. Fore-and-aft vessels are simpler to rig than square rigged vessels, require a smaller crew, and can sail closer to the direction from which the wind is blowing.

forecastle Originally, a built-up structure comprising several decks in the forward part of a ship, from which archers or gunners could fire into an enemy ship. (A sterncastle aft served the same function.) In more modern usage, the forecastle (pronounced and often written *focsle*) is the crew's quarters in the forward part of a ship.

frame A transverse rib that forms part of the skeleton of a ship's hull.

frame-first construction A method of construction in which the internal framework, or skeleton, of a ship's hull is constructed first, with the hull planking being attached afterward. (*See also* "carvel construction," "clinker construction," and "shell-first construction.")

frigate A small combatant ship. In the age of sail, frigates sailed with the fleet as reconnaissance vessels and in battle stood away from the line to relay signals from the flagship to other ships in the line who could not see the flagship because of gunsmoke. Frigates were also used for convoy protection and commerce raiding.

gaff rig A fore-and-aft rig in which the primary sails abaft the mast are trapezoidal in shape: the bottom of the sail is attached to the boom, the luff (or forward edge) to the mast, and the head to a spar called a gaff. (*See also* "Bermuda rig.")

galleass A hybrid type of sixteenth-century vessel employing both a full sailing rig and oars for propulsion.

galleon A full-rigged vessel that evolved in Europe around the sixteenth century and is the immediate ancestor of the full-rigged ship. Galleons had a higher length-to-beam ratio, lower fore- and sterncastles, and greater maneuverability than carracks.

galley A relatively narrow vessel driven primarily by oars. Galleys evolved in the ancient Mediterranean, and the galley *par excellence* was the Greek trieres, or trireme. Although used primarily for warfare, galleys of various kinds also served as dispatch boats, and in the fourteenth century, Venice began to use great galleys for carrying cargo and people.

gun A generic term for a carriage-mounted gun in sailing warships. Guns were rated according to the weight of shot fired, anywhere from one-pound antipersonnel guns to forty-two-pounders and above. The colorful names of the early guns designated specific types, based on the weight of shot. The following table, adapted from Clowes's *Royal Navy*, shows the characteristics of a few of the guns in use at the time of the Spanish Armada:

Gun	Caliber (inches)	Gun Weight (pounds)	Weight of Shot (pounds)	Range (feet)
Culverin	5.5	4,500	17.3	2,500
Demi-culverin	4.5	3,400	9.5	2,500
Saker	3.5	1,400	5.3	1,700
Minion	3.25	1,000	4	1,600
Falcon	2–2.5	660–800	2.5–3	1,500
Serpentine	2	500	0.3	1,300

In the sailing navy, guns were mounted along the sides of the ship — in broadside. The ability to train or elevate the guns was extremely limited, and they could be aimed only by turning the ship so that it was parallel to the target. In the seventeenth century, fleets began to fight in a line-ahead (bow-to-stern) formation, which became known as the battle line. When "crossing the T," one maneuvered one's fleet so that it passed in front of the enemy's battle line, allowing it to rake the enemy ships, which would be able to reply with only a handful of guns mounted in the bows.

Developed in the nineteenth century, rifled guns (measured by the caliber, or internal diameter of the gun barrel) were housed in rotating turrets that gave ships greater flexibility of maneuver.

horsepower A measure of mechanical power. A vessel's horsepower is measured in various ways, depending on the type of engine. The power of a steam engine is expressed as *indicated horsepower* (ihp), the work of the steam in the cylinder, or *nominal horsepower* (nhp), an expression of power derived by formula. Steam turbines are measured by *shaft horsepower* (shp), the power at the crankshaft as indicated by a torsion meter. Diesel engines are often measured by *brake horsepower* (bhp), determined by a brake attached to the shaft coupling. *Effective horsepower* (ehp) is the actual work done by an engine propelling a vessel.

ironclad A warship with a wooden hull sheathed in iron for protection against gunfire.

jib A triangular sail carried on a stay leading from the topmast head to the bow or bowsprit.

jury rig A temporary rig used to replace a damaged or broken mast or spar.

ketch A two-masted yacht with a tall mainmast and a shorter mizzen mast.

knot A unit of measure used to express the speed of a ship in nautical miles per hour. One international nautical mile is defined as 6,076.1155 feet, or approximately 1.15 statute (land) miles or 1.85 kilometers. A knot is generally taken to mean a rate of speed, and some argue that "knots per hour" is an incorrect expression. The argument is a pedantic one; many ship's logs record speeds in knots per hour. The accompanying table shows the time (in days and hours) required to travel a given distance at various speeds.

Nautical Miles	5 KTS.	10 KTS.	15 KTS.	20 KTS.	25 KTS.	30 KTS.
10	0d 02h	0d 01h	0d 01h	0d 01h	—	—
50	0d 10h	0f 05h	0d 03h	0d 03h	0d 02h	0d 02h
100	0d 20h	0d 10h	0d 07h	0d 05h	0d 04h	0d 03h
500	4d 04h	2d 02h	1d 09h	1d 01h	0d 20h	0d 17h
1,000	8d 08h	4d 04h	2d 19h	2d 02h	1d 16h	1d 9h
5,000	41d 16h	20d 20h	13d 21h	10d 10h	8d 08h	6d 23h
10,000	83d 08h	41d 16h	27d 18h	20d 20h	16d 04h	13d 21h

lapstrake See "clinker construction."

lateen A triangular fore-and-aft sail set from a long spar attached to a short mast, found in the Iberian Peninsula, the Mediterranean, and the Indian Ocean.

mast A vertical pole or spar from which sails are set. In a square rigged vessel, masts are often composed of separate sections: lower mast, topmast, topgallant mast, and royal mast. Masts are named, from bow to stern, foremast, mainmast, mizzen mast, and jigger mast. In some five-masted vessels, the middle mast is so named. Driver and spanker masts are also found on six-masted vessels.

paddle steamer A steamboat driven by a paddlewheel. The most common arrangement is a pair of wheels mounted amidships on either side of the hull, although many steamboats have single wheels mounted in the stern.

plank A long piece of sawn timber used in the construction of the hull and for decking. A strake can be made up of one or more planks.

quadruple-expansion engine A steam engine in which the steam expands through four cylinders.

rate A class of sailing warship, particularly in the Royal Navy, dependent upon the number of guns mounted. The number of guns carried by a ship of a given rate changed from time to time. In 1779, it was:

1st rate	100 guns
2nd rate	84–98 guns
3rd rate	64–80 guns
4th rate	50–60 guns
5th rate	32–44 guns
6th rate	20–30 guns

Ships of 60 guns or more were considered fit to lie in the battle line and referred to simply as vessels "of the line." Fourth- and fifth-rates were classed as frigates. Smaller combatants included sloops (ship-rigged, mounting 8–18 guns), bombs (fitted with mortars for bombing shoreside targets), and fire ships, older vessels set on fire and sailed into an enemy fleet to destroy their ships. (*See also* "carronade.")

round ship A medieval merchant sailing ship, as distinct from a longship or an oared galley.

rudder A device hung on the centerline at the stern and used to turn a vessel. (*See also* "steering oar.")

schooner A vessel of two to seven masts, fore-and-aft rigged on each. A topsail schooner also sets square sails on the foremast. (*See also* "barkentine.")

shell-first construction A method of hull construction in which the hull is formed without a frame. The two primary methods of shell-first construction are clinker construction, in which the overlapping strakes are clenched together with iron nails, and carvel construction, in which the strakes are connected by a complex system of mortise-and-tenon joinery.

ship A generic term usually referring to any large seagoing vessel.

ship, full-rigged A vessel having three, four, or five masts and setting square sails on each. These are, from the deck up: course, topsail (sometimes split into lower and upper), topgallant (sometimes split), royal, and skysail.

sloop A single-masted vessel setting a mainsail and a single jib, or headsail.

sloop of war A three-masted, full-rigged warship, smaller than a frigate and mounting 8 to 20 guns.

spar torpedo A nineteenth-century explosive device carried at the end of a spar and placed against an enemy ship before being detonated.

square sail A quadrilateral sail set from a yard. Although a square rigger can carry more sail than a fore-and-aft rigged vessel of comparable size, it is more dependent on favorable (following) winds.

staysail A triangular, fore-and-aft sail set from a stay, a piece of standing rigging leading forward from, and used to provide longitudinal support for, a mast.

steering oar An oar mounted on the side of a ship (usually the right — steering board, or starboard — side) toward the stern and used for turning a ship. (*See also* "rudder.")

strake A continuous row of hull planking (in a wooden ship) or plating (in an iron or steel ship) running fore and aft.

submarine A warship capable of operating underwater for long periods.

thole pin A vertical piece of wood against which a rowing oar pivots.

tonnage In merchant ships, tonnage is usually an expression of a ship's capacity or volume. The word has its origins in the medieval *tun,* or wine cask, tunnage being the number of tuns a vessel could carry. Tonnage rules vary enormously. In the eighteenth century, tonnage was referred to as "burthen." This was replaced by "builder's old measurement," abbreviated bm., or later om., to distinguish it from "new measurement" (nm.). One ton is now generally understood to equal 100 cubic feet.

Gross register tonnage (grt.) is the whole cubic capacity of all enclosed spaces of a ship, including all the room under the deck from stem to sternpost as well as that of the poop or bridge-house, a forecastle, or any other erection. *Net register tonnage* (nrt.) is the capacity under deck available for stowing cargo only, and not including engine room spaces, passenger accommodation, or crew spaces.

Unlike cubic measures of tonnage, *deadweight tonnage* (dwt.) is a measure of the weight of a vessel's cargo. This is determined by calculating the volume of water displaced by a vessel when "light" and when full of cargo. Because the water displaced is equal to the weight of the object displacing it, the difference in displacement figures is equal to the weight of the cargo. (*See also* "displacement tonnage.")

torpedo A self-propelled, underwater explosive device launched from surface ships, submarines, and aircraft. Developed in the late nineteenth century, torpedoes proved enormously effective against both merchant shipping and warships.

triple-expansion engine A steam engine in which the steam expands gradually and successively through three cylinders. Steam is first supplied to a high-pressure cylinder. It passes into an intermediate cylinder at a lower pressure, and finally into a low-pressure cylinder.

weather gauge In the age of fighting sail, if a ship was upwind of another, it was said to have the weather gauge; the downwind or leeward ship had the lee gauge. The advantage of the weather gauge was that its guns could be aimed at the enemy's hull, often below the waterline. The guns of the leeward ship fired into the rigging, where damage was less serious.

yard A spar fastened to a mast perpendicular to the centerline of a vessel and from which square sails are set. The ends of a yard are called yardarms.

yawl A two-masted yacht similar in appearance to a ketch but with a smaller mizzen mast set abaft the rudderpost.

Bibliography

The bibliography includes complete publication data for every work cited in the article source notes. It can by no means be considered exhaustive, although it is helpful in providing the serious researcher with a solid basis for further inquiry. The following journals are devoted to maritime history: *American Neptune, International Journal of Nautical Archaeology, Mariner's Mirror,* and *Warship.*

There are many interesting avenues of research in maritime history on the Internet. One in particular that is quite useful is Maritime History Virtual Archives, owned and administered by Lars Bruzelius: http://pc-78–120/udac.se:8001/www/Nautica/Nautica/html. An excellent forum for online discussion is the maritime history discussion list, MARHST-L, maintained by Maurice D. Smith, curator of the Marine Museum of the Great Lakes in Kingston, Ontario.

Aimone, Alan Conrad. "The Cruise of the U.S. Sloop *Hornet* in 1815." *Mariner's Mirror* 61 (1975): 377–84.

Allen, Francis J. "The Story of the USS *Vesuvius* and the Dynamite Gun." *Warship* 45 (1986): 10–15.

———. "USS *Katahdin:* Fighting Ram." *Warship* 47 (1988): 10–19.

Allen, Joseph. *Battles of the Royal Navy from A.D. 1000 to 1840.* 2 vols. London: A. H. Baily, 1842.

Anderson, Bern. *By Sea and by River: The Naval History of the Civil War.* New York: Alfred A. Knopf, 1962.

Anderson, R. C. "Henry VIII's *Great Galley."* *Mariner's Mirror* 6 (1920): 274–81.

Anson, George, ed. *A Voyage round the World in the Years MDCCXL, I, II, III, IV* by Glyndwr Williams. London: Oxford University Press, 1974.

Arenhold, Capt. L. "The Nydam Boat at Kiel." *Mariner's Mirror* 4 (1914): 182–85.

Athenaeus. *Deipnosophistai* (The Learned Banquet). Translated by C. B. Gulick. Cambridge, Mass.: Loeb Classical Library, 1957–67.

Bailey, Richard. *A Manual for Sailing aboard the American Tall Ship "Rose."* Bridgeport, Conn.: HMS Rose Foundation, 1994.

Ballard, Adm. G. A. *The Black Battlefleet.* Lymington: Nautical; Greenwich: Society for Nautical Research, 1980.

Barrow, Sir John. *The Mutiny and Piratical Seizure of HMS "Bounty": Its Causes and Consequences.* 1886. Reprint, London: Folio Society, 1976.

Bartlett, Merrill L. "Commodore James Biddle and the First Naval Mission to Japan, 1845–46." *American Neptune* 41 (1981): 25–35.

Basch, Lucien. "The Athlit Ram: A Preliminary Introduction and Report." *Mariner's Mirror* 68 (1982): 3–9.

Baxter, James Phinney. *Introduction of the Ironclad Warship.* Cambridge, Mass.: Harvard University Press, 1933.

Beach, Edward L. *The United States Navy: 200 Years.* New York: Henry Holt, 1986.

Bearss, Edwin C. *Hardluck Ironclad: The Sinking and Salvage of the "Cairo."* Baton Rouge: Louisiana State University Press, 1966.

Beattie, Judith, and Bernard Pothier. "The Battle of the Restigouche." In *Canadian Historic Sites: Occasional Papers in Archaeology and History.* Ottawa: Parks Canada, 1977.

Bellabarba, Sergio, and Giorgio Osculati. *The Royal Yacht "Caroline" 1749.* London: Conway Maritime Press, 1989.

Bennett, Geoffrey. *Nelson the Commander.* New York: Charles Scribner's Sons, 1972.

Bernard, W. D. *The "Nemesis" in China: Comprising a History of the Late War in That Country, with an Account of the Colony of Hong-Kong.* London: H. Colbourn, 1847.

Bevan, David. *Drums of the "Birkenhead."* London: London Stamp Exchange, 1989.

Bligh, William. *Narrative of the Mutiny on the "Bounty."* 1792. Reprint, New York: Airmont, 1965.

Blow, Michael. *A Ship to Remember: The "Maine" and the Spanish-American War.* New York: Morrow, 1992.

Bonde, Niels, and Arne Emil Christensen. "Dendrochronological Dating of the Viking Age Ship Burials at Oseberg, Gokstad, and Tune." *Antiquity* 67 (1993): 575–83.

Boudriot, Jean. *John Paul Jones and the "Bonhomme Richard" 1779: A Reconstruction of the Ship and an Account of the Battle with HMS "Serapis."* Annapolis, Md.: Naval Institute Press, 1987.

Bovill, E. W. "The *Madre de Dios.*" *Mariner's Mirror* 54 (1968): 129–52.

Boxer, C. R. "The Taking of *Madre de Dios.*" *Mariner's Mirror* 67 (1981): 82–84.

Bradford, Ernle. *The Story of the "Mary Rose."* London: Hamish Hamilton, 1982.

Bradford, Richard H. "And *Oregon* Rushed Home." *American Neptune* 36 (1976): 155–69.

Breyer, Siegfried. *Battleships and Battle Cruisers 1905–1970.* London: Macdonald & Jane's, 1973.

Brown, D. K. "Seamanship, Steam and Steel: HMS *Calliope* at Samoa, 15–16 March 1889." *Mariner's Mirror* 49 (1953): 193–208.

———. "The Paddle Frigate *Guadeloupe.*" *Mariner's Mirror* 58 (1972): 221–22.

———. "The Introduction of the Screw Propeller into the Royal Navy." *Warship* 1 (1977): 59–63.

———. "*Nemesis:* The First Iron Warship." *Warship* 8 (October 1978): 283–85.

———. "The Design of HMS *Inflexible.*" *Warship* 15 (1980): 146–52.

———. *Before the Ironclad: The Development of Ship Design, Propulsion, and Armament in the Royal Navy, 1815–1860.* London: Conway Maritime Press, 1990.

Brouwer, Norman. *International Register of Historic Ships.* 2d ed. Peekskill, NY: Sea History Press, 1993.

Brownlee, Walter. *"Warrior": The First Modern Battleship.* Cambridge: Cambridge University Press, 1985.

Bugler, Arthur R. *HMS "Victory": Building, Restoration and Repair.* London: HMSO, 1966.

Bulkeley, Robert J. *At Close Quarters: PT Boats in the United States Navy.* Washington, D.C.: Naval History Division, 1963.

Cain, Emily. *Ghost Ships "Hamilton" and "Scourge": Historical Treasures from the War of 1812.* New York: Beaufort Books, 1983.

Canney, Donald L. *The Old Steam Navy: Frigates, Sloops and Gunboats 1815–1885.* Annapolis, Md.: Naval Institute Press, 1990.

———. *U.S. Coast Guard and Revenue Cutters, 1790–1935.* Annapolis, Md.: Naval Institute Press, 1995.

Casson, Lionel. *The Ancient Mariners: Seafarers and Sea Fighters in Ancient Times.* 2nd ed. Princeton, N.J.: Princeton University Press, 1991.

———. *Ships and Seamanship in the Ancient World.* Baltimore: Johns Hopkins University Press, 1995.

Casson, Lionel, and J. Richard Steffy. *The Athlit Ram.* College Station, Tex.: Institute of Nautical Archaeology, 1991.

Cavaliero, Roderick. *Admiral Satan: The Life and Campaigns of Admiral Suffren.* London: I. B. Tauris, 1994.

Chance, Franklin N., Paul S. Chance, and David L. Topper. *Tangled Machinery and Charred Relics: The Historical and Archaeological Investigation of the CSS "Nashville."* Orangeburg, S.C.: n.p., 1985.

Chapelle, Howard I. *The History of the American Sailing Navy: The Ships and Their Development.* New York: Bonanza Books, 1949.

———. *Fulton's "Steam Battery": Blockship and Catamaran.* Washington, D.C.: Smithsonian Institution, 1964.

Chesneau, Roger, and Eugene M. Kolesink, eds. *Conway's All the World's Fighting Ships 1860–1905.* London: Conway Maritime Press, 1979.

Clarke, Arthur C. *Voice across the Sea: The Story of the Deep-Sea Cables and the Men Who Made Possible a Century of Ever-Improving Communication.* New York: Harper & Brothers, 1958.

Clowes, William Laird. *The Royal Navy: A History from Earliest Times to the Present.* 6 vols. 1897. Reprint, London: Chatham, 1996.

Coates, John F. "The Trireme Sails Again." *Scientific American* 260 (April 1989): 96–103.

Cochrane, Thomas. *Autobiography of a Seaman, by Thomas, Tenth Earl of Dundonald.* London: R. Bentley, 1860–61.

Compton-Hall, Richard. *Submarine Boats: The Beginnings of Underwater Warfare.* London: Conway Maritime Press, 1983.

Cottell, G. A. "The Gokstad Viking Ship: Some New Theories Concerning the Purpose of Certain of Its Construction Features." *Mariner's Mirror* 69 (1983): 129–42.

Cox, Lee J., and Michael A. Jehle, eds. *Ironclad Intruder: USS "Monitor."* Philadelphia: Philadelphia Maritime Museum, 1988.

Crumlin-Pedersen, Ole. "The Skuldelev Ships." *Acta Archaeologica* 38 (1967): 73–174.

Culver, Henry B. *Forty Famous Ships: Their Beginnings, Their Life Histories, Their Ultimate Fate.* New York: Garden City, 1938.

Cussler, Clive. *The Sea Hunters.* New York: Simon & Schuster, 1996.

Dalzell, George W. *The Flight from the Flag: The Contin-*

uing Effect of the Civil War upon the American Carrying Trade. Chapel Hill: University of North Carolina Press, 1940.

De Kay, James Tertius. *Chronicles of the Frigate "Macedonian" 1809–1922.* New York: Norton, 1995.

Delgado, James P. *Encyclopedia of Underwater and Maritime Archaeology.* New Haven: Yale University Press, 1998.

———. *A Symbol of American Ingenuity: Historical Context Study, USS "Monitor."* Washington, D.C.: National Park Service/National Oceanic and Atmospheric Administration, 1988.

———. "Rediscovering the *Somers.*" *Naval History* 8 (March-April 1994): 28–31.

Delgado, James P., and J. Candace Clifford. *Great American Ships.* Washington, D.C.: Preservation Press, 1991.

Dennis, D. L. "The Action between the *Shannon* and the *Chesapeake.*" *Mariner's Mirror* 45 (1959): 36–45.

Dunne, W. M. P. "The Frigate *Constellation* Clearly Was No More: Or Was She?" *American Neptune* 53 (1993): 77–97.

Dye, Ira. *The Fatal Cruise of the "Argus": Two Captains in the War of 1812.* Annapolis, Md.: Naval Institute Press, 1994.

Earle, Peter. *The Wreck of the Almiranta: Sir William Phips and the Search for the Hispaniola Treasure.* London: Macmillan, 1979.

———. *The Last Fight of the "Revenge."* London: Collins & Brown, 1992.

Einarsson, Lars. "The Royal Ship *Kronan* — Underwater Archaeological Investigations of a Great Swedish 17th Century Man-of-War." *VIIth International Congress of Maritime Museums, Proceedings 1990.* Stockholm: National Maritime Museums, 1990.

Emerson, William C. "USS *Olympia.*" In *Warship 1989.* London: Conway Maritime Press, 1989.

———. "The Armoured Cruiser USS *Brooklyn.*" In *Warship 1991.* London: Conway Maritime Press, 1991.

Evans, Angela Care. *The Sutton Hoo Ship Burial.* London: British Museum Press, 1986.

Fairburn, Thayer. *The "Orpheus" Disaster.* Waiuku, New Zealand: Western Publishing, 1987.

Fay, Leonard. "Career of the *Conway.*" *Sea Breezes* 7 (new series): 42 (June 1949): 342–60.

Flanagan, Lawrence. *Shipwrecks of the Irish Coast.* London: Gill & Macmillan, 1988.

Fowler, William M., Jr. *Rebels under Sail: The American Navy during the Revolution.* New York: Charles Scribner's Sons, 1976.

Fox, Frank. *Great Ships: The Battlefleet of King Charles II.* Greenwich: Conway Maritime Press, 1980.

Franzén, Anders. "*Kronan:* Remnants of a Mighty Warship." *National Geographic* (April 1990): 438–66.

Fraser, Edward. "H.M.S. *Victory.*" *Mariner's Mirror* 8 (1922): 194, 232, 258, 297, 337.

Frazier, Donald A. "Cottonclads in a Storm of Iron." *Naval History* 8, no. 3 (May-June 1994): 26–33.

Frost, Honor. "How Carthage Lost the Sea: Off the Coast of Sicily, a Punic Warship Gives Up Its Secrets." *Natural History* (December 1987): 58–67.

———. "The Marsala Punic Ship, An Obituary." *Mariner's Mirror* 83, no. 2 (May 1997): 207–11.

Frost, Honor, et al. *The Punic Ship: Final Excavation Report.* Rome: Lilybaeum, *Notizie degli Scavi di Antichità,* serie ottava vol. 30, 1976 (1981).

Fryer, John. *The Voyage of the "Bounty" Launch.* Introduction by Stephen Walters. Guildford, Eng.: Genesis, 1979.

Gardiner, Robert, and Andrew Lambert. *Steam, Steel and Shellfire: The Steam Warship 1815–1905.* London: Conway Maritime Press.

Gardiner, Robert, and Brian Lavery, eds. *The Line of Battle: The Sailing Warship 1650–1840.* Annapolis, Md.: Naval Institute Press, 1992.

Gardiner, Robert, and John Morrison, eds. *The Age of the Galley: Mediterranean Oared Vessels since pre-Classical Times.* Annapolis, Md.: Naval Institute Press, 1995.

Gardiner, Robert, and Richard W. Unger, eds. *Cogs, Caravels and Galleons: The Sailing Ship 1000–1650.* Annapolis, Md.: Naval Institute Press, 1994.

Gifford, Edwin, and Joyce Gifford. "The Sailing Performance of Anglo-Saxon Ships as Derived from the Building and Trials of Half-Scale Models of the Sutton Hoo and Graveney Ship Finds." *Mariner's Mirror* 82 (1996): 131–53.

Gillmer, Thomas C. *Old Ironsides: The Rise, Decline, and Resurrection of the USS "Constitution."* Camden, Me.: International Marine, 1993.

Glasgow, Tom, Jr. "The Navy in the French Wars of Mary and Elizabeth I, Part III: The Expeditions of Le Havre 1562–1564." *Mariner's Mirror* 54 (1968): 281–96.

———. "List of Ships in the Royal Navy from 1539 to 1588 — The Navy from Its Infancy to the Defeat of the Spanish Armada." *Mariner's Mirror* 56 (1970): 299–307.

Goldberg, Joyce S. *The "Baltimore" Affair.* Lincoln: University of Nebraska Press, 1986.

Golovnin, V. M. *Memoirs of a Captivity in Japan during the Years 1811, 1812, and 1813; with Observations on the Country and the People.* 3 vols. London: Henry Colburn, 1824.

———. *Detained in Simon's Bay: The Story of the Detention of the Imperial Russian Sloop "Diana" April 1808– May 1809.* Cape Town: Friends of the South African Library, 1964.

Goslinga, Cornelis Ch. *The Dutch in the Caribbean and*

on the Wild Coast, 1580–1680. Gainesville: University of Florida Press, 1971.

Grissim, John. The Lost Treasure of the "Concepción." New York: Morrow, 1980.

Guérout, Max. "The Engagement between the C.S.S. Alabama and the U.S.S. Kearsarge 19 May 1864: The Archaeological Discovery 1984–1988." Mariner's Mirror 74 (1988): 355–62.

Hagan, Kenneth. This People's Navy: The Making of American Sea Power. Annapolis, Md.: Naval Institute Press, 1991.

Hainsworth, Roger, and Christine Churches. The Anglo-Dutch Naval Wars 1652–1674. Stroud, Eng.: Sutton, 1998.

Hakluyt, Richard. The Principal Navigations Voyages Traffiques & Discoveries of the English Nation. 12 vols. 1598–1600. Reprint, Glasgow: James MacLehose & Sons, 1905.

Hall, William Hutcheon. Narrative of the Voyages and Services of the "Nemesis," from 1840 to 1843. . . . London: H. Colburn, 1844.

Hampden, John. Francis Drake, Privateer: Contemporary Narratives and Documents. University: University of Alabama Press, 1972.

Hancock, C. H. "La Couronne," A French Warship of the Seventeenth Century: A Survey of Ancient and Modern Accounts of This Ship. Newport News, Va.: Mariners' Museum, 1973.

Hardin, Craig. "Notes." American Neptune 11 (1951): 73–76.

Hawkey, Arthur. Black Night off Finisterre: The Tragic Tale of an Early British Ironclad. Annapolis, Md.: Naval Institute Press, 1999.

Heaton, Peter. Yachting: A History. New York: Charles Scribner's Sons, 1956.

Heine, William C. Historic Ships of the World. New York: G. P. Putnam's Sons, 1977.

Heinrichs, Waldo H., Jr. "The Battle of Plattsburg, 1814 — The Losers." American Neptune 21 (1961): 42–56.

Henderson, James. The Frigates: An Account of the Lighter Warships of the Napoleonic Wars, 1793–1815. London: Leo Cooper, 1994.

Hepper, David. British Warship Losses in the Age of Sail, 1650–1859. Rotherfield, Eng.: Jean Boudriot, 1994.

Herd, R. J. HMVS "Cerberus": Battleship to Breakwater. Sandringham, Australia: City of Sandringham, 1986.

Hetherington, Roy. The Wreck of H.M.S. "Orpheus." Auckland: Cassell New Zealand, 1975.

Heywood, Thomas. His Majesty's Royal Ship: A Critical Edition of Thomas Heywood's "A True Description of His Majesties Royall Ship." Edited by Alan R. Young. New York: AMS Press, 1990.

Höckmann, Olaf. "Late Roman Rhine Vessels from Mainz, Germany." International Journal of Nautical Archaeology 22 (1993): 125–35.

———. "Late Roman River Craft from Mainz, Germany." In O. L. Filgueiras, ed., Local Boats, Fourth International Symposium on Boat and Ship Archaeology, Porto 1985. Oxford: BAR International, 1988.

Hollins, Holly. "Fragata from the Fire." Classic Boat (July 1998): 38–42.

Hopkins, Fred. "Chasseur: The Pride of Baltimore." Mariner's Mirror 64 (1978): 349–60.

———. "The Six Baltimores." American Neptune 39 (1979): 29–44.

Horan, James D., Jr., ed. C.S.S. "Shenandoah": The Memoirs of Lieutenant Commander James I. Waddell. New York: Crown, 1960.

Horton, Brian. HMS "Trincomalee." Windsor: Profile, 1979.

Hoste, Lady Harriet, ed. Memoirs and Letters of Captain Sir William Hoste, Bart. 2 vols. London: Bentley, 1833.

Jackson, Kenneth T. "The Forgotten Saga of New York's Prison Ships." Seaport (Summer 1990): 25–28.

James, Wendy, Gerd Baumann, and Douglas Johnson. Juan Maria Schuver's Travels in North East Africa, 1880–1883. London: Hakluyt Society, 1996.

Jameson, Edwin Milton, and Sanford Sternlicht. Black Devil of the Bayous: The Life and Times of the United States Steam Sloop "Hartford," 1858–1957. Upper Saddle River, N.J.: Gregg Press, 1970.

Jamieson, Alan G. "American Privateers in the Leeward Islands." American Neptune 43 (1983): 20–30.

Johnson, R. F. The "Royal George." London: Charles Knight & Co., 1971.

Johnson, Robert Erwin. Thence round Cape Horn: The Story of United States Naval Forces on Pacific Station, 1818–1923. Annapolis, Md.: Naval Institute, 1963.

Jones, Gwyn. A History of the Vikings. New York: Oxford University Press, 1968.

Kemp, Peter, ed. The Oxford Companion to Ships and the Sea. New York: Oxford University Press, 1976.

Kennedy, Gavin. "Bligh and the Defiance Mutiny." Mariner's Mirror 65 (1979): 39–51.

Kjølsen, F. H. "The Old Danish Frigate." Mariner's Mirror 51 (1965): 27–33.

Kloepel, James E. Danger beneath the Waves: A History of the Confederate Submarine "H. L. Hunley." College Park, Ga.: n.p., 1987.

Klooster, Wim. Dutch in the Americas 1600–1800. Providence, R.I.: John Carter Brown Library, 1997.

Knight, C. "H.M. Armed Vessel Bounty." Mariner's Mirror 22 (1936): 183–99.

Kvarning, Lars-Åke, and Bengt Ohrelius. Swedish Warship "Wasa." London: Macmillan, 1973.

———. The "Vasa": Royal Ship. Stockholm: Atlantis, 1998.

Lambert, Andrew. Battleships in Transition: The Creation of the Steam Battlefleet 1815–1860. London: Conway Maritime Press, 1984.

———. "Warrior": Restoring the World's First Ironclad. London: Conway Maritime Press, 1987.

———. The Last Sailing Battlefleet: Maintaining Sailing Mastery 1815–1850. London: Conway Maritime Press, 1991.

Lane, Frederic Chapin. Venetian Ships and Shipbuilders of the Renaissance. 1932. Reprint, Baltimore: Johns Hopkins University Press, 1994.

LaRoe, Lisa Moore. "La Salle's Last Voyage." National Geographic (May 1997): 72–83.

Larrabee, Harold A. Decision at the Chesapeake. New York: C. N. Potter, 1964.

Laughton, L. G. "Report: The Henry Grace à Dieu." Mariner's Mirror 17 (1931): 174–80.

Leary, William M., Jr. "Alabama vs. Kearsarge: A Diplomatic View." American Neptune 29 (1969): 167–73.

Lipscomb, F. W. The British Submarine. Greenwich: Conway Maritime Press, 1975.

Loades, David. The Tudor Navy: An Administrative, Political and Military History. Aldershot, Honats.: Scolar Press, 1992.

Longridge, C. N. The Anatomy of Nelson's Ships. Annapolis, Md.: Naval Institute Press, 1981.

Lundeberg, Philip K. The Gunboat "Philadelphia" and the Defense of Lake Champlain, 1776. Vergennes, Vt.: Lake Champlain Maritime Museum, 1995.

Lyon, David. The Sailing Navy List: All the Ships of the Royal Navy, Built, Purchased and Captured 1688–1860. London: Conway Maritime Press, 1993.

Lyon, Eugene. "Santa Margarita: Treasure from the Ghost Galleons." National Geographic (Feb. 1982): 229–43.

———. The Search for the "Atocha." New York: Harper & Row, 1979.

Maber, John M. "Nordenfelt Submarines." Warship 8 (1984): 218–25.

McBride, Peter W. J. "The Mary: Charles II's Yacht. 2. Her History, Importance and Ordnance." International Journal of Nautical Archaeology 2 (1973): 59–73.

McCready, Lauren S. "The Emery Rice Engine." Sea History 46 (Winter 1987–88): 20–21.

McCusker, John J. "The American Invasion of Nassau in the Bahamas." American Neptune 25 (1965): 189–217.

———. "Alfred," the First Continental Flagship, 1775–1778. Washington, D.C.: Smithsonian Institution Press, 1973.

Macdougall, Norman. James IV. Edinburgh: 1989.

———. "'The Greattest Scheip That Ewer Saillit in Ingland or France': James IV's Great Michael." In Norman MacDougall, ed., Scotland and War A D 79–1918. Savage, Md.: Barnes & Noble, 1991.

McFarland, Philip J. Sea Dangers: The Affair of the Somers. New York: Schocken Books, 1985.

Mach, Andrzej. "The Chinese Battleships." Warship 8 (1984): 9–18.

McKay, John. The 100-Gun Ship "Victory." London: Conway Maritime Press, 1997.

McKay, John, and Ron Coleman. The 24-Gun Frigate "Pandora," 1779. London: Conway Maritime Press, 1992.

McKee, Alexander. King Henry VIII's "Mary Rose": Its Fate and Future. London: Souvenir, 1973.

Mackenzie, Robert Holden. The Trafalgar Roll: The Ships and the Officers. Annapolis, Md.: Naval Institute Press, 1989.

McLeay, Alison. The Tobermory Treasure: The True Story of a Fabulous Armada Galleon. London: Conway Maritime Press, 1986.

Mahan, Alfred Thayer. The Influence of Sea Power upon History 1600–1783. 5th ed., 1894. Reprint, New York: Dover, 1987.

Mallard, Victor F. L. "Ships of India, 1834–1934." Mariner's Mirror 30 (1944): 144–53.

Maloney, Linda McKee. "A Naval Experiment." American Neptune 34 (1974): 188–96.

March, Edgar J. British Destroyers. London: Seeley Service, 1966.

Marden, Luis. "Wreck of H.M.S. Pandora." National Geographic (October 1985): 423–51.

Marder, Arthur J. From the "Dreadnought" to Scapa Flow. 5 vols. New York: Oxford University Press, 1961–70.

Marley, David F. "The Last Manila Galleon." In Warship 1991. London: Conway Maritime Press, 1991.

Marsh, A. J. The Story of a Frigate: H.M.S. "Trincomalee" to T.S. "Foudroyant." Portsmouth, Eng.: Portsmouth Museum Society, 1973.

Martelle, Mickey. "Novgorod and Rear-Admiral Popov, the Black Sea's Round Battleships." Nautical Research Journal 39 (June 1994): 83–97.

Martin, Colin. Full Fathom Five: Wrecks of the Spanish Armada. London: Chatto & Windus, 1975.

———. "La Trinidad Valencera: An Armada Invasion Transport Lost off Donegal — Interim Site Report 1971–76." International Journal of Nautical Archaeology 8 (1979): 13–38.

Martin, Paula. Spanish Armada Prisoners: The Story of the "Nuestra Señora del Rosario" and Her Crew, and of Other Prisoners in England, 1587–1597. Exeter Maritime Studies No. 1. Exeter: University of Exeter, 1988.

Martin, Tyrone G. A Most Fortunate Ship: A Narrative

History of Old Ironsides. Rev. ed. Annapolis, Md.: Naval Institute Press, 1997.

Martous, V. V., and G. Palmer. "The Reconstruction of Russian Maritime History: The Building of a Replica of Peter the Great's Frigate *Shtandart*." In *International Conference on Historic Ships: Design, Restoration and Maintenance, 24 May 1996, Bristol.* London: Royal Institution of Naval Architects, 1996.

Masefield, John. *The "Conway": From Her Foundation to the Present Day.* New York: Macmillan, 1933.

Massie, Robert K. *"Dreadnought": Britain, Germany and the Coming of the Great War.* New York: Random House, 1991.

Mathewson, R. Duncan, III. *Treasure of the "Atocha."* New York: E. P. Dutton, 1986.

Mattingly, Garrett. *The Armada.* Boston: Houghton Mifflin, 1959.

May, W. E. "The *Gaspee* Affair." *Mariner's Mirror* 63 (1977): 129–35.

Mead, Hilary. "The Loss of the *Victoria*." *Mariner's Mirror* 47 (1961): 17–24.

Millar, John Fitzhugh. *Early American Ships.* Williamsburg, Va.: Thirteen Colonies Press, 1986.

Miller, Edward M. *USS "Monitor": The Ship That Launched a Modern Navy.* Annapolis, Md.: Naval Institute Press, 1978.

Miller, Nathan. *Sea of Glory: A Naval History of the American Revolution.* Annapolis, Md.: Naval Institute Press, 1974.

Millett, Richard. "The State Department's Navy: A History of the Special Service Squadron, 1920–1940." *American Neptune* 35 (1975): 118–38.

Milligan, John D. *Gunboats down the Mississippi.* Annapolis, Md.: Naval Institute Press, 1965.

Mitchell, C. Bradford. *We'll Deliver: Early History of the United States Merchant Marine Academy, 1938–1956.* Kings Point, N.Y.: U.S. Merchant Marine Academy Alumni Association, 1977.

Morison, Samuel Eliot. *Admiral of the Ocean Sea: A Life of Christopher Columbus.* 1942. Reprint, Boston: Northeastern University Press, 1983.

———. *John Paul Jones: A Sailor's Biography.* Boston: Little, Brown, 1959.

———. *"Old Bruin": Commodore Matthew C. Perry, 1794–1858.* Boston: Little, Brown, 1967.

Morris, Richard Knowles. *John P. Holland 1841–1914, Inventor of the Modern Submarine.* Annapolis, Md.: Naval Institute Press, 1965.

Morris, Roland. *HMS "Colossus": The Story of the Salvage of the Hamilton Treasures.* London: Hutchinson, 1979.

Morrison, J. S., and J. F. Coates. *The Athenian Trireme: The History and Reconstruction of an Ancient Greek Warship.* Cambridge: Cambridge University Press, 1986.

Morrison, J. S., and R. T. Williams. *Greek Oared Ships 900–322 B C.* Cambridge: Cambridge University Press, 1994.

Murphy, Larry E. *"H. L. Hunley" Site Assessment.* Santa Fe, N.M.: National Park Service, 1998.

Naish, George P. B. *The "Wasa": Her Place in History.* London: HMSO, 1968.

Nash, Howard P., Jr. "Civil War Legend Examined." *American Neptune* 23 (1963): 197–203.

Nelson, Daniel A. *"Hamilton* and *Scourge:* Ghost Ships of the War of 1812." *National Geographic* (March 1983): 289–313.

Nikolaysen, N. *The Viking Ship Discovered at Gokstad in Norway.* Christiania, Norway: Alb. Cammermayer, 1882.

Nutting, Anthony. *Gordon of Khartoum: Martyr and Misfit.* New York: Clarkson N. Potter, 1966.

O'Driscoll, Patricia E. "The Ship with Seven Names." *Sea Breezes* 110 (1955): 134.

Olsen, O., and Ole Crumlin-Pedersen. *Five Viking Ships from Roskilde Fjord.* Copenhagen: 1978.

Osbon, H. A. "Passing of the Steam and Sail Corvette: The *Comus* and *Calliope* Classes." *Mariner's Mirror* 49 (1963): 193–208.

Owsley, F. L., Jr. *The CSS "Florida": Her Building and Operations.* Tuscaloosa: University of Alabama Press, 1987.

Parkes, Oscar. *British Battleships 1860–1950.* London: Seeley Service, 1957.

Parkinson, John, Jr. *The History of the New York Yacht Club from Its Founding through 1973.* New York: New York Yacht Club, 1975.

Pepys, Samuel. *The Shorter Pepys.* Edited by Robert Latham. Berkeley: University of California Press, 1985.

Perry, Matthew C. *Narrative of the Expedition of an American Squadron to the China Seas and Japan Performed in the Years 1852, 1853, and 1854.* New York: AMS, 1967.

Perry, Milton F. *Infernal Machines: The Story of the Confederate Submarine and Marine Warfare.* Baton Rouge: Louisiana State University Press, 1965.

Philip, Cynthia Owen. *Robert Fulton: A Biography.* New York: Franklin Watts, 1985.

Phillips, Michael. *The Royal Navy.* Vol. 1. CD-ROM. Saltash, Cornwall: Michael Phillips, 1998.

Pope, Dudley. *At Twelve Mr. Byng Was Shot.* Philadelphia: J. B. Lippincott, 1962.

———. *The Black Ship.* Philadelphia: J. B. Lippincott, 1964.

———. *The Devil Himself: The Mutiny of 1800.* London: Secker & Warburg, 1988.

Porter, David. *Journal of a Cruise.* 1815. Reprint, Annapolis, Md.: Naval Institute Press, 1986.

Powell, J. W. Damer. "The Wreck of Sir Cloudesley Shovell." *Mariner's Mirror* 43 (1957): 333–36.

Prynne, M. W. "Annual Lecture of the Society for Nautical Research: *Henry V's Grace Dieu.*" *Mariner's Mirror* 54 (1968): 115–28.

———. "Notes: The Dimensions of the *Grace Dieu* (1418)." *Mariner's Mirror* 63 (1977): 6–7.

Pullen, H. F. *The "Shannon" and the "Chesapeake."* Toronto: McClelland & Stewart, 1970.

Ragan, Mark K. "Union and Confederate Submarine Warfare." *North and South* 2:3 (1999).

Randolph, Evan. "USS *Constellation, 1797–1979.*" *American Neptune* 39 (1979): 235–55.

———. "Fouled Anchors? Foul Blow." *American Neptune* 52 (1992): 94–101.

Rattray, Jeannette Edwards. *The Perils of the Port of New York: Maritime Disasters from Sandy Hook to Execution Rock.* New York: Dodd, Mead, 1973.

Rawson, Geoffrey. *"Pandora"'s Last Voyage.* New York: Harcourt, Brace & World, 1963.

Reynolds, William. *Voyage to the Southern Ocean: The Letters of Lieutenant William Reynolds from the U.S. Exploring Expedition, 1838–1842.* Edited by Anne Hoffman Cleaver and E. Jeffrey Stann. Annapolis, Md.: Naval Institute Press, 1988.

Rickover, H. G. *How the Battleship "Maine" Was Destroyed.* Washington, D.C.: Naval History Division, Department of the Navy, 1976.

Rider, Hope. *Valour Fore and Aft.* Annapolis, Md.: Naval Institute Press, 1976.

Ritchie, Robert C. *Captain Kidd and the War against the Pirates.* Cambridge, Mass.: Harvard University Press, 1986.

Robinson, Charles M., III. *Shark of the Confederacy: The Story of the CSS "Alabama."* Annapolis, Md.: Naval Institute Press, 1995.

Robinson, Gregory. "The Great Harry." *Mariner's Mirror* 20 (1934): 85–92.

Robinson, William Morrison, Jr. *The Confederate Privateers.* New Haven, Conn.: Yale University Press, 1928.

Rodger, N. A. M. *The Safeguard of the Sea: A Naval History of Britain 660–1649.* New York: W. W. Norton, 1998.

Rodgers, William Ledyard. *Naval Warfare under Oars 4th to 16th Centuries.* Annapolis, Md.: Naval Institute Press, 1940.

Rodríguez-Salgado, M. J., et al. *Armada 1588–1988: An International Exhibition to Commemorate the Spanish Armada.* London: Penguin Books, 1988.

Rogers, Woodes. *A Cruising Voyage round the World.* 1712. Reprint, New York: Dover, 1970.

Roosevelt, Theodore. *The Naval War of 1812, or, the History of the United States Navy during the Last War with Great Britain.* 1882. Reprint, Annapolis, Md.: Naval Institute Press, 1987.

Rose, Susan. "*Henry V's Grace Dieu* and Mutiny at Sea: Some New Evidence." *Mariner's Mirror* 63 (1977): 3–8.

Rowse, A. L. *Sir Richard Grenville of the "Revenge."* London: Jonathan Cape, 1935.

Rubino, Thomas C. "*Dom Fernando II:* A Fragata Reborn." *Wooden Boat* 128 (January-February 1996): 26–28.

Rule, Margaret. *The "Mary Rose": The Excavation and Raising of Henry VIII's Flagship.* London: Conway Maritime Press, 1982.

Sandler, Stanley. "'In Deference to Public Opinion': The Loss of HMS *Captain.*" *Mariner's Mirror* 59 (1973): 57–68.

Sawtelle, Joseph G., ed. *John Paul Jones and the "Ranger": Portsmouth, New Hampshire, 12–November 1, 1777 and the Log of the "Ranger" November 1, 1777–May 18, 1778.* Portsmouth, N.H.: Portsmouth Marine Society, 1994.

Schäuffelen, Otmar. *Great Sailing Ships.* New York: Frederick A. Praeger, 1969.

Schom, Alan. *Trafalgar: Countdown to Battle, 1803–1805.* New York: Oxford University Press, 1990.

Schurz, William Lyle. *The Manila Galleon.* New York: E. P. Dutton, 1939.

Seeger, Martin L. "The Ten-Cent War: Naval Phase." *American Neptune* 39 (1979): 271–88.

Selfridge, Thomas O., Jr. *Memoirs of Thomas O. Selfridge, Jr.: Rear Admiral, U.S.N.* Introduction by Captain Dudley W. Knox. New York & London: G. P. Putnam's Sons, 1924.

Semmes, Raphael. *Memoirs of Service Afloat.* 1868. Reprint, Secaucus, N.J.: Blue & Grey Press, 1987.

Senior, William. "The *Bucentaur.*" *Mariner's Mirror* 15 (1929): 131–38.

Sherman, Constance D. "An Accounting of His Majesty's Armed Sloop *Liberty.*" *American Neptune* 20 (1960): 243–49.

Shomette, Donald. *The Hunt for HMS "De Braak": Legend and Legacy.* Durham, N.C.: Carolina Academic Press, 1993.

Silverstone, Paul F. *Directory of the World's Capital Ships.* London: Ian Allen, 1984.

———. *Warships of the Civil War Navies.* Annapolis, Md.: Naval Institute Press, 1989.

Sjøvold, Thorleif. *The Oseberg Find and the Other Viking Ship Finds.* Oslo: Universitets Oldsaksamling, 1966.

Smith, D. Bonner. "Some Remarks about the Mutiny of the *Bounty*." *Mariner's Mirror* 22 (1936): 200–237.

Smith, Philip Mason. *Confederates Downeast: Confederate Operations in and around Maine.* Portland: Provincial Press, 1985.

Smith, Sheli. "Life at Sea." In Peter Throckmorton, ed. *The Sea Remembers: Shipwrecks and Archaeology.* New York: Smithmark, 1961.

Snorri Sturluson. *Heimskringla, or, the Life of the Norse Kings.* Translated by Erling Monsen and A. H. Smith. Cambridge: W. Heffer & Sons, 1932.

Sokol, Anthony E. *The Imperial and Royal Austro-Hungarian Navy.* Annapolis, Md.: Naval Institute Press, 1968.

Sondhaus, Lawrence. *The Habsburg Empire and the Sea: Austrian Naval Policy, 1797–1866.* West Lafayette, Ind.: Purdue University Press, 1989.

Soop, Hans. *The Power and the Glory: The Sculptures of the Warship "Wasa."* Stockholm: Kungliga Vitterhets Historie och Antikvitets Akademien, 1986.

Spencer, Warren F. *The Confederate Navy in Europe.* University: University of Alabama Press, 1983.

Spratt, H. Philip. *Transatlantic Paddle Steamers.* Glasgow: Brown Son & Ferguson, 1951.

———. "The First Iron Steamer." *American Neptune* 13 (1953): 157–61.

Staples, William R., ed. *Documentary History of the Destruction of the Gaspée.* Providence: Rhode Island Publications Society, 1990.

Stefansson, Vilhjalmur, ed. *The Three Voyages of Martin Frobisher.* 2 vols. London: Argonaut, 1938.

Sténuit, Robert. *Treasures of the Armada.* New York: E. P. Dutton, 1971.

Stephens, Hawley. "C.S.S. *Georgia*: Memory and Calling." *American Neptune* 45 (1985): 191–98.

Sternlicht, Sanford. *McKinley's Bulldog: The Battleship "Oregon."* Chicago: Nelson-Hall, 1977.

Stewart, W. Roderick. "Seppings Survivor." *Warship* 6, no. 22 (1982): 81–87.

———. *Welcome aboard the Frigate "Unicorn."* Dundee: Unicorn Preservation Society, 1982.

Still, William N., Jr. "*Monitor* Companies: A Study of the Major Firms That Built the USS *Monitor*." *American Neptune* 48 (1948): 106–30.

———. *Iron Afloat: The Story of the Confederate Ironclads.* Columbia: University of South Carolina Press, 1985.

Strum, Harvey. "The *Leopard-Chesapeake* Incident of 1807: The Arrogance of Seapower." *Warship* 43: 157–64.

Sugden, John. *Sir Francis Drake.* New York: Simon & Schuster, 1990.

Sullivan, Catherine. *Legacy of the "Machault": A Collection of 18th Century Artifacts.* Hull: Parks Canada, 1986.

Swanson, Bruce. *Eighth Voyage of the Dragon: A History of China's Quest for Seapower.* Annapolis, Md.: Naval Institute Press, 1982.

Switzer, David. "Privateers, Not Pirates." In Peter Throckmorton, ed., *The Sea Remembers: Shipwrecks and Archaeology.* New York: Smithmark, 1991.

Tacitus. *Tacitus on Britain and Germany.* Translated by H. Mattingly. Baltimore: Penguin Books, 1948.

Taylor, Thomas E. *Running the blockade; a personal narrative of adventures, risks, and escapes during the American Civil War.* Introduction by Julian Corbett. 1896. Reprint, Freeport, N.Y., Books for Libraries Press, 1971.

Tennyson, Alfred Lord. "The *Revenge*." In *Ballads and Other Poems.* Boston: James Osgood, 1880.

Throckmorton, Peter, ed. *The Sea Remembers: Shipwrecks and Archaeology.* New York: Smithmark, 1991.

Trask, David F. *The War with Spain in 1898.* New York: Macmillan, 1986.

Tucker, Spencer C. "U.S. Navy Steam Sloop *Princeton*." *American Neptune* 49 (1989): 96–113.

Tucker, Spencer C., and Frank T. Reuter. *Injured Honor: The "Chesapeake"-"Leopard" Affair, June 22, 1807.* Annapolis, Md.: Naval Institute Press, 1996.

Turner, Mrs. W. J. Carpenter. "The Building of the *Grace Dieu*, *Valentine* and *Falconer* at Southampton, 1416–1420." *Mariner's Mirror* 40 (1954): 55–72.

Twitchett, E. G. *Life of a Seaman: Thomas Cochrane, Tenth Earl of Dundonald.* London: Wishart, 1931.

Tyler, David P. "Fulton's Steam Frigate." *American Neptune* 6 (1946): 253–74.

Uden, Grant. *The Fighting "Temeraire."* Oxford: Blackwell, 1961.

U.S. Navy. *Dictionary of American Naval Fighting Ships (DANFS).* 8 vols. Washington, D.C.: Naval History Division, Department of the Navy, 1960–81.

Van der Molen, S. J. *The "Lutine" Treasure: The 150-Year Search for Gold in the Wreck of the Frigate "Lutine."* London: Adlard Coles, 1970.

Waddell, James I. *CSS "Shenandoah": The Memoirs of Lieutenant Commander James I. Waddell.* New York: Crown Publishers, 1960.

Warren, Gordon. *Fountain of Discontent: The "Trent" Affair and Freedom of the Seas.* Boston: Northeastern University Press, 1981.

Webber, Bert. *Battleship "Oregon" . . . Bulldog of the Navy (An Oregon Documentary).* Medford, Oreg.: Webb Research Group, 1994.

Wegner, Dana M. "An Apple and an Orange: Two *Con-*

*stellation*s at Gosport, 1853–1855." *American Neptune* 52 (1992): 77–93.

Wegner, Dana M., Colan Ratliff, and Kevin Lynaugh. *Fouled Anchors: The "Constellation" Question Answered.* Washington, D.C.: U.S. Government Printing Office, 1991.

Wells, John. *The Immortal "Warrior": Britain's First and Last Battleship.* Emsworth, Eng.: Kenneth Mason, 1987.

Wilson, David M. *The Bayeux Tapestry: The Complete Tapestry in Color.* New York: Alfred A. Knopf, 1985.

Winton, John. *"Warrior" — The First and the Last.* Liskeard, Cornwall: Maritime Books, 1987.

Wise, Stephen R. *Lifeline of the Confederacy: Blockade Running during the Civil War.* Columbia: University of South Carolina Press, 1988.

Wood, Gerald. "The Ironclad Turret Ship *Huascar.*" *Warship* 10 (1986): 37–38.

Wood, Robert D. *The Voyage of the "Water Witch": A Scientific Expedition to Paraguay and La Plata Region (1853–1856).* Culver City, Calif.: Labyrinthos, 1985.

Wyllie, Harold. "H.M.S. *Implacable.*" *Mariner's Mirror* 34, no. 3 (1948): 147–55.

Yanaway, Philip E. "The United States Revenue Cutter *Harriet Lane,* 1857–1884." *American Neptune* 36 (1976): 174–205.

Index